Diaries of an
English Rogue
ABROAD

Diaries of an
English Rogue
ABROAD

Kevin Courtney

Library of Congress Control Number:		2012920948
ISBN:	Hardcover	978-1-4797-4627-9
	Softcover	978-1-4797-4626-2
	Ebook	978-1-4797-4628-6

To order additional copies of this book, contact:
Xlibris Corporation
0-800-644-6988
www.Xlibrispublishing.co.uk
Orders@Xlibrispublishing.co.uk
305008

This book is dedicated to my brother—Kev

I would like to thank the following people for making this book possible to publish: first of all, my parents, who have backed me up all the way. My mum has spent endless hours scanning photos for the book, and my father has sorted the relevant folders, photos, diaries for me at such short notice. Janet Stock, Paula Blow, and Fiona Kelham (the girls in the office) for advice and much-needed support. Claire (my best friend), who gave me the idea to look into getting it published. Also, Neil Kerfoot, for his invaluable advice and support. I would also like to thank Mary Lopez and Emily Laurel from Xlibris for their full support and professional advice. I apologise to my partner and especially my daughter, whom I have neglected since working on this project, and I thank you for your patience and support.

Last of all, I want to thank Kevin for leaving us with such a beautiful insight into his life. I hope I have done you proud.

I love and miss you, Kev.

Xxx

Michelle

CONTENTS

Introduction (an insight into who Kevin was)

World trip 1990-91 (Kev at the age of twenty-one to twenty-two years old)—Kev's first real adventure of four hundred and fifty days of travelling from London through to Asia including India, Australia, New Zealand, Hawaii, and America—most of it drunk! Should the book have been called *Diaries of a Drunkard Abroad*?

Africa—1992-93 (Kev at the age of twenty-four to twenty-five-years old)—hitch-hiking from London and travelling through France, Spain, and down to Africa, ending up in South Africa (includes being sent to jail in Africa).

Central America 1996-97 (Kev at the age of twenty-eight years old)—Kev travels through Central America to reach the bottom of Panama.

Darién Gap, 1997 (Kev at the age of twenty-eight years old)—the most dangerous of all Kev's travels, travelling through the Darién Gap jungle to reach Columbia. Not many travellers have survived this adventure to tell their tale!

South America, 1997 (Kev at the age of twenty-eight years old)—one man and his tent, exploring Columba right down to Chile.

Epitaph—a few words from some of Kev's closest friends.

Kev's last words

INTRODUCTION

This book is in memory of my wonderful brother Kevin Courtney. He died in a tragic diving accident in Hong Kong on 2 November 1998, aged only thirty years. His body was lost in the ocean for five horrendous days until a fisherman found him and we were able to get him home and lay him to rest. This part of my life is something I wouldn't want to live through ever again.

Kevin (born in Lincoln UK) was a born traveller, and from the age of seventeen, travelled as often as he could, visiting places such as America, India, Australia, New Zealand, etc. His travels were not of the norm though; oh no, Kevin liked to take risks, and he often went where nobody else would dare. During his travels, he kept personal diaries and also sent home thousands of postcards to his parents to keep them informed of his whereabouts.

He was a risk taker from an early age. I remember when we biked to the newsagent to do our paper round in the early mornings, and Kevin would just fly across the road on his bike without checking if a car was coming.

As his younger sister, I wouldn't say it was easy to live with Kevin: like the time when he learnt to kickbox, after a falling-out (as often brothers and sisters do!), I had to hide in the bathroom till my parents came home so he didn't beat me up! Also, when I was in my third year at school (age thirteen), Kevin was in the fifth year, and when I returned to school after a little operation on my nose, everyone seemed extremely concerned and asked me if the rumours were true! Kevin had told everyone that I had had a termination (abortion); he thought it was highly amusing. He had such a mischievous sense of humour!

As with most brothers and sisters, we didn't really bond properly until we had both left school and we had matured a little. When Kevin came home from his travels, I loved to hear of where he had been, and he was always so pleased to see his family. I was so proud of him. Always the joker, once, my brother, for my birthday, had sent me a cheque (signed and dated). I was so excited as I had never received money from him before; I thought he had finally grown up. Then I noticed the amount; it was for 'naught pounds and naught pence'! Thanks, Kev. I recently found a letter he had sent me while away on his travels. On the envelope, he did not address it to me but to 'Kev Courtney's big sexy sister'. He ended the letter by stating 'May your sex be safe and your orgasms be frequent'. Kevin had a great sense of humour; he was wild and crazy, such a party animal, well, when he could be. The ladies loved him—a proper Jack the Lad!

Later on in his life, he began a career in diving and worked for a company that could employ you wherever you were in the world. Kevin worked as a diver in Hong Kong for the last three years of his life, all the time saving up for his next travelling adventures.

Sadly, the last time the family saw Kevin was in England, August 1998. It was a special time for us as he took us all for a meal (a first!) at the Grand Hotel in Lincoln, and we had a photo taken of the four of us together, which, though we didn't realise at the time, would be our last family photo. I remember him packing to go home again to Hong Kong, and we were saying our goodbyes, and I kissed him and hugged him, and he told me he loved me. That was the first time he had ever told me that and the last.

For a long time, I have wanted to do something creative with Kevin's diaries, postcards, and photos. I wanted to document them in some way so we could share his stories with family and friends.

Then I decided to create a website, where I added some of his later travels. I had some interest from his friends, and one of my friends (thanks, Claire) suggested I get it published. I wasn't sure if any of it would be what people wanted to read, so I contacted a publisher, and they called me back after taking a look at his website, saying that they would love to publish, and so now, I can finally honour Kevin and have his story told. Some of the places he visited, I am not sure if he spelt correctly, but I have just rewritten all his diaries as he wrote them. The words are his very own. The sketches in this book have been taken from his diaries, sketched by him, and all the photos are from his camera. Some names within this book have been changed for privacy.

Kevin wasn't shy about his antics, so I don't feel guilty in publishing his stories; in fact, most of the diaries have taught me things that I never knew about him and things I never knew he did. As his diaries progress through the years, it reflects how he matured and how he became the man he finally was. The early days, he spends most of his time drunk and partying, whereas later on, he develops his sense of adventure. He never boasted about his travels, so I never really knew exactly what he was up to. Upon reading this book, I would like you to accept Kevin for who he was: a young lad travelling, looking for adventure and excitement; hence, the title of the book, *Diaries of an English Rogue Abroad*.

Kevin was an adventurer and was always seeking thrills; his stories range from funny to shocking. I am so proud of him; he was my hero. This is my tribute to Kev.

I have thoroughly enjoyed writing up Kevin's diaries, and I hope you enjoy reading them just as much.

Enjoy!

WORLD TRIP, 1990-91

13 March 1990, Lincoln, England

Well, today's my last day in England, and I still have a million things to do. I feel very reluctant about going on my own, but I know I must go because if I don't, I will greatly regret it later on in life.

Day 1: 14 March 1990, London Heathrow

Got up at 6 a.m. in order to catch the 7.15 a.m. coach to London, getting me there at 11.40 a.m. (£9). From then on, it was panic stations as I had to pick my tickets up from the STA travel agents the other side of London before catching the 45-minute-long tube journey to Heathrow in order to check out by 1.30 p.m. latest. I made it on time, only to discover that the flight had been delayed 1½ hours and was now leaving at 4.30 p.m. This didn't bother me as, for compensation, I was given a £5 food voucher to spend at the restaurant.

The plane ended up leaving at 6 p.m. (3 hours late), which could mean that I might miss my connection flight at Karachi (Pakistan) tomorrow. The adventure begins.

Day 2: 15 March 1990, Pakistan, Nepal

I'd finally got to sleep when we arrived at Karachi (Pakistan) at 6 a.m. (Pakistan is 5 hours ahead of England). We then had to wait 4 hours to catch our connecting flight to Katmandu (Nepal) arriving at 2 p.m., the time being 45 minutes ahead of Pakistan. I had to obtain a visa, costing me £20, before catching a taxi with two girls I met on the plane. We went to a guest house in the heart of the city, costing Rs 60 cash, but I haggled it down to Rs 50, which, at Rs 46 to the pound, worked out at about £1.08.

After a quick shower, I went exploring with the 2 girls and found the streets to be bustling with life. It got dark at 6 p.m. and we spent an hour trying to find our way back. I bought a small bottle of vodka for Rs 65 and drank it with the chap behind reception. By the time the bottle was empty, we were both pissed. He then bought me a Chinese meal and some beers (Rs 55 each). By the time I got back to my room at 10.30 p.m. I went straight to bed for a good night's sleep.

Day 3: 16 March 1990, Katmandu, Nepal

Woke up with a hangover at 11.30 a.m. and then booked myself on a 2-day white-water rafting expedition and a 3-day jungle safari, plus 2 nights' accommodation for $95 in Pokhara, then hired a bike for 40 pence and rode round the city, dodging traffic approaching me from all directions. I made my way up to the Monkey Temple and paid a local child 10 pence to look after my bike for an hour. The temple was crowded with monkeys. After walking around topless for 3 hours, I was told that if the police saw me, I would get fined $50.

I biked to the Tibetan Refugee Centre, where they made handmade carpets to sell to the public. I got friendly with one of the refugees, and she invited me back to her pad to sample some Tibetan beer. It is made from rice and only takes 4 days to brew and is about as strong as wine.

I biked back to the main square, and some bloke came up to me and asked if I wanted my ears cleaned. He gave me a free sample and wiped the wax on to his finger to show me.

I brought my bike back one hour after the shop had closed, and some poor lad was sitting on a stone, waiting for me. Got to bed at 9.30 p.m.

Day 4: 17 March 1990, Nepal, White-Water Rafting

Got up at 5.30 a.m. and, after a quick breakfast, got picked up to go on a 2-day white-water rafting expedition. Spent the first 3½ hours on a bus travelling through Nepal until we got to the starting post.

The water was a bit tame at first, but then it soon got better, especially when we hit the rapids. When there were no rapids, me and another English guy (Phil), started to swim, getting pulled along by the very strong current. We came to some rapids, and the guide said it was OK to swim down them. It wasn't. The water was about 1 metre deep, with huge rocks everywhere. It was very hard to dodge them because of the current. My legs smashed against them a few times, and we were very lucky to get away with just cuts and grazes.

We stayed in the raft after that, and the rapids got worse. On the last rapid (the biggest), we had to stop and check it out beforehand. The guide said it wasn't safe, but Phil and I talked him into it. It was very rough. We went straight down, and when I looked up, I saw a wall of water in front of me. When we hit it, Phil and I went arse over bollock, along with a couple of other people, into the middle of the raft.

Got pissed up at night with Phil and the guides and slept under the stars next to the fire.

Day 5: 18 March 1990, Nepal, White-Water Rafting

Woke up and was still pissed from last night. After breakfast, we began rafting again.

We had 4 Chinese on our raft, and they hardly paddled. Our guide stood on the raft with only his kegs (pants) on, so I went up and ripped them off. He looked a sight standing on the raft with no clothes on. Phil and I began swimming again, and I nearly got my leg ripped off on a really sharp rock that was just below the surface.

It was another brilliant day white-water rafting through breathtaking scenery with eagles soaring above us. We had travelled 50 km by raft in the last 2 days.

I caught the bus to Pokhara. It was crammed full of people who wouldn't stop staring. I began talking to 2 Canadian birds. We were the only white people on the bus. When it began to get dark, I went to shut the window and then realised that there was no glass, so I had to sit there freezing, Arrived at 8 p.m. and went straight to my accommodation, which I had already booked.

Day 6: 19 March 1990, Nepal, Pokhara

Got up at 10 a.m. and hired a bike for the day (30 pence). I spent half an hour biking to find a famous waterfall, when I finally found it. I paid my entrance fee of Rs 3 and went in—and there was nothing there as it's only a waterfall in the wet season. I'm running very low on my Nepal money and don't want to change another traveller's cheque until Thursday, when I reach India, so for every meal, I've had either plain rice or noodles, and I'm more than pissed off with it.

Got a fairly good view of the mountains and lakes of Pokhara today on my bike ride, but I was sweating my bollocks off because I had to wear trousers and a long shirt to avoid my sunburn getting any worse. A fairly lazy day.

Day 7: 20 March 1990, Nepal, Jungle Safari

Got up at 5.30 a.m. as I'm catching the 6 a.m. bus to Chitwan, where I'm going on a 3-day jungle safari costing me £40, including transport to and from the camp. The 6 a.m. bus was jam-packed, so I had to get on to the next one. There were thousands of people on the bus, and I was cramped up in the corner, with no room to breathe. After half an hour, my legs went numb. I was the only white person on the bus and wasn't really sure I was going in the right direction. Then the bus broke down for half an hour. In total, I was on the bus for 6 hours.

I got dropped off at a village near to the park and got taken the rest of the way by jeep. When I got to the camp, I bumped into Phil and shared a hut with him. After our lunch, I went canoeing in a wooden dugout and went through the jungle looking for crocodiles, but we didn't see any. Then we went on a trek through the jungle and saw a group of rhinos as well as a few deer, eagles, etc.

After dinner, we had some dancers come and do a display for us. At the end, Phil and I got picked to go up and have a go—we made right twats of ourselves, especially me, who kept standing on the toes of the lads who were dancing next to me barefeet.

Day 8: 21 March 1990, Nepal, Jungle Safari (Chitwan)

Got up at 7 a.m. and, after breakfast, went on a breathtaking tour through the jungle for a couple of hours and saw a large variety of birds, including parrots, eagles, vultures, etc. Then we had a look at a small tribal village near by. After dinner, Phil and I were in our hut, and he went out for a shit outside round the back, then I went for one (as we couldn't have bothered to walk to the toilet). After 5 minutes, the hut was covered in flies and stunk really badly, so in the end, we had to move to another hut.

After that, we went on a 5-hour safari by jeep and saw rhinos, sloths, crocodiles, etc. We had a crappy jeep that kept breaking down. There was a fairly big bush fire, and we had to drive through it—a good day.

Day 9: 22 March 1990, Nepal

I left Chitwan today, and Phil and I nearly got charged for a table we broke, but we got away with it by pretending we couldn't understand them. I said goodbye to Phil and caught a jeep to a nearby village (Tardy), where I'm catching the bus to Sanauh (Indian border). I met an American lad who was going there too and joined him. It was too crowded on the bus, so we both sat on the roof, which was great fun.

Two bus changes later and 5 hours on the road, we arrived at the border, where we both caught a bus to the train station (4 hours in a very cramped, uncomfortable, hot, and sweaty bus). I started to feel weak and sick.

Got to the train station at 7.30 p.m. I'm going to Agra but have to change at Lucknow. However, my train to Lucknow doesn't leave until 12.30 a.m. (another long wait—5 hours). I had a brief walk around the busy town centre and couldn't believe it when I saw some oxen asleep in the middle of the road, with all the traffic driving round them.

Day 10: 23 March 1990, Lucknow, India

I caught the 12.30 a.m. train and went straight to sleep. My train arrived in Lucknow at 6 a.m. and my watch was packed in my bag, so I didn't know what the time was. I woke up when we arrived at a station. I got up quickly and ran outside to look and see if it was my station. I couldn't find anyone, and when I looked round, my train was leaving. All I had on was my shorts. All my bags etc. were on the train, so I had to run and jump on to the train. I was lucky as Lucknow was the next station.

I spent the day at Lucknow, my worst and loneliest yet because I never saw a white person all day. I was like a freak to all the locals, as wherever I went, they would stare at me and laugh because they hardly saw any tourists in this hole. There were kids shitting in the street and people pissing everywhere. I spent most of the day counting the hours down to 9 p.m. when I caught the train to Agra (9 hours). When I was walking through the town, some idiot threw a rock—which smacked me on the head!

Day 11: 24 March 1990, Agra, India

Got to Agra at 6 a.m. totally shattered. I dropped my baggage off at the station before hiring an auto-rickshaw with a driver to guide me for Rs 30 (£1.10) for the day. I saw the Taj Mahal at sunrise and was desperate for a shit. There were no toilets, so I had to hide in a bush. I had a shit with loads of people walking past me.

When I got back, the guide took me to Agra Fort. While I was inside, I put my bag down to get something out. I put a packet of biscuits on the floor next to me, and a big monkey ran up and pinched it. Then all his mates came, and I was stuck in a corner.

I had a go at driving the rickshaw and nearly rolled it. Went for a walk round town for a couple of hours and couldn't get over the fact that everyone kept staring. Apart from the Taj Mahal, I didn't see a white person all day until I went to the train station, where I met 2 English birds. I sat next to them on the train and got pissed out my head on a bottle of whiskey. Can't remember anything else.

Day 12: 25 March 1990, Delhi, India

Woke up at 6 a.m. on top of a pile of mailbags inside the station. After a quick shower, I went into the town and booked myself on a day's sightseeing trip in the hope of meeting some other white people. I went to the bus stop, and when I got on the bus, it was full of Indians. I was the only white person on the bus and stuck out like a sore thumb. I was really pissed off, especially when the tour began speaking in Indian.

The first stop was at the Red Fort, which was OK, but after that, we kept stopping at various monuments and temples etc., and I didn't have a clue what they were—apart from where Gandhi was cremated. Saw a motorbike accident. Some poor lad was lying in the middle of the road, with blood everywhere, and 2 chaps just came up and dragged him to the side of the road. After the tour, I went in and complained to the tour officer and nearly had a fight with the manager.

Caught the night bus from Delhi to Jiapur at 9 p.m.

Day 13: 26 March 1990, Jiapur, India

Got to Jiapur at 4 a.m. A bicycle rickshaw picked me up and took me to a hotel, where I had to barter really hard in order to get a room for Rs 30 (£1.10). Woke up at 8.30 a.m. and went to book the night train to Jadpher, which was full, and so had to go on the 2 p.m. train, leaving me little time to see Jiapur.

I got on a rickshaw and saw the city before catching a bus to see the famous city fort. I saw some snake charmers and had a photo of me having a go and then one with the snake round my neck. I caught a minibus back, which was crammed with people. I was in the middle and couldn't tell when it was time to get off. I got off miles before my stop.

I caught the 2 p.m. train to Jadpher. I had some weirdo sit next to me, just staring at me for 2 hours solid before I moved. I kept shouting at him, but he didn't understand. Got to Jadpher at 10 p.m. and went straight to the station, and after a 10-minute push and shove in a so-called queue, I managed to book myself on tonight's train to Jaisalmer at 10.30 p.m. with some other Brits.

Day 14: 27 March 1990, Jaisalmer and Kruri, India

I got to Jaisalmer at 9.30 a.m., a town in the heart of the Thar Desert. I went straight to the 15th-century city inside the castle grounds on the mountain. I got a room in the original building of the castle for Rs 20 (80 pence), a fascinating place. I went for a walk round the town. It was a bit like being in the 15th century, with camel-drawn carts.

They do camel expeditions here, but I was told they are a lot better at a remote village 1½ hours away, called Kruri. Only a few thousand tourists have ever been, and I had to obtain a permit to go there. I went back to my room, packed my bags, and left in order to catch the 3 p.m. bus to Kruri. The bus was very crowded and uncomfortable—especially for me as the roof was only 5 feet high, and I'm 6 feet tall. The bus was full of desert nomads from the village. When I got to my village, there were only a few mud huts. I made my way to the only guest house for miles and met a few English people.

In the evening, after a massive dinner, the village band played for us. It was brilliant, lying under the stars in a desert village, listening to songs that have been passed on from generation to generation.

Day 15: 28 March 1990, India, 4-Day Camel Safari (Thar Desert)

I got woken up at 8 a.m. with a pot of tea being delivered to my hut. After a really filling breakfast, I left on a 4-day camel trek in the Thar Desert, along with 4 other tourists. My camel was about 8 feet tall, giving me an excellent view of the desert. We travelled for a few hours before coming across a small and remote desert village, where the people were very friendly. We bought a bottle of millet wine off them for tonight. We carried on for a few more hours before stopping for dinner, freshly cooked chapattis and vegetable curry.

After dinner, we came across a camel with its baby. One of the guides went up and milked the mother and gave us a taste of fresh camel milk. I had a shit in the desert, and before I had finished, I had about a thousand flies hovering round my arse. We stopped for the night in the sand dunes. After tea, the guides sang us a few of their traditional songs while we got pissed on millet wine and hash.

Day 16: 29 March 1990, India, 4-Day Camel Safari (Thar Desert)
Got up at 7 a.m. and watched the guides baking the chapattis and porridge for breakfast against the desert sunrise.

After travelling for a couple of hours on the camels, we came across another rural village, in which half the kids had eye infections. We carried on travelling a bit longer, seeing wild peacocks on the way. After dinner, I left the rest of the group (who were only on a 2½—day trek). We stopped at a small village, and they were having some festival. I got invited in and had a red stripe painted on my face. I was then sat down with the rest of the village men, and I had to hold some millet seed in my hand for 5 minutes before throwing it into the centre of the road with everyone else. Then I had a home-made cigarette: tobacco held together by a leaf. It was brilliant. 2 women were beating drums and singing. I showed them my camera, and most of them didn't know what it was. I was given some food and ate it with the rest of the men. I had to crush my chapattis up with my hands and mix it with some liquid curry until it was one big sloppy mess on my plate. Then I had to scoop it up with my fingers and eat it. Some men were even sharing their plates. After the food, I was invited to go and visit the women (a great honour). They were all crammed into a little mud hut, with traditional music being played in the background.

It was, by far, my best experience of my trip so far, being treated like a king in a small desert village in the middle of nowhere, where only a few white people have visited before—fantastic. They offered to put us up for the night, but we had to get off—slept in the sand dunes again.

Day 17: 30 March 1990, India, 4-Day Camel Safari (Thar Desert)

Friday, and another brilliant day trekking through the Thar Desert, watching the wild gazelles, peacocks, and prairie dogs. Then we noticed a large flock of vultures in the sky, circling round, so we went to investigate and saw about 40 vultures ripping a dead camel to pieces. I had a closer look, and its head had been eaten, and it had only one side, allowing me to see inside its ribcage.

The temperature really got hot, 35°C approx., and I could only walk about 20 feet before getting out of breath. In the afternoon, we saw more gazelles etc. before cooking some chapattis and sleeping under the stars.

Day 18: 31 March 1990, India, 4-Day Camel Safari (Thar Desert)

Don't know what time we got up as neither of us had a watch. It is the last day of my trek today, and I'm going to miss the desert life and getting our water from a 50—foot-deep well and cleaning the pots and pans with sand (very effective).

During the night, a snake had been sniffing around us, and we could see its trail in the morning.

We carried on, heading back to Kruri, and on the way, I saw a dead ox being eaten by wild dogs. One of the dogs had eaten a big hole in the ox's side and had his head right inside the ox in order to get more meat. During my stay in the desert, I have seen falcons, vultures, peacocks, gazelles, and prairie dogs.

I stopped off at my guide's village for a couple of hours before returning to Kruri. I caught the bus to Jaisalmer (2 hours). I spent it on top of the bus, which was a mistake as we drove through a sandstorm, and it got very cold and dark quickly.

I caught the night train to Jodhpur at 9.15 p.m.

Day 19: 1 April 1990, Jodhpur, India

Arrived at Jodhpur at 9 a.m. and walked half a mile to the reservation office in order to book a ticket to Delhi. I met another English bloke doing the same, and we were both told to come back at 11 a.m. so we both went for a pot of tea with some Swiss bloke. We went back at 11 a.m. and booked our 2nd-class sleeper before making our way up to the top of Jodhpur castle, which is on a massive hill, giving an excellent view of the city with all the houses painted blue. We spent most of the day up there waiting for our train, getting hassled every 5 minutes by bastard kids coming up and asking for money and pens. Had a couple of beers before catching the 3.45 p.m. train to Delhi.

Day 20: 2 April 1990, Delhi, India

Arrived at Delhi about 6.30 a.m. and then took a cycle rickshaw to New Delhi station, where I dropped my bag off at the luggage room. On the way, we passed a brothel, where I bartered with them and was offered a shag for about £1.80 but turned it down.

Went to the tourist booking office at the station, waited 40 minutes to buy a ticket before finding out I was at the wrong place (typical of India).

Got talking to a couple of birds from England—it was their first day abroad, so I took them under my wing and showed them the ropes. One of them knew a girl my age whom I went to primary school with and who lives half a mile from me at home.

Saw a tramp walking round with no clothes on and his eyelid hanging down his face about 5 inches.

Caught my train to Varanasi at 2 p.m. for a fairly boring 16-hour train ride.

Day 21: 3 April 1990, India, Varanasi

I got here at 6.30 a.m. a complete physical wreck. I got a cycle rickshaw and went to the Ganga River in order to have a look at an Indian cremation. It was fantastic. They carry the dead bodies through the street on a stretcher, with the body draped in silk, and take them down to the river, submerge the body underwater, before placing the body on a pile of logs and then burning it. After a short while, the silk covering the body has burnt away, exposing the burning flesh of the body. The body is burned for about 3 hours until only cinders remain, which are then put in the river.

As I walked along the river, I saw a couple of vultures picking at a log in the middle of the river. As the log drifted towards me, I realised that it was a human body. It was pale blue and stunk as it was covered in sick. What made it worse was that there was a group of men swimming and washing in the river and acted as if it wasn't even there. It must have been in the water for over a week.

I got to the train station to catch the 9 p.m. train to Calcutta, and the bicycle rickshaw man whom I had hired this morning was waiting for me. I hired him this morning on an hourly basis. When I went off to look at the river, I couldn't be arsed to go back, so I left the poor bloke waiting for me. I'd told him I was catching the 9 p.m. train, and so he was waiting for me at the station. I had little money left and owed him a fortune as he'd left his meter running all day—I had to run off and hide, a bastard thing to do, but this is India.

Day 22: 4 April 1990, Calcutta, India

Spent most of the day on the train, getting to Calcutta at 12.30 p.m. I didn't even try to get a flight to Bangladesh. I just went straight to book my train ticket to Madras tonight. I waited in a queue for over an hour before being told that there were no reservations left. So I had to run about 2 miles through really bad crowds and traffic to the tourist office in order to see if they had any reservations left. They said no but that I might be able to get on the 3 p.m. train, so I ran back to the station, and I bought an open ticket. There were no reservations left. I was running around the station like a twat but did no good, so I just got on the train.

Day 23: 5 April 1990, Madras, India

Shit or bust—well, it only paid off yesterday. There were about 700 people on the train, and only 1 person didn't turn up, allowing me to have his sleeper. Otherwise, I would have been thrown off the train at 9 p.m.

Train journeys in India, although very time-consuming, can be quite interesting. For example, every 5 minutes, vendors come past in really scruffy clothes, selling tea and refreshments. Then beggars wriggle past with no legs or have arms missing or are blind. Today, one bloke walked past selling second-hand zips and grotty doorknobs—I don't think he got much business. At every station, kids will jump on the train and sweep all the rubbish from under your feet and then no one will give them any money.

I got to Madras at 7.30 p.m. and got straight on a rickshaw to the Broadlands Hotel for a desperately needed shower. Went for something to eat and a quick look around before getting stoned with a few other travellers on our hotel roof. Went to bed at 2 a.m.

Day 24: 6 April 1990, Madras, India

Woke up at about 8 a.m. It was 28°C in the shade. Went for some breakfast with a lad called Simon, whom I met on the train from Calcutta and whom I'm sharing a room with. It felt good waking up in a bed for a change, without worrying about which station to get off at.

Went to the Air Lanka office and booked a flight to Sri Lanka for tomorrow night. The woman at the office told me I had to go to the bank, which was 1½ miles away, to change my traveller's cheques. I ran down to the bank, sweating my bollocks off in the heat, then had to wait 40 minutes in various queues before getting my money and running back to Air Lanka, where I spoke to someone else, and they told me that I could cash them there. Typical India.

Went to the beach. It was brilliant just to relax after spending so much time rushing about. Had a shit in the sea before going to a restaurant where they did continental food. We ordered fish and chips and ended up with a small piece of fish and only 4 chips—wankers.

Day 25: 7 April 1990, Madras, India

Got up during the night to go to the toilet, and a massive rat the size of a cat ran past me.

I got up at 8 a.m. and paid some local woman £1.50 to wash 3½—weeks' worth of my clothes. Most of them had been stuck in my bag for weeks, growing mouldy.

I went to the beach with Simon (big-headed twat), and we stayed there for a couple of hours, watching the water buffalo's bathing in the sea and the local fishermen at work. I can't get over the poverty in India. Everywhere you look, there are beggars and homeless people. As soon as it gets dark at about 6 p.m. the pavements and sides of the road are lined with homeless people trying to get to sleep for the night.

I had to get a public bus to the airport, which was like mission impossible as there were hundreds of buses. I got on a bus and wasn't sure if it was the right one until it passed the airport an hour later. I flew out at 10 p.m. arriving in Sri Lanka (Colombo) an hour later. Got talking to a local man who was going to Mount Lavinia (20 miles away) in a taxi. He gave me a lift and wouldn't accept any money. Got to bed 2 a.m.

Day 26: 8 April 1990, Mount Lavinia, Sri Lanka

Last night in Colombo, armed police were stopping traffic due to lots of terrorist attacks by the Tamids. Then this morning, I was walking along the beach, thinking how scenic it looked, then I spotted a soldier sitting behind a pile of sandbags, with a big machine gun. Then I got approached by a queer on the beach, so I packed my bags and went to Colombo. I spent an hour there sweating my bollocks off until I caught the 3.45 p.m. train to Hikkaduwa.

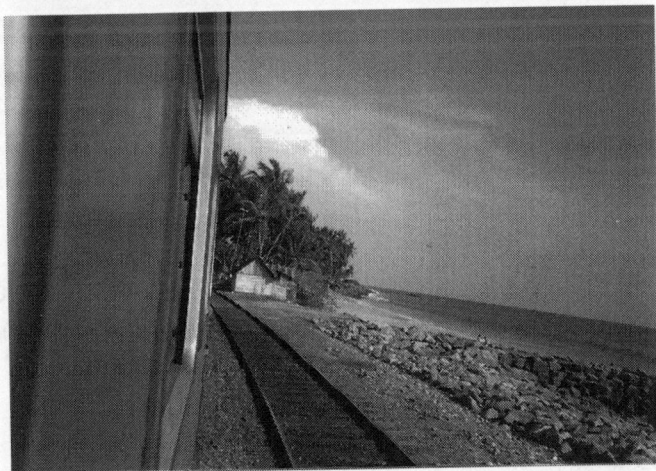

The journey was one of the most scenic I've ever been on. It ran right along the golden beaches, with palm trees everywhere, and every now and then, we would pass a small village where the houses were made of palm-tree leaves (paradise), then a massive black could came along and it pissed it down.

Got to Hikkaduwa after 2 hours, watched the sunset over the beach and palm trees before renting a room for Rs 50 (85 pence). It should have been Rs 125, but I did some hard bargaining. I stayed up half the night talking to 2 Dutch guys and one Belgium lad.

Day 27: 9 April 1990, Hikkaduwa, Sri Lanka

Woke up at about 7.30 a.m. and went for breakfast with the 2 Dutch lads. We went outside next to a small river and watched the giant iguanas swimming past—some of them nearly 2 metres long.

Then I hired a face mask and snorkel and went snorkelling in the reefs. It was great watching the large and colourful fish swimming virtually right under me. Then my ring slipped off my finger and went to the bottom of the sea. I managed to swim down and get it—*whew.*

In the afternoon, I had a scuba-diving course, £8 for 1½ hours. I learnt a lot and went swimming around with the instructor up to 2 metres (fantastic). The second lesson is tomorrow, and I will be going to 10 metres. The course lasts 4 days, after which you dive 30 metres or more. I might get my flight to Thailand postponed in order to do the diving course.

Had a massive plate of fried rice and squid tonight. I was really enjoying it until I realised that about 20 squid died for my one meal.

Day 28: 10 April 1990, Welligamma, Sri Lanka

Got up and went down to the diving club for my second lesson (diving down to 10 metres), but the sea was too rough, so I couldn't go today, so rather than hanging about waiting, I packed my bags (once more) and caught the train to Galle.

At Galle, I bought a fresh pineapple (massive) for 30 pence. It still had the stem on, and I ate it on the side of the pavement. I spent a few hours roaming round the 16th-century Dutch town before cramming into a bus for a 17 km (1 hour) journey to Welligamma, a quiet little village on the south coast, which is supposed to be home to the famous stilt fishermen (but I didn't see any). I booked myself into a family guest house for 85 pence before having a swim in the sea and watching the sunset at the same time.

Had a big plate of fried rice and tuna before going to bed at about 8.30 p.m.

Day 29: 11 April 1990, Tissamaharama, Sri Lanka

Got up early and caught a bus to Mitre Gamma. I stayed here for a while, watching the famous stilt fishermen, then I went back to the road, when a car picked me up and took me to Motora (45 minutes away).

I was lying on the beach on my own, not another person in sight, apart from someone in the distance walking towards me. He carried on walking for a couple of minutes until he was a few metres from me, then he crouched down and had a shit (right next to me), wiped his arse in the sea before walking off.

Then I caught the bus to Tangalla, a really tough journey. I was hanging on to the outside of the bus for half an hour, whizzing round all the corners, then someone started throwing up out of the window next to me.

When I got there, I went to look for a famous lagoon. I followed someone's directions and ended up going across other people's gardens. I asked someone which bus went to Tissa. He told me he was going on the same bus, so I waited for half an hour with him and got on the same bus. I was very lucky as I was one of the few who got a seat. I asked someone else on the bus, and they said it wasn't going to Tessa (bastard), so I had to get off.

Got to Tissa in the end.

Day 30: 12 April 1990, Tissamaharama, Sri Lanka

Got up at about 8 a.m. and had breakfast, then wrote about 11 postcards to various people (all saying the same).

Today was my last chance to confirm my flight, a fairly easy task (I thought). After 2 hours, I discovered that there were only about 4 phones in the town, and after visiting them all at least twice, I discovered that none of them were working.

Got stoned after dinner and was giving some lad a backy down the road. I swerved and nearly knocked a policeman off the road.

In the afternoon, I went on a jungle safari in Yala National Park, saw giant iguanas, a giant yellow tortoise, wild elephants (one with a tusk which is pretty rare), crocodiles, peacocks, etc. Didn't see any leopards or anything like that, but I still enjoyed it.

It is Sri Lanka's New Year's Eve tomorrow. I don't know where I'll be, but I'm going to try and gatecrash a party!

Day 31: 13 April 1990, Nuwara Eliya, Sri Lanka

Got up at 5 a.m. and had a quick Sinhalese (Sri Lankan) breakfast and nearly threw up.

Went to the bus stand to be told that there probably weren't any buses today. There were though, and I went through half an hour of serious brain ache, trying to find which bus went to Wellawaya. It was a near-impossible task even though there were only 2 buses. It was definitely one of them.

I got to Wellawaya and then went through the same routine to get to Ella, by which time I had given up and decided to stay here tonight. I booked into a guest house before spending the afternoon relaxing next to a massive waterfall with a Scottish lad. Then I met a minibus full of a Sinhalese family. They were pissed and offered me some whiskey. I got pissed up and ended up going to their house in Nuwara Eliya (2 hours away). I began to regret it when I sobered up, but how often do you get to spend New Year's Eve Sinhalese style, watching a 3-hour Sri Lankan opera while waiting for someone to get the booze out? It came out in the end, and I got a bit merry.

Day 32: 14 April 1990, Kandy, Sri Lanka

Got up at 6 a.m. (I slept on the floor with 5 other people).

Their New Year began at 5.40 a.m. and we weren't allowed to eat until 7.10 a.m. when we had to be facing south. There were about 15 in the family, together for New Year, and I was lucky enough to experience these traditions and friendship.

We left the home early in the morning as they were travelling north and were dropping me off at Kandy. On the way, we stopped off at (another) relation's house for some food and a piss-up for the men, while the women waited next door. When we got back in the van, it had a flat tyre, so all the men were pissed up trying to change the wheel with no jack.

They dropped me off at Kandy after giving me hundreds of addresses from them all so that I would write to them, and all the men were trying to marry me off with one of their daughters. I saw a 6-foot-long snake down a lane. I was still pissed and ran after it in order to get a photo of it. It went like a rocket, but I was nearly on top of it when it dived into a bush. Then someone told me that it was a giant cobra which is very poisonous, which put a couple more skids on my kegs.

Day 33: 15 April 1990, Colombo, Sri Lanka

Got up at 6.30 a.m. and had fresh pineapple and avocado for breakfast.

I went down to the river and watched the old men washing the working elephants. I had a go at riding on them bareback and nearly crashed it.

I caught the train to Colombo. I paid second class, but all the seats were full, so I had to sit in the aisle along with about a hundred other people. Then the guard told me I could go in the luggage carriage (luxury). The train was so full that there were loads of people hanging off the train, then someone got hit by something and fell off. The train stopped to pick him up, and he was brought to the same carriage as me. He was in a right mess. Then some woman next to me collapsed and was unconscious for quite a while.

Got to Colombo and then went to Mount Lavinia to collect my mailbag. Back in Colombo, there was a group of lads pissed up. One grabbed me, so I pushed the twat away and walked off. I can't risk any trouble as I leave for Thailand tomorrow.

Day 34: 16 April 1990, Bangkok, Thailand

I had to get up at 5.30 a.m. to get to the airport on time. I haven't had a watch for 3 weeks and so had to keep getting up during the night, going downstairs, dodging all the tramps on the way in order to find the time.

Caught the bus to the airport (45 minutes) and got to the airport on time, only to find that the plane had been delayed 1½ hours. In the end, the plane didn't leave until 4½ hours later. I had a bottle of arrack (coconut whiskey) with me so drank that and got pissed up and knocked the empty bottle over, smashing glass everywhere. When we eventually got on the plane, I made the most out of the free beer, wine, etc. on board.

Got to Thailand 9 p.m. their time (7 hours in front of GMT), spent another hour travelling to Kiwa Chang Road, where all the tourists are. I got a dormitory room (sharing with 8 others). Went up on the roof and couldn't believe it. There were about 50 people just sitting there smoking away. Got stoned and went to bed.

Day 35: 17 April 1990, Bangkok, Thailand

Got up at 8.30 a.m. The room was like a fucking sauna and stank of sweat, BO, and stale farts. Picked my rucksack up, and there was a massive hole in it, where a rat had been chewing. I pulled all my clothes out, and there was a hole the size of a fist on the front of my tracksuit top—bastard.

Went for a walk and ended up going for miles. I visited a snake farm, palace temples, etc. Went to a cafe in the evening, full of tourists, and watched *Aliens II*, after which I went to Pat Pong with an Aussie lad. There were strip clubs and tarts everywhere. Went in one bar, and there were 10 birds dancing on the stage, bollock naked. They had various acts like opening a bottle with a fanny, ping-pong balls, fanny farting with pee shooters, smoking fags out of their fannies, blowing horns by fanny farting and shagging onstage. I got to bed at 2.40 a.m.

Day 36: 18 April 1990, Bangkok, Thailand

I had to be up at 6 a.m. but I had no alarm clock, so when I woke up at 5 a.m. I had to stay awake in case I didn't wake up again before 6 a.m. I was knackered after having only 2 hours' sleep but caught the sightseeing bus to see the very famous 'Bridge over the River Kwai'. It took about two hours to get there in the minibus, stopping off to see a huge temple (Papadong) on the way. We saw the museum first before being taken to the actual 'Bridge over the River Kwai' that the British POW built 45 years ago, with thousands of them dying in the process. Then we went to a steam train across the bridge and down the original death railway for 1½ hours before having lunch. We saw the cemetery of all the dead soldiers and then we came back.

A very interesting and patriotic day.

Went for something to eat and bumped into the Aussie lad I was with last night. We went to Pat Pong again. I spent half the night bartering over a couple of T-shirts, which I got in the end, then I left the bastard T-shirts in the rickshaw on the way home.

Day 37: 19 April 1990, Bangkok, Thailand

Had about 4 hours' sleep (2 more than the night before) and managed to get up before 6 a.m. in order to go on another excursion trip. This time, to the floating markets 30 miles from Bangkok.

There were a lot of tourists there, but apart from that, it was like going back 200 years in time. The floating market is like a small town with canals rather than roads, and all the villagers come to the floating market on their boats to buy meat, vegetables, etc. The highlight of the trip was a boat ride through the market.

It is getting very hot and humid here in Thailand, where the temperature reaches 40°C in the day and about 35°C during the night. It should reach a lot higher in the next few weeks when it's at its hottest.

I went to watch Thai boxing with a couple of other lads from the same dormitory/sweat hole as me. The boxers are more traditional than in England, doing prayers, sometimes even dancing in the ring before the fights.

Day 38: 20 April 1990, Bangkok, Thailand

Got up at 7.30 a.m. as today's my first official rest day, and I have too much to do. Sent a parcel home to the family. It included 1 turban, 1 mask from Sri Lanka, 2 T-shirts, a teaspoon from Nepal, a *Waterboys* tape for Dad in remembrance of last year's Land's End to John o'Groats bike ride, and one pair of cheesy, sweaty well-worn kegs (pants). It cost me around £10.

I found out today that I'm in the year 2533, which is the Thai year, and if you think that was good, the Saudi Arabians are still in the 14th Century.

I got talking to some bird from Taiwan, and she offered me a modelling contract in Taiwan—wow, I had to turn it down as my trip comes first. Rushed around and got a few posties sent before catching the 6 p.m. bus to Chiang Mai.

Day 39: 21 April 1990, Chiang Mai, Thailand

Arrived at Chiang Mai at about 9 a.m. and checked into a guest house. Then I went for a walk round the town and ended up walking round all the monasteries where all the Buddhist monks live in their ancient and beautiful buildings.

Then I met a Thai girl and got talking to her. She invited me back to her hotel room. I asked her if she was a prostitute. She said no. So I went with her, and we got in a taxi. I was beginning to get a bit suspicious. I said I would pay, then I realised that I'd forgot my wallet, so she paid. Went into her room, and the waiter came in and brought 2 bottles of coke. I watched him open them in case he put any tablets in them. I had a few sips, and she started getting a bit heavy on drugs, asking me for some. I wanted to get out, so I told her to come back to my pad—she agreed and got up off the bed. I got up quickly off the bed and fucked right off and never looked back. I'll never know what she wanted. Was it sex? Was she a prostitute? Or an undercover policewoman trying to get me for drugs—fuck knows.

Day 40: 22 April 1990, Thailand, 4-Day Jungle Trek (North Thailand)

Excellent day. Got picked up at 9.30 a.m. as I'm going on a 4-day and 3-night jungle trek in the north of Chiang Mai.

We drove by jeep for 1½ hours before stopping off at a really tropical waterfall for a swim (brilliant), then we carried on driving for another hour before stopping for lunch and then beginning the trek. Initially, we came across the Meo tribe before heading off deep into the jungle. It is the hot season at the moment, and there were quite a few fires. We even walked through one. In the wet season, though, there are loads of leeches.

We came across a hot spring where boiling water shoots out from a hole in the earth. There was steam coming off the stream. We walked further down about 200 hundred yards, where the water was as hot as a bath. It was great lying in a hot stream (similar to a Jacuzzi but with jungle surroundings). We stopped off at a traditionaly dressed Karen tribe village for the night—great.

Day 41: 23 April 1990, Thailand, 4-Day Jungle Trek (North Thailand)

I got up at 7 a.m. with a really bad back after sleeping on the bamboo floor in our bamboo-stilt Karen-village hut.

After breakfast, we set off in the scorching sun, yet only 9 a.m. in the morning. It was hard work going up and down the hills in the jungle when it gets to over 40°C during the day. The next village we came across, I saw a baby who had died last night. It was a sad sight, seeing it lying there with its family crying.

We carried on trekking through the jungle before stopping for lunch and a nap as it's too hot to even think. Then we went the next 1½ hours on elephant, which was even worse than the trekking as I had to hold on for my life, getting rocked everywhere.

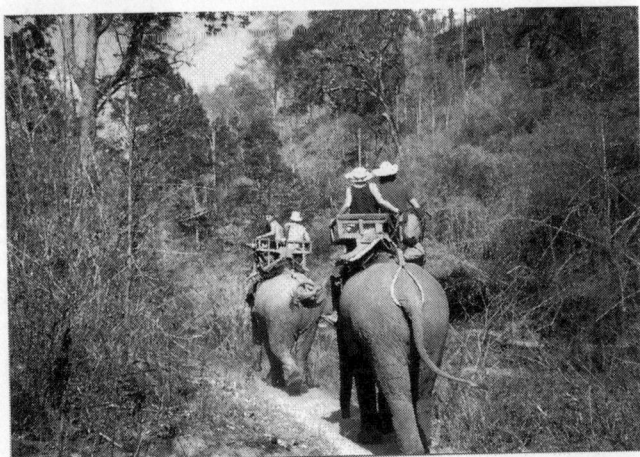

We got to another Karen tribe, where we're sleeping tonight, dived in the river to cool off, and stayed there for ages. Had fried rice and baby deer before smoking opium and going to bed.

Day 42: 24 April 1990, Thailand, 4-Day Jungle Trek (North Thailand)

Got up at 8 a.m. Didn't sleep too well last night as it was fucking cold.

We left the camp soon after breakfast by a raft made entirely out of bamboo. It was even tied together from thinly cut bamboo. It was great fun, but the raft was far from stable, with it nearly overturning at one rapid. Saw a poisonous snake (3 feet long) just basking in the sun on a rock by the river. We got fairly close before being told that it was poisonous.

We stopped off at another tribe. They were having a BBQ. They had baby wild boars about 6 inches long on a stick. They were very tasty. Helped wash an elephant in the river and got a photo of me standing on its head.

Nearly lost my legs when I got trapped between some rocks and the raft in the rapids. We rafted for 6 hours today, and after 3 hours, the raft was virtually in pieces, and the bags got soaked—we were lucky not to lose them. A fairly dangerous day.

Day 43: 25 April 1990, Thailand, 4-Day Jungle Trek (North Thailand)

Got up with a bad back again from sleeping on the floor. Had a quick wash, shit, etc. in the river before trekking off to see some more tribes. I bought a pipe for £1.50.

Saw the Akha tribe in their village before moving on to the Lahu tribe. It was really hot (about 40°C), and the trek was hard going, but Jez and I were having a laugh, so it wasn't so bad. I've known Jez for 4 days, and we get on really well (he's Irish but working in Saudi Arabia as a dentist. He's about 40 years old). As I was getting out of the jeep, he asked me my surname, and it was the same as his mother's, so maybe we are related—I don't know.

I'm totally shattered and caught the bus back to Bangkok at 6.30 p.m. Again, I was the only white person on the bus.

Day 44: 26 April 1990, Bangkok, Thailand
The bus broke down in the middle of the night and then when we finally got going. Again, we got a flat tyre. I was virtually too tired to sleep and had a fairly rough journey. When we finally got to Bangkok, I had to wait for a bus to take me to Koh Siang Road. The bus was jam-packed with people, and I didn't have a clue where I was or where to get off. I got there in the end after spending over an hour on the bus.

Koh Siang Road is great, just a street full of tourists. It's like being in Spain. I got talking to a Scottish lad, Jerry, and we walked down to Pay Pong (red-light area). We got lost, and it took us 1½ hours. Went to see a show and saw the usual perverted acts: pulling a chain of razor blades out their fannies, shagging, dripping hot candle wax all over their naked bodies.

Day 45: 27 April 1990, Bangkok, Thailand

Got up early in order to write out a load of postcards etc. Met Jerry, and we went to the massage place. I had a nice bird, while Jerry had the short fat one. Mine couldn't speak any English though. I was expecting a nice relaxing massage—I was wrong. I spent most of the hour gripping my teeth in agony as she bent, twisted, and pulled every limb of my body. At one stage, I was lying on my front while she walked up and down on my back, then, while still standing on my back, she grabbed my arms and pulled me towards her—all the bones in my back cracked.

Cashed another traveller's cheque and went on a spending spree, sent *Jive Bunny* tops to Stuart and a small parcel to the family. I caught the bus at 6.30 p.m. to take me to Penang in Malaysia.

Day 46: 28 April 1990, Penang, Malaysia

The night coach was a bit rough as I had eventually gotten to sleep when the bus stopped at a garage, and everyone got off for something to eat. Then when I finally got to sleep again, I was woken up as I had to change buses (6 a.m.). The bus drove for about 5½ hours before dropping me and a few others off at some town, where we had to wait 1½ hours to catch a minibus to Penang Malaysia.

There was quite an array of travellers, 2 French, 1 Brazilian, 1 Korean, and 1 Bangladeshi. We got to the border at 3 p.m. The lad from Bangladesh nearly didn't get in as he didn't have a visa, so he had to bribe them. It was an interesting journey watching all the people working in the paddy fields and the rubber plantations.

Got to Penang via a 15-minute ferry and then couldn't find anywhere to stay because it is the Muslim New Year, and lots of the Malaysians are on holiday. Found a place in the end for £1.20. I had a massive pig out before having a quick look round and going for a well-deserved sleep.

Day 47: 29 April 1990, Penang, Malaysia

I went round with the South American guy today. We went exploring round George Town. There are lots of Chinese people here, which means great food. We went round the local market, where I tried out various tropical fruits, like star fruit and coconut water, etc.

My camera broke, so I ended up buying a new one for $40. Got talking to an Aussie girl and spent the rest of the afternoon walking round the shopping centre with her, then she introduced me to her mates. We all went for something to eat before going out on the piss. Then a group of buskers joined us, by which time there was a massive gang of us. When the bar closed at 12.30 a.m. we went to another one. When I was staggering home, I saw a big rat in the street, so I stood still and watched it, and it came in my direction and stood about 6 feet away from me. I scared it away in case it decided to bite me.

I got back to the hotel at 2.30 a.m. and had to bang on the front door. I woke the staff up as after 1 a.m. they lock the door and go to bed.

Day 48: 30 April 1990, Penang, Malaysia

I got a new zip sewn on my money belt today, costing me about 65 pence. Then got my watch strapped, glued together for free.

I met Sarah (the Australian girl), and we went to the beach together. It took us an hour to get there with 2 bus rides. The beach was great, with massive hills covered in trees behind us. When we left, we decided to hitch it back to George Town (10 miles). We got a lift with the first vehicle that came past—an open-back lorry. We climbed into the back, and it was fun until it began pissing down really hard.

The rain carried on pouring down for a few hours, after which the whole town was flooded with water 6" deep in the road. I was wading through it and fell down a manhole in the middle of the road. I went straight down up to my chest and smashed my legs and side on the way down. I was soaking wet, and now my new camera wouldn't work—bollocks.

Went out tonight with the same crowd as last night and got absolutely arseholed. Some old bloke got pissed up with us, and he stuck a safety pin through his arm. He was going to do it through his cheek. Everyone went to bed at 1 a.m. so I went round with a big group of English lads to a disco bar. It was great, but I can't remember any more. I don't know what time I got to the hotel, but I must have woken up the staff again.

Day 49: 1 May 1990, Penang, Malaysia

Great day. Woke up with a massive hangover from last night. I hired a cast-iron bicycle with no gears, along with 2 other lads, and we set off on a 50-mile bike ride around the island. I felt like shit for the first couple of hours and nearly threw up.

First stop was the Snake Temple in which poisonous viper snakes roam around freely inside. We then went through a few scenic fishing villages along the coast before reaching a rubber plantation, in which rubber is drained off the trees. Then came the hills. One hill took nearly an hour to bike up, and I was sweating my bollocks off. The way down was good as I didn't have to peddle for 5½ kms. I just rolled down and watched the great view. Then we stopped off at a waterfall before going to the Butterfly Farm, where giant butterflies fly around, saw grasshoppers 6" long and scorpions the same size. Saw a great sunset on the coast but couldn't take a photo as my camera broke (again). We did the last 10 miles in the dark, and it began to absolutely piss it down, I was drenched and nearly got run over a few times as I had no lights.

Day 50: 2 May 1990, Penang, Malaysia

I wrote another batch of postcards out this morning (I'm getting pissed off with it). My camera still won't work after I fell down a manhole, and it got wet, so I took it back to the shop and bullshitted like mad and swapped it for a new one.

I decided to go to the top of Penang Hill in order to get a great view of the island. It took me an hour to get there, then I found out that the train that takes you to the top wasn't working, so I had to go back to George Town.

I met the Australian girl and went round with her for the rest of the afternoon. She bought a bottle of vodka, and we shared it between us. I went back to my doss hole to check out. The manager had charged me for an extra day because I didn't check out at noon. I could see his point, but I had no money left, and someone wanted to take my room, which meant that he wouldn't lose any money. We had a very big argument, and he wasn't going to let me leave. We were very close to having a fight but didn't. Got the bus at 8.30 p.m. and went over Penang Bridge, the 3rd longest bridge in the world at over 8 miles long.

Day 51: 3 May 1990, Singapore

I hardly got any sleep on the bus. In the morning, we got delayed due to a couple of accidents etc. One of them, a young lad had been knocked off his bike and was lying there dead by the side of the road.

When I got to Singapore, I had to catch 2 underground trains in order to get me to a cheap doss house. The station, streets, etc. are very clean, with no litter. My bag is on its last legs with the stitching coming out everywhere. I got to the doss house in the end. I'm sleeping on the balcony on the 6th floor, along with hundreds of other travellers.

I went to explore the island—I think I've found paradise at long last. There are no golden beaches here with palm trees, but they have a McDonald's where you can get 2 double cheeseburgers and a large chocolate milkshake for just over £1. I went to the cinema and watched *Born on the Fourth of July*.

Civilisation again—who needs it?

Day 52: 4 May 1990, Singapore

I had my free breakfast this morning on the 13th-floor balcony, watching the world pass by, then it began absolutely pissing it down.

There are lots of pathetic yet stupid rules here in Singapore—smoking in a public place, £200 fine, not flushing the toilet, £300 fine, even crossing the road at the wrong place. I daren't leave my doss house. Saw a tramp being arrested for sleeping on the pavement.

Spent the whole day running round like a twat, trying to find out when the boat sails to Jakarta—I went to the port and got passed on to about 10 people before getting sent somewhere a bus ride away. I was getting nowhere slowly, so I bought a plane ticket for £60.

Went round the town tonight, and the streets were just full of white people (most of whom work here). There are also some great-looking Chinese women here, and they all wear mini skirts.

Day 53: 5 May 1990, Singapore
    It was pissing it down again this morning. I went round all the electrical shops today (there's thousands of them) and got a good-quality walkman for £40. Spent the rest of the day walking round Singapore, listening to my new friend. I still can't get over how spotless and clean the city is—I'd love to come and work here one day. There must be at least 20 McDonald's here in the city—they are on almost every corner.

Went back to my doss house and watched the sunset from the 13th floor—a great sight. Then I went out round the town for a pig out. I saw loads of people going out on the piss for their Saturday night out (as I would in England), yet my Saturday night here in Singapore was spent sewing. Yes, trying to sew my fast-deteriorating bag together.

Day 54: 6 May 1990, Jakarta, Indonesia
    I just lazed around today on the balcony until midday, when I caught the bus to the airport in order to fly to Indonesia. I finally got to Jakarta (capital of Indonesia). I booked into a youth hostel for 67 pence. I'm in the dormitory.

I went out on the piss with an Aussie and a guy from New York (ex-DJ from the Hippodrome). We bought a litre of whiskey each for 50 pence. We started drinking in the street and were soon paralytic. We started talking to a couple of prostitutes. I fell asleep in the back of a cycle rickshaw. The driver got pissed off because he couldn't wake me up. Then we lost Dan. No one can remember anything else, but Dan woke up with a lass from the slum area and had no money left, and his necklace was gone. I woke up in the youth hostel. My bed was soaking wet with piss. I had no money left, and my necklace and camera (less than a week old) were gone. Bob woke up in a right mess, half his face ripped off. His neck was all grazed, and his shoulder and knees were all ripped apart.

We thrown out of the youth hostel. An American lad was laughing at us, so Bob pissed on his bed.

Day 55: 7 May 1990, Jakarta, Indonesia

We got thrown out the hostel, so we checked into another one. We were all still pissed and went straight to sleep. I woke up at 2 p.m. and stood up and nearly threw up everywhere, so I had to go back to sleep again.

We all got up at about 3.30 p.m. and could hardly move. Our hangovers were that bad from last night's cheap whiskey. No one knows what happened last night. We spent all day trying to work out what happened, and here is our most logical guess—Dan went back to a bird's house, leaving me and Bob. We went into the back streets, where I went off leaving Bob with my valuables. Bob, who was then on his own, got mugged, put up a fight, and got beaten up very bad and ended up being dragged along the floor, where he ripped half his face off.

I had one of my worst ever hangovers in living memory. A Chinese man gave me a 2-hour reflexology massage for £3.

Day 56: 8 May 1990, Jakarta, Indonesia

I've still got my hangover from 2 nights ago. Found out today that Jakarta is in the top 10 of roughest cities in the world, alongside the Bronx in New York. There is a number 70 bus here that rides around the town and is full of muggers, where no end of tourists get on the bus and have been pinned down by half the bus and have had all their valuables removed before being thrown off.

I pulled a local girl this afternoon (very pretty) and spent the rest of the afternoon with her, walking round the streets. I took her back to my hotel but couldn't get into my room because Bob had walked away with the key. I really enjoyed the intimate company of the other sex again. Dan touched the woman in charge of the guest house, and she went mental (as she's a Muslim). All he did was touch her shoulder. Her husband came out and nearly hit Dan. We all had a big argument, and they were going to call the police but kicked us out instead.

I, Dan, and 3 other lads went to a disco tonight. All the birds were very good-looking but all prostitutes, slags, and transvestites. A bird came up and pulled me. We were talking for a bit, then I asked if she wanted to go outside. She said no but that if I wanted to sleep with her, I would have to provide a room. I couldn't take her back to my hotel as I was locked out. A room above the disco was £9. I needed an extra £6. I tried to borrow, but no one had any money. I went to reception, but they wouldn't let me have the room for anything less, so we decided to go in the toilet. I went first and waited ages, but she didn't come. Then I realised that I was in the wrong toilet, by which time she'd fucked off home. At the end of the night, we went outside, and all the birds wanted to sleep with us. I got a taxi with 2 other birds and went to their place, and here I was, shagging all night for the price of a taxi fare £1.20. She was very good-looking with a great figure. Caught a taxi home, which broke down halfway. Dan and the Swedish guy got a free shag as well but had to pay for a hotel room. There were 4 birds trying to sleep with the yank, but he didn't believe them when they said it was for free. They were virtually demanding sex from him. He ran away in the end, and they chased him. Dan had another argument with the hotel woman and got arrested.

Day 57: 9 May 1990, Jakarta, Indonesia

I caught the train to Yogyakarta at 6.30 p.m. Another rough and hot journey during which I slept on the floor.

Day 58: 10 May 1990, Yogyakarta, Indonesia

Finally got to a Yogyakarta guest house at 8 a.m. and went straight to bed. I was knackered.

Got up at 1 p.m. Dan and Bob were still asleep, so I went off on my own. I wrote a letter to Stuart in England, explaining about when we got robbed and about the birds in the nightclubs coming up to us and asking us for sex (free of charge). Even though it's all true, I doubt he will believe it.

Bob walked out into the road today without looking, and a bicycle rickshaw ran him over. Bob was OK, but the rickshaw nearly crashed into a car before falling off.

I had a walk round Yogyakarta and found it pretty boring after Jakarta. Went round the street markets in the evening before having an early night at 11 p.m.

Day 59: 11 May 1990, Yogyakarta, Indonesia

I went to the beach today with Bob. We caught the bus to Paragannthis. The bus took an hour and cost 20 p—on the way, it began pissing it down with rain but had stopped by the time we got to the beach. The beach isn't made up of sand but volcanic dust and debris from all the volcanoes. We had a walk along the beach, and someone stopped us because they wanted their daughter to have a photo next to us. The next thing we knew, there was a massive crowd of Indonesians coming towards us. We ended up having our photo taken about 20 times—next to mums and dads, brothers and sisters.

Saw a tramp lying on the side of the road, with only a T-shirt on. His balls were hanging out for everyone to see.

We caught the bus back, and there were about 10 old women sitting at the back, chewing betelnut leaves—all their teeth were red and falling out. They let me have some. It was vile.

Went to the cinema in the evening and watched an English film shot in Chicago. It was just like being at home. When we came out, it was a really big shock to see all the dirt and poverty again. Went round some local lad's house after for a joint.

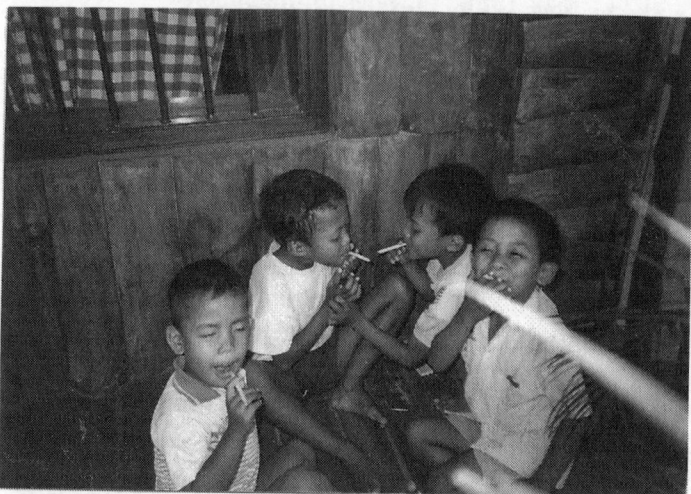

Day 60: 12 May 1990, Probalingo, Indonesia

Got up at 5.30 a.m. in order to catch the 6.30 a.m. train that didn't leave until 7.30 a.m. Some fat cunt came and sat next to us and began practicing his English on us—the twat was there for about 8 hours and was driving me round the bend. I had to go to another carriage. I was really tired and went into the luggage compartment. I went to sleep between 2 motorbikes and got covered in shit, but I needed my sleep desperately.

Went past Mount Merapi—the second most active volcano in the world. Got to Probalingo at 8 p.m. and went to a very good-quality hotel for 60 pence each a night, with breakfast included.

Day 61: 13 May 1990, Probalinggo, Indonesia

Had a lie-in today and got up at 10.30 a.m. I went round the small town and never saw another white person all day. All the people are very friendly, and when you walk down the street, everyone is waving and saying hello.

We decided to go to Mount Bromo—a very famous volcano, but the accommodation is very expensive (over £1), so we decided to sleep on the top of the volcano. We caught a minibus to a nearby village and then spent another 2 hours walking up to the top of the volcano. It was fairly cold, and we were way above the cloud line (3,000 metres above sea level). We got there in time to see the sunset. It started to piss it down before we went to sleep, so we broke into the tourist centre. Bob slept on the settee, Dan slept on the floor, while I slept on the coffee table.

Day 62: 14 May 1990, Mount Bromo, Indonesia

I woke up at 2.30 a.m. after only a few hours' sleep. We all left the tourist centre and went for a walk round the volcano and waited for sunrise. It was freezing but worth waiting for. When it got lighter, we realised how dangerous it had been walking round the top of the volcano in the dark. There was a massive drop in the centre from which steam was coming out, a fantastic sight.

I lost Bob and Dan so went back on my own. I was waiting back at the hotel for them and got talking to a couple of local Indonesian girls, who invited me back to their house. I went back and met their family and was treated like a king, with them forcing tea, fruit, and biscuits down my throat for a couple of hours. Bob and Dan were at the hotel when I got back—we went out for a meal from one of the many street vendors. Bob and I got on a bicycle rickshaw each and had a race down the street.

Caught the midnight train to Bali—nearly missed it.

Day 63: 15 May 1990, Bali (Kuta), Indonesia

The train to Bali was crammed, packed with people and standing room only. I was getting pissed off with it, and so when we stopped at a station, I went to find somewhere better. I got to the back of the engine room before the train pulled away. It was very bumpy, but at least I had a seat. At the next stop (an hour later), I went to get Dan and Bob. We took all our bags out of the train in order to move into the engine room, but just as we'd moved our bags outside, the train began to pull away, so it was a quick panic to get back on the train into our original place.

At the next station, we all ran with our bags and were just climbing into the engine room when the driver caught us and threw us out, so we went into another carriage.

Caught a bus to the ferry. The ferry took half an hour before a 2-hour bus ride to Dempesar in Bali. All this travelling, 11 hours on a train, bus and ferry only cost about £1.60. Spent about 2 hours in Kuta, asking for cheap accommodation, but everything is expensive because of all the tourists.

Day 64: 16 May 1990, Bali, Indonesia

Went down to the beach today and ended up arguing with a man selling watches. We were so close to having a fight.

Dan and I had an omlette topped with magic mushrooms, and we got so stoned, it was unbelievable. We couldn't even find our way back to the room. We didn't have a clue where we were. Bob took us to a bar and left us there while he went for a meal. We just sat there hanging on to the bar. Everywhere I looked, I saw mirrors. It took me half an hour to find the toilets. When the effects began wearing off, we got a bottle of whiskey and downed it. I got paralytic and ended up climbing a massive totem pole in the middle of the disco, with no clothes on. I got thrown out and ended up falling asleep in the middle of the road. All the traffic got held up for about 5 minutes. I lost Dan and Bob and fell asleep on the side of the road, where a bird (from Borneo) picked me up and took me back to her house.

Day 65: 17 May 1990, Bali, Indonesia

I didn't know where I was when I woke up. I looked round and saw a bird lying next to me. I left her and began walking home. It took me 45 minutes as she lived in the next town.

I got back at 2.30 p.m. and was totally fucked, with a bad hangover. I spent the rest of the day walking round like a zombie. Went out again tonight on the piss and had another great night. I spent most of it dancing away in a disco pub, along with a load of Australian pissheads. Bob and I nearly had a fight with 2 massive Australians who kept giving us some abuse. I can't remember anything else. The next thing I knew, I was walking home, and it was about 8 a.m. I don't know where I'd been.

Day 66: 18 May 1990, Bali, Indonesia

Dan is going back to Sydney tonight, so Bob and I moved to a cheaper room. We found a cheap room last night—looking for a double room with breakfast and tea. We went back today with our bags, and the bloke told us the room was 10,000. We had a massive argument with him because the price had gone up. We were shouting at him for 10 minutes. All his mates came, and we were so close to a fight, when we realised we were at the wrong place.

Went out on the piss again tonight with Bob. I took a bottle of whiskey with me and got totally smashed. I ended up falling asleep on the dance floor for over an hour, while everyone danced around me. Bob ended up in a swimming pool with 3 birds—all naked, he ended up poking one of them. Bali is about half the size of a Spanish resort yet twice as wild. Bob and I have already got a reputation for being crazy, and the birds love us.

Day 67: 19 May 1990, Bali, Indonesia
Woke up this morning next to the bird from Borneo. She found me asleep again last night.

I was pissed up for most of the day and pissed off because I lost my T-shirt last night. I got home at 3.30 p.m. from my night out.

Went out for another crazy night with Bob. I've taught him my sprog trick, and everyone loves it. I was supposed to be sober tonight because we're going on a trip tomorrow, but I ended up getting out of my face again. I had some mega mushrooms as well.

Day 68: 20 May 1990, Bali, Indonesia
I couldn't believe it when I woke up this morning as I was lying next to the bird from Borneo again. That's 3 times she's found me asleep on the street and brought me back to her place.

I got home at 3 p.m. and had missed my trip.

Went out on the piss again tonight with Bob. We went outside the Crazy Horse, where they had a competition to climb a massive coconut tree. There was a massive crowd, and I took my clothes off before climbing up it. I met a Swedish bird tonight. At the end of the night, she said she was going to the toilet, but she never came back.

On the way home, Bob and I saw an Australian being beaten up by 3 Indonesian guys. We ran over to help, and Bob ended up getting a black eye.

Day 69: 21 May 1990, Bali, Indonesia

I've been in Bali for 7 nights now, and last night was the first time that I'd actually slept in my bed as I usually sleep in the street or with the bird from Borneo. I got to bed last night at 5 a.m. and got woken up by the German guy at 8 a.m. in order to go to some place with Bob so he can get his Australian visa. We were going to go to a tattoo place but didn't have time.

At night, we went out on the piss again. I drank in the street with a group of Indonesians playing guitars before going to the Crazy Horse and winning an arrack drinking competition. I nearly had a fight with 3 Aussie guys who began taking the piss out of England. I got talking to an English lad, paralysed from the neck down. I held his drink and fags for him. Got pissed out my face and fell asleep down an alley.

Day 70: 22 May 1990, Bali, Indonesia

Woke up at 9 a.m. down an alley and had lost my wallet.

Spent most of the day with the Indonesian bird. She's moved hotels so that she is nearer to me. She wants me to move in with her, but I don't. I slept at her place all afternoon and began having hallucinations.

Went on the piss again. Bob and I went to a disco. We pulled a couple of Indonesian girls but couldn't be arsed today, so we did a runner. We went to Crazy Horse. I saw the 3 Aussies whom I nearly had a fight with last night. I offered one of them to go outside, but he wimped away. We spent most of the night drinking and dancing. We got in the nightclub for free. There were no spare birds, so I danced on the stage until it closed. We had a great sing-song with a load of English football hooligans. I ended up jumping head first into a hedge. We stopped off for a meal and ordered rice. They gave us rice with egg, which cost more, and we didn't have enough money, so all the local heavy mobs moved in. In the end, we had to scrounge some money.

Day 71: 23 May 1990, Bali, Indonesia

Woke up next to the Indonesian bird. I spent most of the day with her until she fell out with me because I've been with her for one week and never taken her out at night, and I've only spent 20 pence on her.

Went to Crazy Horse tonight, and I won the 'climbing the coconut tree' competition. There was an Italian bird's party 3 miles away, so we went to it. We got there via motorbike taxi, excellent fun, pissed out my face and drinking my bottle on the back of the bike.

The party was a Yuppie do, full of Italians, great music. I danced all night. Bob had a go at DJing and messed it up. All the yuppies were moaning. Then about 10 local rogues stormed in, and because the music was too loud, they nearly hit Bob. It got a bit crap after, so I left and went back to my local. I met Micky, and we went to the Pink Panther, and we got drenched as it was pissing it down.

Day 72: 24 May 1990, Bali, Indonesia

Got to sleep at 6.30 a.m. last night and up 2 hours later because I'm supposed to be getting a jeep. I was supposed to be catching the jeep with 6 other lads, but only 1 turned up, and he only turned up to tell me that he wasn't going. I went back to his place for a sleep.

Got back to my room at 5 p.m. Bob got pissed tonight and went with a prostitute. After he finished, he told her he only had 70 pence. She went barmy and brought her pimp in. Bob nearly had a fight with him.

I went out and got paralytic again. I ended up drinking arrack in the street with Big Will before meeting all the English lads. I can't really remember anything else apart from falling asleep on the street—*again*, and I woke up at the bird-from-Borneo's house *again*.

Day 73: 25 May 1990, Bali, Indonesia

I just couldn't believe it when I woke up at the bird-from-Borneo's house again. I got home at about 1 p.m. Bob had only been home a few hours himself. I can't get over how crazy this place is. It's full of people like me who keep trying to get out of Bali but drink too much the night before and keep delaying it.

Got arseholed again tonight with Geoff and Kenny (paralysed lad in a wheelchair). I needed the wheelchair more than he did on the way home. I was pushing him and nearly crashed it several times. I had to stop at every prostitute so he could chat them up. I bumped into Borneo (the prostitute who always takes me home for free). She wanted me to go back with her, so I did, again!

Day 74: 26 May 1990, Bali, Indonesia

Woke up and walked back home, got back at 12 p.m. The Indonesian bird was waiting for me and wanted to know where I had been. I told her I had slept in the street again.

I went to pick up my photographs, but 17 of the negatives got chewed up in the machine, so I didn't get them. I had a massive argument with the bloke, so he gave me a free film. Then he tried to charge me for the 22 photos that did develop, but I just walked out the shop. I was supposed to be meeting Mike, but by the time I got there, he had gone.

Spent the rest of the day walking round with a hangover. Went out and got totally pissed out my face again tonight with Kenny and Geoff. At the end of the night, I saw Borneo. I didn't want to stay at her place, so she was pissed off and chased me down the street. I was pissed and kept falling down.

I went to call for Jingles (another bird) at 6 a.m. and she burst out crying. She had been raped in the disco. She went for a piss, and some lad followed her into the toilet.

Day 75: 27 May 1990, Bali, Indonesia

Woke up with Jingles at about 2 p.m. and then fucked off. Had a few games of pool (lost).

Went out on the piss, drank half a bottle of whiskey, and went on the beer. Spent most of the night in Kwala Blue and Crazy Horse, drinking and dancing. I pinched a motorbike helmet and wore it for the rest of the night. I was running round, drinking, dancing, and chatting up the birds, with a motorbike helmet on my head. I looked a right twat but was too pissed to care. I went round with Kenny (great lad who is paralysed from the neck downwards). I can't remember anything else but ended up falling asleep down an alley and got robbed for the 3rd time in 2½ weeks. This time, they got my gold ring (18th-birthday present) and my helmet.

Day 76: 28 May 1990, Bali, Indonesia

I got home at 7.30 a.m. after waking up in the street. Geoff came round at 9.30 a.m. as we're hiring a jeep. I felt like shit and was still pissed. Bob, Kenny, and Geoff, and I hired a minibus for £20 for 2 days.

We got lost in Dempesar (the capital) as there are no signposts. It took us 4 hours to go about 45 minutes. We got to Lake Batur, a massive volcano in the mountains. It was really foggy, and we could not see more than 20 yards in front. We hired a speedboat to take us across Lake Batur to a cemetery, and it took me half an hour to get Kenny into the boat from his wheelchair. It was good fun driving a speedboat cross a massive volcano with beautiful scenery. We got to the cemetery, a very spooky place—they didn't bury these dead or burn them but left them on the ground to rot. There were rotting bodies lying around—one of them had flip-flops on. There were magic mushrooms growing around the bodies. There were skulls and bones everywhere. Next to the cemetery was a tree, 1500 years old. Then we visited an ancient temple.

Went on the magic mushrooms tonight. We got a buzz but nothing too big.

Day 77: 29 May 1990, Bali, Indonesia

Got up and went for a bath in the hot springs down the road. Everywhere you look, there are giant volcanoes. We drove around for a bit and ended up at Lovina Beach. It was pretty shit, so we headed back to Kuta. We got back at 9 p.m. and I went round to see Jingles.

Went on the piss with Kenny tonight—he may be paralysed from the neck down but has travelled around the world, been arrested several times, and had a few fights, knocking someone out with a headbutt once. We bought a bottle of arrack for 66 p and drank it in the street. We were both soon arseholed. Kenny was really bad and could hardly speak. We went back to Kwala Blue, and Kenny ended up unconscious and threw up all over himself and the table. We got into Peanuts, and I was pushing him around and kept crashing. In the end, he woke up, and I took him for a dance on the dance floor and nearly dropped him a few times. Called for Jingles at the end of the night and spent the night with her.

Day 78: 30 May 1990, Bali, Indonesia

Woke up with Jingles and went home, then hired a surfboard. I was quite far out in the sea, and there was no one about, so I had a tug. The next thing I knew, I had drifted out about half a mile. I was shitting my pants as I didn't think that I'd make it back to land. The tide was pulling me further and further out. I swam like fuck and made it in the end. *Phew.*

Jingles came around again to clean up for us—bless her. I spent most of the day surfing, and then I went for a 5-mile run with Royston. It was a fast pace, and I was fucked after. I bumped into Phil (a lad whom I met 11 weeks ago in Nepal) and had a few joints with him.

Kenny and I went on the arrack again tonight, another bottle between us. We were all pissed. I could hardly walk and kept crashing Kenny's wheelchair. He fell out at one stage when I bumped into the curb, but he was too pissed to notice. We went to Peanuts again and made twats of ourselves. I ended up falling asleep on the road—*again*.

Day 79: 31 May 1990, Bali, Indonesia

Woke up on the street and staggered home. Jingles came around to see me. I was pissed out my face still and bought lots of clothes for Australia. It wasn't until I sobered up slightly that I realised that I didn't like any of the stuff I bought.

I spent the whole day walking round like a zombie, my whole body on reject—2 weeks on the piss, and I've only slept in my bed twice, and I've been robbed 3 times in the last 3 weeks.

It's our last day as we fly to Perth tonight. I felt like shit and could hardly breathe.

When we got to Perth, we had 4 birds and 2 lads waiting for us (Bob's mates), and within 5 minutes of being in Australia, we were on the piss. There were 8 of us in one car. The boot wouldn't open, so we had to squeeze the bags in as well. We all piled round to Bob's bird's house for a party. I was really fucked and fell asleep after a few beers.

Day 80: 1 June 1990, Perth, Australia

Typical—my first day in Australia, and it's also the first day of winter. My whole body is stiff. I feel very weak and run-down and have a bad chest.

Caught the bus into town with Bob and Karen (Bob's bird). It was my first taste of Perth, and I was impressed. It's a very clean and modern city yet with a lot of spotless older buildings. We went to a pub (the Brass Monkeys) for a quick beer before going home. There were now 8 people living in the house that's supposed to be for 2 people, and another person is arriving in a few days. Went around a few pubs tonight and got pissed up, went for a kebab, which was shit. Then we went to the Firm, which is a disco. It was good, but I couldn't dance as I kept getting a stitch. I was really tired and fell asleep—the disco closes at 6 a.m. but we left at about 2.30 a.m.

Day 81: 2 June 1990, Perth, Australia

I still can't believe I'm actually in Australia after nearly 12 weeks of travelling. Now that I'm in Australia, it means that I've been to all 5 continents by the time I'm 21.

I caught the bus into town today and then again to Riversvale, where I called for my aunty and uncle. They were out, so I went down to the river and fell asleep on the jetty. I woke up a couple of hours later and called for them again. They were in this time, and they had been expecting me for the last week. I read all my mail that had been sent and phoned my mum up—I didn't know what to say. They cooked steak for me, delicious.

I went to a pub with Karen and Bob tonight and got a stitch walking only 5 metres. Felt rough as fuck and went home after one beer—really bad stitch.

Day 82: 3 June 1990, Perth, Australia

Got up at 10 a.m. and still felt really fucked. Woke Bob up, and we both walked down to the launderette with a big dustbin liner full of cheesy washing. It was the first time I'd ever done my own washing, and it was a piece of piss.

My aunt and uncle picked me up at 2.30 p.m. as they are taking me to a friend of my dad—he travelled around Africa with my dad. They live in a very posh house in a very posh area near the river. We went for a bike ride along the river, about 5 miles, before having a big pig-out. My aunt and uncle have never seen my dad's friends before, and I was looking through some old photos at a stranger's house and saw a picture of me, and what's worse is that my aunt and uncle took the photo.

Got back at 10 p.m. and my chest was playing up. I could hardly breathe. Watched a few shitty programmes on TV.

Day 83: 4 June 1990, Perth, Australia

Still feel run-down and weak, and now I've got a mouth ulcer.

It's Bank Holiday today, and the whole town is dead. Amy's boyfriend arrived today, meaning that there were 9 of us in the house.

I went down to the beach (Scarborough Beach) today with Bob. The beach was fairly shit after Asia but still OK. The sea was freezing cold, so I didn't stay in for long. As soon as I came out, my chest and stitch felt a lot better. Watched the sun set along the coast before catching the bus back to Mount Hawthorn (Perth). I had about 20 slices of toast today and a big bag of fish and chips—there's nothing like a good healthy diet. Half the people in the house got pissed tonight on gin.

Day 84: 5 June 1990, Perth, Australia

Got up at 8 a.m. in order to start work (I've only worked 7 days this year). Bob was ill, so I went on my own. I went for the job selling papers in the street—it's shite pay but a good laugh. I turned up at the office, and it was full of other people who also do the same job. I got my papers and my stand and got sent to a war memorial on Victoria Street. I felt a right prat to start off with, standing on a street corner, shouting, 'Daily News'. I get $10 a day and then 10 c per every paper I sell. I was pissed off when I worked hard all morning and only sold 17 papers. In the afternoon, I got a bit pissed off and started getting a bit cheeky to people. I started to sell loads after about 4 o'clock, when people started coming out of the offices. Chatted up a few birds, worked for 8 hours, and sold 95 papers (very good), yet I only earned about $22 (about £11). I spent half my money on food and drink and getting to work and back.

Day 85: 6 June 1990, Perth, Australia

Woke up with a massive headache—I couldn't move as it was so painful. I had a few painkillers, which improved it a bit. I've got a mouthful of ulcers as well. Bob is also in a lot of pain. His balls feel like they're on fire—he had an AIDS test yesterday. I might get one.

Went to the supermarket and bought some food—I've been living off toast the last 5 days. I'm not doing the paper-selling job any more as it's fairly hard work and very low paid. I need to earn some big money fast as I might be heading off to Darwin in a few weeks' time. I'm going to look for a proper job on Tuesday, when I'll, hopefully, be feeling 100 per cent better.

Day 86: 7 June 1990, Perth, Australia

Got up feeling like a bag of shit again and spent most of the day throwing pills down my throat. Caught the bus into town and bumped into my uncle when I was on my way to my aunt's office to pick up a letter from home.

Popped into the job centre. I saw an advert for working behind a bar for £7.50 an hour. I phoned up, and it was for a topless bar. I told them that I have no morals and would be prepared to go topless, but they only wanted girls. I phoned up for another job, and I've got an interview tomorrow at 1 p.m.

Everyone went out on the piss tonight, except me and Fay. I didn't go out as my headache was coming on strong again. I slept in Shelly's bed as when everyone came back from the pub, they all had a party in my bedroom (the lounge) until 4.30 a.m.

Day 87: 8 June 1990, Perth, Australia

I had an interview at 1 p.m. today but didn't get up until 1.30 p.m. so bollocks to that job. Everyone else got up at about 2 p.m. It's Shelly's 25th birthday, so we went for a pub lunch. We'd only been up 3 hours when everyone was getting tired again, so everyone ended up in bed.

We went tenpin bowling tonight, all 9 of us. We were all late in getting ready as everyone was watching the TV and couldn't be arsed to move. All 9 of us squeezed into the car. It got worse when we drove through town as everyone had to duck down so that we didn't get pulled over by the police. Had a couple of games of bowling before going to the Queens (pub with a band). We all ended up at the house, passing the joints around and getting stoned. It was the first match of the World Cup—Argentina lost to Cameroons 1-0.

Day 88: 9 June 1990, Perth, Australia

I got up at about 2 p.m. with the rest of the gang. It's the big party tonight: mine, Shelly's, Karen and Fay's birthday party, and Neds leaving do. We spent most of the day cleaning the house up. We needed some more wood for the fire, so Ned and I got the supermarket trolley out of the garage and went on a collecting mission. We walked down the street, pushing the trolley, ripping up any loose fences we came across.

Had some speed before the party, to keep myself awake. The party soon livened up, but there were hardly any spare birds. The bath was full of beer and ice. Had a few joints and more beer and got out my face—the next thing I knew, Dan was bringing his band inside the house. He set his stuff up, and the band began playing. I fell asleep later in the chair, and when I woke up, this bird was snogging me. I couldn't believe it—I pulled a bird in my sleep.

Day 89: 10 June 1990, Perth, Australia

At half past 7 in the morning, Shelly couldn't sleep, so we had a few joints together. I couldn't get to sleep and didn't finally nod off until 2 p.m. in the afternoon.

Woke up at 5 p.m. The house had more or less been tidied up, which was good news. Everyone was walking around the house like a zombie. Its Ned's last night, so he and Marc came home pissed out their heads.

Day 90: 11 June 1990, Perth, Australia

My 22nd birthday.

I got up at 7 a.m. to say goodbye to Ned, who is off to Sydney. I stayed up, it's my 22nd birthday, and I feel really old and past it.

I went up town with Fay to look for a job. We couldn't find one, so we got a bottle of cheap champagne each. We sat in the middle of town and hit someone with the cork when we opened the bottle. We nearly got arrested by the police, so we went down by the river and finished the bottle off there. My bastard camera broke again. By now, we were both arseholed and went back for another bottle. We drank it on the bus on the way home, with everyone staring at us. We went to the off-licence for some beers. On the way, we saw Matty in the launderette, so we talked to him for a bit.

We staggered back home. I didn't have a clue where I was. My aunt phoned. I talked with her for 10 minutes and can't remember. Then my dad's friend phoned up, and I was talking with him for 10 minutes before I realised who he was. I ended up crashed out on the lounge floor for the rest of the night.

Day 91: 12 June 1990, Perth, Australia

Got up and went for a run. I was going to start my collecting job today—collecting for charity door to door, but it was raining (shame), so I didn't bother. We had to be there for 2 p.m. and Bob never even got up in time. I'll go tomorrow, I promise.

Spent most of the day lazing around, doing nothing.

Day 92: 13 June 1990, Perth, Australia

Got up and went for a run and then woke Bob up as we are both starting our collecting jobs today, collecting for battered and unwanted dogs. We keep 30% of what we collect. I picked up a birthday card from Greg Dawson at my aunt's office on the way—she gave me a birthday present, a $5 lottery card, which I lost.

We all got in the van and got dropped off at various suburbs of Perth. I hated the fucking job, going around to people's houses and begging for money. It began pissing it down. I was soaking wet and kept getting doors slammed in my face. I had only been doing it for an hour when I knocked on a big posh house. 2 lads lived there (their parents were out at work). They told me that they had no money, only beer, so I more or less invited myself into their house. I drank a large bottle of beer in one go and then had another one—bollocks to the job. There were a couple of birds in the house, but they belonged to the lads. We started to run out of beer, so I went to the off-licence and got a couple of bottles of wine with one of the lads. I got wrecked out my face. The van picked us up at 6 p.m. I didn't know where I was. I had half a bottle of wine left when I got picked up. I was talking really loud, and everyone knew I was pissed. I only collected $20, meaning I earned $7. I spent more on that getting to work and back and on the wine. Had a good day though.

Day 93: 14 June 1990, Perth, Australia

Walked into town, took an hour, and went to the job centre and got a job for Monday morning. I visited my aunt at work and ended up going back for a meal. She had a loaf of bread that was slightly stale, so she fed it to the ducks. I was nearly crying as it was a day's worth of food for me.

When I got back to the house, everyone was going out, so I joined them. We went to a few pubs before going to the Aberdeen. It was full of US sailors as a massive carrier had ported with 6,000 of them on board. Shelly pulled a black lieutenant. At the end of the night, we all ended back at his hotel room as he had a fridge full of beer. Once the beer had run out, we went home, taking Jack with us. We stopped for a burger on the way (Jack paid). Jack stayed at our pad tonight and has invited us all to the ship on Saturday for a meal as it's Karen's birthday. Went to bed at 2.30 a.m.

Day 94: 15 June 1990, Perth, Australia

Matty woke me up when he went to work. Some bird came round today. I'd been talking to her for over an hour at the party last Saturday, but I'll be fucked if I can remember.

My dad's friend came round and took me out in the car today. We went around the outskirts of Perth for my first real taste of Oz. We visited a large dam and various other places of interest, a good day out.

Marc, Ryan, and I went to a strip do tonight. It cost $25 (£12) for as much as you drink and eat. There were topless barmaids giving the free beer out. The strip tease bird was like a fucking model and knew the ropes. First time, she stripped off in a small bathtub. Then some poor bloke got picked out of the crowd. She stripped him off and gave him a bath. Then the next time she came on stage, she did a similar thing to another guy. She was supposed to come on again, but someone nicked one of her stockings, so she stormed out in a mardy and never did the last act. We were all pissed as twats and left at about 12.30 a.m.

Day 95: 16 June 1990, Perth, Australia

Supposed to be going to the US Navy carrier for a free meal and a tour, but Jack didn't phone up—Yanks!

Went around town with Marc and bumped into Claire (Ned's old bird). It's Karen's birthday today, so we all went out on the piss. Everyone was skint, so we got pissed at home first. Marc and I drank 2½ bottles of wine and can hardly remember leaving the house. We got a taxi to the Brass Monkey, where I fell asleep on the floor after only being there for 5 minutes—I nearly got thrown out. Then we all staggered to Limbos (nightclub). As soon as we got there, Matty and I fell asleep next to each other and looked a right pair of twats. I was asleep there for over 3 hours.

Went home at 3 a.m. and watched the World Cup football with Matty, fell asleep at 5 a.m.

Day 96: 17 June 1990, Perth, Australia

Woke up at 9.30 a.m. on the lounge floor. Helped Shelly sand her car down before cleaning my room. I wrote to Greg, which took all afternoon, so the bastard better write back. Everyone was on wine tonight apart from me as I've got to get up at 4 a.m. tomorrow to start my new job—so I went to bed early, 12 a.m.

Day 97: 18 June 1990, Perth, Australia

I didn't know where I was when my alarm clock went off at 4 a.m. I biked into town in order to start my job at 5 a.m.

Met another English lad. We had to unload a lorry full of acoustic insulator walls and take them up to the 6th floor. We had a lift, but it was murder as the panels were really big, heavy, sharp, and were bastards to get into the lift. It took ages to get them to the 6th floor, by which time my hands were ripped to shreds, and there were dents in all the corridor walls. All the gear was for an ear-testing room for the old biddies. Began assembling the room for the rest of the day—very hard and physical day, but it was nice watching all the office birds go past. Worked hard for 13 hours and earned $160 (about £80), but after tax, I took home £65. I was about fucked by the time I got home.

Day 98: 19 June 1990, Perth, Australia

Got up at 7 a.m. and biked to town in order to carry on with the job I started yesterday. I worked for 1½ hours until the job was finished, earning $15 after tax. Went straight to the job centre after but couldn't find any jobs.

Went home and got changed. Matty leaves for Sydney tonight, so Fay and I went out on the piss together—we were all skint so bought a cheap bottle of champagne each and got pissed in the park. We all had party hats on and must have looked a right bunch of twats. We got another bottle before going home in a pissed-up state on the bus. I went to the local chippy, pissed out my face—the third afternoon in 8 days. I've been pissed up in the chippy. I still had my party hat on. We went down to Brass Monkey and then got some wine. I was pissed up and can't remember saying goodbye to Matty—never mind.

Day 99: 20 June 1990, Perth, Australia

Got up at 7 a.m.—still pissed and went down to the job centre with Bob in order to get some casual work, but there was none available, so we had to go back home again. I phoned up about an electronic-assembly job. They were supposed to phone me back but didn't.

I went swimming with Fay today before biking 4 miles for a job interview, promoting a discount card. I start tomorrow at 10 a.m. My 4th job in just under 2 weeks. I need it as I've only got £170 left, and jobs around Perth are as tight as a duck's arse in a frozen pond. Biked home and then went for a run. I was going to go kick-boxing afterwards, but I didn't know where to go, so I had a big bag of chips instead. Had a bit of a slobby night watching the TV.

Day 100: 21 June 1990, Perth, Australia

Started my 4th job (in 2 weeks) today, and I biked down to the office down near the beach. I had a quick training session before starting off in the car to the other side of Perth. We ended up at an industrial site. I had to go around the different factory sites and talk to the workers to try to get them to buy a discount card for $99—it's worth it, but no one was interested. After a while, I couldn't be arsed to do it any more and spent the rest of the time talking to another bird who is also doing the same sales rep as me, and she used to be a stripper. I fucked off down the pub with her. We ended up drinking champagne on the beach. Before long, we were both pissed as twats. We ended up buying a 4-litre cask of wine and going back to her place.

Day 101: 22 June 1990, Perth, Australia

Didn't know where the hell I was when I got up. There was still some wine left at the bird's house, so I drank about 2 litres of the stuff. I ended up pissed out my face *again*. We left her house at 9 a.m. I had to catch the bus down to the beach to collect my bike. I was wobbling all over the road on the way home. When I got home, I phoned up to see if I'd got an electronics job. I hadn't got it, and they wouldn't tell me why, so I argued with him, so he hung up. I phoned him back up and gave him a mouthful.

I went to town and picked up some mail from my aunt—2 postcards only, one from Penny and the other from Stuart. Phoned up for a job at a kebab house and went round for an interview. I find out tomorrow.

Got home and went mental on the sports field opposite our house, running and doing press-ups, sit-ups, etc. I didn't go out tonight as I was tired. I had just got to sleep at 1.30 a.m. when Fay and Karen

came home pissed up. They came into my room and woke me up.
We all chatted and drank champagne for about an hour.

Day 102: 23 June 1990, Perth, Australia

Spent most of the afternoon dossing around town with
Karen—I'm getting pissed off as I've only got £115 left and have no
chance of getting a job.

We all went out to a Vietnamese restaurant tonight (all 7 of us in
one car again). We brought our own wine with us, so it was fairly
cheap. We got rat-arsed and drove to a party. We were there for a
couple of hours, then I went back into town with Shelly. We went to
Networks nightclub. I had only been there half an hour, when I was
thrown out because I was asleep on one of the tables. It was about
to collapse. I didn't know where I was and walked around the streets
for a bit. I went through a car park, and some lad was beating his
bird up in the car. I ran over and stopped it. I started shouting at
the twat and told him to get out the car so I could hit him. He was
shitting his pants and wouldn't come out, and his stupid bitch of a
girlfriend was on his side, so I fucked off and left.

I went back to the nightclub, but they wouldn't let me in. I was arguing
when Bob, Ryan, Karen, etc. turned up.—we ended up at some shitty
disco. I went around pinching drinks. We got back at about 4 a.m.
and had a few joints in the lounge. The next thing I knew, it was 9
a.m. when I woke up on the lounge floor, so I went to bed.

Day 103: 24 June 1990, Perth, Australia

It's Fay's birthday today. I felt generous and gave her tea and
toast in bed.

We both went to Fremantle for the afternoon. We tried to hitch it
into town, but no one would stop, so I rolled up my trouser leg and
stood in the road. The next car that came past stopped. It was a
queer granddad, but we still got a lift. Fremantle was OK. Saw a bit
of a scuffle in the street.

Everyone went out on the piss again tonight. I stayed at home in order to save some money. When everyone got home, we all got stoned on joints. It turned out to be a good night after all.

Day 104: 25 June 1990, Perth, Australia

A bit of a shitty day. I helped Shelly take the TV back to the rented shop before going into town. I was pissed off as I'm running out of money, and we are all going up to Darwin on Monday (4200 km away).

I went on the charity-collecting job and got a bollocking because last time I did it, I got pissed out my face, and there were a few complaints. I collected $43 in the afternoon. I only handed in $16 and kept $27—I need it more than the fucking dogs, that's for sure. They were pissed off when I only gave them $16 as everyone else gave around $60 to $90.

I've got a week's free membership at an aerobics class, so I walked to the class. By the time I got there, it was too late, so I had to walk home.

We've finally bought our car, a massive 6-seater, white Holden. It's more of a minibus than a car. It goes like a rocket. Not long till Monday, when we shoot off to Darwin. It only cost $1200.

Day 105: 26 June 1990, Perth, Australia

My aunt phoned up at 8.30 a.m. to tell me that she had a letter for me from Michelle (my sister). I couldn't get back to sleep, so I woke Fay (who's now moved into my room) and talked to her.

Went for a ride in the car with Fay and Ryan, to City Beach and then Cotlslow Beach. I got back in time to start my 5th job in 2½ weeks—another collecting job, this time for a lifeboat. I went on Fay's bike and nearly didn't make it in time as I had to go via my aunt's office on the fucking one-way bastard system and nearly got run over a dozen times. I started my collecting job, and I was in a pretty poor area so didn't do that well.

Day 106: 27 June 1990, Perth, Australia

Everyone's really skint—times are hard. Owning your own tea bag has now become a status symbol in the house, and each is used at least 3 times. Bob found one in the ashtray today and used it. Everyone's food in the house (what there is) keeps getting nibbled at. I'm very tight with my money at the moment and only spent 60 c yesterday, and that was on a pint of milk. I'm now experiencing life as a pauper.

Went uptown with Fay and joined the RAC, then fucked off on my own around the shops. I went round to my aunt's office and invited myself for tea. My uncle picked us both up and took me to their new home. It's massive, with a huge swimming pool. I phoned Mum, and from what she told me, I realised how boring life was in England. Mum and Dad offered me £100 for my birthday, but I turned it down because of pride as I want to be independent, but I had to admit defeat tonight and asked my uncle for it. He just pulled £100 worth of dollars out his wallet and gave it to me.

Had a joint with Fay before going to sleep.

Day 107: 28 June 1990, Perth, Australia

It's the coldest winter here in 31 years, and the temperature dropped to an all-time low last night, 2.9°C. Everyone's talking and moaning about the cold, yet I'm still going around in my shorts.

I went collecting again. I was in a very posh area. I went to one house, and it was massive, swimming pool etc., 3 posh cars outside. I asked for a donation, and the reply was, 'Sorry, but we're penniless and can't afford it'. Bastards. When I got in, I handed in $14.50, and the bloke sacked me because I wasn't collecting enough. It was my last day so didn't give a fuck.

We all went out tonight to see a band. I smuggled a cheap bottle of champagne in. Amy and her boyfriend Ryan keep falling out. Went to another pub and went around pinching drinks and got plastered. Spent most of the night dancing with Shelly. Got a bollocking when I got home because I pissed all over the toilet seat and floor.

Day 108: 29 June 1990, Perth, Australia

Woke up with a hangover. Last night, when Ryan fell out with Amy, Ryan decided he was going to leave, so he gave me all his food. He was pissed off this morning when he changed his mind and all his food had gone.

Went around town with Amy, and it pissed down. One of Shelly's friends had a cocktail party tonight. There was food laid out, so we all had a pig-out. The party was pretty tame compared to an English one. I had cocktail after cocktail and was soon out my tree. I fell asleep on the settee. When I woke up, I didn't know where I was. We got home at 4.30 a.m. I had my usual pig-out of fish-finger butties.

Day 109: 30 June 1990, Perth, Australia

Woke up still pissed. Felt a bit bad last night. The girls spent an hour lecturing me on drinking too much, but I was pissed and can't remember.

Went down to the launderette today—my first time in a month. I had a sleeping bag wedged full of dirty washing.

Went to Fremantle tonight to meet someone the girls met in Goa (India). I bought a couple of bottles of wine and drank them on the way. We had a few beers in the house before going to an Irish pub, where they had an old boy playing the piano, so we all had a good sing-song. Then we went to a trendy pub, and I got chatting with a couple of Portuguese birds and ended up going to their car for a smoke. They kept giving me a pipe full of grass. As soon as I'd finished, they would fill it up and give it back to me—I was off my face and had about 10 pipes. I could hardly talk, I was that stoned.

Then they asked me if I wanted to go somewhere else with them. I couldn't as I had to get back to the pub in order to get a lift home with the others (it takes a half-hour drive, so I didn't fancy walking).

I didn't know where I was, and I couldn't find the others, so I hitched it home. It took me 2 lifts to get there, and on the second, lift I made him stop off at the chippy. Got home, and the others had been worried.

Day 110: 1 July 1990, Perth, Australia

My aunt was supposed to phone me this morning but never did, so I phoned her. She was ill—that's my Sunday dinner out the window. They both came down to say goodbye. We all spent the day cleaning the house up for when we leave on Tuesday.

England play Cameroon tonight in the World Cup quarter finals. I went with Fay to Café Sport to watch it, but the match didn't start until 3 a.m. so we went to a nightclub, which was full of druggies—we had a really good time, seeing as I was sober and had no money. When we got back, we had a couple of joints and got pissed on champagne.

Day 111: 2 July 1990, Perth, Australia

A busy day today as we're heading off to Darwin tomorrow. I was really tired and went shopping with Amy and Fay to get a few final things. We got the RAC to check the car out. The bloke laughed when we told him we were going to Darwin in it and said that he wouldn't take it. No matter what happens, it's going to be a laugh a minute and an adventure.

We're all virtually skint so will probably have to stop off on the way (of the 4,200 km journey) and do some fruit picking in order to raise more money. Bob went collecting today. Paris came round tonight, and we all bought a foil of grass for the journey. Got stoned off my face before going to bed.

Day: 3 July 1990, Perth, Australia

We left Perth this morning to head for Darwin, but the car wouldn't start, so we had to phone the RAC. He fixed the car, and we were soon on the way and out into the big, wide world, with fuck all money. As I always say—shit or bust, it's only 4,200 km.

Within a few minutes from Perth, we were out in the bush, with straight roads and flat scenery. After 2½ hours, we got to the Pinnacles, a desert full of natural limestone pillars up to 10 feet high. We all had a spliff in the middle, took a few photos, and fucked off quick before it got dark. We spotted a group of kangaroos hopping around. We'd already seen loads of dead ones by the roadside, but these were our first live ones.

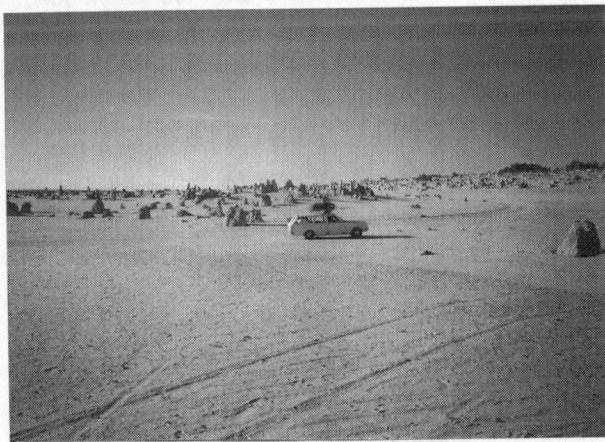

We left the main road and went down a dirt track and set up camp. Sausages and beans for tea followed by a few spliffs beside the campfire. It was freezing, and I didn't have a sleeping bag with me, so I wore 3 pairs of trousers and 6 tops. One of the worst nights I can ever remember. I spent most of the night shivering in the back of the car.

Day 113: 4 July 1990, Near Kalbarri, Australia

Had a really rough night with Bob, freezing myself silly with no sleeping bag.

The car is still poorly. It blows it's horn every time we go round a corner, which is funny when we're driving through a small town and people stare because they think that we are hooting at them. We stopped off at a small town in order to fill up with petrol, food, etc. Fay took the big gas lamp to the camping shop to get a spare part and ended up leaving the lamp in the camping shop. We didn't realise until we set up camp 200 miles away.

Bob tried out his new machete tonight and chopped down a couple of trees for our campfire. We camped illegally again, this time in Kalbarri National Park. I cooked for everyone—beans, cabbage, and noodles with potatoes. It only cost 50 c each.

Day 114: 5 July 1990, Near Kalbarri, Australia

The girls were going to go back and collect the gas fire that Fay left yesterday, but they decided that it wasn't worth it. We packed up camp and head to Kalbarri and gatecrashed the campsite there. Had a wash and shower etc., then took off without paying. We went down a bumpy dirt track in order to see some gorges—a smaller version of the Grand Canyon. Bob couldn't be arsed to have a look, so I went with the 3 girls.

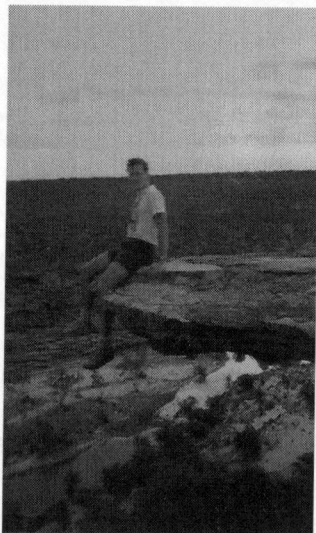

On the way, we saw a massive termite nest 9 feet tall and built like a wall. I threw massive rocks at it, but it wouldn't smash. The next thing we knew, there were thousands of termites all around us, so we fucked off sharply.

After visiting the gorge, we all rolled a spliff in the car park and drove back to town. We watched the World Cup semi-final (England vs Germany). We were in a typical local Aussie bar. It went to penalties, and England lost—bollocks. Drove out of town and set up tent again, illegally, along a dirt track. Got pissed and stoned, went to bed.

Day 115: 6 July 1990, Near Monkey Mia, Australia

I had my first decent night's sleep last night as I had 4 pairs of trousers and 12 tops on and slept between Fay and Amy.

It was my turn to drive today, and I drove for about five hours and never got bored. We stopped off at a remote garage that was full of men dressed as cowboys. They have big ranches and farms here, up to 1-2,000,000 acres. Bob was complaining because we always eat the same food, so Amy cooked us all a spaghetti bolognaise. It took ages to make. It had just been served up when Bob dropped his in the fire.

Went to a shell beach today (1 of only 3 in the world). The whole beach was just made up of tiny little shells. I drove the car on to the beach. We all had a spliff and then found somewhere to camp—in some red sand hills near a deserted beach.

Day 116: 7 July 1990, Carnarvon, Australia

Packed up camp and went down to Monkey Mia. Was supposed to pay $5 to get in, but we got out of it by driving straight through. There were wild dolphins swimming right up to the beach—2 of them, plus one baby. 1 of the adults came up to me and let me stroke it.

Spent the rest of the day driving up to Carnarvon, another small country town. Bob and I had a massive argument with the girls because he wanted to camp on a rubbish tip, but they didn't want to because it was right near an aboriginal slum area. In the end, the girls drove off and left us in the middle of nowhere, with our bags and tent. We built a fire and set up camp, not knowing if we would ever see the girls again. Bob and I were halfway through a 4-litre cask of wine when the girls came back in the car, and we were all friends again (for the time being). I got arseholed and fell asleep next to the fire—Bob had to put me to bed.

Day 117: 8 July 1990, Fishing Trawler Carnarvon, Australia

We've finally reached warmer weather, so I can go to bed without wearing 13 layers of clothing. Had a look around in daylight and found out that we'd been camping on a rubbish tip.

Everyone's pissed off with being skint, and there's a big rodeo on today, but it costs $10 to get in, and a big barn dance tonight is $5, and we can't afford to go to any of them. We need to find work very soon.

We spent most of the day on the beach, lazing around. I went for a run along the beach and down to the pier (about 1 km out to sea). Went for a swim after. We drove to town—I was driving as everyone else had been drinking. I got pulled up by the police for doing a U-turn in the wrong place—$50 fine and 1 point. Bastard. My first point ever. I was shitting myself as I'd been drinking, and the car was full of grass. This happened outside the pub, so when we went in, everyone knew. We got talking to a fisherman and ended up going back to a massive fishing trawler that he is looking after. It's worth nearly two million dollars. We all got pissed and watched a few videos and then the World Cup final—West Germany beat Argentina 1-0.

Day 118: 9 July 1990, Carnarvon, Australia

There might be work on the fishing trawler for me and Bob. We'll find out at 12 p.m. tomorrow.

Carnarvon has a population of 4000 to 5000 Aboriginals and 1000 whites. There is also 1 policeman per two hundred people. Everywhere you look in town, you see Aboriginals.

We drove around about 50 plantations today looking for work on the land. They grow crops such as bananas, oranges, peppers, etc. We couldn't find any work but managed to pinch enough vegetables from the fields to hold us out in salads for a few days. I went into the disabled toilets in the supermarket with all the dirty pots and pans and gave them a good clean. Exhausted from going around all the farms, we sat by the old campfire in the rubbish tip (that we're staying in) and got pissed.

Day 119: 10 July 1990, (Rubbish Tip) Carnarvon, Australia—Week 17

Times are hard when you have to camp illegally on rubbish tips and steal your food from local farmers. I'm that poor that I can't even afford to brush my teeth. The car is getting really bad—hooting at least twice everytime you go round a corner.

We all went down to the docks to see if Bob and I had a job on the fishing trawler. We waited on the boat for about 4 hours to find out, but the skipper missed his plane from Perth, so now the ship won't leave until tomorrow. We won't find out until then.

Bought a 4-litre casket of wine between Amy, Karen and me. Drank it in the car park while we made cheese sandwiches on the bonnet of the car. Pissed up, we all went to the Port Hotel and played a few games of pool against the Aboriginals. They were all pissed and high on dope. I kept going back to the car to have a drink of wine. We all went to another pub, but I never made it as I fell asleep in the car, and neither did Karen as she was next to me in the car, throwing up everywhere. Eventually, we made it back to the rubbish tip and set up camp. I was off my tree and can't remember anything else.

Day 120: 11 July 1990, Australian Sea

Everyone was still pissed up in the morning due to last night's session. We packed our bags and left the rubbish tip—hopefully for the last time. Went down to the docks with Bob and the girls in order to see if we had got the job, and there was another bloke (ex-rodeo) waiting for the same job—bastard. We had to wait for another 3½ hours for the skipper to fly in from Perth as his plane was delayed. He couldn't make up his mind whom he wanted to take on, but it looked like the other bloke, so we told him that Bob and I could work for 1 wage between us. We got the job. We set sail half an hour after being told that we had the job. We only just had time to say goodbye to the girls.

The sea was really calm this evening, like a lake, which was good as it was Bob's and my first night. Started work at 5.30 p.m. after our first decent meal for ages and worked right through the night on the fishing nets, sorting out the scallops and prawns, then shuckling the scallops. This is where you need speed as you get $3 per kilo.

It was a bad night. Bob and I only got $22 between us during the night.

Day 121: 12 July 1990, Australian Sea

It was my turn to make breakfast—sausage, egg, bacon, beans, and toast for 6 people. During the night, we caught 1 shark and 2 massive stingrays (at least 6 feet wide) that had to be wrestled with in order to get them off the boat.

After breakfast, spent the morning doing repairs on the boat before going for a well-deserved sleep at 1 p.m.

Got woken up at 5 p.m. in order to begin work again. I brushed my teeth for the first time in 5 days today and feel like a new man. The full moon affects the catch due to it's effect on the tides etc. The moon is still fairly full, hence, we got a fucking shit catch tonight and worked on and off through the night and only earned $9 (£4.50) for the scallops, plus a bit more for the prawns. My hands are red raw now and full of cuts due to the scalloping and general boat work. Our boss (Warrick) is becoming an absolute twat and bollocks us for the slightest little thing, yet I suppose he's only doing his job. Went to bed at 11 p.m.

Day 122: 13 July 1990, Australian Sea

Woke up at 5.3 p.m. (6½ hours' sleep, not bad). Put out the nets and then time for tea.

The first couple of nets were pretty shit—no scallops or prawns, although after that, it picked up a lot. Warrick kept bollocking Bob and me as we kept making a few mistakes, although I thought we did pretty well, seeing that we're new to this game. Saying that, Bob grabbed the net as it was going in the water, got dragged down the boat, bumped into me, and we both went arse over tit and fell over, nearly into the water, and I got elbowed in the eye.

Caught a couple of massive sea turtles, ¼ tonne each, and had to wrestle with them to get them overboard. We dropped the second turtle off the table and on to the floor and then couldn't throw it back in because the nets were out, so we had to leave it for an hour until the nets were back in. It kept waddling around the boat. We had to be careful because although it was slow, it had a very powerful mouth and could easily take a big chunk out of your leg.

Day 123: 14 July 1990, Australian Sea

Got up at 5.30 p.m. It's my turn to cook dinner, and I've never cooked anything in my life, and today, we were having chicken. Fuck me—was everyone pissed off when I told them that I hadn't taken the chickens out of the freezer! I had to leave them in the engine room to thaw out while everyone went hungry. I couldn't even peel the potatoes properly. In the end, Pat (the skipper) had to do it all. I felt a right twat, believe me!

Caught a massive sea snake (very poisonous and can kill). I thought it was dead and started playing with it and looking into its mouth. Then I realised it was still alive. I told Pat, who then threw it at me, and it bounced off my head and into the sea. He could have killed me.

Day 124: 15 July 1990, Australian Sea

I was exhausted during the last hour of scalloping, and it was pissing it down. I was really tired, and after breakfast, even the smallest of jobs were hard to complete. Bed 12 p.m.

After a big slap-up meal of steak etc., it was back to work. Everyone's pissed off with me because I'm eating too much food, and we might even run out. I couldn't give a toss. After living on a rubbish tip for a week, with no food, I'm making the most of it.

We caught a massive hammerhead shark 8-10 feet long, weighed a tonne. We all had to wrestle with it to get it off the boat before it bit someone. Then a 5-foot sea snake got loose and was drifting around the floor of the boat—1 bite can kill you. I had to get its tail and throw it overboard.

Tonight was my worst yet, I was really fucked and my hands are red raw due to cuts and wet sores.

Day 125:—16 July 1990, Indian Ocean, Australia

Got up after 5 hours' sleep—I don't know if I can last another 2½ weeks with fuck all sleep. The sea was really choppy tonight, and poor old Bob was trying to cook tea, and the pots and pans were going all over the shop. He smashed the plate from the microwave. Pat wasn't impressed.

Another long night working our bollocks off for fuck all. Got another massive giant stingray. Bob and I had to pull it off the table with a hand each in either nostril. We caught about 4 sharks tonight. Each time, Bob and I would have to jump on to the table, grab it by the gills without getting bitten, lift it up, and throw it overboard. They were about 5 feet long, and I dropped one of them on the floor.

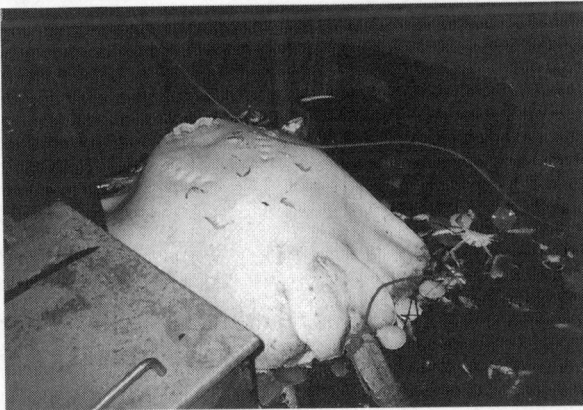

Spent most of the night as usual slagging the 3 Aussie guys off while they slagged the Pommes off.

Day 126: 17 July 1990, Indian Ocean, Australia

We finished early today and went fishing for yellowfin tuna, just loading the line up, throwing it overboard, and then pulling it back in. Caught a few 1½ feet long.

I had to cook tonight, fried chicken—fuck, I didn't have a bastard clue how to cut the chicken up, but I managed to do them both OK, although everyone was moaning as I took the skin off.

God was I fucked tonight. I had the flu, no skin on my hands, and then I got some chemical in my eye and could hardly see for the rest of the night. As usual, everyone spent the night slagging people off. Bob and I dropped a big bollock tonight and ended up ripping the fishing net more or less in half. The whole boat had to stop for an hour while it was changed. Everyone was really pissed off with us. Later on, we caught another massive sea turtle We couldn't get it off the table as it grabbed hold of it with its mouth, so Pat the twat came along and smashed its eye in with a wooden post until it let go. Hardest night of my life. Never been so tired. Walking round like a zombie. Bed at 1 p.m.

Day 127: 18 July 1990, Indian Ocean, Australia

The next thing I knew, it was 5.20 p.m. and I was being woken up to start work again. How am I going to survive 23 bastard-long nights, working about 20-hour days non-stop, no days off? I don't know where I am half the time and can hardly see the words that

I'm writing in this diary. Spent 10 minutes in the freezer down in the hull to wake myself up before work.

Pat bollocked Bob and me as we keep going into the kitchen for cups of coffee to wake ourselves up. Everyone else is really fucked as well, which makes me feel better. Can hardly use my hands as they're ripped to pieces and won't heal as they are constantly wet. Got an eye infection and a big rash around my bollocks due to Bob and me not washing or changing our clothes for the last 1½ weeks. Feel really dirty, but no time to wash. We're having a competition to see who is the dirtiest after this nightmare of a slave camp is over, but I had to call it a day as I'm covered in spots, have a foot infection, and a big rash around my bollocks. Had my first shower in two weeks and still keeping the same clothes on.

Day 128: 19 July 1990, Indian Ocean, Australia

Caught a 9-foot shark and couldn't get it by the tail, so Darren the twat kept smashing it on the head with a hammer. An easy night compared to previous nights. Pat (skipper) bollocks me and Bob at least a couple of times a day, but we couldn't give a shite. In fact, we've been bollocked so many times (usually for nothing) that we find it funny. Now he won't even speak to Bob and me. Warrick had an argument with him as well, and now he won't speak to him either.

Day 129: 20 July 1990, Indian Ocean, Australia

Wrote a quick letter to my parents as believe it or not, the postman is coming round later on to pick up any mail.

The hours of this job are as long as fuck. We get up at 5.20 p.m. to begin at 5.30 p.m. and watch the sunset and work all the way through the night, pulling the nets in, emptying them on the table, putting them back out, sorting out the prawns and scallops, boxing the prawns and putting them down the deep freeze, shucking the scallops, then start all over again.

Day 130: 21 July 1990, Indian Ocean, Australia

Bob and I can't be arsed any more and spend most of the time working half as fast as everyone else. Everyone used to keep moaning at us to work harder, but now they realise that we couldn't give a fuck if we stay on the boat or not so are just putting up with us until we reach land.

Day 131: 22 July 1990, Indian Ocean, Australia

We're about halfway through the trip at the moment and counting the days down—can't wait to get back to land. Caught another massive stingray tonight and couldn't get it off the sorting table. It was 6 feet long, plus tail, and 4 feet wide. We had to tie some rope around its tail and hoist it up in order to get it off the boat, but it was so heavy, it broke its tail. In the end, we had to string a rope through its nostrils, from one through to the other, and hoist it up that way, then cut the rope, letting it fall into the water. My hands are full of splinters from the spike on the back of the fish and crab bites.

Day 132: 23 July 1990, Indian Ocean, Australia

Caught a massive shoals of fish about 2 feet long, and they got everywhere. Pat was pissed off as there were no scallops or prawns, yet Bob and I were pleased as it meant a lot less work for us both to do.

The atmosphere is getting better on the boat, although you can still cut it with a knife. Bob and I got bollocked for treating the place like some sort of holiday cruise which we're on I suppose. We couldn't give a toss about the money any more, so long as we have an easy ride—a bad attitude to have, I know, but when you're on a working holiday, it's a lot harder to get yourself motivated into doing any actual work.

Day 133: 24 July 1990, Indian Ocean, Australia

Caught a couple of 6-foot-long sharks again tonight. Bob and I had to wrestle with them in order to get them off the boat along with the usual turtles, stingrays, etc. Had to cook breakfast today, fried fish. I had to gut them first etc., and I didn't have a fucking clue but soon learnt. I've learnt quite a few useful little skills on the boat so far.

Was sitting down quietly having a shite today, when the bastard toilet door flung open, and Darren with the hosepipe gave me a good soaking. I've come to the conclusion that everyone on this boat is a cunt in some form or another. Scott is an arse licker and a moaner, Warrick is a miserable bastard, Pat likes the sound of his own voice too much, while Darren, who is the best of the lot, could still be an arsehole.

Day 134: 25 July 1990, Indian Ocean, Australia

Had a big argument with Warrick tonight and nearly smacked the twat. Later on, Bob stole one of his fags and nearly got caught.

Caught a massive stingray tonight, about 6 feet wide and 8 feet long, plus tail. Darren the twat cut its tail off before throwing it back in. Had about 20 minutes off after each slot had finished tonight (7 slots altogether) and time just enough to get my head down for 5 minutes. Felt worse for it, though, everytime I got woken up, as 1 minute I'd be asleep and the next minute I'd be outside in the cold and wet, hauling the nets in again. It's a hard life at sea, believe me.

Day 135: 26 July 1990, Indian Ocean, Australia

The weather was really rough tonight. The boat was really rocking from side to side, each time sending a massive wave flying across the boat, soaking everyone. It made the work on the boat even harder as everything that was not tied down flew all over the shop. Kept having to hang on to the boat to stop myself from getting washed away.

Went for a quick piss off the side of the boat, got hit by a wave—1½-foot-high water—and ended up pissing all over myself.

Counting the days as always until I get off this boat. The nights are long, and the crew is a bunch of old women moaning and arguing all the time.

Day 136: 27 July 1990, Indian Ocean, Australia

We've been fishing right above Port Hedland near Broome, and we're now on our way south. We were supposed to be stopping off at Exmouth today for 20 minutes, but no one woke up in time. It was my turn to sleep on the couch today. I closed my eyes, and the next thing I knew, it was 5.30 p.m. and time to get up again. When I get back to land, I'm going to sleep for a whole week. The only thing that's keeping Bob and me going is the fact that we're nearly at the end of the trip (6 nights left).

We're working like twats but earning fuck all as we're getting tons of shit in the nets but no scallops.

Bob opened the fridge tonight, and Pat's last bottle of wine fell out and smashed on the floor. Pat went crazy as now he'll have to go without for the rest of the trip. It was worth it just to see his face.

Day 137: 28 July 1990, Indian Ocean, Australia

Later on, we were all outside. I was running around like a twat, trying to do ten jobs at once. Then Pat came on the scene and bollocked me for not doing the job that he wanted me to do. I turned around and stuck one finger up at him and carried on. He went wild, and now, as punishment, he's going to take off the tax from the money we earn. That's over half—the short-arse little cunt. I've got no motivation left after being told that.

I'm doing a scientific experiment on my hair. I haven't washed it for 2½ months (since I was in Bali), and for the last 2½ weeks on the boat, I have not brushed it or let water on it, and I use my hair as a dirty rag. Whenever my hands are dirty and shitty with fish blood and guts, I wipe them in my hair.

Day 138:—29 July 1990, Indian Ocean, Australia

We caught a family of stingrays tonight, about 8 of them on the table. Had to get them off by sticking my hands up their nostrils and pulling them off the table. They have the slimiest nostrils you can imagine.

Apologised to Pat for sticking a finger up at him, but he didn't want to know and is still taking off the tax on our wages (49%).

We were fishing in the reefs tonight, which meant that we pulled up a lot of brightly coloured fish as well as a lot of stonefish that can kill a man if their spikes puncture your skin. I picked one of them up without realising. Talk about skid marks. Later on, we caught a massive fiddler shark, 7 feet long and 3 feet wide. Got all the nets tangled up in the water, and when we winched up, they were all ripped to fuck.

Day 139: 30 July 1990, Indian Ocean, Australia

Pat still won't talk to Bob and me, which is bad news as it's looking like he's still going to tax us. We've both been a bit of a jinx on the boat as the nets have been nearly written off at least twice due to Bob and me. We've broken almost everything breakable, and we've virtually run out of food and water and are now on rations for both, and this is their worst fishing trip that they've ever had all season in terms of what we've caught (they usually catch at least 5 times the amount that we've caught).

Day 140: 31 July 1990, Indian Ocean, Australia

Had sausage, egg, beans, and king prawns for breakfast. A waste of prawns, I suppose, but we've got to make the most of our food as we'll be paying for our own soon when we get back on the road. Can't wait. 2 days left. I've even begun counting the hours down.

We moved to an area tonight where there are supposed to be no scallops but loads of prawns. Yet when we started pulling in the nets, they weren't full of anything. Bob and I were pleased as it meant we could have a well-deserved fairly relaxed night after working on an average of 135 hours per week for the last 3 weeks, with no breaks. It's been all work and no sleep.

The boat is full of the biggest twats I've ever met. They spend all their time slagging everyone else off.

Day 141: 1 August 1990, Indian Ocean, Australia

It's our last full day today, so after work, we all had to give the boat a good clean-up. I had to clean the oven. It was a right mess. Had about 5½ hours' sleep and felt totally fucked when I got woken up to start work (as usual), although at least tonight is our last night on the boat. Everyone was taking the piss out of Bob as I work twice as hard as he does.

Day 142: 2 August 1990, Carnarvon Land Ahoy! Australia

Worked through the night and arrived back at Carnarvon Port at about 5 a.m.

It was great to be back on land again after 3½ weeks at sea. I couldn't walk in a straight line as I was so used to the boat rocking. I'll miss the life out at sea in some respects—such as the colourful sunrises at about 6.30 a.m. and the schools of dolphins that follow the boat whenever we're fishing, usually about 15 of them who are after all the dead fish that we throw back in off the shit shute. Had to unload the freezer, which was a twat of a job as it's—40°C, and we were inside it for half an hour, then another hour hosing it down in order to defrost it—nearly froze my balls off.

Pat didn't have the heart not to tax us, so we got the full whack $2190 between us—fuck all compared to all the hours we've done, over 400, and earned about £600 each.

Went around Carnarvon for a bit. Phoned my aunt up in order to get my mail sent onto me in Darwin. My friend Stuart has sent me a parcel for my birthday—a blow-up doll. I was too stunned for words when my aunty told me.

Met Darren and Scott in town and nearly had a fight with Darren. They were both pissed already. I was totally fucked and went to bed at 5 p.m. at the backpacker's hostel. Been awake now for 24 hours and had only 5½ hours' sleep in 2½ days.

Day 143: 3 August 1990, Carnarvon, Australia

Got up at 9 a.m. in order to hitch-hike it to Broome (1000 miles away). It was pissing it down with rain, and my washing was still out on the line, so I went straight back to bed and didn't get up till 1 p.m.

Bob had his head shaved today and left a 3-inch square patch on the top, which has a ponytail down his head. We keep helping ourselves to everyone else's food etc. in the fridge. Naughty, I know, but we are still on a tight budget. Drank 2 litres of wine tonight and

then went to the local disco, sneaked in, and avoided paying—it
was shite. Pissed as a twat, I fell asleep in the hostel lounge. Bob
came home 2 hours later and took me to my bed. We were both
arseholed.

Day 144: 4 August 1990, Port Hedland, Australia

Woke up 9.30 a.m. Still pissed but also with a massive
hangover. Went into the lounge, and some dirty twat had left
their shoes right in the middle for people to trip over—they were
my shoes.

I was supposed to be hitch-hiking, but it was pissing it down. When
it had virtually stopped, I got a lift to the road out of Carnarvon,
hitched for half an hour before getting a lift 80 miles down the
road—good to be on the road again. Waited in the middle of
nowhere for an hour for my next lift, who was going to Broome
(1,000 miles away), same place as me. He'd just spent 1½ days
solid driving from Perth. I'd only been in the car for half an hour
when it broke down—the wheel fell off. The last car I'd been in had
broken down when he dropped me off, and I had to give him a bump
start. We had broken down in the middle of desert. So he hitched
it to the next garage while I stayed in his car and waited for him to
come back with help. The car was in a right mess. He arrived back
with some help, and we got towed for 40 km. We had to go really
slow as the back wheel kept catching on the wheel arch. 2½ hours
and 2 flat tyres later, we got to the garage. The bloke whose car
it was got offered a couple of weeks' work while his car would be
repaired, while I got a lift on a massive juggernaut road train with
2 massive trailers.

Day 145: 5 August 1990, Broome, Australia

Drove through the night in the front of the cabin. Weird
feeling driving through the desert about 8 feet high above the
road, with a full moon shining away. Loads of kangaroos, but we
didn't hit any.

Arrived at a roadhouse outside Port Hedland at 3.30 a.m. Tried to get a lift for the next couple of hours—no luck. Fell asleep in the roadhouse for an hour, with my face resting on a magazine. Woke up with print all over my face. Spent another 2 hours hitching before I got picked up by a perverted weirdo, a complete arsehole, although he did take me 640 km to Broome while I smoked all his dope for him. It took us 8 hours to do 400 miles. It took so long as he was paranoid about his engine overheating.

Arrived in Broome at 8 p.m. totally shagged. I just found a spare bed in the dormitory and went straight to sleep without paying or registering.

Day 146: 6 August 1990, Broome, Australia

Soon as I woke up, I got talking to a Pomme, and within half an hour, I had a job—picking up litter from the streets (my 7th job in Australia). We get $1 per bag, and I worked for 2 hours in the sun, sweating my bollocks off, and got 16 bags—half of them filled from the dustbins I passed. $16 dollars cash in hand. Still pissed off with living like a pauper, eating bread and apples. I've got $1200, but I'm trying not to spend that.

Went for an interview at the Roebuck for a barman—find out tomorrow. Went to bed early but didn't get much sleep as the lad sleeping in the bunk below me had about 10 epileptic fits during the night, keeping me awake.

Day 147: 7 August 1990, Broome, Australia(21 Weeks)

Got up at 7.30 a.m. in order to begin work at 8 a.m. I had to collect all the shit and litter from the Aboriginal camp. It was a cold and foggy morning, and there were Aboriginals all over the shop, pissed out their brains. Some of them were still there from last night, drinking. The others were on the first beer of the day. Even so, all of them were pissed, and I had a good laugh with them as I ran around them, picking up all their empty cans and bottles. Got 12 bags in 1½ hours and then had to stop as I ran out of bags.

Spent the rest of the day walking around everywhere in Broome, looking for work, and couldn't find a thing. Saw a couple of pissed-up Aboriginal grannies having a fight in the middle of the street tonight. One of them ended up getting her top ripped off.

Went to see 'Staircase to the Moon' tonight, a strange effect with the full moon that only happens 5 times a year.

Day 148: 8 August 1990, Broome, Australia

Didn't get much sleep last night again due to Wez having his epileptic fits. Went out on the shit, collecting around with Wez. I was working my balls off and filling my bags to the full, while he was going slowly and only half-filling his bags, then the twat pretended that he'd done more bags than he'd actually done, which made it look like I was lying as I'd done more bags. Then the little fat fucker grassed me up for getting rubbish out of people's gardens—and he couldn't understand why I took offense. Finished at midday after 4 hours' work and spent the rest of the day by the pool in the sun, listening to my radio. Got a postcard from Fay in Darwin with the rest of the girls. They're working on a plantation for peanuts. Went to bed at about 7.30 p.m. again tonight.

Day 149: 9 August 1990, Broome, Australia

Got up early and collected 13 bags before the ranger came up and asked me where Wez was as he's the main suspect for stealing $400 from the church. He's also a suspect for stealing $50 from the bunkhouse. Went out on the highway with Thomas and got some more bags before hitching it back to town. Found out that Wez had done a runner and left town.

I hitched it down to Cable Beach with Thomas and went out on the nudist beach (we kept our shorts on). A couple of birds, bollock naked, waved me over and got me to take a photo of them—the best photo I've ever taken.

Everyone got pissed up by the pool in the afternoon before going to the Pimp and Prostitute ball. I fell asleep for most of the night before pulling some bird and ended up going back to her tent with her mate and another lad from the bunkhouse. We smoked all of their grass between us, about $20. I've never laughed so much. We just smoked it all and then fucked off. They gave us a lift home. A really good night out, and I only spent $3.

Day 150: 10 August 1990, Broome, Australia

Woke up early for work and then couldn't be arsed, so I went back to bed until about 3.30 p.m. Finished my wine off and then went into the beer garden, where they had a band playing. It cost $5 to get in, so I crawled through a really small hole in the fence. I got stuck halfway through and ended up ripping my jacket to pieces. The band was OK. Went down to the Divers disco, pretty shit, pinched a few more drinks, got even more pissed, and went to bed.

Day 151: 11 August 1990, Broome, Australia

Woke up still pissed and began work with Thomas on the rubbish, collecting around. I got one bag and then couldn't be arsed any more, so we both went back to bed.

They had a bit of a festival on this afternoon as part of the Shinju festival. Just lazed around in the sun all afternoon with the lads. Thomas had his eyebrow off a couple of nights ago when he was pissed, so when Larry was arseholed last night and fell asleep, Thomas shaved his eyebrows off, plus his armpits, legs, and cut a bit of hair from his head. They were going to shave him bald, but he's got an important interview on Monday. Got pissed as a fart and went to the divers disco with Pete. Had half a joint that someone had given to Pete. Went to a party with Lucy, which was shite, so I raided the fridge, had a massive pig-out, and then fell asleep in the kitchen. Went to bed 3.50 a.m.

Day 152: 12 August 1990, Broome, Australia

Got up at 6.50 a.m. Still off my face from last night. Went straight down to the park to start collecting the rubbish. I felt like a bag of shite and was nearly sick several times when picking up cold, greasy leftover food. Worked for an hour until I began to sober up, which made me feel worse, so I fucked off and went back to bed.

Lazed around the pool for the rest of the day. Got pissed on my wine again tonight and went down to the beer garden, where they had a wet T-shirt competition. Got invited to a beach party afterwards and got a lift down there. Free beer at the party. Hitched it home paralytic.

Day 153: 13 August 1990, Broome, Australia

Woke up at 8.30 a.m. and was sick everywhere. I checked out today but actually leave tomorrow morning, saving myself $10. I'll just sleep in a spare bed tonight. I was sick a couple more times during the day. Couldn't afford any food, so I pinched a load from the fridge with Pete.

Went to the beer garden tonight to watch the talent competition. It cost $2 to get in. Fuck that. I sneaked in through a really small hole at the back. It was like an SAS mission as I ended up backstage and sneaking past the bouncers. I pulled an Irish bird (24) and took her and her mate back to the bunkhouse. Some other lad had pulled her mate. Then Shaun came along and talked to us for 2½ bastard hours! I was embarrassed to kiss this girl as I haven't brushed my teeth for 4½ days, and my hair is really greasy. A nice bird. I will probably meet up with her in Sydney.

Day 154: 14 August 1990, Great Sandy Desert, Fitzroy Crossing, Australia

Went to bed at 4.45 a.m. today. Found out that Pete came home at 6.30 a.m. He'd been down at the beach with Lucy. We got ready to go. I raided the fridge for food. Then we were off.

Hitching it to Darwin with Pete. Got a lift to Roebuck and then Derby, each time leaving our names etc. on any signpost. Waited another hour and then got another lift to Fitzroy Crossing. After arriving at Fitzroy Crossing (a small shanty town in the Great Sandy Desert full of Aboriginals), we tried hitching for another 4 hours, without getting a lift. Spent all day hitching and only got about 300 miles down the track—only another 1000 long and hot miles to Darwin.

Camped in Pete's tent along the roadside on some waste ground full of empty beer cans. Cold beans and bread for tea, again!

Day 155: 15 August 1990, (Northern Territory) Kununurra, Australia

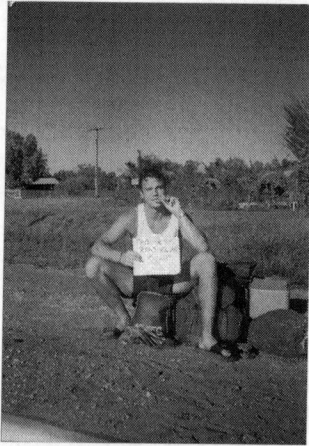

Got up early, took the tent down, and began to hitch-hike again in the baking-hot sun. Waited 3½ bastard hours before getting a lift—that's 7½ hours hitch-hiking in the same spot after a lift. We were lucky, though, as the bloke who gave us a lift was only going 1000 miles down the road to Darwin. His name was X-Ray, or so he said. His car was full, so all 3 of us had to cram into the front seat. It was really hot, sweaty, and uncomfortable, but at least we were moving again.

We drove through the Great Sandy Desert before reaching the Kimberleys, a more lush and more mountainous area. Pulled into a lay-by after it got dark and camped out.

Day 156: 16 August 1990, Darwin, Australia

Another early start. Driving past the gorges and creeks of the Kimberleys. Massive bright-red termite mounds everywhere, up to 3 metres high. Saw my first dingo—a wild Australian dog. We drove through Timber Creek. It was dole cheque day, so all the Aboriginals were pissed up, and a fight broke out between 2 tribes. I saw one bloke throw a brick at someone a metre away from him.

It bounced off his head, and he fell to the floor. There was going to be a riot, and we had to drive through it. It was a bit scary, but we got through OK.

My arse was killing me as it's really uncomfortable squashed up in the car. We arrived at Darwin at 8 p.m. after 3 days solid hitch-hiking (1,300 miles). That's about 2,300 miles I've hitched from Carnarvon. Found a backpacker's hostel—$12.50, rip off. Spent the night there.

Day 157: 17 August 1990, Darwin, Australia

Moved into another backpacker's hostel this morning, a cheaper one, and then went down for my post. 4 letters and a parcel from Stuart—it was my 22nd-birthday present from him, a blow-up doll! I couldn't believe it. I blew it up in the dormitory and left it on someone's bed. It got a few stares and comments, believe me.

Spent most of the afternoon walking around the shopping mall with Pete. Bought a cask of wine (4 litres) and drank it with Pete and Neil (another Pomme). I got arseholed and can't even remember leaving the hostel, let alone remember where I went and what I did. We lost Pete, and he ended up at a charity auction with free beer. I met up with him later on, and I had a big cut on my hand and ended up getting blood all over his shirt.

Day 158: 18 August 1990, Darwin, Australia

Pete went around looking for jobs this morning, while I was in bed—no luck. We hung around the pool in the morning and then around town in the afternoon. Pete showed me the car he tried to steal last night. We spent a couple of hours rooting around the dustbins at the back of the shops and did pretty well as we found 3 potatoes, 2 loaves of fairly stale bread, a shaver, some sandwiches, magazines, etc. We were rooting in the bins and eating some sandwiches that we'd just found and got some really dirty looks.

Went on the piss tonight with Claire (hostel cleaner). Pete fell asleep, so we left him and went to a club. I was paralytic, and Claire couldn't understand me. I ended up falling asleep next to her. She couldn't wake me up, so she left me. The next thing I knew, I was being thrown out by the bouncers. I went to another club and was still staggering around and spent about 4 hours solid dancing on the dance floor until it closed at 6 a.m. and I had sobered up by then.

Day 159: 19 August 1990, Darwin, Australia

Got to bed at 6.30 a.m.—great night. Woke up at 9 a.m. Really tired. Fay phoned me up and invited me to the rodeo for the day at Humpty Doo 40 km away. We began hitching, and I had 2 litres of wine with me, and Pete had some beer. We began getting pissed while waiting for a lift. I was soon pissed again. It took us about 3 hours to hitch and about 4 different rides. I can't even remember getting the last ride, let alone getting to the pub where they had a big drinking competition. I can't even remember meeting the girls whom I haven't seen since Carnarvon a few months ago, a bit of a shame as I was looking forward to meeting them. They took us to the rodeo. I didn't know where the fuck I was. 7 in a car to the rodeo.

It was $7 to get in, so Pete and I climbed over the fence—I don't know how I managed it in my state. The rodeo was supposed to be pretty good, but I can't remember much about it. I lost everyone and ended up hitching it to the hostel and raided the fridge for another free meal.

Went out again with Pete in the evening to a bar with a rock band playing. Some bird tried to chat her way into my pants, but she was too ugly, so we (Pete and I) both fucked off. On the way home, we stopped off at another backpacker's hostel in order to raid the fridge. Couldn't find it—bed 2 a.m.

Day 160: 20 August 1990, Darwin, Australia

Posted a parcel back home today, full of clothes and the blow-up doll that Stuart had sent me. Then we went to the pub in the shopping mall and got talking to a couple of nice Australian girls, Sharon and Tess. We invited them to come on holiday with us for four days around Kakadu National Park as we had a couple of spare seats in the car. They agreed to come. Tess got really pissed and was sick everywhere while I got off with Sharon. At the end of the night, I took her back to the hostel. Pete was drunk and got out of his bed and pissed out the window and then got back in the wrong bed, with another man.

Day 161: 21 August 1990, Litchfield National Park (Wangi Falls), Australia—(23 Weeks)

I checked out of the hostel 2 days ago and have still been staying there but without paying. Pinched some pots and pans plus food from the kitchen this morning before collecting the hire car and picking up the 2 girls for our 4-day holiday around the National Park.

We drove for a couple of hours before arriving at Litchfield National Park, where we went to Wangi Falls—the best natural beauty I've ever seen, a massive lagoon with 2 waterfalls entering it. We camped right next to it and went skinny-dipping into the lagoon during the night. We both couldn't sleep in the tent, so we slept under the stars for a while but got bitten to fuck by the bastard insects—ended up back in the tent.

Day 162: 22 August 1990, Jabiru, Australia

Got up fairly early. Everyone was shattered due to fuck all sleep last night. We drove to another isolated lagoon with a couple of waterfalls. I went for a swim in it before moving on. Driving past massive termite mounds up to 5 metres tall. Went to the tropical rainforest and were supposed to pay to get in, but we drove straight past the man collecting the money. I went for a walk with Sharon through the jungle to an old spitfire that had crashed during WW II. Nearly stood on a black snake 5 feet long as it slithered around on the path.

The girls drove to Kakadu National Park while Pete and I got pissed in the back. It was about a 3-hour drive, and we had to stop off on the way to buy some essentials (like condoms). By the time we got there, Pete had drunk himself unconscious, and I wasn't far behind him. Four of us camped but only paid for 2. Pete remained unconscious for the rest of the night. Sharon and I wanted to be on our own. The ground was too hard, so we decided to go up a tree and spent half an hour walking around the campsite, looking for a descent tree to climb. In the end, we had to settle for the car bonnet.

Day 163: 23 August 1990, Kakadu National Park, Australia

Got up, and there were a few wild kangaroos hopping about and cockatiels flying past. Went swimming in the crocodile-infested river. There were lots of signs saying no swimming as it was too dangerous but fun. Then I noticed an 8-foot crocodile on the riverbank, and it was getting into the river. I nearly messed my pants and couldn't get out fast enough.

Went to Barramundi falls and had a swim there. Pete climbed up the side of the gorge 100 feet high and nearly killed himself. I climbed up the waterfall and swam around the small lagoons and saw a lizard about a foot long, swimming around. I looked it up in the book later on and found out that it was fairly rare.

Camped out in the wilderness again and got pissed next to the fire.

Day 164: 24 August 1990, Kakadu National Park, Australia

Thrashed the bollocks off the poor old hire car again today. Down all the four-wheel-drive tracks, and the fucking thing seized on us in the middle of nowhere. We had to hitch a tow to Jabiru—the car is really fucked up bad, red wine stains all over the upholstery, all the paint has been scratched down one side, and Pete had taken the mileage cable off so we didn't have to pay for so many miles. He couldn't put it back on as he'd lost the nuts and bolts for it. We didn't know if we should just forget about the car and just hitch it straight to Cairns, but the hire company had a branch in Jabiru, so we told them, and they gave us another one. They didn't even check the car out. We got a 4-wheel-drive jeep and drove to a uranium mine and went on an hour-long tour in a bus. I fell asleep after 5 minutes and woke up after the tour had finished. Camped out in the woods tonight—heard loads of animals running around during the night.

Day 165: 25 August 1990, Darwin, Australia

I'm beginning to get pissed off with Sharon as she is getting far too serious and keeps telling me that she loves me—I just can't handle it.

Stopped off at some marshlands on the way back to Darwin, and I saw a 2-foot-long lizard run past me. Got back to the hostel and washed some clothes. Sharon wanted to travel around the world with me, but I had to tell her that she couldn't—I felt a bit of a bastard, but I had to do it. I've been pissed every night since I arrived in Darwin 1½ weeks ago, and tonight was no exception. Got arseholed on cheap wine again and went to an acid party with Pete—Sharon and Tess tagged along as well. I spent most of the night dancing and pinching drinks—can't remember anything else.

Day 166: 26 August 1990, Darwin, Australia

Woke up and looked around and realised that I was in bed with Sharon. I said my goodbyes and left.

Fay, Amy, and Karen took me out today—we went to the nudist beach. They only went topless, so I kept my shorts on too. Got pissed again on wine when I got back and, about 10 of us climbed into a small combi van and drove down to a jazz concert at the casino. I went through the restaurant and pinched a bottle of wine from one of the tables and then went back half an hour later and pinched another one. Can't remember much about coming home in the combi van. I was supposed to be going to a nightclub but fell asleep on the settee.

Day 167: 27 August 1990, Crab Island, Australia

Woke up in the morning on the settee in the reception and was covered from head to toe with flea bites and spent most of the day scratching myself silly.

Supposed to be hitching it down to Cairns today with Pete, but 10 minutes before we were due to leave, someone phoned up, offering us jobs on a deserted tropical island for 2 weeks. I decided to go on that and hitch it down to Cairns later on. I went with Daniel, who also got the job—the catch was that we had to hitch it down there, 200 miles away. Most of it was down dirt roads in the middle of nowhere. We got a lift for over half the way and got dropped off in the middle of nowhere, trying to get a lift down a road where only a couple of cars a day come down. A stupid place to be left at. Believe it or not, we got a lift after 10 minutes, a country bumpkin and his wife and 3 kids. It was squashed but at least a lift. He didn't want to drop us off in the middle of nowhere so gave us a lift to Crab Island. We weren't sure where it was and spent over an hour going down really rough four-wheel-drive tracks in his Holden. We had to stop about 6 times to move trees that had fallen on to the track.

Day 168: 28 August 1990, Crab Island, Australia

Began working on Crab Island—a tropical island with only 7 people on it. A nice island, but you can't swim in the sea as it's full of crocodiles, sharks, etc. Spent the day digging holes on the beach—nice view but sweating like a twat. Worked for 7 hours.

Day 169: 29 August 1990, Darwin Harbour, Australia

The boss told us that we would be working for $7.50 an hour rather than $10 as we were first told. We told him where to go and left. Ross was going to Darwin and gave us a lift on the back of his truck. He felt sorry for us and said he would let us stay on his boat ($140,000) free for as long as we wanted. Not a bad bloke.

Day 170: 30 August 1990, Darwin Harbour, Australia

As I've jacked my job in digging holes on a tropical island, today was just another day just lazing around the swimming pool all day in the sun—it's a hard life. I'm fed up with living on a tight budget and eating beans all the time.

I'm going to have to go to the doctors soon about my rash on my bollock that I got in Bali as it's getting worse. Today, I realised what a slob I've been, drinking all the time, so I went for a 5-mile run. Sweated like a twat but felt a lot better after.

Met Sharon and Tess tonight and went out with them—all the bottle shops were shut, so I went to the backpacker's hostel and pinched some wine from the fridge. Danced all night at Beachcombers Disco, then took Sharon back to the boat. On the way, I raided the fridge at the backpacker's hostel and got a couple of bags of food.

Day 171: 31 August 1990, Darwin Harbour, Australia

Sharon went home in the morning while I stayed on the boat for a while. We've got no electricity, gas, water, etc. on the boat, so I went to the transit centre and used their kitchen. Spent the rest of the day doing fuck all again, lazing around the pool. Pete and I are hitching to Cairns on Monday, nearly 2000 miles away—I'm looking forward to being on the move again.

I went down to the transit centre tonight and ended up in Sarah's (who works there) room, playing a drinking game called 'drink driving' and got arseholed within about 20 minutes. Then a few people came round, and we had a small party—I ended up unconscious on the bed. I was that pissed.

Day 172: 1 September 1990, Darwin Harbour, Australia

Woke up this morning in bed with Sarah. She had to go to work. I stayed in bed and went back to sleep. I was walking around pissed up from last night for most of the day. Sat outside the transit centre, writing some postcards, when 2 lads started smacking the shit out of each other and ended up fighting right by my feet—blood everywhere, even on me.

Bumped into Fay tonight and couldn't get rid of her—she fancies me but hasn't got around to asking me out yet. I don't want her to as I treat her more like a mate than a girlfriend. Spent most of the night dancing and pinching drinks. Fell asleep for a couple of hours in the disco. Fay had nowhere to sleep, so I took her back to the boat, and she slept in my bed—I didn't try it on.

Day 173: 2 September 1990, Darwin Harbour, Australia

Got up still arseholed and had to rush down to Nimble Beach as it's the 'Beer Can Regatta' today, and I was supposed to be in it. Got down there and found out that I wasn't—bastards. Daniel was on his way back to the boat last night when some queer tried it on. Daniel smacked the shit out of the cunt.

Sharon was at the beach, so I had to keep a low profile in case I bumped into her. $2 to get in, so we climbed the fence. Good day. Everyone was pissed drinking beer and smoking joints in the sea. A few drunken slobs were getting washed up on the beach as if they'd been shipwrecked.

Hitched back to the Harry Christner meeting as it was free food. Met Amy and Fay and got pissed with them. Fell asleep on some grass on the way home for a couple of hours. Pete came home and woke me up. He began winding me up as I wanted to go to sleep and ended up throwing his T-shirt down the hatch and on to my face. I threw it back, and he did the same thing again, so I threw it out the porthole, and it sunk. Pete was really pissed off as he's only got 2 T-shirts now—serves him right.

Day 174: 3 September 1990, Darwin Harbour, Australia

Got up and went round to wake Pete up as were due to hitch-hike down to Cairns today, and the cunt had packed his bags and fucked off without me. I couldn't go now as I haven't got a tent. Spent most of the day really pissed off, trying to buy a tent. Sarah (who works in the transit centre) was trying to get me into bed this afternoon and was tying everything, but I wasn't having any of it. She's good-looking etc., but I just couldn't be arsed.

Went out with Yvonne tonight (Dutch girl)—too boring, so I left her and went out with Sarah. Went back to her room for a 'drink driving' game—drank nearly 4 litres of wine between us.

Day 175: 4 September 1990, Katherine (Football Pitch), Australia

Sarah woke me up at 5.30 a.m. when she went to work, while I stayed in bed for a few more hours. Bought a tent. Was $40 but got it down to $25—*bargain*. Kept a low profile around town, avoiding Sharon as I've got a love bite on my neck. Went back to the boat, packed my bags, and began hitching to Cairns.

I spent all afternoon hitching and got 6 lifts in all, only taking me 330 km down the road to Katherine. I went to camp on some wasteland and then noticed a bush fire about a mile away, coming towards me, so I fucked off quick. Walked around for half an hour, and in the end, I broke into a football ground and camped on the pitch. Putting the tent up in the dark was a job as it's the first time I'd used it. Loads of Aboriginals sniffing around but no trouble.

Day 176: 5 September 1990, Tennant Creek, Australia

Got up early to begin hitching at 7.30 a.m. after a rough night camping. Got my first lift (7th so far) after only half an hour by the road—some chap heading in the same direction as me but ended up dropping me off 400 km down the track. I think he was pissed off as he wanted me to chip in with the petrol—no chance.

Waited another half hour before getting picked up by a German woman (late 20s), not bad-looking, who took me 450 km down the track to Three Ways. I was supposed to be turning off in order to go to Cairns but decided to carry straight on for a return trip of 1,800 km in order to see Alice Springs and Ayres Rock. I left her and got a lift within 5 minutes, 20 km down the track to Tennant

Creek, where, after trying for 1½ hours without a lift, I called it a day. Not a bad day's hitching.

Day 177: 6 September 1990, Alice Springs, Australia

Heard loads of spooky noises last night as I was trying to get to sleep. I left a small bag of rubbish outside the tent door last night, which had gone by morning—some Aboriginal or wild animal must have taken it.

Started hitching at 7 a.m. and was soon passed by Yoseph (Israeli guy from Darwin). He was on his motorbike. We had a quick chat, and he went. Half-hour later, I got picked up by a massive juggernaut. It was going 500 km down the road to Alice Springs. The driver was pissed last night and couldn't keep his eyes open so had to keep stopping. At one stage, he stopped in the middle of nowhere and went to sleep for an hour.

Got to Alice Springs in the end and met Yoseph. We went out together to some disco, which was shit, so I had an early night.

Day 178: 7 September 1990, Ayers Rock, Australia

Found some loose strands of spaghetti in the kitchen, so cooked it up for breakfast. Went to see Ayres Rock today and got there on the back of Yoseph's motorbike (Yamaha 550). It seems to take twice as long on a motorbike as you're cramped up, and your arse goes numb after half an hour, and it gets really uncomfortable.

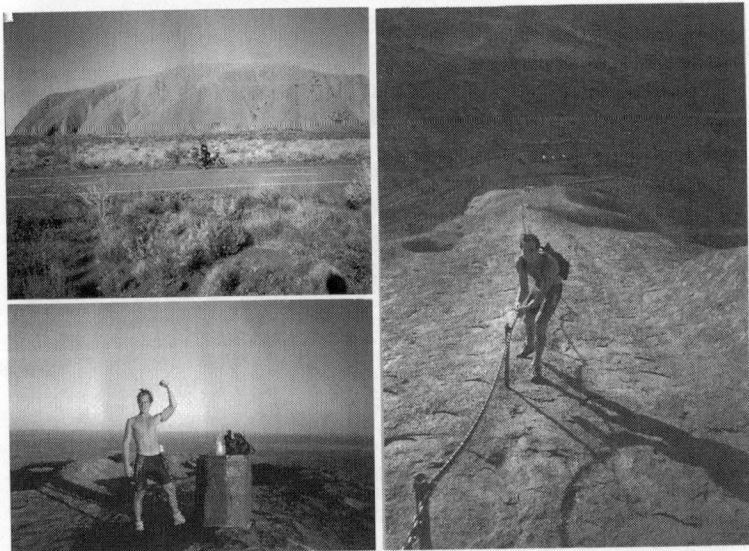

Got there in the end at about 5 p.m. so we had to climb the rock quickly in order to see the sunset. I ran up it (or at least I tried). I was fucked after running up half of it. The best natural beauty I've seen in Australia. The sunset was excellent as well to watch as the rock changes colour. Drove about 20 km away from the rock and camped on the driveway on some farm.

Day 179: 8 September 1990, Alice Springs, Australia

Froze my bollocks off last night in the tent. Had the standard meal for breakfast—cold baked bean sandwich.

We hadn't been going for long on the bike when it broke down. He got it going again, but it wasn't safe enough to take 2 people plus bags, so I decided to hitch. Got a lift straightaway, but it was a clapped-out Land Rover that was about ready for the knacker's yard. We chugged along through the desert at the pathetic speed of 45 miles an hour. il took forever, but we got there in the end.

Fucking beans again for tea—I'm pissed off with the fucking little things. Chatted to a few people in the hostel before going to bed but couldn't get to sleep due to some loud-mouthed twat snoring.

Day 180: 9 September 1990, Middle of Nowhere, Australia

I'm hitching to Townsville today, over 2,000 km away, so I bought a big stock of beans for the journey.

I left Alice Springs at 10 a.m. and had a bastard of a job getting out as my bags were far too heavy. I was sweating my bollocks off and getting nowhere fast. After 2½ hours of agony, I got a lift to the outskirts of the town, where I had a better chance of getting a lift. I waited 5½ bastard hours before I managed to get a lift from Alice Springs, and that was only because I hid all my bags behind a bush so it looked like I was stranded. Got a lift from a gay teacher, who took a fancy to me and bought me a couple of beers at a pub on the way. Some local yob came up and accused me of being queer due to me wearing earrings. I threatened him, and he soon backed off. Got dropped off in the middle of nowhere.

Day 181: 10 September 1990, Three Ways, Australia

The block of cheese that I pinched from the backpacker's yesterday is going sweaty, so I decided to have cheese on toast for breakfast. I built a fire and put the sandwiches on the fire—the bread burnt and the cheese didn't melt (a complete flop). I'll stick to beans in future.

Waited an hour and got a lift to Tennant Creek 125 km away, where I only wanted to go a further 25 km in order to get on the right road to Townsville. I had to wait a bastard 3½ long and sweaty hours before I got a lift off an Aboriginal truck full of Aboriginals.

Arrived at Three Ways (a famous bottleneck for hitch-hikers) at 3 p.m. I saw some hitcher going the other way, who had been waiting 4 hours. I just got settled on my patch when 2 hitchers going the same way as me walked past—luckily they went 100 metres down the road.

Day 182: 11 September 1990, Queensland, Cloncurry, Australia

I was getting worried about getting stuck at Three Ways, waiting 2 hours yesterday and an hour today before I got a lift. The flies were driving me crazy, swarming around my face while I waited for a lift.

I got a lift off a guy who'd been hunting ferrule pigs—he'd got 2, and their rotting jawbones, complete with tusks, were on the dash bar, drying out. I don't know what smelt more, those or my now festering socks I've had on solid for 9 days and which have gone hard.

I got dropped off at Cloncurry and had to walk 2 km to get out of town in order to pitch my tent, passing a rival hitcherhiker on the way. I had my twice-a-day meal of cold baked beans before nodding off to sleep. Camped in someone's garden (didn't ask).

Day 183: 12 September 1990, Australia

What a bastard of a day (my first in Queensland). I was woken up at 4.30 a.m. when my tent collapsed due to gales. Bastard! I had to pack my tent away before it received further damage, so I ended up sitting by the roadside at 6 a.m. frozen cold due to the wind, trying to hitch a lift. Hour after hour, and still no lift. I didn't get a lift until 1 p.m. (after 7 hours solid hitching), from a battery sales rep—loads of free batteries. Driving through the outback, I saw an eagle swoop down and grab a 1½-foot snake off the ground before flying off. Then I saw an emu with a bunch of chicks.

Couldn't find anywhere to camp tonight—ended up in a small bunch of trees. Huge cobwebs everywhere, with massive spiders in their webs—spooky. Watched the sunset before having my beans and then to bed.

Day 184: 13 September 1990, Townsville, Australia

I'd only been waiting by the side of the road for an hour when the sales rep who gave me a lift yesterday picked me up again, this time taking me down to Townsville. I fell asleep in his car. I was asleep leaning against the door when the bastard flung open. I woke up to find myself half hanging out of the car, with no seatbelt.

I was glad to get to Townsville as I've been hitching solid for 10 full days—I'm shattered, stink, and my clothes are virtually rotting away as they've not been washed for over a month. I've hitched 4,500 km in 10 days. It was good to get back to civilisation again and away from the outback even though I really enjoyed it.

Day 185L 14 September 1990, Cairns, Australia

Got woken up during the night when the German lad below me decided to have a wank. The whole bed was shaking like fuck. I thought I was going to fall out.

My final day hitching today. It took me ages to walk out of Townsville to get to an ideal hitching spot 5 km away. It nearly killed me carrying my bags that far. Easy hitching—got 4 lifts without hardly trying. Now I've hitched nearly 5000 km in 11 days. It's time to let my hair down.

Got *free* hamburgers tonight at the hostel before going out on the piss with a crowd of crazy English hooligans. We sat around the hostel getting arseholed on wine. A couple were shagging in one of the dormitories, so we all went to watch—can't remember much more, but I ended up taking all my clothes off and climbing up a large palm tree in the middle of the High Street. We all went to a nightclub, where I got thrown out, can't remember what for. I managed to get back in and was thrown out again. I ended up at another club, where I slept for most of the night. I came home at 6 a.m. but I was locked out, so I to climb a barbed-wire fence and a roof in order to get in through the back way.

Day 186: 15 September 1990, Cairns, Australia

There's a Japanese bloke in our dormitory, and everyone just takes the piss out of him, so he moved to another dorm today. Skunky's got crabs, and so he's had to shave all his pubes off to get rid of them.

We all got pissed on wine again before going out to a nightclub. Ended up at a party on the way at some bird's pad—pretty shit. Flash got smacked at the nightclub and ended up on the floor—got home 5.30 a.m.

Day 187: 16 September 1990, Cairns, Australia

Spent the whole day lazing around like a fat slob. The most energetic part of the day was walking to Vinnie's (similar to the Salvation Army, where all the tramps go for a free meal). Had a pile of sandwiches and a pie.

Got a massive hangover from last night, which soon went when we all went on the piss again—cheap wine again. I got thrown out of the nightclub for falling asleep on a table. I found a nice grassy roundabout and went to sleep in the middle of it for a couple of hours before going back to the nightclub.

Day 188: 17 September 1990, Cairns, Australia

The boys were supposed to be driving to Darwin today but postponed it until tomorrow as Stan wanted to take his car to the auction today. He'd got so pissed last night that by the time he'd got up today, he'd missed the auction.

Had an excellent night tonight with the lads. We all got pissed up in the dorm, and everyone was totally off their faces.

Day 189: 18 September 1990, Cairns, Australia

All the lads were supposed to head off in a bit convoy up to Darwin at 10.00 am today, but 4 of them didn't get home from last night until 11 a.m. Great bunch of lads and was sorry to see them go.

I won a 'spitting the baby's dummy across the swimming pool' competition, winning a *free* white-water rafting day trip. Raymundo and I played a game of 'Truth or Dare' tonight with a couple of birds, excellent game. The dares got out of hand though. I had to put my hands down Raymundo's pants, grab his bollocks, and tell him I loved him. Another dare was to strip bollock naked and climb a pole, pretending to be a monkey, etc.

Day 190: 19 September 1990, Cairns, Australia

At the moment, I'm living for free as I checked out of the hostel yesterday and am still living there for free, sneaking in and out. My food is all free as I go down to the Salvation Army for free meals. The nightclubs are free and so is alcohol as I pinch all my drinks.

Went on the piss at 11 a.m. today for a full-day session and was also stoned for most of the day. Had a great laugh. Went out and bumped into Fay. She was after my bollocks tonight, and I couldn't get rid of her. She kept trying it on, but I wouldn't have any of it. I had to tell her to go in the end. Joe and I pulled a couple of Swedish birds and took them back to the dorm for a game of 'Truth or Dare'. I had to run up to some Japs with my pants around my ankles, waving my bollocks at them. We got bollocked for being too loud.

Went to a nightclub with my bird, but she wasn't interested in anything because of her boyfriend back home, so I walked her home. On the way back, I raided one of the fridges at a hostel—loads of food. Was pissed off when I found out Joe ended up shagging his bird on the pool table last night while I got the tight one.

Day 191: 20 September 1990, Cairns, Australia

Spent the whole day slobbing around doing sweet FA. There was another free wine function at the backpacker's hostel tonight. Joe and I had 10 cups each before I pushed him in the pool. He got me back later on and pushed me in. We were both arseholed, got changed, and went out again. I lost Joe and went to Magnums, where I pulled a really nice bird. I was with her for half the night, and she kept moaning because I was drinking too much. I couldn't remember her name. She fucked off in the end. The bird who hands out the leaflets for Magnums wanted to dance with me at the end. I told her it would cost her 4 beers (she gets them free). She agreed, and by the time we got on the dance floor, the record had finished. Went to bed 5 a.m.

Day 192: 21 September 1990, Cairns, Australia

Got up at 8 a.m. a physical wreck to begin my 6-day scuba-diving course, and swimming around in a cold swimming pool isn't what I'd call fun.

Excellent night tonight. Free wine and hamburgers at an excursion promotion. I had 4 massive burgers (stole a few more for breakfast) and loads of wine. Got talking to a bird. We ended up at Joe's pad, getting pissed and smoking joints. I was with this bird in Magnums when I bumped into the Swedish bird I was with a couple of nights ago (the tight one), so I went off with her to Magnum II. We really got on well together, but she still wouldn't let me near her.

Day 193: 22 September 1990, Cairns, Australia

I had to get up for my course. Bastard. I was tired yesterday and now have to go through today with no sleep in 2 days (only 3 hours' sleep in 3 days). It was a really rough day. I spent endless hours sitting in a classroom, spending all 100% of concentration on trying to stay awake. I fell asleep no end of times. It was hell. I kept nodding off every 5 minutes.

Another free food promotion night at one of the backpacker's hostel tonight. Spent ten minutes walking there. It was pissing it down with rain, and I got drenched, only to find out that it was only cheese and biscuits. Went home to bed at 8 p.m.

Day 194: 23 September 1990, Cairns, Australia

Got up at 7 a.m. Still feeling like a bag of shite. Went for my day-3 diving course, in which we went out to Green Island today and then another hour from there on to the reefs (the Great Barrier Reefs). The ocean was really rough on the way out to the reefs, and loads of people were throwing up everywhere. Got kitted up etc. with the scuba tank and gear, and jumped off the boat ten feet down into the water. Excellent feeling swimming around at the bottom of the ocean—saw a giant sea clam over 1 metre across and put my hand on it. The fucking thing closed, nearly taking my fingers off. Stopped off at Green Island on the way back—a small deserted tropical island. Saw a stingray in the water.

Went out tonight but came home early (about 2 a.m.) as I've got a few big days coming up.

Day 195: 24 September 1990, Great Barrier Reef, Australia

Today is the first of a 3-day, 2-night scuba-diving trip in the outer Great Barrier Reef, which means that I had to get up at the crack of dawn again.

Spent 4 hours sailing out to the reefs (Sudbury Reef), where we had 2 dives during the day with Vince (instructor), practising various scuba-diving procedures. Excellent fun and a great laugh at the same time.

Went out for a night dive tonight in pitch darkness—a mind-blowing experience swimming around in the dark, 50 feet underwater, with only a small torch for light. Chased a large crab on the ocean floor with Paul (my dive buddy).

Had a massive pig-out for a dinner before going to bed.

Day 196: 25 September 1990, Great Barrier Reef, Australia

Up early again on the boat in order to spend another day diving on the reef. Today was the first time that we were allowed to dive on our own. Paul and I saw a big manta stingray plus a few barracudas and loads of fish etc. down there. We did 3 dives during the day and 1 at night, each lasting about half an hour. The night dive was great as Paul and I switched our torches off and swam around in complete darkness. Several people saw a 6-foot reef shark swimming around, but Paul and I missed it.

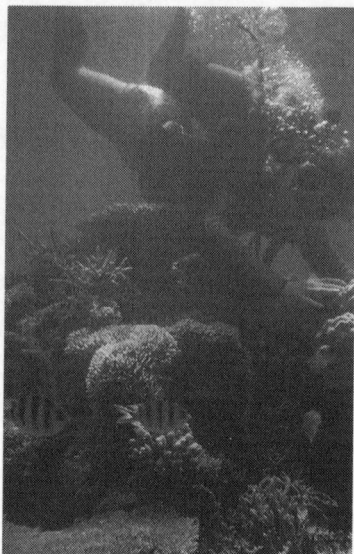

There was a talent show tonight. Paul, Ashley, and I did a little sketch. I was dressed up as a fat slag and ended up doing my condom trick. Everyone got rat-arsed and ended up stripping bollock naked and jumping off the boat for a swim. Great night. I collapsed unconscious again, and the girls took me to bed after first stripping me naked.

Day 197: 26 September 1990, Great Barrier Reef, Australia

Got up and did a couple of dives while I was still pissed from last night. I went down 12 metres today with one purpose in mind—to have a shite while Ashley took a photo. Steve and Lindsey came down to watch. I had a shit and then a big school of fish came up and began eating it. Paul and I were supposed to be going down to a maximum depth of 18 metres but ended up going down to a depth of 25 metres (80 feet).

Got back to land in the afternoon and sneaked back into the hostel, where I've already had 8 nights' free accommodation. Steve and Lindsey are doing the same thing. We had about 7 people around tonight, getting pissed on the wine. I can't even remember going to

Magnums at 9.30 p.m. where I was drinking beer through a snorkel. I ended up rolling around on the floor and couldn't be arsed to go to the toilet, so I just lay there and pissed myself. I ended up getting thrown out. I walked down the street and got talking to a group of Aboriginals who were sparring in the street. I was pissed and had a spar with one of them. I was winning, so the bloke smacked me.

Day 198: 27 September 1990, Cairns, Australia
Got woken up by the manager of the hostel, who threw me out as I was asleep in the girl's dormitory.

Went out tonight with the people from the diving course. Went into a club—kept getting free bottles of champagne from the bar (8 altogether).

Day 199: 28 September 1990, Cairns, Australia
Spent another day lazing around doing fuck all. The hostel now knows that I'm staying here and keep coming around, trying to find me, but I'm always out.

Free hamburgers and wine tonight. I ended up winning a horse riding trip in Cape Tribulation. You had to put your name in a hat. I put several tickets in under different names and won under the name of 'Steven Briggs'.

Went out with Lindsey again tonight. we got a free bottle of champagne. I was really pissed—I don't know why, but I spat a whole mouthful of champagne in her face. She went wild and ran off. I went to Magnums until 5 a.m.

Day 200: 29 September 1990, Cairns, Australia
Another day living on the edge of poverty—the only money I spent today was on a couple of postcards for England. I leave the hostel in the morning and don't come back until the early evening, so the hostel can't catch me. During the day, I spend my time at the hostel next door by the pool, even cooking my food there.

Went to the Verandah Bar again tonight (getting pisssed on the verandah outside my hotel room). We had about 5 people around with their casks of wine as well as a few bottles of Sam Buca. I got arseholed and went into Bob and Karen's (from Perth) dorm and ended up collapsing in their room on someone's bed.

Day 201: 30 September 1990, Cairns, Australia

I was really pissed off this morning when I woke up and realised that I'd missed my Saturday night (last night) out as I got pissed and fell asleep before going out.

Went around town with a couple of barmaids from Magnums today.

Chatted some bird up around the pool and invited her to the Verandah Bar. There're so many birds here, it's unbelievable. Went to Magnums tonight. Bob was there, and I had to keep pinching drinks for him as well as myself. Walked around the streets with Paula until it got light, with a couple of small dogs following us wherever we went.

Day 202: 1 October 1990, Cairns, Australia

Got home about 9.30 a.m. and went to sleep for a few hours before leaving the hostel before the cleaners came in and found me. Got talking to 3 Canadian girls next door. They only arrived in Oz yesterday. I got on really well with them and ended up getting pissed in the afternoon on beer and wine. I took them all to Vinnie's for a free feed with all the tramps. They all came round to the Verandah Bar this evening, and we all got totally pissed. I ended up unconscious on the floor and got carried to Magnums and only just got in. I got off with Monica. She wanted to go to Magnums II later on, but I couldn't go as I was supposed to be meeting Paula there.

Went back to my room with her, and Joe was there with some bird he'd been after for ages. He was just about to poke her one when I got back with Monica—he'd left a sign on the door telling me not to come in, but I was too pissed and didn't see the sign. Monica and I fell asleep straightaway, leaving Joe and Jackie very pissed off.

Day 203: 2 October 1990, Cairns, Australia(29 Weeks)

Met Monica tonight and went to the Verandah Bar before going to Magnums. I was shitting myself as I thought Paula would be there, but she wasn't. Lindsey was though and thought she was going out with me until she saw me with Monica. She came over and embarrassed me a bit. Monica was tired, so I took her home but went back and danced with Amy till 4.30 a.m.

Day 204: 3 October 1990, Cairns, Australia

Bollocks—I've been caught in the room yesterday morning and this morning by the cleaners. The management came up later on when I was out and saw all my bags etc. They told Joe that if I didn't pay, they would throw him out.

Spent the day with Lindsey, had a massive joint, and got totally stoned. Took Lindsey to Vinnie's for free food. I was tripping and trying to eat my meal. Bob came in as well for his daily meal. He's only got 20 cents left.

I moved into Monica's room tonight and spent the evening with her. I was still stoned. She was too tired to come out, so I went on my own and met Paula and went to Magnums II with her until 5 a.m. before coming home to Monica. I had to have a wash first to get all the lipstick and perfume off. I feel a bit bad about what I'm doing, but I like both girl's a lot and need a bit of time to decide.

Day 205: 4 October 1990, Cairns, Australia

Monica got up early to go on a dive course while I stayed in bed. I was supposed to be going around to Paula's place this afternoon but ended up getting some casual work unloading beer barrels off a road train at the brewery. The road train picked me up, and on the way, we stopped outside Paula's flat to let her know.

Sweating my bollocks off unloading the beer kegs. I had 5 cans of beer halfway though and was pissed for the rest of the afternoon and nearly fell off the top of the truck several times. Got dropped off at Paula's place. Stayed there before going back to see Monica. I was covered from head to toe in dust.

Took Monica for a meal tonight (keeping a low profile in case I met Paula). Monica's going away tomorrow and went home early, so I went off to meet Paula. She left at 3 a.m. as she was going on a cruise for 4 days. I was homeless and had nowhere to sleep, so I went in the 24-hour launderette, locked the door, put some newspapers down for a bed. I couldn't turn the lights off as there were no switches because the lights are permanently on, so I took the fuse out and went to sleep.

Day 206: 5 October 1992, Cairns, Australia
Woke up in the launderette and went off to call for Amy and Fay and slept with them for a while before meeting the bloke and his road train at 1.30 p.m. to do a couple of hours' work at the Brewery. Hard physical work made harder with a hangover. Worked until 4 p.m. (2½ hours for $30) and then went into the workers bar for a free beer, drinking as much as I could for a couple of hours. Free food as well. Picked Fay up on the way back for a ride in the truck. Pissed as a fart, I went to bed for a sleep. Got up at 10 p.m. and started all over again. It's my dad's birthday today, so I came out of the nightclub at 4.30 a.m. to phone him. Pissed off my face. He wasn't in, so I talked to my sister. Went back to the nightclub before going to sleep in the launderette.

Day 207: 6 October 1992, Cairns, Australia
I woke up at 9.30 a.m. on the launderette floor to find someone in there doing some washing, so I went into some hostel and slept on the settee for a couple of hours.

Joe left this morning to work on a fishing trawler, so I've half moved in with Fay and Amy. I went out with them tonight to Magnums and spent most of the night dancing. I was really tired so went for a sleep on the settee. I lay down on it, covering 3 seats, and went to sleep. I got woken by the bouncers. I couldn't be arsed to go to the launderette so decided to hide in Magnums and sleep there until midday tomorrow, when the cleaners come in, so I pulled the settee about 6 inches away from the wall and slept between the settee and the wall in the small gap. I was asleep when some fat bird woke me up and took me home to hers.

Day 208: 7 October 1990, Cairns, Australia

Woke up next to the ugliest and fattest bird in Cairns—I was nearly sick. Had a few bucket bongs with her and her sister, getting really stoned before walking home. I was really embarrassed when she went out of the bedroom and left the door open and her dad walked past and saw me. I was lying there bollock naked. Then she had the cheek to ask him if he'd give me a lift home—he refused!

Took me an hour to get home as I took a few wrong directions. The 3 Canadian girls get back today—Monica, Richard, and Racheal. I wanted to cook them a meal but couldn't as the supermarkets were all closed as it was a Sunday. Went back to Fay's and Amy's room to get changed (I think they're getting pissed off with me hanging around there). Went out with Monica tonight and slept in her room.

Day 209: 8 October 1990, Cairns, Australia

I've managed to get a day's work at the bungee site in exchange for a free jump. I was supposed to be there at 7.30 a.m. but didn't get up till 8 a.m. when Monica woke me up. Bollocks—I ran straight down and had missed the bus. The next one was at 9 a.m. I was very lucky as, when I got there, they still needed me to work. Did fuck all work, just a bit of shovelling—which was hard with a hangover. Finished at 3 p.m. and did my bungee jump—it was pretty scary jumping off a 44-metre (150 ft) structure with a rubber rope tied to my legs.

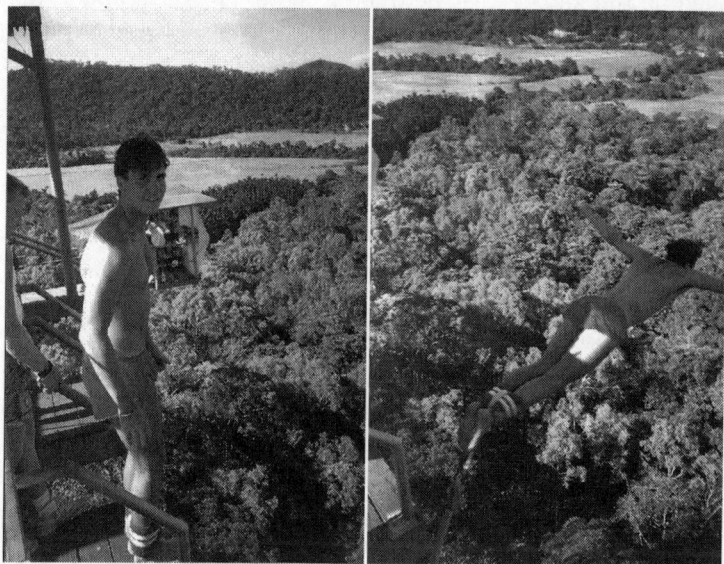

Hitched it back and ran around like a twat for over an hour in order to cook a meal for the 3 girls, only to find out that they had already eaten. The girls were tired tonight so stayed home while I went out and met Paula. Stayed with her till about 5 a.m. before coming back to Monica's room.

Day 210: 9 October 1990, Cairns, Australia(30 Weeks Away)

Didn't have a clue when I woke up this morning at 7 a.m. as I've only had 5 hours' sleep in the last 2 nights. Worked on the bungee site again today, which was even pissier than yesterday. Found some witchetty grubs while I was digging—they are really ugly and about the size of my thumb. The Aboriginals eat them in the bush, so I tried one. I held it up, and it was wriggling about and had a shit in my hand. I put it in my mouth and ate it live! It tasted gross.

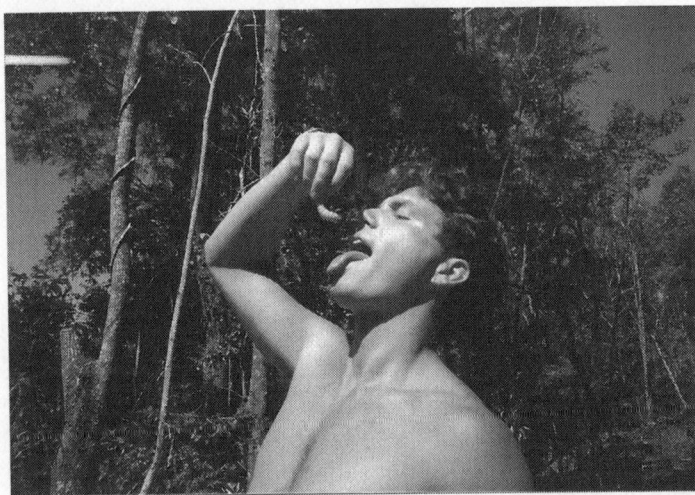

I cooked a meal for the girls tonight (3-course)—soup, pasta with mayonnaise, salmon and pepper, followed by a Swiss roll. My first sober and only night in for nearly 4 weeks. I was shattered. Someone had moved into Monica's room, so I was homeless again. I walked past one of the rooms in the hostel, and the door was open, and there was no one in there, so I sneaked in and went to sleep.

Day 211: 10 October 1990, Cairns, Australia

Another day of slobbing around doing and spending nothing. I'm only spending about $30 a week, even though I'm going out every night and getting blind drunk. I've moved in with the Canadian girls although I've still got a bag in Fay and Amy's room and spent the afternoon with them.

Went on the piss tonight while the 3 Canadian girls stayed at home. I took half a cask of wine out with me and stuffed it down my pants. Everytime I wanted a drink, I'd unzip my flies and open the nozzle and pour it out. In Magnums, I had about 4 people holding their glasses around my bollocks while I filled their glasses up. Everyone thought I was pissing. Got home 5 a.m.

Day 212: 11 October 1990, Cape Tribulation, Australia

Got up at 8 a.m. after another night with fuck all sleep. Monica kept waking me up as I kept snoring.

I'm off on a dirty weekend with Monica today. We hitched it to Cape Tribulation—a small place in the middle of a rainforest with deserted beaches. We got lifts straightaway each time. I was getting on really well with Monica and was set for a good weekend until we arrived at the ferry, where she bumped into Stig (someone she knew), and he tagged around with us for the rest of the time. I was so pissed off. I found out that he went out with Amy, so I've heard all about him and he's heard all about me although we've never met.

Set my tent up with Monica before going out on the piss.

Day 213: 12 October 1990, Cape Tribulation, Australia

I was a bit moody this morning as I was frozen last night in the tent while Monica had most of the blankets.

We went down to the beach—a real tropical beach with no one on it apart from me, Monica, and, of course, fucking Stig. I was pissed off and went for a run. In the afternoon, I went on a horse-riding trip that I'd won in Cairns. It was excellent going through tropical rainforests on horseback. We ended up on a tropical beach and rode the horses into the sea, up to their necks in water. Great fun.

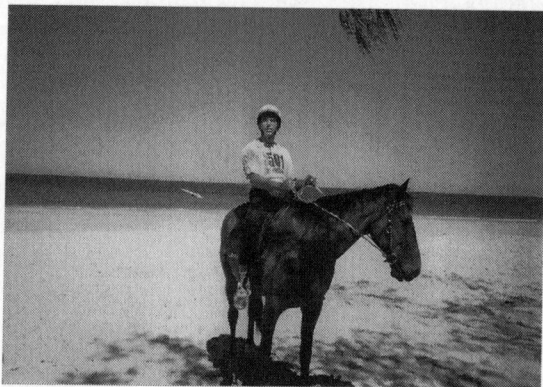

Went out tonight and got pissed. Everyone ended up down the pool after the bar closed. Jumping in with their clothes on. Paul and I nearly had a fight in the kitchen when 3 men walked in and tried to pinch some food.

Day 214: 13 October 1990, Cairns, Australia

I nearly entered into a rodeo today, riding steer bulls, as I thought it was $10 to enter. Got down to the rodeo, and it was $60.

Got a lift back to Cairns with Monica. We were supposed to be going to Kuranda together, but I couldn't be arsed. She was pissed off etc. as she had to go on her own. Met up with Fay and Amy again, which was good, as I'd thought they'd gone, and I had left my bag with them. I bought a cask of wine for Bob tonight as a belated birthday present. We drank it with Karen and Todd by the pool before going to Magnums for another night of serious dancing. The fat slag I was with the other night kept hanging around me and started crying when she saw me with Paula.

Day 215: 14 September 1990, Cairns, Australia(7 Months Away)

Only had an hour's sleep as Paula and her mates are going to Kuranda for a few days. She wanted me to come, but I've fuck all money.

I did my second free bungee jump today. They wouldn't let me do a somersault, so I did a back dive instead.

Went out with no money again tonight, sober, and ended up at Jamie's pad for a joint with about 7 others. We all then went to Magnums for a really rowdy sing-song. Went to the Playroom Club, where I entered the wet boxer short competition. I went on last, with my boxer shorts pulled up to my nipples and with my arse and balls hanging out the bottom. The crowd went wild. I jumped into the bathtub, and water went everywhere. I came second as the winner was a bodybuilder. Went back to Magnums II and can't remember anything else.

Day 216: 15 October 1990, Cairns, Australia

I didn't know what happened last night. All I can remember was waking up on a small island in the middle of the road. My hand was bleeding and I was covered in shit and my shirt was missing. Haven't got a clue what happened. Bumped into Bob—he got beat up last night.

Monica is off today, so I took her to the bus stop. Went to Vinnie's again tonight for another meal with all the tramps. Went out completely skint and sober tonight and pinched all my drinks, got rat-arsed. Pinched for about 4 other people as well. Went mental with all the lads tonight (7 out of 9 people I lived with in Perth are here in Cairns at the moment). I met Paula and spent the rest of the night with her. Good-looking and a great laugh, likes getting pissed as well, so it goes without saying that we get on like a house on fire. Walked her home. It was light when we got back.

Day 217: 16 October 1990, Cairns, Australia

I'd been up all night and had no sleep. I left Paula's at 6.25 a.m. and ran like fuck to Fay and Amy's place. It took 10 minutes, and I nearly threw up. I got changed and ran in order to catch the bus for a day's white-water rafting down the Tully River, which I had won in a competition. I managed to get a half-hour sleep on the bus but was too tired and hungover to appreciate the day's rafting. I felt really fragile, especially when stupid twats were going around splashing other boats.

The bus broke down twice on the way back, and it took us 4 hours to get back. Had another crazy night out with Paula, Amy, etc. Took her home at 5 a.m.

Day 218: 17 October 1990, Cairns, Australia

I slept on a mattress on the lounge floor with Paula last night and woke up in the morning at 8.30 a.m. with her 3 friends and 1 American bloke (whose flat it is) walking around.

I spent most of the day walking around town with Paula. I took her to my daytime accommodation for a coffee. I was really fucked as I've had fuck all sleep for the last 5 weeks, so I had a little sleep in Amy's bed before meeting Paula at 11 p.m. The next thing I knew, it was 1 a.m. and Amy and Paula came around and woke me up. I didn't know where I was. They had a taxi waiting, so went back to Magnums while I got ready. They didn't have enough money to pay the taxi so ended up at the police station. We got to Magnums in the end and spent most of the night dancing.

Day 219: 18 October 1990, Cairns, Australia

I stayed with Paula all morning and didn't get back to Amy's until 2 p.m. and she was pissed off with me as we were supposed to hitch out of Cairns today, but now it's too late. It was Ned's birthday today, so we all went out on the piss tonight. At the hostel, 20 of us were in the pool, and all the lads stripped bollock naked and had a game of piggy back, etc., plus 'whose got the whitest bottom' contest. After that, I got dressed and went down to the International Backpackers with Pam and Amy to drink a cask of wine. We got pissed on the wine and then went to Magnums. Paula was pleased to see me as I was supposed to be leaving today. I'm off tomorrow now and will miss Paula, although we're going to meet up again in Sydney before Christmas.

Day 220: 19 October 1990, Australia

Woke up at 10 a.m. and said goodbye to Paula and her 3 crazy friends and went to see Amy as we're actually leaving Cairns after being here for 5 weeks. I've only paid for 4 nights' accommodation and, apart from my dive course, have only spent about $300.

Began hitching with Amy at 12.30 p.m. It took half an hour to find a good hitching spot. We got 5 lifts today, and I only managed to travel 190 km. I fell asleep during most of the lifts. I was fucked—5 weeks on the piss with only 2 nights off—plus I'm averaging 2-3 hours' sleep a night and eating fuck all food. It will do me good to get out of Cairns. Camped in a lay-by with Amy, bed 7 p.m.

Day 221: 20 October 1990, Airlie Beach, Australia

Woke up at 7 a.m. in order to pack the tent up and begin hitching again to Airlie Beach. We got 4 lifts during the day, and I fell asleep during every lift and let Amy do all the talking. We got a lift from a couple of hippies who were artists and took us to visit their art exhibition on the way.

We finally arrived at Airlie Beach mid-afternoon, where I met Sooty and Wendy (from my diving course in Cairns). Fay has been here for a couple of nights, and she came around tonight with a cask of wine and 3 new girlie mates of hers. We all got pissed on the wine before going down to the bar for a few party games. Then we all caught the bus into town and ended up in Magnums. Went around a few more bars before deciding to go home. It was at least a 45-minute walk, so we decided to break into Magnums's accommodation. I broke into the toilet window to let Fay in. Found a room.

Day 222: 21 October 1990, Airlie Beach, Australia

I was lying on the bed bollock naked this morning (7 a.m.) when the front door opened, and 6 people walked in. I was still pissed and didn't have a clue where I was. Fay and I got dressed and fucked off. The courtesy bus was parked down the street, and I found a brand new packet of tobacco on the seat. The driver took us home. We got back at 8 a.m. I was still pissed and stayed awake.

Chad and Jeremy (my room mates) went on the piss, so I had a few shots of whiskey and rum with them. Played a game of trivial pursuit in the 3 girls' room—had a good laugh. I went to town to get a cask of wine, which took 2 hours as it was pissing it down, and I missed the bus back. I had to help the girls out tonight as they had a big green tree frog in their room. Went around a few pubs with my wine down my pants. We got pissed and broke into Magnums again.

Day 223: 22 October 1990, Airlie Beach, Australia

Got up at 6 a.m. feeling like a bag of shit, and walked home with Fay. Managed to get a lift. I checked out of my accommodation and then went to bed. I'm still staying here, just not paying. Had a joint and spent the rest of the day stoned out my face. Fay went away for a couple of days on a boat trip today. I was knackered and stoned and had a night in.

Day 224: 23 October 1990, Airlie Beach, Australia(32 Weeks!)

Got up at 11 a.m.—my best night's sleep in months. I bumped into Paula by the pool. She's travelling down to Sydney with her 3 mates and is staying here for a few days. I haven't seen her for a few days, so it was good to see her again.

I spent the rest of the day lazing around with her. We got 4 casks of wine in tonight (16 litres). All the girls came around as well as Amy and Fay. We all got pissed on the wine before catching the 11 p.m. bus into town. I had half a cask of wine down my pants while Bone had one in her bag. It was a good night until Pete started slagging everyone off and upset Paula. I was going to smack the cunt but couldn't find him. I took Paula to Magnums Motel and broke into an empty room, turned on the TV, and went to bed. There were no sheets, so I had to rip one of the curtain rails off the wall in order to use it as a blanket.

Day 225: 24 October 1990, Airlie Beach, Australia

We left the motel room that we had broken into last night and went back home to our daytime accommodation, where we are squatting as well. Fay, the girl I was with a couple of nights ago, is back. I'm ignoring her. I hate being a bastard, but I can't help it this time. Paula is worried that she might be pregnant as one of my condoms split last night. Another really embarrassing problem—I've just realised that I've got crabs. I caught them in Cairns when I borrowed Skunky's boxer shorts as he had them. The bad thing is that I've given them to Paula, and she's given them to her 3 mates—one of whom is only here on holiday and goes back home to her boyfriend in 2 weeks. They think its funny though, but it's embarrassing when we all sit together, and everyone's scratching their genitals.

Got a cask of wine with Paula tonight and drank it with her and then took it around town with me. I had it shoved down my pants again. I got caught, though, so the bouncer looked after it for me until I left. We both got really pissed and broke into one of Magnums's rooms again. Paula was really pissed and threw up in the toilet several times.

Day 226: 25 October 1990, Airlie Beach, Australia

Got up feeling like a bag of shit again and went to catch the bus home with Paula. We had to wait half an hour until the bus came and then another half an hour for the bus to leave. Then we realised that we were on the wrong bus as we went off in the wrong direction, so in the end, we ended up hitching home.

Amy and Paula's mates left today, hitching down to Sydney. We'll all catch up with them soon—I've still got £40 left so don't have to get down there until a couple of weeks. I'm only spending about £1 a day, living on noodles.

Caught the bus into town tonight. I'm fed up with getting pissed, so we found an empty room, and I broke in by climbing through the toilet window. We made ourselves at home, switched the TV on as well as the kettle to make a pot of tea. There were no cups, though, so I had to break into next door in order to get a couple of cups. I squeezed through the bathroom window and was hanging on to the shower rack to support myself, when it snapped off the wall and went crashing to the floor. I tried to fix it, but it was too fucked.

Day 227: 26 October 1990, Airlie Beach, Australia

Woke up and watched TV for a while before going home before the cleaners caught us. My crabs are playing up and so are Paula's. We've got some cream for them but haven't used it yet. I'm pissed off with eating 2-minute noodles. I have about 5 packets a day, but at 29 cents a packet, I can't complain.

Went to Magnums again tonight with Paula for a couple of hours. We had a few drinks without getting pissed—that's 2 sober nights in a row. Later on, we had a look around and found another empty room. I broke in and let Paula in, made a pot of tea, and watched TV for a while.

Day 228: 27 October 1990, Airlie Beach, Australia

I've been squatting at Reef Oceana for a week now and only spent one night there. I went for a 5-mile run today with Adam and left him miles behind. He'd previously been boasting about how fit he was. I ran out of condoms today. There weren't any family planning clinics here, so I had to buy some from the chemist. I was buying some when Annie and Sally Ann (Paula's mates) walked I., I was a bit embarrassed. I put on the anti-crab cream that Paula bought, and it stung like fuck. I thought my balls were on fire.

I went out tonight with Paula and Annie—we bought a cask of wine and then broke into one of the rooms, where we got pissed on the wine before going out. Went to Magnums and had a great laugh! I got really pissed and fell asleep next to Paula, so she had to take me for a walk in order to sober me up, but I was too pissed.

Day 229: 28 October 1990, Airlie Beach, Australia

Woke up feeling a bit sick from last night. Walked around town with Paula before catching the bus home. I'm eating 2-minute noodles for every meal, and it's really getting to me. Spent most of the day with Paula, a great girl, and we're really getting on well. We both stayed in tonight and watched TV in one of the rooms we're squatting in, until 3 Germans moved in, meaning there were no beds for Paula and me to sleep, so we went next door, where Annie's squatting.

Day 230: 29 October 1990, Airlie Beach, Australia

Another lazy day doing nothing. Hung around the pool for a while before going for a 5-mile run in the midday heat.

Went into town with Paula in order to get more wine. We're both hitching down to Brisbane tomorrow (1,200 km away), which should be a good laugh. Chad, Jeremy, and Pete are getting fed up with Paula and me as they are paying for their room while we squat in it.

Went on the piss again tonight with Paula, Annie, and Sally Ann. Went out with the infamous cask of wine shoved down my front—we all got really arseholed and went to Tricks and danced the night away before going back to Magnums Motel and breaking into another spare room again.

Day 231: 30 October 1990, Roadside Near Mackay, Australia

Had the biggest shock of my life this morning at 7 a.m. when a gang of cleaners tried to get in through the front door. We both woke up still pissed, asleep, and bollock naked. We ran round in circles trying to get dressed while the cleaners tried to get in the front and back door. We just opened the door and ran like fuck, leaving the room in a right state. We broke the bed last night. We both ran down the road and caught the bus home—got back totally knackered, packed our bags, and then left to hitch to Brisbane.

We caught the bus into town and then were told that we were going in the wrong direction so had to come all the way back again. Got a lift straightaway in a car and then had to wait 45 minutes to get our second and last lift of the day. It was hard to get a lift as there were 4 other couples within 100 yards, trying to get a lift—we got the first lift as well. Got dropped off just before dark and put the tent up on some waste ground by the road. Then got rat-arsed on a cask of wine.

Day 232: 31 October 1990, Australia

Paula's getting worried about becoming pregnant as I've had 4 condoms split on her, and she was due to come on last week. I've already given her crabs, so I don't want to give her a baby as well.

Got a lift off some smelly hippies with 3 kids first and then by a bloke, who took us 400 km down the road and bought us loads of drinks plus a hamburger each. Then we got a lift 20 km from a young Aussie bloke and ended up at his place, smoking bongs and getting really stoned. I was off my face and couldn't stop laughing. The bloke dropped us off near some wasteland, where we camped for the night. It was hard work trying to put the tent up in the dark while I was still floating about.

Day 233: 1 November 1990, Brisbane, Australia

Our 3rd day of hitching—we got our first lift in a sugar-cane lorry after waiting for an hour and then another lift in a road train going all the way to Brisbane.

We left our bags In the transit centre (Brisbane) while we had a look around the town centre. It was a bit embarrassing as we bumped into Monica. We caught the courtesy bus to the hotel that Annie and Sally Ann were staying in, but they had checked out this morning and gone to Surfers Paradise, which meant that we couldn't squat in their room and had to pay for the first time in 10 days.

Went out on the piss tonight with Paula—she kept warning me not to get too pissed as we were both in a big city that we'd never been in before. I took a cask of wine out (down my pants) again, and we walked into town, taking us 20 minutes. Paula asked a taxi driver where the best place was, and he said he'd give us a free lift. He took us, and we ended up near our hostel again at some hole of a pub. By now, we were both pissed, and I had to take Paula home as she was feeling sick—that's women for you. She told me not to get too drunk and then got arseholed herself.

Day 234: 2 November 1990, Surfers Paradise, Australia

We're hitching down to Surfers Paradise today (70 km) but had to go around town first to the family planning clinic in order to get some free condoms. Paula was too embarrassed to go in, so I went in on my own and got some. Paula was worried about being pregnant, so I asked the woman about it and ended up booking her in for a pregnancy test there and then. She was waiting outside and nearly died when I told her. She had the test and knows that she wasn't pregnant 2 weeks ago, so she's got to have another one in 2 weeks. By now, it was too late to hitch to Surfers, so I went against my morals and caught the bus instead ($9). We got there at 5 p.m. and walked around for an hour until we found where Annie and Sally Ann were staying and squatted in the hostel with them.

We got 8 casks of wine and got pissed before going out. I took the wine with me, went to a pub, and then a nightclub, where we danced for most of the night—I got pissed while Paula got really drunk. Got home at 4 a.m. and made her some noodle toast and a coffee. By the time I'd made it all, she was fast asleep.

Day 235: 3 November 1990, Surfers Paradise, Australia

We all went down to the beach today, and I was bored stupid, so I went for a run along the beach. I got carried away and ended up running non-stop for 1 hour 50 minutes, covering about 11 miles. Felt a lot better for it. I want to join a boxing club in Sydney and so have to get fit.

We got a cask of wine tonight and sat on the beach and got totally wasted. I can't remember coming home. I fell asleep in the lounge and was snoring really bad while Paula shoved toast and black coffee down my throat.

Day 236: 4 November 1990, Surfers Paradise, Australia

Woke up feeling great, and no one could understand why I didn't have a hangover—the reason is I had drunk so much last night that my hangover didn't come on until late afternoon.

Annie and Sally Ann caught the bus to Sydney tonight, while Paula and I are going to hitch down tomorrow.

Day 237: 5 November 1990, Surfers Paradise, Australia

Got up late and went around town in order to get some money out etc. I've fuck all left ($40). By the time we got back, it was 2 p.m. We were supposed to be hitching down to Sydney today in order to meet up with everyone, but by the time we were ready, it was too late, so we went down to the beach instead.

I can't believe how well Paula and I are getting on as we are together 24 hours a day and have been like that for about the last 3 weeks. We went for a walk down the beach tonight—we ended up back at the squat, watching TV.

Day 238: 6 November 1990, Australia

We both managed to leave Surfers Paradise today after a couple of packets of 2-minute noodles. We got a lift off a boy racer, who was speeding around the corners. I was really enjoying myself while Paula was shitting herself in the back. We got dropped off in a town on the border of NSW. We had to walk about 2 miles to get out of town, so we pinched a supermarket trolley and put our bags in it and pushed it down through town to a good hitching spot. We got some stares. Managed to get a lift off a truck carrying raw copper going to Sydney. We stopped when it got dark and put the tent up in the middle of a forest. Paula was pissed off with me as I fell asleep in the truck. We both got pissed on wine.

Day 239: 7 November 1990, Sydney, Australia

Paula came on this morning, which was good news as she is over a week late. Woke up this morning with a big hairy spider about a foot away from my head. I thought nothing of it and threw it out of the tent. I found out later that it was a funnel-web spider, and if bitten by it, I would have only 4 hours to get to the hospital before I'd kick the bucket. I nearly messed my pants.

We had to wait an hour for a lift before getting one off a perverted truck driver with flu, going all the way to Sydney. He felt really sick and would drive for an hour and then stop for about 2 hours. It took fucking ages.

We got to Sydney at 2.30 a.m. totally knackered, and all 3 of us slept in his cabin.

Day 240: 8 November 1990, Sydney, Australia

Got woken up at 7.30 a.m. and then tried to hitch 26 km into the city centre. It was murder as we were stuck on a busy highway and couldn't get a lift. We tried for an hour and a half before deciding to catch the train. We got to the city centre at about 12 p.m. (Kings Cross). Paula and I called for Amy and Fay and left our bags with them while we went around Sydney. I bumped into Skunky and his mob whom I knew from Cairns. He couldn't believe that I caught crabs from his boxer shorts.

We visited Sydney Opera House Bridge etc. I've arrived in Sydney with only $17, no visa card, not even a ticket out of the country, which means I can't afford to have a roof over my head. Paula checked into a hotel but couldn't manage to sneak me in. We both went around to a backpacker's hostel and drank a cask of wine in the TV lounge. The next thing I knew, it was 3 a.m. and I woke up on the floor with Paula. She went back to her hotel while I stayed in the TV lounge until 6 a.m. Then I left before getting caught.

Day 241: 9 November 1990, Sydney, Australia

Felt like a tramp today, walking around at 6 a.m. and trying to sleep on the park benches along with the down-and-outs. I couldn't get to sleep, so sat in the park and watched all the prostitutes, queers, pimps, and alcoholics. I've no money. I'm homeless, hungry, and have fallen out with Paula. I've never been so pissed off and depressed with life. Spent all day walking around, trying to get a job and getting fucked off each time. Managed to get accommodation by handing my passport in as a deposit of payment at a later date.

Got pissed with a cask of wine with Paula, Annie, Sally Ann, and Gary. We all got paralytic and went to a free club—we'd only been there 5 minutes before going back to Paula and Annie's place. We ended up in the kitchen and had a massive food fight—raw eggs, peas, even milk. Everywhere, and everyone, it was covered in food—the walls, windows. And the floor was a lake of milk. It was a right state. We all ran away—Sally Ann stole a cask of wine and a massive bag of food. Paula was so scared that she moved into my room with me.

Day 242: 10 November 1990, Sydney, Australia

Annie came down this morning saying she'd been thrown out with Paula because of last night's food fight. They've got Gary's description, and the police are out looking for him. Dwaine, Joel, and Fay, who weren't even there but know us, have been thrown out as well. I got back to my hostel, and I was thrown out because he said I was too lively, and I'm staying at a quiet hostel. I moved to the one next door, with Paula and Annie. Later on, Neil (the lad I know well from Bali) came in looking for someone. I couldn't believe it as I haven't seen him for 6 months. We went to his mate's house, who was having a party, so I got pissed there before coming back to go out with Paula, Annie, and James. We went to a bar first, where I smuggled in a cask of wine before going to a nightclub called Tramps, miles from anywhere. We got in for free as James knew the bouncers. It was a good night until I got woken up by the bouncers as I had fallen asleep. They were going to throw me out, but on the way, I bumped into James, who knew the bouncer, so I was allowed to stay. Paula wasn't exactly impressed—got home 5 a.m.

Day 243: 11 November 1990, Sydney, Australia

Got up this morning, Paula was going down the beach and wanted me to come with her. I couldn't as I was clearing the shithouses out at $6 an hour. She went down the beach, and I was going to meet her after. The manageress said I could do the job tomorrow, so I went down the beach to meet Paula. She and the rest of the mob weren't there, so I spent most of the day walking around Bondi Beach, looking for them. I was pissed off as they weren't there. Came back to the hostel, and Paula was waiting for me. She'd come home early as it was cold.

We stayed in tonight and watched a film on the TV.

Day 244: 12 November 1990, Sydney, Australia
Paula moved out today to a penthouse suite down the road, with Annie, Joel, Dwaine and Billy, while I stayed at the hostel and cleaned and scrubbed the showers down. After that, I got changed and began my interviewing job. I did it for a couple of hours and got 10 questionnaires filled in—easy work and good money. Had to run down in time to get to the Harry Krishna for a meal for 20 cents. Neil came around and has got me a job starting tomorrow.

I went out with him and Paula for a couple of drinks before coming back to my pad to watch a film. Afterwards, I went to her pad. We both slept in the double bed while Annie slept on the lounge floor.

Day 245: 13 November 1990, Sydney, Australia
Got up at 6.15 a.m. really fucked up as I'm not used to getting up so early, and I didn't get much sleep last night. I caught the train to Arncliffe and began work at 8 a.m. as a forklift driver in a storeroom, moving materials about. Had a good laugh working with Neil on the forklifts. It's a cushy job, easy work, and not much of it, plus, when you've finished your work, the boss (Roy) doesn't mind you sitting around. I did 1½ hours overtime today and earned $92 for the day. Caught the underground train home and stopped off at Harry Krishna's for a free meal. Called for Paula (who was pissed off as she didn't find a job today) and spent the night with her. We had the double bed while Annie slept on the settee again.

Day 246: 14 November 1990, Sydney, Australia

The alarm went off at 6.15 a.m. I didn't have a clue where I was. I said something to Paula (who was in a bad mood), and she told me quite bluntly to piss off, so I did—the cheeky bitch. I had to run home, change my clothes, and run to the train station in order to catch my train. Began at 7.30 a.m. this morning. I'm doing half an hour overtime every morning with Neil, and the boss doesn't get here till 8 a.m. so we just sit around drinking tea for half an hour.

Went to Harry Krishna's for another free feed on the way home. I'm getting pissed off with Paula messing me around, so I didn't call for her. I was thinking about finishing it between us when she came around. I couldn't be arsed to speak with her at first, but we made up in the end. I had to scrounge another alarm clock in order to wake up tomorrow morning. Went around to Paula's place. We slept on the floor as Annie and James had the bed tonight.

Day 247: 15 November 1990, Sydney, Australia

I was completely fucked this morning as I'm only getting about 4 hours' sleep a night. I had to run over to my hostel. I didn't have a key, so I had to break in. I got changed, ran to the tube station, and missed my train.

Work's going well, driving the old forklift truck. I drove a big van to the shops today with Neil. Went to Neil's house and drank beer and watched TV for an hour before coming back to work in order to take our dinner break.

It's James's last night tonight, so about 8 of us went out on the piss to a club called Players, where Paula and Annie had got jobs. Pissed as a twat, came home with Paula at midnight and slept with her on the lounge floor.

Day 248: 16 November 1990, Sydney, Australia

Woke up and gave Paula a poke and ended up missing my train as a result. Neil and I had big hangovers today and kept making loads of mistakes. We were driving the forklift down the road, with 12 big boxes of yarn. We turned a corner too fast and dropped the lot. We looked a right bunch of twats. Supposed to be working until 2 p.m. today, but Neil and I did 4 hours overtime and finished at 6 p.m.

Paula and Annie went to work tonight, starting their new jobs handing out leaflets for Players Nightclub, at $30 an hour. I was knackered and went for a sleep for a couple of hours before going down the gym at Paula's pad, then going up to see Dwaine, Billy, and Joel. Paula came home pissed as a twat as she gets free drinks all night.

Day 249: 17 November 1990, Sydney, Australia

Slept at Paula's place last night. I've slept with her every night since she moved in on Monday—I'm hardly at my hostel. I went to the post office today and got a letter from Dad. Had a lazy day. Now that I'm working for a living, I appreciate my weekends a lot more. Went down to the gym with Paula after she'd finished work and then had a swim, Jacuzzi, and sauna. I'm off out with Neil and Dan (whom I haven't seen since being in Bali 6 months ago). I got back to my hostel and met Neil—Dan had to work, so couldn't come, so Neil and I got a cask of wine with some Yorkshire twat, got arseholed, and went out to Taboo's with the cask rammed down my pants. Neil and I got arseholed, and I fell asleep, so Neil fucked off home. I staggered home and put some 2-minute noodles on the go and then went to sleep in the wrong bed. Next thing I knew, some chap was waking me up as I was in his bed, and my noodles had burnt dry.

Day 250: 18 November 1990, Sydney, Australia

Got up still pissed as a twat. Paula came around and couldn't believe that my night out with the lads ended up in a drunken mess at the pathetic hour of only midnight (I'd only been drinking for 3 hours). Went down to the gym with Gary in the afternoon—he's pissed off as Sally Ann doesn't want to move in with him. Went to Welasooh bar tonight. It was excellent, jam-packed with people inside and out, and was like a bar in Spain, with everyone going mental, singing and shouting and dancing on the tables.

Day 251: 19 November 1992, Sydney, Australia

Had to borrow another alarm clock from someone in order to get up in time this morning. Found out that when Neil went home on the last train on Saturday night, he fell asleep and ended up 6 miles from home and ended up getting a taxi costing him $10. I'm really looking forward to getting paid as I'm $100 in debt. I really need a new pair of shoes as well, as the ones I've got have holes in them. It's bad walking around town in them as there is lots of hypodermic syringes lying around everywhere.

Went around to Paula's. She was pleased to see me until I told her I was off down to the gym—again. Fay came around tonight. It was Annie's turn for the bed, so Paula and I slept on the lounge floor.

Day 252: 20 November 1990, Sydney, Australia

Got up and had to run home and break into my hostel again. Got changed and ran off in order to get the train to work. I really like living in Sydney as it's my first time in a big city. I'm living in Kings Cross, which is the Soho of Sydney—puffs, prostitutes, tramps, druggies, pimps, and perverts everywhere. I get a real buzz out of it. The sad thing is all the druggies around with syringes all over the street.

Popped off at Harry Krishna's on the way home for my 20-cent meal. Went down to the gym at Paula's place before going out. Paula took me out to the pictures tonight to see the film *Ghost*. Excellent film, even though Paula cried. We had to run to catch the last train home. Jumped on it just in time, only to find out that we were on the wrong train and had to get a taxi home.

Day 253: 21 November 1990, Sydney, Australia

I stink like a rat's arsehole as I had put the work clothes I wore last week in a plastic bag on Friday for Paula to wash for me and forgot about it till Monday morning, so now I smell twice as bad. My trainers are becoming really cheesy as well—I'm embarrassed to sit next to anyone in the train. Spent most of the day walking around like a zombie—couldn't keep my eyes open. Did 3 hours overtime today with Neil and, because of it, missed dinner (my Harry Krishna meal). I'm really fucked and couldn't get to sleep in my hostel so went around to Paula's flat for a while but couldn't keep my eyes open there either. Slept in the bed with Paula while Annie slept on the settee.

Day 254: 22 November 1990, Sydney, Australia

Pinched a big pot plant last night for Paula's balcony. Pissed off at work today as last week I did 38 hours of work plus 8 hours overtime and only got paid $350—by the time I've paid my bills, I'll be skint again.

Caught the train to Kings Cross and went to Harry Krishna's again for my meal. Got back to my hostel to find that I'd been moved to another dorm and had no bed. Went out to Players with Paula, Annie, and Sally Ann. I got some stares walking down the street with 3 good-looking blondes. It seemed strange buying drinks from a bar in a nightclub, as apart from last Thursday, I've only bought about 6 drinks in as many months. Everyone kept chatting up the girls, so I had to pretend I was going out with all of them at different intervals during the night. Caught the last train home.

Day 255: 23 November 1990, Sydney, Australia

I was still pissed up at work and nearly crashed the forklift several times. Neil and I did 5½ hours overtime today, in which time we only did about an hour's work—good skive but shit money.

Got home at about 8 p.m. and had a shower and went to call for Paula. I'm not getting on too well with her at the moment, which isn't too good as I'm moving in with her tomorrow. She went to work with Annie and took Joel and Dwaine with her. They all came back pissed. I was really pissed off with Paula as she was told to get 2 lads to hand leaflets out for the nightclub at $15 an hour, and she got Dwaine and Joel to do the work even though she knew I was desperate for work.

Day 256: 24 November 1990, Sydney, Australia

Woke up and left Paula in order to move my stuff in. I think I'm doing the wrong thing here as we're not getting on too well at the moment.

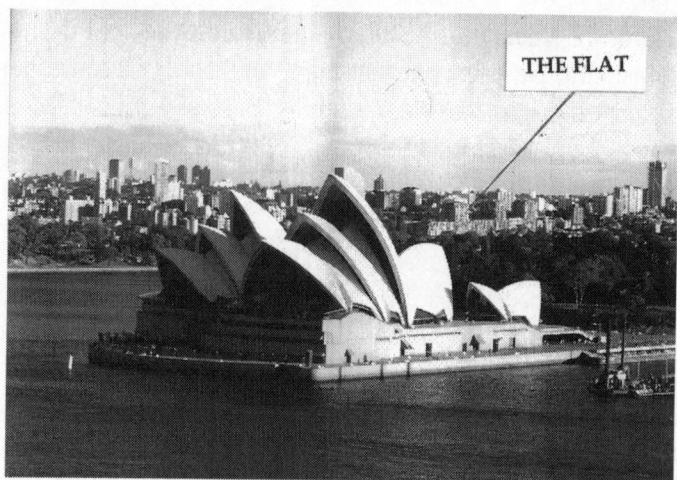

THE FLAT

We all went down to the market—Paula, Annie, Joel, Dwaine, Billy and I. Dwaine is a first-class lad who will do anything to help you out. Billy is OK, while Joel is a slimy bastard trying to creep around the girls all the time. Went down to Bondi Beach to the kick-boxing club there for 1½ hours and surprised myself at how fit I was before running home. Had a Jacuzzi with Paula before getting pissed. Neil came around, and I went to Players with him. Smuggled some beer in. Paula came in later after handing out leaflets. Caught a taxi to a party, where we all got paralytic. Can't remember much more, neither can Paula—must have been a good night.

Day 257: 25 November 1990, Sydney, Australia

I was in bed with Paula when Neil and Dan came around. I haven't seen Dan since Indonesia 6 months ago. Everyone fucked off down the beach while the 3 of us stayed in and got some beers in. I got rat-arsed while the other 2 talked about politics etc. After a while, we all staggered down the park and got some more cans on the way down. I got a cigar as well. We began talking to some druggies in the park, where I ended up falling asleep for over an hour. When I woke up, everyone had fucked off, so I tried to make my way to Harry Krishna's for a 20-cent meal but bumped into Neil and Dan on the way. Had some more cans of beer with them before swimming across Sydney Harbour—took fucking ages, and I swallowed about half the water. Stupid thing to do as I was paralytic, and the harbour is renowned for sharks. Got back pissed and wet. Supposed to be going out that evening but never made it.

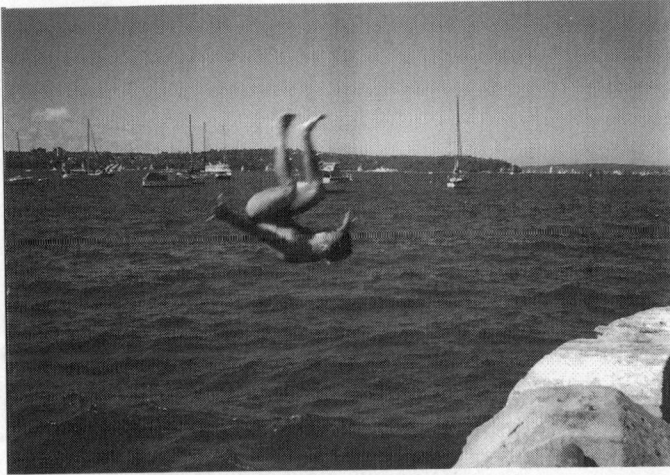

Day 258: 26 November 1990, Sydney, Australia

I was still pissed when I got to work today and nearly rolled the forklift when I was going around a corner too fast. Neil was hanging on the side and shat himself. The factory is full of foreigners such as Vietnam boat refugees, Chinese, Arabs, Lebanese, etc. I only know a couple of Aussies who work here.

Went for a swim when I got home, then spent the rest of the evening with Paula. I drew her a map of her travels through Asia for her to send home. We're getting on really well now, which isn't too good as we both go off in separate directions at the end of February.

Day 259: 27 November 1990, Sydney, Australia

I was like a zombie again today at work after only getting 3½ hours' sleep last night. It was my and Paula's turn for the bed, so we made the most of it. I regretted it today at work as I felt like shite—nearly fell asleep on my forklift. Just had to keep myself awake drinking coffee all the time. Drove past a giant skip, and it was on fire. I dived off the forklift and got a fire extinguisher and tried to put it out. After 20 seconds, the extinguisher had run out. The Chinese had got the hosepipe out. I got drenched by it. The fire brigade had to come and put it out. I got hold of a box of clothes and pinched half of them (about $400 worth). I walked out of the factory and found 2 stolen handbags. I couldn't hang around, so I hid them in a bush until tomorrow. I had a bag full of hot clothes, so I couldn't stop. Took the clothes home for the girls, and they were really nice and expensive clothes—nothing for the lads though. Paula bought me a nice T-shirt today.

Day 260: 28 November 1990, Sydney, Australia

Went to work and picked up the 2 stolen handbags that I found on the way home yesterday. I went through them and found $300 in one of them. I got the phone number for one of the owners and phoned her up. No reply, so I took them to the police station. Worked late tonight until 7 p.m., another 11½-hour day. I saw 4 people sniffing around the outside of the factory. It was the woman who had lost her handbag. I told her that I found it and took it to the police station etc. I felt really bad about pinching the $300 but as she never even thanked me for handing her bag in, I was glad I'd swiped it. Pinched some more clothes for the girls. Got home, and about 20 people were getting pissed in our flat, so I got pissed with them. Ended up with Dwaine in the sauna, drinking beer—good laugh.

Day 261: 29 November 1990, Sydney, Australia

I've got another job. The pay is 50% better than my present job ($420 a week to take home). Roy wasn't pleased when I told him. I'm getting pissed off with working with the Vietnamese, Chinese, etc. as I can't understand the fuckers. Did 3 hours overtime today in which I wrote a couple of letters.

Went out on the piss tonight with Paula, Sally Ann, Gary, and Jack. Went to Players again, where Annie was working on the till. We all got pissed on beer. Some German boxer started chatting Paula up at the bar. I got really pissed off, and when he put his arm around her, I grabbed hold of him and swung him around. spilling his pint everywhere. I offered him outside for a fight, and he agreed, but Paula stopped it, and the cunt had all his mates with him anyway.

Day 262: 30 November 1990, Sydney, Australia

Woke up for work when Annie came home (6 a.m.). I slept on the settee last night and was paralytic when I got home—when I got up this morning, I'd pissed myself, and the settee was soaking wet.

Went to work and was still arseholed. I could hardly walk. I had to leave at 4 p.m. to get my union ticket for my new job ($113). Neil didn't leave work until 7 p.m. and clocked me out then. That's an extra 3 hours of double time for doing fuck all.

Went out on the piss with the lads. Had some wine before going out and had too much. I can't even remember getting to Players. I was that pissed. I was supposed to meet Paula there at 12.30 a.m. When she got there, I was unconscious in a chair, dribbling. Paula was upset and tried unsuccessfully to wake me up several times. Each time, I'd swear at her, making her even more pissed off with me. I didn't wake up until 3.30 a.m. when we all caught a taxi back to Kings Cross—we went for a pizza. Paula gave me a bollocking for telling her where to go. I couldn't remember, so she stood up and threw the keys at me before fucking off home—I got home at 5.30 a.m.

Day 263: 1 December 1990, Sydney, Australia

Woke up, pissed as a fart, next to Paula and apologised. I was supposed to be doing questionnaires in the street today but couldn't be arsed. Caught the train to the post office, and some bird on the train kept staring at me. Then I realised that she was a French-Canadian bird I got off with in Cairns—not bad at all. My parents phoned up today, and it was great to hear from them again. They really have strong accents, something I must have lost.

Went down the beach, where Paula and Annie were working, handing out leaflets. Had half an acid tab tonight. Dwaine was supposed to take half as well but didn't come home from the pub, so I was hanging around for him like a twat on heat. In the end, I turned down a party and a couple of other offers in order to get him from the pub, but he wasn't there. I went back to the flat but was locked out—bollocks. I was really pissed off with Dwaine and ended up going to Players on my own, where Paula was working on the till. I danced for most of the night until Paula finished at 3 a.m.—got a cab home.

Day 264: 2 December 1990, Sydney, Australia

Felt like a bag of shite all day and spent most of it in bed. Got woken up by 4 fire engines and an ambulance as the church opposite caught fire. Did fuck all today as I'm not feeling 100%. I slept in the same bed as Joel tonight. He came home pissed and thought I was Annie, while I thought he was Paula, as I'm used to sleeping with her. So without realising what was happening, we kept putting our arms around each other during the night and then waking up to realise what was going on—this happened several times.

Day 265: 3 December 1990, Sydney, Australia

It's my last day today working with Neil as a forklift driver in a Yarn Warehouse. I've worked for 3 weeks and have taken home about $1000 after tax and overtime as well as pinching $500 worth of clothes for Paula and Annie. I've only been working here for 3 weeks and will be glad to move on.

Came home, and Paula had made a curry—best thing I've tasted in ages. Getting on really well with Paula. I only wish I'd met her in England, where we could have more of a future together—great-looking and great personality, what more could I ask for?

Day 266: 4 December 1990, Sydney, Australia

Got up at 5 a.m. in order to start my new job. I was really fucked. Went down with Dwaine, Gary, and Jack. It took an hour on the train, so we all sprawled out on the seats and went to sleep. I'm doing laboring work, putting up large storage racks at a massive warehouse—hard work but a good laugh.

Went down the gym, sauna, etc. with the rest of the lads. Paula started another temp job today. I don't know what's going to happen at the end of February when we both go separate ways.

Day 267: 5 December 1990, Sydney, Australia
I had to phone Paula up today in the morning to wake her up and nearly got the sack as I was away for half an hour. Had to work my bollocks off for the rest of the day in order to prove myself.

Dwaine borrowed a video camera tonight, so he and I went out to make a video for back home. Paula was ill and couldn't come—she gave me $5 for some fags. Dwaine and I bought some wine with it and got completely arseholed while making the video. I can't remember coming home. I was that pissed. Paula was fuming as she'd been waiting for me to come back with her fags, and I came home paralytic drunk and gave her loads of abuse.

Day 268: 6 December 1990, Sydney, Australia

Woke up still arseholed, and Paula was more than pissed off with me and pissed off with Gary as he fell out with Sally Ann last night, and he told her that I didn't like her either. Got a massive bollocking from Paula tonight when I got home, for last night's performance, and I thought I was going to lose her. I don't know why the fuck I came home and gave her loads of abuse.

The girls went out tonight for a girlie night out. They went out while we ended up with about 20 people in our flat, getting pissed. Fay came around to see me with Bob and Karen, who had just arrived from Cairns. Went out on the piss with them and can't remember coming home.

Day 269: 7 December 1990, Sydney, Australia

Been arseholed the last 2 nights and paid for it today at work. Worked my bollocks off all day before having a sleep on the train on the way home. We all took our shoes and socks off and stunk the whole carriage out.

Finished my video off tonight. Filmed the gym downstairs and said a few Christmas words to the family with Paula and Sally Ann. I worked with Paula and Annie tonight, standing on the street corner like a rent boy, handing out leaflets for Players nightclub. Only worked an hour, got loads of abuse, a couple of free drinks, and $15. Stayed at Players for a bit before catching a taxi home. Paula was pissed and wanted a massage, so I got the baby oil, and when I came back, she was fast asleep—women!

Day 270: 8 December 1990, Sydney, Australia

Went down to Paddy's Market today with Paula and got loads of cheap fruit and veg. Had to rush around like a twat on heat in order to get to the post office to collect any mail. Sweating my bollocks off when we got there, and no bastard mail. If I don't get any mail from Stuart or Adam soon, I'm going to send them a big fuck-off letter each.

I cooked a really nice pasta dish for Paula and Annie tonight. Annie and I went out with the lads tonight, about 8 of us on the piss. I had to meet Paula at 3 a.m. when she finished work and so had to be awake at that time. We all got pissed on wine before moving on to room 24, where they had a party. We had more beers there, and the lads and I had half a tab each to keep us buzzing through the night. We all moved on to a backpackers Christmas party. We were all rat-arsed. Mark kept going around picking birds up off the dance floor and carrying them to our table. He did it to some bloke he didn't know and dropped him on the floor. He got thrown out in the end because he was rolling about on the floor and began chewing on someone's ankle. He hasn't a clue how, but he woke up at the airport miles away from the party. Another lad got thrown out for pissing everywhere. I was dancing on the dance floor and ended up stripping off. I got down to my boxer shorts when the bouncers walked past, so I got dressed quickly. Paula wasn't impressed, although she thought it was funny afterwards.

Day 271: 9 December 1990, Sydney, Australia

We got in at 6 a.m. and then couldn't sleep as we were all still affected by the trip.

Day 272: 10 December 1990, Sydney, Australia

Dwaine had to physically drag me out of bed this morning as I was still a wreck from the weekend. All four of us, Dwaine, Gary, Jack and I, took up all the seats in the compartment on the tube as we fell asleep on the hour-long train journey to Liverpool, where Glenn picks us up in the van ready for us to start at 7 a.m. Dangerous work on the top of a 4th-level storage rack when you can't keep your eyes open. Nearly fell off several times.

Got home really fucked. Looking forward to a quiet night in with Paula, but Sally Ann had just moved into flat 131, so we had to go around for a few drinks.

Day 273: 11 December 1990, Sydney, Australia

Up at bastard 4 a.m. again. I've never been so fucked in all my life (apart from working on the fishing trawler off Carnarvon). I can't cope with a daytime job and being with Paula at night-time. However, I can't give up the job as I desperately need the money, and there is no way I'm going to give Paula up. I can't win. Fucked up at work again and keep scratching my head, legs, etc. as a result. Can't carry on like this.

Fell out with Paula tonight as she spent 1½ hours cooking tea for me, and I didn't appreciate it as I was really knackered and in a ratty mood.

Day 274: 12 December 1990, Sydney, Australia

Joel leaves for England tomorrow—I can't wait to see the cunt piss off home. He's too slimy with the girls in the flat.

We all went down to Bobby McGee's down at Darling Harbour. Yuppie place full of Italians, Greeks, etc., all posers, with their shirts unbuttoned and chests hanging out. I nearly smacked one of the cunts who tried it on with Paula. I pushed him away, but he never started anything. Got a taxi home with Sally Ann and Gary. Paula and I slept in the lounge tonight as it was Annie's turn to sleep in the bed.

Day 275: 13 December 1990, Sydney, Australia

Fucked as a cunt today. I'm like a zombie at work as I'm burning the candle at both ends, which makes working on the high beams (4-floors high) dangerous as it only takes one slip to kill myself. I was on the top beam today and nearly killed Dan (the boss) when I dropped my mallet and only just missed him. I thought the fat cunt was going to sack me. Slept on the train on the way to work, during dinner, and in the train on the way home.

Went for a walk around Sydney tonight with Paula and took some photos of the sights—Harbour Bridge, Opera House, etc. Good night out.

Day 276: 14 December 1990, Sydney, Australia

Typical tube journey to work again today—asleep for an hour on the way to Liverpool. We never buy train tickets as we always climb over the fence at Liverpool Station. Dwaine gets pissed off as he daren't do it, so he always buys a ticket. He bought a weekly ticket on Monday ($18) and only used it twice before losing it, so he had to fork out again while we paid fuck all.

Phoned Steve and Lindsey up tonight, whom I haven't seen since my diving course. They wanted to see me tonight, but I couldn't as we've hired a car for the weekend, and Sally Ann is taking us all out for a spin around Sydney tonight, but then she changed her mind.

Day 277: 15 December 1990, Kiama, Australia

I got fuck all sleep last night as Dwaine had a trip (acid) and spent all night lying in bed in hysterics.

We're going on a dirty weekend today. Gary and I are taking Sally Ann and Paula away for a surprise. Got a really cheap shitty car that really stunk of stale piss. We all nearly threw up when we got in. We drove down south to Kiama and then broke down. It took an hour for some chap to fix it for us. Then we drove down to Seven Mile Beach, which is a very scenic, almost deserted beach. We spent the afternoon lazing around on the beach before setting up camp in the woods alongside the beach (the perfect spot for a romantic night). Put the tents up, built a fire, cooked some sausages and beans, and got pissed on wine. A good evening.

Day 278: 16 December 1990, Sydney, Australia

Woke up during the night to find the tent soaking wet! There was a massive thunderstorm, and my tent wasn't waterproof, so I had to run outside bollock naked and put a plastic sheet over the top. I got soaking wet. Gary's tent was like a Wendy house and blew down, so Gary and Sally Ann ended up running through the woods with fuck all on, looking for the car, where they spent the rest of the night. Meanwhile, the rain brought all the mosquitoes out, and as the front zip on my tent is fucked, we ended up with a swarm of mosquitoes inside. Paula couldn't get to sleep as they kept biting her all over while I couldn't get to sleep as my sleeping bag was soaking wet, and I was freezing cold.

What was meant to be a great romantic weekend ended up as one of the worst nights in my life.

Woke up feeling as rough as fuck. Shit night—really glad it was morning and the night was over. Gary managed to get the fire going, so Paula and I had sausage and beans in bed. Everyone was tired and pissed off. I ended up falling out with Paula—I left her crying while I went for a run along the beach. I felt sorry for her, though, as she got bitten completely from head to toe last night by a swarm of mosquitoes while I didn't get bitten at all. She's reacted badly against them, and it's made her sick. We packed the camping gear away and drove to a place call Green Patch on Jervis Bay, where there were flocks of wild parrots, 'rosellas'. They would come up and eat out of our hands. Then we drove over to Cave Beach—a beautiful and scenic beach with tropical caves and cliffs on either side.

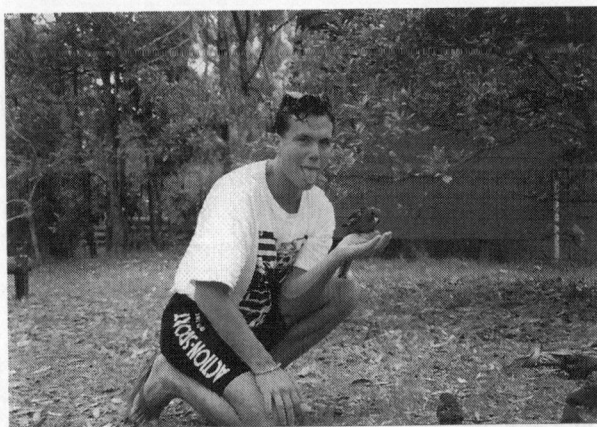

It took 3 long hours to drive back home, in which time we drove through a massive hailstorm, and the hails were the size of large marbles. We couldn't stop the car as the car was on its last legs and probably wouldn't start up again. Paula's bites had all swollen up on her face and everywhere. She caught some form of fever from them, so when we got back, I did her job for her (handing our leaflets). At closing time, I got loads of abuse from all the pissed-up cunts coming out. I nearly ended up smacking a few of them.

Day 282: 20 December 1990, Sydney, Australia

Coming home from work today (I hardly ever pay my rail fares),
I handed over an invalid ticket to the ticket officer. He realised and
took me in his office, where he asked me loads of questions. I knew
I was going to get a $50 fine (I've saved that over the last few
weeks by climbing over the fence etc.), so when he asked me to
come with him, I shoved him out of the way and ran like fuck. I had
my safety boots on, which were too big and kept hanging off my feet
as I ran through Kings Cross on my way home.

Jack pinched a $70 hat tonight from a shop in Kings Cross and got
chased down the street by a gang of Chinese with baseball bats.
He ended up cornered on a building site but climbed over the wall
and escaped.

Day 283: 21 December 1990, Sydney, Australia

What a fucking day. Got up at 5 a.m. and went to work as
normal, jumping the fence at Liverpool Station to avoid paying the
train fare. Worked until 1 p.m. before going out on the beer. We
all piled into the works van and drove to St Mary's, getting pissed
on the way. Stopped off a few times on the way for a piss etc. We
drove through a town, giving abuse out of the window to everyone.
Gary threw a beer bottle out of the window, and it smashed on
the road.

We went to some club. I wasn't allowed in with my singlet, so had
to put on a pair of overalls. We got rat-arsed in the club, singing,
shouting, etc. We all drove back to Glenn's house and continued to
get pissed there, abusing all his neighbours before driving to the
train station. On the way, while we were driving down the main road,
Jack climbed out of the window and on to the roof. I half climbed out
of the window and grabbed hold of Jack. I was wrestling with him
on the roof while we sped down the main road. I ripped his shorts
off, so he was lying on the roof bollock naked. Jack climbed down

on to the bonnet, then back on to the roof when Glenn slammed his brakes on. Jack had smashed into the windscreen, cracking the window. Jack was OK and ran down the road bollock naked, chasing his shorts while I went for a piss. We all got back in the car and drove off to the station. On the way, we passed a field in which some birds were horse riding. We stopped and gave them some abuse, and they ran off. Then some bloke in a BMW pulled up and gave us some shit about the girls and then threatened us with an iron bar. Jack and I chased him around the field, but we couldn't catch him. Gary found a cricket bat and threw it at the BMW window. We jumped back into the car and caught the train home.

I went to tell Paula, but she wasn't home as she'd gone on her work's Christmas Party, so I went back out on the piss again.

Day 284: 22 December 1990, Sydney, Australia

Got home in the morning, and Paula still wasn't home. The bitch. I was furious. She didn't come home till 10 a.m. and I went up the fucking wall. She had got pissed at the party and couldn't come home on the train, so she slept at Maria's (her boss) house.

Day 285: 23 December 1990, Sydney, Australia

Went out today and bought a few things for Christmas. I've got Paula a gold ring with a sapphire in the centre and a cluster of 8 diamonds on the outside, plus some small presents.

Day 286: 24 December 1990, Sydney, Australia

Christmas Eve today, and I still haven't got in the Christmas spirit yet. Got pissed in the flat tonight with Paula and Annie and ended up phoning home and spoke to Dad. We went downstairs after and got pissed with everyone else. I took half a trip and got arseholed in the flat before going through Kings Cross and catching a taxi to Rocks. The Rock was jam-packed with people. We went to an Irish pub and had more beers there, and I can't remember anything else.

Day 287: 25 December 1990, Sydney, Australia (43 Weeks)—Christmas Day

Woke up still pissed from last night and opened my presents. I got a children's kite from Dwaine as well as a pair of 6-year-old-girls' Ninja Turtle bikini bottoms. I went downstairs to room 131 for a champagne breakfast while Paula cooked sausage and beans. I got arseholed. I can't remember opening Paula's present as I got it last night when I was rat-arsed. It's a gold St Christopher with 'Thinking of you always, Paula' written on the back.

Already pissed, we all staggered down to the train station and caught the tube and then the bus to Bondi Beach. I took my kite with me and hung it out of the bus as we went down the road. I pinched a massive can of coke and was walking around with it for most of the day. All I was wearing was my Ninja Turtle girls' bikini bottoms. They were only meant for a 6-year-old, so you can imagine how tight they were—all my fishing tackle went numb after a while. I kept them on all day and got really bad sunburn around various parts of me that had never seen the sun before. Excellent day—everyone pissed and partying on the beach, loads of Christmas trees, Union Jacks everywhere, even a settee and TV on the beach. Steve brought his blow-up doll with him. My best Christmas day ever. I got arseholed and took half a trip as well. I climbed up a massive lamp post to hang a big Union Jack from the top. I got halfway up but couldn't get any higher as it was red hot and burning my legs really bad. I came down with friction burns everywhere. Paula wasn't too happy with me today as I spent most of the day with the lads and hardly saw her.

Some poor cunt drowned on the beach today.

Day 293: 31 December 1990, Sydney, Australia— New Year's Eve

Got up at 5 a.m. in order to go to bastard work. I started on a new site, and it took 1½ hours to get there and the same coming home.

We all went down to Sally Ann's room to watch the fireworks over the Opera House. Steve got a phone call from the police, who told him that they've got a warrant out for my arrest and that I can't leave the country (because Gary threw a cricket bat through a BMW windscreen, and they think it's me). We all got arseholed and caught a taxi to the Rocks (an old area of Sydney next to Sydney Bridge). I couldn't believe how packed it was. You couldn't even walk down the street. Had an excellent night even though I was worried about the police warrant out for my arrest. We kept sniffing am nitrate, sending us high for a couple of minutes each time. A great night out. I got really pissed off with Gary and smacked him twice only seconds before midnight, giving him a black eye. Sally Ann went wild and chased me down the streets, which were cram-packed with people snogging, celebrating the New Year. Neil got arrested at 12 o'clock as he started dancing on a car, which turned out to be a police car.

Day 294: 1 January 1991, Sydney, Australia— New Year's Day

Woke up next to Paula, who was complaining about her hangover. All the lads came around the flat as we're all going to see the England vs Australia one-day test match. We all got 'St George's Crosses' painted on our faces. Got pissed on wine and half a tab before marching down the streets in our full glory, with Union Jacks everywhere. Steve had his blow-up doll on his shoulders. We stopped off at a pub on the way to the cricket match, which was full of English hooligans. Several beers later, about 60 of us marched down the street, chanting English songs and waving flags. Jon went into the grounds while I finished my beer. Before I'd finished it, he'd already been thrown out. He bought another ticket, and we both went in. Great atmosphere, singing all afternoon with all the fans. Dwaine and Steve got thrown out just after the game started. Dwaine managed to get back in again but got thrown out after several minutes. I didn't see much cricket as I spent most of the day arseholed in the bar. I pinched an Aussie flag from some lads sitting about 10 feet in front of us. I shouted at them, and when they turned around, I ripped the flag in half. They were pissed off as they realised I was defacing the Aussie flag and then even more pissed off when they realised it was their flag. Had a great day and ended up getting thrown out, but I managed to sneak back in.

We all staggered back to the Darlo Bar for some more beers—I hardly saw the cricket match, but I think we lost. I had a few more beers and pinched a hat and a Union Jack before crawling home pissed as a twat. Crashed on the settee. Paula and Annie came home pissed as farts half an hour later. Paula had to strip me off in the shower and wash all my face paint off. It took her ages as I couldn't even stand up.

Day 295: 2 January 1991, Sydney, Australia

Got woken up at 5 a.m. still pissed from yesterday's day out at the test match. Can't remember making my sandwiches. I staggered down to Kings Cross tube station to catch the train to work. Gary was down there, and I hadn't seen him since I smacked him at 12 o'clock New Year's Eve. I was sitting on the floor, and he came over to me and punched me on the head and then kicked me. I stood up and started smacking him back in the face. He already had a black eye from when I punched him. When I'd finished with him today at the train station, all his face was swollen, and he was bleeding. I thought he'd had enough and dropped my guard and was just about to walk away when he smacked me. I slipped and fell over and then he kicked me in the face. My teeth got pushed through my cheek, leaving a big hole in it and blood everywhere.

The train arrived. I got on and fell asleep on the seat. I woke up half an hour later at Parramatta Station, with blood everywhere. I jumped the fence at the station to avoid paying and then went to the hospital to get it stitched up. I haven't got any medical insurance, so the tight twat of a doctor only put one stitch in it and didn't use any antiseptic. It hurt like fuck. Walked back and caught the bus into town. I didn't have a clue where to go as I've only worked at this site once before and couldn't remember the way. I had to phone the operator up to get the address and walked around like a twat for over an hour. In the end, I had to wake someone up to ask them directions. It turned out to be some senile old fart, who sent me in the wrong way. I ended up getting to work 2½ hours late, pissed off and with a mouthful of dried blood.

Day 296: 3 January 1991, Sydney, Australia

Neil came round tonight and told me about himself on New Year's Eve. When it struck 12 o'clock, he jumped on a car and started dancing on it—it turned out to be a police car. He got arrested and ended up spending the night in the cells for the night.

Day 297: 4 January 1991, Sydney, Australia

Paula went to Players tonight, handing out leaflets again, so I met her there after work. I got there an hour late as I was enjoying myself in the pub next door. Got home 3.30 a.m.

Day 298: 5 January 1991, Sydney, Australia

Woke up at 9 a.m. when someone knocked on the door. I got up and answered it. It was some bloke who had come around to look around the flat. I showed him around while still bollock naked.

I took Paula to Marley Beach today. We went down to Circular Quay and caught a half-hour ferry there. On the way, got a very scenic view of Sydney Bridge, Opera House, etc. By the time we got to the beach, the sun had gone down, and it started to rain—still a good day out.

I went out with Paula and Annie tonight. We got pissed on wine before going out. I got pissed off with them as they took ages to get ready. Went to Ziggy's and then the Coliseum. On the way, some cunt tried to mug me down Kings Cross. I ignored him and carried on walking. He didn't know what to do, so he fucked off. Paula and Annie handed out leaflets for Players for an hour while I got arseholed in the Cock n Bull. I went outside to talk to the girls, when someone went past with a supermarket trolley. I got in, and they pushed me down the street and down a hill. When they fell over and left me to freewheel down the hill, I nearly shat my pants. I can't remember much more as I got paralytic drunk. Paula had some bloke take me for a piss as I was too drunk to go myself. Then she had to get 2 blokes to get me out as I fell asleep in there. Annie and Paula took me for a dance, and I had to hold on to them to keep myself up. They took me home in a taxi. When we got out of the taxi, the girls went into reception and then realised I was missing. I was lying on the pavement unconscious.

Day 299: 6 January 1991, Sydney, Australia

Woke up at 10 a.m. still feeling pissed, had a cup of tea, and went back to bed. Didn't get up till 3 p.m. as I was so fucked. I went for a walk with Paula. We walked past the Opera House, past the Rocks (old part of Sydney), and up to Harbour Bridge (the one that my grandad's brother helped build). We walked across the bridge, getting an excellent view of Sydney. Sean (my workmate) went to court last week for trying to climb the bridge when he was arseholed and got fined $200. Walked for miles. Got home to cook tea, when Annie and Jane came home pissed as twats with an Aussie steward, whom they'd met today. Jane ended up taking him back to her room for some sex! The dirty slag—she slept with Billy last week and someone else the week before.

Day 300: 7 January 1991, Sydney, Australia

Got up at 5 a.m. again to go to work. Everyone's pissed off with the job as we spend about 3½ hours a day travelling to work and back, catching 2 trains, a bus, and then walking 10 minutes just to get there. Jack and I never pay for our train tickets, but today, the conductor came around on the train, so we had to pay (only $2.50, but I've only got 20 cents left now).

Day 301: 8 January 1991, Sydney, Australia (43 Weeks)

Had a lie-in this morning as I got up at 5.30 a.m. before running around like a twat on heat in order to catch my first train. The cunt of a ticket collector came around again this morning, meaning we had to pay for the second day running. Pissed off as I've got no money left, and I need to save like mad for New Zealand. I've been working for 2 months now and only saved $500 (£200). I pinched a load of milk from the warehouse at work with Jack as well as a few jars of peanut butter.

Got caught on the way home on the train with no ticket again! They're cracking down at the moment, and I would have got a $50 fine, but the conductor had just fined some poor chap and wasn't in a rush to check everyone else's tickets. That's the second close shave I've had, the first being when I had actually been found out at Kings Cross, and I pushed the conductor away and ran off.

Day 302: 9 January 1991, Sydney, Australia

Pissed off with my job—It's not so much the job but getting there and back each day.

Bob came around to visit me tonight as he'd actually got his photos developed from when we both worked on the fishing trawler. The worst and hardest job of my life—out at sea for a month, working 18 hours every day (no days off). I'm so glad I did it, though, as the memories are for life. The photos are excellent, some of me wresting with man-eating sharks, etc. on the boat and of turtles, sea snakes, stingrays, etc.

Day 303: 10 January 1991 Sydney, Australia

Had a cunt of a day at work as I'm really fucked. I haven't really had a good night's sleep in months. I kept asking Jack the time every 5 minutes, and the day really dragged on.

I was looking forward to going out with Paula tonight and being alone together for a change. I couldn't believe it when, just before we went out, Sally Ann invited herself to come along and brought Gary with her—the lad whom I've had 2 fights with in just over a week. I couldn't believe that the girls thought that it would be OK to go on a foursome after what happened. We split up as soon as we got there. I got as pissed as a twat and caught the last train home with Paula. We were the only people in the carriage. I started kissing Paula, and before I knew it, we were both bollock naked from the waist down. Paula climbed on top of me, only to find I had brewers droop—I've never been so pissed off.

Day 304: 11 January 1991, Sydney, Australia

Had a lie-in today, getting up at 6 a.m. as we're working on a new site only 20 minutes from home. I was still pissed from last night and can't believe what happened on the tube during the way home.

Got home from work at 4 p.m. I was bored stiff as I've never been home so early before. Jon phoned up some bird, pretending to be Dwaine, and invited her around to the flat tonight. Dwaine was in a state of shock when one of his ex-lays turned up. She brought a cask of wine with her, so we all got pissed. Jack, Jon, Dwaine, and I were all singing dirty songs for half the night. I went to Players with Paula. She was pissed handing out leaflets for an hour while I kept popping off to the bottle shop to get the beers in. We stayed at Players for a couple of hours before getting a cab home. Paula wasn't too impressed with me as I wanted to walk through Kings Cross and see all the prostitutes and transvestites etc.

Day 305: 12 January 1991, Sydney, Australia

Dwaine slept with his bird on the lounge floor last night while Jon and Billy watched. They occasionally grabbed Dwaine's feet so he knew they were there. He threw her knickers at them as he wanted them for his trophy cabinet (he's got a collection of girls' underwear on his headboard in the bedroom, about 5 pairs of knickers and 3 bras). Dwaine was a right bastard to the old girl as when he woke up in the morning, he had left her on the lounge floor and gone to his bed. I felt really sorry for her as I was in the kitchen and could see her in the lounge, running around looking for her knickers.

We were all supposed to be going to a BBQ downstairs tonight, but as it was broken, we went to a party downstairs. Jane (the slag) was after every man in sight, especially poor old Billy, who nearly got raped by her when he walked her home. The poor lad was scared stiff. Annie's Lancashire hotpot was there, and we all went to Players so that Paula and Annie could hand out the leaflets for an hour. I was so pissed, I could hardly stand, so Paula laid me down on a bench in the High Street and left me for an hour while she went to work. When she came back, I'd gone—she spent an hour looking for me before giving up and catching a taxi home as she was as pissed as a twat as well. I woke up a couple of hours later down an alley. I didn't have a clue where I was as the last thing I could remember, I was at the party. I had to walk from Bondi Junction to Kings Cross, which took 1½ hours, getting me home at 4 a.m. It goes without saying that Paula wasn't too pleased.

Day 306: 13 January 1991, Sydney, Australia
Woke up with Paula, with a hangover, and still feeling pissed from last night. Took Paula to the Botanical Gardens for a relaxing day, winding down from a drunken weekend. Dwaine didn't get home till late afternoon as he slept with a horse that he pulled at the party last night. He stole her pants and bra for his trophy cabinet. Steve got lucky as well and pinched her knickers also and gave them to Dwaine for displaying on his headboard.

Day 307: 14 January 1991, Sydney, Australia
I've been travelling for 10 months now. Even though I've done so many things, it still seems like I left yesterday. Had a lie-in today, getting up at 6 a.m. as we're still on the new site. We're all skint at work, so we've joined a club at work called 'The Tight Fist Gang', in which we can't spend any money at work on food or drink etc. It's

all in a bid to save money and a good laugh at the same time. I got told today that there isn't enough work until next week, so Jon and I have been laid off until then. This pissed me off as I'm desperately trying to save up for New Zealand. Jon and I are now going to Blue Mountains tomorrow for a few days to get away from it all. Paula wasn't too pleased.

Day 308: 15 January 1991, Sydney, Australia

Jon let me down and couldn't come away with me today as he had to get his visa for Thailand. Dwaine and I went down to see Steve and ended up as lookouts for him while he stole a radiator from someone's car. Went down to the gym afterwards for a workout and swim. I got caught having a piss in the Jacuzzi by the cleaner, but she never said anything. A lazy and relaxing day walking around the Botanical Gardens with Jon.

Day 309: 16 January 1991, Sydney, Australia

Got woken up at 5 a.m. with a phone call from the folks back home. They had phoned so early because they thought I was going to work. They hadn't realised I was off this week. I went to see Amy, who was working as a waitress—she gave me a free cappuccino and chocolate gateau.

I felt like a housewife today as I washed all my and Paula's dirty clothes before going down to the supermarket to buy some groceries. I bought a nice pizza for dinner and put it in the oven before going down to Kings Cross Station to meet Paula from work. I wanted to surprise her with a nice pizza for dinner, but by the time we got home, it was burnt and had gone rock-hard (the thought was there).

I went around to Sean's house for a beer and to get some information about the Blue Mountains, where I'm going camping with Paula on the weekend. Went to Magnums with Paula and had a few beers and a cigarette (naughty boy).

Day 310: 17 January 1991, Sydney, Australia

The start of World War III. What a day. It all started at 11 a.m. while watching TV, when a newsflash came on stating America and England had started a massive bombing raid on Iraq. Jon and I spent the whole day watching the progress reports on TV. All day, every channel had its programme postponed as they were covering the Iraq War instead. The British boys were one of the first in, with 5 successful bombing missions.

I took Paula to Players tonight—we caught the tube there. We didn't have a ticket and sneaked past the ticket collector on the way out. Annie was working on the till at Players, so she let us in for free. We had a good night out, drinking and dancing all night. The trouble came when we left to go home. We were very late for the last train home, so had to run to the tube station. I ran off in front, which pissed Paula off. When she met me on the train, she went wild and hit me several times and ripped off the necklace that she had bought me for Christmas. That's some women for you.

Day 311: 18 January 1991, Blue Mountain Katoomba, Australia

I was really pissed off with Paula when I woke up because of the way she behaved last night. We made up though. She went to work while I stayed at home and packed our bags as we're off camping in the Blue Mountains for the weekend.

I got to central station at 1 p.m. and had to wait an hour for Paula to turn up, by which time we'd missed the train. We had to wait for the next one. We caught that train, fell asleep, and missed our stop. We ended up at the end of the line, 45 minutes away from Katoomba, and had to wait nearly an hour to catch the train back. So what was supposed to be a 2½—hour trip ended up being a 6-hour trip.

Once we got there, we asked someone directions to the campsite and ended up getting a sightseeing tour around Katoomba. We got dropped off at the Three Sisters (a famous rock formation) in the

Blue Mountains. We watched the sunset before finding somewhere to camp, which was on a sort of playing field among all the 'no camping' signs. There were other tents there as well as ours—we put the tent up, and I got the wine out and got pissed.

Day 312: 19 January 1991, Blue Mountain Katoomba, Australia

Woke up and had a couple of glasses of wine, which fucked me up for the rest of the day. I've got a big rash around my balls and can't stop scratching. Everyone packed up their tents this morning while I left mine locked up as it was too heavy to carry.

We went for a nice scenic walk through the Blue Mountains and down to Katoomba Falls. It took a couple of hours to get down to the bottom. From there, we got the scenic train back to the top. The train runs vertically up one side of the mountain, reaching an angle of 52 degrees. When we went back to the tent, we realised that we'd camped on the boundary line of a cricket pitch, and a match was in play.

Spent the rest of the day lazing around doing nothing. We were supposed to be going to Wentworth and camp the night there, but we couldn't be arsed. Got the wine out instead and got pissed. My bollocks are getting sorer by the minute. Made a little fire and cooked sausages and beans. By the time it was ready, we were in the middle of a swarm of flies and so had to run to the tent and eat it inside. Woke up in the middle of the night with the sounds of thunder and lightening. I got out and saw a massive storm heading towards us. There was nothing we could do but stay in our tent and wait. First of all, the wind came. I thought the tent was going to blow down as it had bent down to an angle. We had to hold the tent up. Then the rain came. My tent might as well be made out of toilet paper as when it rains its not waterproof. We got drenched in the tent but were lucky as we only got the tail end of the storm!

Day 313: 20 January 1991, Sydney, Australia

I woke up in agony. I've got an infection in my balls. They've gone septic and have stuck to my leg. I could hardly walk. I was in pain every time I moved. It was so bad that we had to come home early. I couldn't even lie out in the sun as I had about 1000 flies sniffing around my poor swollen and septic plums.

I haven't had a shower since last Friday, and with puss all around my sack and leg, you can imagine how smelly the train got on the way home—especially as it was really humid inside, and there were no windows to open. We came back without a ticket and got away with it. It took years to walk from the tube station to our flats. My testicles are now red raw. To make it worse, we were locked out of our flat and had to wait for an hour to be let in. I limped over to a doctor's in the Cross. It was full of prostitutes and druggies—it was a right shithole. I played with the cockroaches on the floor while I waited my turn. It was a woman doctor, really scruffy, and she seemed really surprised when I slapped my balls at her. My puss stunk the surgery out.

Day 314: 21 January 1991, Sydney, Australia

Pissed off at the moment as I wasn't at work last week, and now it looks like there is no more work at all. Totally pissed off—I've only got $800 to my name and have no air ticket out of the country. I'm going to have to look for a job tomorrow (it'll be like looking for a needle in a haystack).

Steve (whom I met on my dive course) came around today. He brought his mate around, and we had a large joint between us. Got stoned off my face.

Day 315: 2 January 1991, Sydney, Australia (45 Weeks)

Went to the supermarket with Jon, and we bought a pizza each. I pinched a chocolate bar and ate it at the checkout. I paid for the 2 pizzas and fucked off. The lady behined the checkout shouted to me to come back. I thought I was going to get done for pinching the chocolate bar, but I had only forgotten my change.

My bollocks are still sore, although they are a lot better. I can nearly walk again. Got pissed with Paula tonight, a bit naughty as I'm on antibiotics (you only live once).

Day 316: 23 January 1991, Sydney, Australia

I felt like a housewife today as Paula went to work to earn the money while I stayed in bed, thinking about all the various housework that needed doing and what to cook for tea. Went down to the job centre. Fuck all jobs, so I came back and lay in the sun with Billy and Jon. We only live 50 metres from the biggest naval base in Australia, and one of the supply ships came in today from the Gulf War. They had been miles away from any action and done fuck all, yet they thought they were heroes. That's Australians for you.

Stayed in with Paula tonight, and we both got pissed.

Day 317: 24 January 1991, Sydney, Australia

Woke up feeling like a bag of shite after getting pissed last night while I'm on antibiotics for my septic balls. Paula went off to work while I stayed in bed recovering. I was on my own in the flat later on, walking around bollock naked as I was just about to go into the shower, when Sally Ann walked in without knocking. I felt a right twat. My bollocks are still a bit sore, although my rash is getting better. Billy, Dwaine, and Jon have now all got similar rashes round their wedding tackle as well.

We all sat down today and watched the Gulf War updates, scratching our genitals. Bob came around tonight, pissed off because he'd lost his job, and Karen had left him. Paula and I went to Players again tonight and got pissed as twats before catching the last train home.

Day 318: 25 January 1991, Sydney, Australia

Woke up again feeling rough as fuck—too much alcohol and not enough sleep. Had a slobby day doing as little as possible. Lay out in the sun with Mark, Jodi, Sally Ann, Jane, etc. for a couple of hours, sweating all the alcohol out that I'd drunk in the last few days.

Paula and I got pissed on wine tonight before going to Players, where Paula and Annie handed out leaflets for the nightclub for an hour. I bought a cheap bottle of champagne, and we drank it on the street. Jane came with us. She's slept with at least 5 blokes since I've known her (about 2 months), so I told her that I thought she was a slag. She burst out crying—Paula was pissed off with me because of it and so went to talk to some blokes in the bar next door. I grabbed her and took her back outside. I started arguing with Jane, and Paula hit me and fucked off again. I made up with Jane and went to Players with her. I went back looking for Paula and caught her flirting with some bloke on the dance floor in another pub. I went up and pushed him away and started shouting at Paula. The bloke started acting the big man. I was going to headbutt the cunt, but he had about 4 of his mates next to him. I grabbed hold of Paula and fucked off. When we got to Players, I told her I didn't want to see her again and fucked off. I sat on a bench in the High Street, and some bird who had been giving me the eye all night came up and started talking to me. She lived nearby and wanted me to come back to her house for a quick one. She wasn't bad-looking, but I just wasn't interested (I've had enough of women for one night). I spent 1½ hours walking home. I didn't want to go home to Paula, so called for Amy—it was 4 a.m. and she was still up talking to Karen and another bird. I was already arseholed but had a couple of glasses of wine with them before going to sleep in a spare bed.

Day 319: 26 January 1991, Sydney, Australia

Woke up in Amy's flat and got home about 10 a.m.—still pissed as a twat. Paula went mental because I stayed out all night and ripped my necklace off and burnt me with a red-hot teaspoon and slapped and punched me several times. I had a massive hangover, and it hurt like fuck even though I was trying my best not to show it. We made up in the end, though, and went down to Bondi Beach together, where we worked, handing out leaflets for Players. It started raining after an hour, so we came home (I got paid $30). A massive storm broke out while on the train home. It was so strong that you couldn't see out of the window. By the time we got to Kings Cross Station, it had flooded—it was the worst storm I had seen in my life. Paula and I were already soaked and so walked home through the storm. Victoria Street (where we live) had flooded and was like a raging river with water up to a foot deep in some places. I nearly lost my flip-flops several times.

Jon (our flatmate) is leaving on Friday, so we all went out for a 4-course meal plus as much as you can drink for only $22. There were about 54 of us, and it was a scream, drinking and eating as much as you could and playing stupid games like 'passing the chewed-up sardines from your mouth to someone else's' and taking it in turns to stand up on your chair, pulling your pants down, taking a length of toilet paper, and putting it up your arse. Someone sets the toilet paper on fire while you have to down your beer. Once empty, you can then pull the toilet paper out your arse. Poor old Mark got his ring-piece scorched. I spent half the time smoking joints before going over to Players, where Paula worked for an hour with Annie. I ended up having an argument with Paula and fucked off to the 'Tea Gardens', where some bird began chatting me up and invited me back to her house for some more beers. I was pissed off and drunk, so I went back with her. I didn't want anything to happen, and so, as soon as we got there, I sat on a chair rather than the settee. She was a good-looking bird and was doing her best to get me into bed, but I wasn't interested and left about half an hour later.

Day 320: 27 January 1991, Sydney, Australia

Woke up at 9 a.m. under some stairs miles away from home. I shat myself as that's the second night running that I haven't come home to Paula. I got home at 10 a.m. still pissed as a twat. Paula was upset even though she believed me.

She took me down to Bronte Beach before we both sobered up from the last 4 nights on the piss. I was arseholed and fell asleep as soon as we got there. I woke up a couple of hours later, red raw with sunburn all down one side. It was so bad, I had to come home. My sunburn was really bad. I've even got blisters all over my face through too much sun. I was looking forward to a sober night in tonight after the 4 previous drunken nights. However, there was a party on, so we all went there. The whole bath and fridge was full of beer, so Paula and I got pissed again for the 5th night running. It was a good party, and we stayed until 3 a.m.

Day 321: 28 January 1991, Sydney, Australia

Massive hangover day. My kidneys are pickled, and my body is on reject—too much sex, drugs, and rock 'n' roll for one weekend.

Day 324: 31 January 1991, Sydney, Australia

Fucked off at the moment as I haven't worked for three weeks now. Piss bored all day as I've no money to do anything. I got 2 postcards from home today and a small package with some photos of the family, including my Land's End to John o'Groats bike ride and my expedition to Pakistan.

Tim O'Conner (my mate from home) phoned up tonight—I bumped into him on Christmas day on Bondi Beach, pissed as a twat. He came out with Paula and me tonight. We went to Players as it was Jon's leaving do (another flatmate bites the dust!). There were about 20 of us on the piss. I was pissed when I got there as I'd been on the wine. I did my condom trick (up the nose and out the mouth) for Jon, but he was too pissed and couldn't remember it.

Got the last train home. Paula went for a slash during the night and saw Jon shagging some bird on the settee.

Day 325: 1 February 1991, Sydney, Australia

Another day unemployed—no jobs in the CES (job centre). Jon left today for Thailand—the cheeky cunt fucked off without paying any bills.

I made Paula a 3-course meal for dinner tonight—a cupper soup followed by jacket potato and beans, with jelly for pudding. We got pissed tonight before going out. The girls went to work for an hour while I met Tim and his bird Linda (she used to live 100 yards from me in Lincoln, but I couldn't remember her). I've got absolutely fuck all money and pinched a few drinks in the Cock n Bull before all going to Players. Everytime I see Tim, I am pissed and can never remember much, and tonight was no exception. A good night out with an old mate.

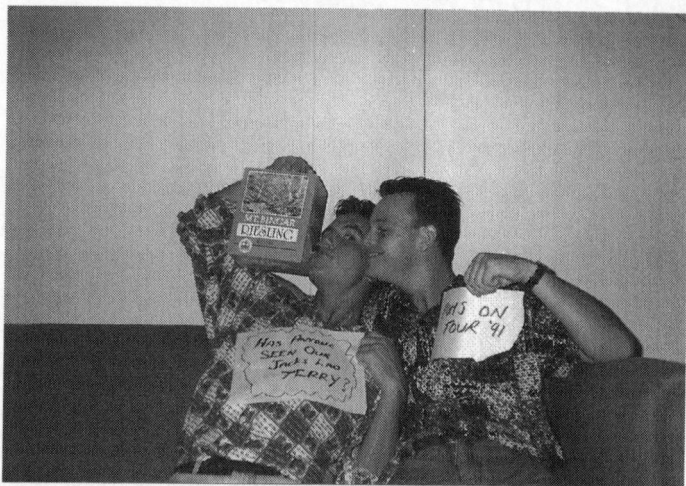

Day 326: 2 February 1991, Sydney, Australia

Paula and I were still pissed when we got up, and so stayed in bed for most of the day, recovering.

Jane is leaving tomorrow, and so we all went down for a farewell piss-up with her tonight at 8 p.m. All the lads were there, and it was a good laugh. Paula and Annie went to work later on, so Neil and I went with. I pinched several beers while the girls handed out leaflets. Paula wasn't feeling too good, so I had a dance on my own. Some bird came up to me and tried it on. I told her that I was going out with someone and walked off. Paula came up and went wild, thinking that I'd shagged her last week. She started slagging me off really bad, so I started on her. The next thing I knew, she grabbed me around my neck, digging her fingernails in at the same time. It hurt like fuck, so I pushed her back. She ended up falling off her chair, banging her head on the floor. She wanted me to come home with her in a taxi, but I was too angry with her and walked away instead.

Day 327: 3 February 1991, Sydney, Australia

Woke up still pissed as a twat and still pissed off with Paula. I went on the grass and lay out in the sun. I only lasted 5 minutes as my head started spinning round due too much alcohol last night. Jane (the slag) left today to go home to England. I went down to the airport with her and Mark, Jodi, and Mike. I had a beer and was pissed as a fart again.

We drove back home before going down to the Botanical Gardens for a piss-up with the lads. We all got bollocked by the ranger for playing cricket. We all got pissed and came home. I made up with Paula. We went for a walk in the park, and she got bitten to fuck by mosquitoes.

Day 328: 4 February 1991, Sydney, Australia

Pissed off again today as I can't find a job, and both time and money are running out fast. I've only got $900 and still have to buy a flight to New Zealand. I want to try and sail there on a yacht or work my passage on a cargo boat. I've got to find a job as I'm walking around like a bear with a sore head at the moment.

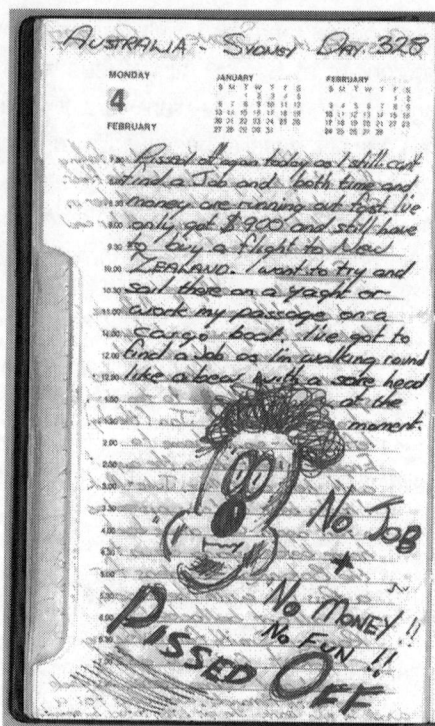

Day 329: 5 February 1991, Sydney, Australia

Paula and I got up early this morning and went down to someone's squat (they're illegally squatting in an empty house), and believe it or not, the phone is still connected. Paula phoned her parents up for 15 minutes before going to work. Then I phoned up my family back home. I was on the phone to England for over half an hour, and it didn't cost me anything!

I phoned up the old boss this morning and managed to get some work, which was walking around town like a cunt, hassling people to get them interested in financial planning. I get $2 per person and managed to get 16 people, although only 10 of the people would probably be genuine—a couple of hours' hard work.

Tim and Linda came around tonight. I showed them around the flats and nearly had a fight with some Aussie twat in the sauna.

Day 330: 6 February 1991, Sydney, Australia

Tim O'Conner—one of my old mates from home (whom I went to playschool with)—and his girlfriend Linda are moving in with Paula, Annie, and me next week. I left home nearly a year ago on my own, and now I'm going to be living with a couple from the same village as me back home. A small world.

I spent about 3 hours today, working for the financial company and couldn't find anyone to complete my survey. Everyone kept telling me that they were too busy. In the end, some Bible-basher came up to me and gave me some religion shit. I pretended that I was interested for 5 minutes. Just as he was about to leave, I got him to fill in one of my forms. The only form I got filled in for 3 hours' work, earning myself $2. This job's doing my bastard head in. I can't do it for much longer.

Day 331: 7 February 1991, Sydney, Australia

I couldn't believe my luck when I phoned my old racking job, and he said I can start back tomorrow. I don't know how long for, though.

Paula came home from work early today as we're off to see an Opera tonight, *Mikado* by Gilbert and Sullivan at Sydney Opera House. I borrowed a shirt, tie, and trousers off Annie's man, Neil—the smartest I've looked since I left England nearly a year ago. We both got dressed up and had a nice walk through Botanical Gardens, smoking joints and getting stoned on the way. We were late for the opera. Paula and I nearly burst out laughing when the first singer came on singing in a high pitch. It was really good for about half an hour, after which it got a bit repetitive. I fell asleep and missed the end of the opera (it went on for 3 hours). We had to walk home in the rain as we had no money for a taxi—a good night out.

Day 332: 8 February 1991, Sydney, Australia

I thought it would be good to go back to work and that I'd appreciate it, but after being back for ten minutes, I was fucked off with it. Steve and I travelled to work on an old ticket—the ticket collector came around on the train (I shat myself as I didn't have any money). Just as he came up to Steve and me, we arrived at Tempe (our stop), so we frank boffed (fucked off). We walked past the ticket inspector at the station without showing our tickets. He shouted to us to come back a couple of time before we gave him our tickets and fucked off quick. He shouted at us to come back as the tickets were out of date, but we ignored him.

Spent all day putting beams up with Steve. We both sweated like twats for the whole day, working our bollocks off.

Went to bed as soon as I got home but was too tired to sleep (believe it or not). Got pissed on wine with Paula, smoked a joint, and then went to Bondi Junction. I met Tim and Linda in the Cock n Bull while the girls handed out leaflets. I bought a cheap bottle of piss and drank it outside with them. We all piled into Players and had another loud night out, singing, shouting, and abusing people. A good night out—can't remember coming home though.

Day 333: 9 February 1991, Sydney, Australia
Got up still pissed from last night and went down to Bronte Beach with Paula before we both sobered up. I was fucked yet

couldn't sleep on the beach. I went for a walk and looked up—Sally Ann and Gary were about 5 metres in front. I'm sure they saw me. I pretended that I didn't see them and carried on walking. The last thing I wanted was to spend the afternoon with them.

It was Paula's turn to cook tonight, yet I ended up cooking it (*again*). We all got pissed on wine again tonight before going out to Players and the Tea Gardens. Got pissed with Paula and smoked loads of fags (pissed off about that as I don't smoke). We got a taxi home via McDonalds.

Day 334: 10 February 1991, Sydney, Australia

Went shopping with Paula this morning to get the weekly groceries. I was pissed off again because I've fuck all money at the moment and have to be really tight with the small amount I've got. I did an hour's work on Bondi Beach today with Paula—the good thing is, I got paid $25 for an hour's work. I had to run down Bondi Beach, hand out tickets for Players, and then run all the way home again. Went to bed—good night.

Day 335: 11 February 1991, Sydney, Australia

Back to work again. Steve and I don't know how long we're going to be working for and so have to work as slow as we can to make the job last longer. I didn't realise how hard it was trying to look busy without doing anything.

Day 336: 12 February 1991, Sydney, Australia (48 Weeks)

Dwaine has found several crabs on himself and can't work out how he got them. He doesn't know, but he got them off me. Mine have come back for a third time since I originally caught them in Cairns. Now everyone else is worried about catching them as he borrows everyone else's clothes. Dwaine went down to the doctor's tonight and got some cream, which we all used, so, hopefully, they've all gone—touch wood.

Day 337: 13 February 1991, Sydney, Australia

Spent all day at work drilling into reinforced concrete floors, getting a headache. There were no earplugs or headphones, so I had to shove toilet paper in my ears to dampen the noise.

I'm getting into too much of a routine at the moment, i.e. go to work, catch the train home, cook tea, wash up, have sex, go to bed.

Dwaine and Billy moved out tonight (peace and quiet at long last). They packed their bags and frank boffed. Tim O'Conner and his girlfriend Linda are moving in on Friday.

Day 338: 14 February 1991, Sydney, Australia, Valentine's Day

Valentine's Day today. I've already received my presents from Paula—a pair of gold earrings and a gold necklace. She gave them to me a couple of days ago as she couldn't wait.

I went to work today and couldn't believe it when we all got sent home at 2.30 p.m. (an hour early) because it was *too hot*—you're allowed to go home if it gets to 42°C, yet today, it got up to 45°C. Everyone back home in England can't get to work because of the snow, yet here am I, getting sent home because it's too hot!

I got Paula the new Righteous Brothers cassette today and took her out for an Italian meal. It was a 'bring your own plonk' place. We got stoned before going and took a cask of wine with us. We both got pissed as farts on the wine. Paula was scratching her head and found a crab in her hair—I thought we'd got rid of them. We had another joint on the way home. I got pissed off with Paula because as soon as we got home, she fell asleep on me.

Day 339: 15 February 1991, Sydney, Australia

Pissed as a twat when I got to work this morning, but I soon sweated it out once I started working. Steve and I spent most of the day asking people the time and counting the hours and minutes down until 3.30 p.m. (home time!)

Paula and Annie moved into the bedroom with me tonight as Tim and Linda are moving into theirs. They completely took over the bedroom. I had about 4 large draws and lots of cupboard space before they moved in. Five minutes after the girls moved in, I was reduced to a shoebox in the corner of the room.

Tim and Linda moved in tonight. We bought a cask of wine and got pissed before going out to Players—the girls handed out leaflets for an hour while the rest of us got pissed on the street. I shared a cheap bottle of champagne with Linda, and she got pissed as a fart. We all went down to Players for more alcohol and stayed there for a couple of hours before coming home. Stopped off at McDonald's down Kings Cross and then walked home from there.

Walking down the road, I stopped for a piss in a bush. Some slag having a meal outside a restaurant saw me and shouted at me. I flashed my trouser snake at her in retaliation. The next thing I knew, she was shouting at the police. I put my pride and joy away and began walking off. The police van drove up beside me, and one of them told me to stop. I ignored them and carried on walking. The police van stopped and a couple of policemen got out, shouting at me again to stop. I ran like fuck down the street with the police chasing me. The next thing I heard was, '*Stop, or I'll shoot*'. I shat my pants and stopped straightaway. The policeman chasing me immediately did a rugby tackle on me. We both went arse over tit in the middle of the road. The next thing I knew, he had a gun to my head. I ended up lying face down in the middle of the road, with my hands cuffed behind my back. He picked me up and shoved me against a wall, with my legs open, and he searched me.

Paula walked round the corner with Tim and Linda. They couldn't believe it. I got shoved in the van and taken to the station. I knew that they didn't have any witnesses, so I denied everything. Then Paula barged into the police station, pissed as a twat, and told them to let me out as I'd only had a piss in the street, so now they know it was me! To cut a long story short, they let me out. They checked me out on the computer. I shat myself as I still have a warrant out for my arrest, so I spelt my surname wrong and got away with it.

Day 340: 16 February 1991, Sydney, Australia

I took Paula out for the day—we went to Cronulla Beach (40 minutes on the train). By the time we got there, the sky was full of clouds, and a strong wind was blowing sand everywhere. It was a similar feeling to sitting next to a sand blaster on Skegness Beach.

It's the Gay and Lesbian Mardi Gras tonight, so we got pissed on wine and went out to see the float parade. I've never seen so many gays in all my life—walking around in leather, with their nipples pierced, holding hands, snogging in the street, etc. I was pissed up and walked down the street holding Tim's hand, with Paula's lipstick on. Paula wanted to go for a piss, so we broke into a little shed. She crouched down and began pissing. I took a couple of photos on her camera. She went mental as her boss was taking the film in to have it developed for free. Tim and I tried to climb on a float, but the bloke wouldn't let us, so when he turned around, we both climbed on to the float. We had a quick dance on stage with some others on the float for some photos, then fucked off quick before we got our bottoms pinched. A real eye-opener.

Day 341: 17 February 1991, Sydney, Australia

Went to Paddy's market with Paula. Bought loads of groceries (fruit and veg). I feel like a bloody married man!

Day 342: 18 February 1991, Sydney, Australia

Pissed off with work as it is so boring at the moment (we're making frames all day). Every day, on the way to work, I climb over the fence at the station in order to save a few dollars on ticket fares.

Day 345: 21 February 1991, Sydney, Australia

Everyone in the flat is pissed off at the moment as Annie's boyfriend Neil virtually lives here. He sleeps here every night (which pisses Paula and me off as we share the same bedroom as Annie, so Neil is sleeping in our room). He's a slob, never cleans up after himself, and everyone's getting fed up with it. So I wrote a message and left it for him to see. Hopefully, he won't be hanging around here so often.

Bought a cask of wine and got pissed with Paula, Tim, and Linda before going to Players as it was $1 a drink night. It was $5 to get in, but Annie was working on the till so let us in for free again. Had another good night out before catching the last train home.

Day 346: 22 February 1991, Sydney, Australia

I couldn't walk straight when I got to work this morning as I was still pissed from last night. Everytime I sweated, it stunk of alcohol. We've spent all week making frames—boring work. I feel more like a robot than a human being. Counted the hours down until 3.30 p.m. (*the weekend*) and fucked off home on the train.

Paula was home when I got there as she didn't go to work today.

Another typical Friday night out—pissed on wine before going out, tube to Bondi Junction, Paula and Annie handing out leaflets outside the Cock n Bull while we all got pissed in the street. I went to the toilet in the Cock n Bull, and someone from Lincoln had written some graffiti on the wall. I couldn't believe it. I'm on the other side of the world, yet I saw 'Brooksy—Lincoln FC' written on a toilet wall. Went to MacDonald's on the way home with Paula. We both wanted a piss, but there were no toilets in MacDonald's as the downstairs was closed, so we both sneaked down and had a piss in a corner next to Ronald MacDonald.

Day 347: 23 February 1991, Sydney, Australia

Another day in the life of a housewife—pushing a fucking trolley around a supermarket with Paula, getting the weekly groceries.

Watched *The Bounty* tonight on TV. A great film, but missed the end as went to Players—pissed and stoned before I went. Pissed as a fart, I started talking to some alcoholic granny in the Tea Gardens. The poor lass could hardly stand up, she was that pissed. The next thing I knew, Paula was having a fit as I'd been talking to her for an hour. I started arguing back, and we had a big argument.

She punched me in the face, and I couldn't believe it. We made up and fucked off home in a taxi.

Day 348: 24 February 1991, Sydney, Australia

I bumped into Jack today. He'd just got back from New Zealand. I spent the day with him. We went around Kings Cross, taking photos of the prostitutes, before walking down to Elizabeth Bay and lay in the sun for a while.

I took Paula for a walk later on tonight. She went hysterical when she looked down and saw a massive spider on her breast.

Our toilets have broken, so we've been given the keys to flat 138 in order to use their toilet as no one lives there. There was no power in the flat, so we couldn't see anything. We pinched a few light bulbs and were going to pinch some of the rungs from the blinds to replace the missing ones from our flat, but they were the wrong colour.

Day 349: 25 February 1991, Sydney, Australia

It was Mike's 21st birthday today, so we all went down to his flat tonight for a party. We got there at 8.30 p.m. by which time he was already pissed as a twat and was walking around bollock naked, with only a Union Jack wrapped around him. He downed another few mouthfuls of whiskey and was sick in the toilet. He ended up unconscious on the settee, while everyone else continued the party. Jules went to the bottle shop and got some more beers, stumbled into the road, and nearly got run over by a police car. He shouted abuse at them and ended up getting arrested (he goes to court for it in a couple of weeks, but he won't be here).

Day 350: 26 February 1991, Sydney, Australia

Paula and I went to the pictures tonight to watch *Exorcist III* as Annie went to watch it last week and said it was good. It was shit.

My visa for Australia ran out yesterday, which means that I'm over here illegally at the moment, although I've got another 28 days left before I will get prosecuted.

Day 351: 27 February 1991, Sydney, Australia
It's Dwaine and Billy's leaving do tonight at Magnums. I took Linda and Tim with me. They both got pissed as farts. Dwaine ended up being sick in the toilet before falling asleep in the cubicle for an hour. Billy disappeared halfway through the night and was found asleep on the pavement when everyone went home.

Day 352: 28 February 1991, Sydney, Australia
Another boring day at work, counting the hours down till home time. Went to work on the back of Steve's motorbike and nearly fell off the back several times.

Went to Players tonight with Paula. Annie let us in for free. We were all set for a good night out with $1 a drink, until I bumped into Gary and Sally Ann and was forced to talk to them for a bit. I've still got a warrant out for my arrest because of Gary. I got pissed off with him as all he could talk about was how much money he is earning in his new job and how little work he does. They caught a taxi home while Paula and I caught the tube.

Day 353: 1 March 1991, Sydney, Australia
Another wild night out tonight. Paula and I had a sleep at 7.30 p.m. for an hour before going out. The next thing I knew, it was midnight, and we'd been asleep all that time. Paula was pissed off as she was supposed to be at work half an hour ago. We couldn't believe it and went around the Cross instead. We went to Taboo's for a drink before coming home.

Day 354: 2 March 1991, Sydney, Australia
Took Paula around Paddy's market today with Tim, Linda, and our Jack-thelad Terry. Bought loads of vegetables, then came back and did loads of cooking (don't tell the lads!).

Tim got sacked from his job last week because he crashed the work's van and then told the secretary to 'Fuck off'. Anyway, to cut a long story short, they are both leaving next week to travel around Australia, so we had their leaving do tonight.

Pissed as cunts on cheap wine before catching the tube down to Bondi Junction. I shared a cheap bottle of champagne with Linda. She ended up feeling sick and came home early with everyone else. I stayed out on my own for an hour (sweeping drinks) before walking home. I got a lift from a gay bloke in a posh car. He dropped me off outside my flat. I think he wanted me to invite him in for a shag.

Day 355: 3 March 1991, Sydney, Australia

Went down to Bronte Beach with Paula, Tim, and Linda. Tim and I were acting like kids on the beach, running around like twats. I got sand all down my trunks and took them off in the sea to wash the sand out of them. Tim chased me, trying to pinch them off me. I ended up running around bollock naked with my trunks in my hand. The next thing I knew, the lifeguard had got hold of me and was bollocking me for running around naked on a family beach and threatened to ban me from the beach.

Took Paula for a sauna and Jacuzzi when we got back to the flats. I cooked a nice stir fry tonight for Paula and me. It was boiling hot. I served it on to the plates, and before I'd even had a bite, I dropped my plate on to my foot and spilt it all over the carpet. Burnt my bastard foot and lost my dinner at the same time.

Later on, Tim made himself a cup of tea, and I pinched it off him. He made another cup for himself. I was in the kitchen with him (all I had on was my swimming trunks). He took his tea bag out of his cup of tea and dropped it down the front of my trunks, burning my bell end, sending the poor thing red raw. If that wasn't enough bad luck for one night, I was sitting on the bed, talking to Paula while she was doing her hair. I lay back on to the bed and scorched my back on her curling tongs, leaving a bright red mark down my back.

Day 358: 6 March 1991, Sydney, Australia
Another typical day at work, dodging the ticket collectors on the train and then climbing over the fence at the station. I switch my brain off as soon as I get to work as it's that easy and boring. I look forward to dinner time, when Steve and I strip off and have a sleep in the sun.

Paula's sister Jane comes over from England today to visit us for a month. Paula and I got pissed before we went out to meet her. We had some wine in the flat, followed by a few beers in Magnums. Caught the tube to Central Station to pick her up. We waited for ages before coming home to find her sat on the settee, waiting for us. The flat's crowded at the moment as Tim and Linda move out on Saturday, and the new people, Mike and Nancy, have already moved in. Plus Jane's here now, so that's 7 people in a 2-bed-room flat. I'm sharing a bedroom with 3 blonde girls at the moment—Paula, Annie, and Jane.

Day 359: 7 March 1991, Sydney, Australia

It's Jane's first night out in Oz, so the girls took her out for a meal at Players. I went to Mike and Steve's leaving piss-up downstairs with Tim and Linda. It was OK, but the police came down in the end and moved us on because we were making too much noise. We all ended up at Players, pissed as twats, making fools of ourselves. Tim and I drank until we couldn't stand up any more before coming home on the last tube—great night out.

Day 360: 8 March 1991, Sydney, Australia

Got up at 6 a.m. pissed as a fart and went to work on the back of Steve's motorbike and nearly fell off several times. Wobbled all over the shop. Straight to bed as soon as I get home from work.

Got pissed on wine with Paula and Jane. While Paula was at work, I took Jane around a couple of pubs before going to Players for some more beers.

Day 361: 9 March 1991, Sydney, Australia

Tim and Linda left today while the rest of us went down to Bondi Beach. I've hardly slept during the last few nights, so I slept like a log on the beach.

I took Jane downstairs to a party tonight while Paula went to work. Had some more wine and went to the Cock n Bull, where I had a few joints. Ended up in Players again.

Day 362: 10 March 1991. Sydney, Australia

Took Paula and Jane down to Darling Harbour around the shops. It's bad enough going shopping with one woman, but it's a nightmare going with two. We must have spent about half an hour in every shop we passed. The girls went into the aquarium. I waited outside as I couldn't afford the $12.50 to get in. I went to the exit of the aquarium and just walked in over the barrier. The guard shouted at me to stop several times. I ignored him and carried on walking. He ran up, grabbed me, and told me to get out. I told him I'd just come out of the aquarium and had forgotten my coat, so he let me in. The girls couldn't believe it when I bumped into them.

Day 363: 11 March 1991, Sydney, Australia

I'm not working today as there is no work on (again), so instead, I booked my flight to New Zealand. Sydney to Auckland return costing me $399. I'll have to find some form of work over there!

Day 364: 12 March 1991, Sydney, Australia

Paula was being a bit of a bitch this morning, so I went to the zoo with Jack today instead of going with her on the weekend. We were going to climb over the fence to get in—once we managed to get there by ferry—but we managed to get some *free* entrance tickets. The zoo was OK, but we were too fucked to appreciate it.

Paula went to the pictures with Jane tonight while I stayed in and got pissed and stoned before catching the tube to Marc Place, where I got out and walked down to Sydney Harbour Bridge. I climbed up to the top of the bridge (80 metres above the road and 130 metres above the water). It was fairly easy, although I did get caught on barbed wire a few times. It took forever to reach the top. I took my Union Jack with me and lit a joint at the top, getting more stoned, looking at an excellent view of Sydney. I had to be careful as Sean got caught trying to climb the bridge before Christmas and got fined $200, but he was at the bottom. Any further up, and he'd have got fined a maximum of $1000. I felt great when I'd climbed down and realised what I had done. Came back home, and our bedroom was crammed full of people drinking. So being the nice sociable person that I am, I sat down and joined them. We carried on till 1 a.m. before everyone staggered off home. Not a bad night at all.

Day 366: 14 March 1991, Sydney, Australia

What a great feeling waking up this morning, as it was a year ago today that I left England, flying to Nepal for the first stage of my 'around the world trip'. Here I am, one year later, in Australia and still going strong. I think that there's about 50% chance of me still travelling next year at this time. I fly to New Zealand next Monday in order to work before, hopefully, getting a lift on a yacht to some of the islands in the South Pacific and then heading to South America.

I soon felt pissed off today as it's my first day back at work this week. There's not much work on at the moment, so Keith and I had to work as slow as possible to make the work last longer. I was standing on top of the scissor lift and ended up ripping my leg open on some sharp metal. Sod's law—it would have to happen near knocking off time. I caught the tube home and got it sewn up at a doctor's surgery down Kings Cross (8 stitches). The doc said that it was good enough for me to go to work tomorrow, but I managed to talk him into giving me a sick note for tomorrow.

I went out on the piss tonight, celebrating my one year's travel with Paula, but sadly, my leg wasn't fit enough to go to work the next day.

Day 367: 15 March 1991, Sydney, Australia

Had the day off work today because of my leg. Paula also had the day off as she had flu. I had lots of things to sort out but couldn't be arsed.

Day 368: 16 March 1991, Sydney, Australia

Caught the tube and bus down to Bronte beach today in a last bid to top up my tan before I go to New Zealand next week. I soon got bored with lying in the sun and so ran down to Bondi Beach and back along the windy footpath along the top of the clifftops. Life is becoming routine again, and I'm getting itchy feet to move on. I don't know whether it's because I've been in Sydney for too long or whether it's because I've been with Paula too long and feel like I'm getting settled.

It's the girls' last night working for Players tonight, so we had a small party back at the flat before catching the tube to Bondi Junction for the last time. I went into the Tea Gardens while the girls were handing out leaflets. The bird who works at the butcher's shop was after me tonight in the Tea Gardens. I felt a little bit tempted, so I left to meet Paula. We all went to Players and went mental on the dance floor. Must have looked a right bunch of twats, but we had a great time. Caught the taxi home with Paula. I went to cook some food while Paula fell asleep on the settee, and I ended up falling asleep next to her. We didn't wake up till 5 a.m. when we crawled to bed.

Day 369: 17 March 1991, Sydney, Australia

Took Paula down to Watsons Bay today (the entrance to Sydney Harbour). Lots of high cliffs, very scenic. There was a nudist beach nearby, but I couldn't find it. I couldn't ask anyone where it was as Paula was with me, and she didn't know about it.

Caught the ferry back to Circular Key and walked home past the Opera House and through the Botanical Gardens—not a bad day out. Pity about the nudist beach though.

Found out tonight that Mike and Steve, who went down near Melbourne a couple of weeks ago to meet Sean, etc., were fruit picking. They both managed to get a job, but on the first day, Steve started chatting some bird up. Her boyfriend was nearby and smacked Mike and beat the shit out of Steve. To cut a long story short, they all got the sack, including Sean etc. who had got Steve the job.

Day 371: 19 March 1991, Sydney, Australia

I've got so many things to sort out this week, it's unbelievable. I made out a massive list and was just about to get my arse into gear and start sorting things out, when Neil and Dan (some mates from Indonesia) came around. Dan bought a massive bag of grass around with him. He rolled up several joints, and we smoked them in the flat, getting stoned off our heads before going down to Kings Cross for a Thai meal. I was fucked and had to go home to bed—I'll start my list tomorrow.

Had a really good night tonight. Paula and I went around Darling Harbour before going for a few drinks.

Day 372: 20 March 1991, Sydney, Australia

Paula went to work this morning (her last day) while I stayed at home. I got my list out and was just about to go off and get things sorted, when Jane came back from a week at Fraser Island. I had a few joints and so got stoned again and then went running about all day like a blue-arsed fly, trying to sort my lift out, getting trains from one end of the city to another, collecting wages, tax forms, certificate forms, etc.

Paula came home pissed tonight from her dinner-time drinking session with the office staff.

Began packing our bags as we leave the flat on Saturday morning, and there are still one thousand and one things that have to be done. The flat is in a right state, and if it's not immaculate by the time we leave, then the girls may lose some of their $400 bond—I haven't paid any of the bond.

Day 373: 21 March 1991, Sydney, Australia

Another day running around like a twat, going around in circles and getting nowhere fast. The girls went down to the zoo this afternoon, while I carried on rushing around (I'm on the verge of a nervous breakdown).

It's our leaving do tonight (mine and Paula's). Several people came around to our flat. We had a few drinks before going around to Annie's boss's house, where we all got really stoned. I was a wreck and couldn't keep my eyes open. We all piled down to Players for the last time. Annie took her video camera with us and filmed us all pissed as farts. Sally Ann was flirting around everyone like a right slag (again). We all went to Kings Cross and were going to go to Porky's (a strip joint), but we were all too fucked and went for something to eat instead. I went off on my own for a Thai meal and fell asleep on the table halfway through. Got woken up when everyone came back to collect me—a good night out.

Day 374: 22 March 1991, Sydney, Australia

Sent a massive parcel home today (8 kg), mostly of the clothes I stole when I was working at the yarn warehouse. We all spent most of the day cleaning the flat up and smoking joints throughout the day before going to see an agricultural show, which was a load of shite. Saw a few pigs, cows, goats, etc. Not bad value for the $8 entrance fee.

Went back to the flat, got changed, and went out for a few drinks with Paula down to the Cross.

Day 375: 23 March 1991, Sydney, Australia

We were supposed to be going off to the Blue Mountains today, but by the time we'd finished off cleaning up the flat, it was mid-afternoon, so we just lay about in the sun for a while. We all went down to Tanya's flat tonight as it's her 25th birthday. Everyone was getting pissed playing party games. We stayed for a while before going off with Paula. We went to the Coliseum for a few drinks and then for some food.

I'm looking forward to travelling on again, but I don't know how I'll feel about Paula once I've gone. We've virtually been with each other constantly for the last 6 months, so it's going to be very hard and lonely at first without her. It's all character-building stuff.

Day 376: 24 March 1991, Sydney, Australia

Woke up early this morning as we're squatting in our old flat. Got ready and headed off to the Blue Mountains for the day. Caught the train to Wentworth and spent the afternoon smoking joints while walking around the Wentworth Falls. I went for a swim under one of the waterfalls and remained soaking wet for the rest of the day.

When we got back to Sydney, I went for a Thai meal along with Paula and Jane. I felt a right twat tonight as I was in Sally Ann's place talking to click. We thought that we were the only ones in and started slagging Gary off, only to find out that Gary was in his bedroom, listening to us.

It's my last night with Paula as we both go our separate travels tomorrow. We're both upset, but in a way, I'm glad as it gives me a lot more freedom when travelling. We might meet up in South Africa in 9 months' time (Jan 1992).

Day 377: 25 March 1991, Auckland, New Zealand

Got up at 6 a.m. after only 2 hours' sleep, completely shattered. Today's the day that Paula and I go off in our separate ways after spending 6 months with each other. Sally Ann took us all to the airport. It was very emotional smoking joints and counting the minutes down. A sad day. Paula and Jane flew to Perth while I went to check in for my New Zealand flight. I nearly shat my pants when I was told that I couldn't fly because my return ticket wasn't valid as I didn't have another visa in which to enter Australia. I spoke to the manager, who phoned up all the big knobs, trying to sort it out. In the end, he said that I could risk going over on the plane, but if caught at the New Zealand end, I would be sent home to England. Shit or bust, I went for it. I couldn't believe it when I saw Pam and Debby on the same plane. To cut a long story short, I managed to get through immigration (whew!) and waited around the airport for 6 hours, getting pissed until Pam's friend arrived and took us back to her house. Typical, it's pissing down.

Day 378: 26 March 1991, Auckland, New Zealand (54 Weeks Away)

Woke up this morning with a bad back as I had slept on the lounge floor last night (I must be getting old).

My first impression of New Zealand is that there is a lot of water (rainwater).

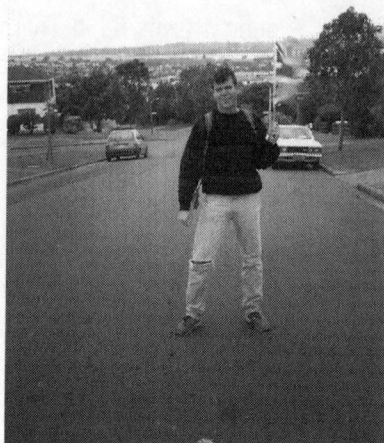

I left Brandon's house and caught the bus into town in order to find a backpacker's hostel. Pam and Debby came to for the ride. I got lost in Auckland, trying to find the hostel, and must have walked for miles before I caught the bus. It was pouring down with rain again. I've been missing Paula throughout the day, which isn't surprising. However, this was short-lived as I met a French bird in the same dorm as me. We got chatting away while I got my wine out and got merry. I slept like a log tonight, catching up on my previous 2 nights' sleep.

Day 379: 27 March 1991, Auckland, New Zealand

Walked into town this morning with the French bird and had a look around the shops and market stalls. I got a load of postcards to send home. I went down to the harbour and enquired about getting a yacht to the South Pacific Islands and, from there, making my way to South America. I've been living in a flat for the last 4½ months and find it hard to adjust back into the backpacker's scene, trying to cook dinner while sharing the stove with about 20 other people.

Day 380: 28 March 1991, Taupo, New Zealand

I finally left Auckland today, heading down to Nelson in order to find work. I got on to the motorway and found it really easy to hitch-hike (a lot better than Australia). I got several lifts today, one being off a couple of guys from a small island in the South Pacific called West

Samoa. They took me to a place called Rotorua that was full of hot geysers and bubbling mudbaths. I felt like I was walking on the moon. It cost $9 to get in, but I couldn't sneak in as I was with 2 blokes.

I then got a lift further south to Lake Taupo, a massive lake. I camped on the grey volcanic sand on the edge of the water, miles away from anywhere, watching a fantastic sunset.

Day 381: 29 March 1991, Wellington, New Zealand

I absolutely froze my bollocks off last night, wearing nearly every piece of clothing I'm carrying with me. I haven't got a sleeping bag, and I found it hard to sleep on the sand as it was very uneven and bumpy.

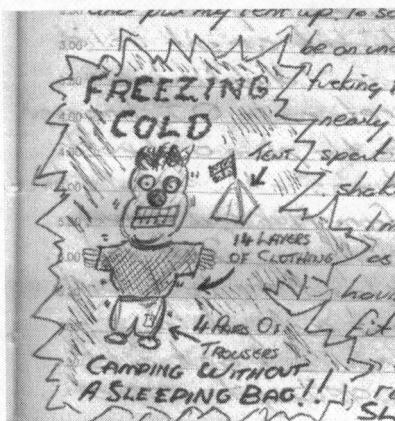

After waiting half an hour for a lift this morning, it began raining.
I managed to get a lift before I got wet. The bloke took me down
the road for a couple of hours. On the way, we drove through the
'Desert Road', past snow-capped mountains. When my lift had
finished, I pulled my bag from out of the back seat, and I realised
that I had managed to get tar all over my bag, which had rubbed off
all over the back seat of the car. The bloke wasn't impressed.

There were 3 sets of hitches on the next stretch (sod's law). All the
Maoris in their biker gangs are heading down to Wellington. Van
loads after van loads of them went past me along the roadside—all
mean-looking bastards from the 'Black Power' gang—similar to the
Hells Angels. A girl hitching near to me got warned by the police to
keep off the road.

Managed to get a lift to Wellington. Arrived in a hostel and watched *Coronation Street* on TV, the first time for over a year. I've been feeling pissed off all day. Finding it hard to get back into the travelling mode. Roughing it again. I even felt like heading home—the first time in months.

Day 382: 30 March 1991, Wellington, New Zealand

Had a walk around town today with Martin (a lad from the hostel). We both went off in separate directions, and I couldn't find my way home. I went off miles in the wrong direction. It took me over 2 hours to get back. Later on, I went to the supermarket. On the way, I helped someone bump start their car. Several minutes later, I was sitting in their front garden, getting stoned off my trolley. I was walking around in a daze afterwards, trying to find the supermarket. I asked someone directions (a young lad) and ended up at his house drinking cups of coffee. I got to the supermarket in the end.

Martin and I bought a cask of wine tonight and braved the streets of Wellington, pissed as farts. We asked someone where a good place to go was and ended up at a gay nightclub, so we sneaked on to another bar. I tried to phone Paula up at 1 a.m. but was too pissed to operate the phone—can't remember coming home.

Day 383: 31 March 1991, Blenheim, South Island, New Zealand

Woke up at 7.30 a.m. with my head still spinning from last night. I managed to get away without paying for my accommodation last night, $12, before catching the 3½-hour ferry to the South Island. When I arrived at Picton (the ferry port), I began hitching to Nelson, only 1½ hours away. I got a lift straightaway from an American woman who had to keep stopping to let her 2-year-old daughter be sick. She dropped me off at a small town called Blenheim half an hour away from Picton.

I spent the rest of the day trying to hitch-hike without any luck. I sneaked into a campsite without paying and put my tent up. To say it was cold would be an understatement. It was fucking freezing. I had nearly all my clothes on and spent the whole night shaking with cold. I must have looked as though I was having an epileptic fit—the worst night of my travels. I must remember to buy a *sleeping bag*!

Day 384:—1 April 1991, Nelson, New Zealand—April Fools' Day

I woke up this morning shaking with the cold, sneaked out of the campsite, and began hitching again with a cold, runny nose and empty stomach. I've been feeling pissed off and lonely for the last couple of days, and getting abuse off drivers while trying to hitch a ride didn't make me feel any better. I tried all morning to get a lift—*no chance*. In the end, I gave up and caught the coach. What made it worse was that the coach went to Nelson via Picton (where I'd originally started off from yesterday but with a few less wrinkles and grey hairs that I have now).

Nelson is supposed to be the sunniest spot in New Zealand—even though it was cloudy and pissing it down when I got here. I ended up at the best hostel I've been to yet—there were no rooms left, so I got the garden shed for $5 per night plus as much tea and coffee as I can drink, a free bike, and free use of the washing machine.

Day 385: 2 April 1991, Nelson, New Zealand (55 Weeks Away)

It was pissing it down for most of the day today, but that's New Zealand for you. Popped down to Post Restante and picked up a couple of letters from the old folks back home. Went to a travel agent's to enquire about going home—NZ to Hawaii to LA, hitch across to New York, and flight to London for only $1300. I only have $1600 left. I'm thinking of going home for early June to celebrate my 23rd birthday back home with all the lads.

I saw an advert for crew sailing the South Pacific, Indian Ocean to East Africa. I pulled the notice off straightaway and applied for a place as crew. Got pissed tonight with a couple of English hooligans from the Hostel.

Day 386: 3 April 1991, Nelson, New Zealand

Went down to the Post Restante and collected some mail from Paula. I made a bad mistake by travelling with a woman for 6 months—it's great while you're with them, but it fucks your travelling plans about when you leave them. I've been walking around like a lost sheep for the last 1½ weeks.

I went for a bike ride today with Ady—a lad from the hostel. We went down to the beach and had a stroll around there for the afternoon. I went to see the owner of a yacht this evening, who is sailing to East Africa in 4 weeks' time and is looking for crew. He's taking about 6 months to get there, stopping off in the South Pacific etc. along the way with a cost of about $20 (£6.50) a day for food etc. An adventure of a lifetime, but he's already got enough crew.

Back at the hostel, after my 2-minute noodles, I was just about to watch *Coronation Street* on TV, when they all put a video on.

Day 387: 4 April 1991, Nelson, New Zealand

After the other night's camping disaster, freezing my bollocks off all night, I decided to buy a sleeping bag. I got £40 from my mum and dad for Xmas and cashed it in today, getting NZ$114. The sleeping bag was reduced from $180 down to $130. I also bought a silicon spray for my tent in order to make it waterproof. I ran out of spray halfway through my tent and couldn't afford to buy another can, so I took the can back to the shop and told him it was faulty and swapped it for another one. I'm going on a 4-day trek tomorrow, along rugged and deserted coastlines.

Day 388: 5 April 1991, Abel Tasman, New Zealand

Got up in the early hours of the morning (6 a.m.) in order to get 4 days' worth of food, clothes, tent, and sleeping bag into a small daysack, pinching a pot, cup, etc. from the backpacker's hostel.

A bus picked me up and dropped me off a couple of hours later at the end of the road. I got together with a couple of English girls and a lad and did the walk with them, going through tropical rainforests and golden deserted beaches. Completely isolated from anything. I had to dodge the ranger a couple of times to avoid paying the park fees. We slept in a wood hut on the beach. Noodles and beans for tea.

Day 389: 6 April 1991, Abel Tasman, New Zealand

Up at 7 a.m.—2-minute noodles and beans for breakfast again. We crossed a couple of estuaries today at low tide—the first crossing went OK, but we arrived at the 2nd crossing too late, by which time the water was already waist-deep and getting worse. We got wet but managed to keep my pack dry. Saw some beautiful coasts and rainforests. I slept in the same bed as 4 women and an old man tonight. The woman sleeping next to me was snoring really loud all night, right in my ear. I had to shove toilet paper in my ears and wrap a towel over my head.

Day 390: 7 April 1991, Abel Tasman, New Zealand

Another day trekking through the Abel Tasman National Park, completely isolated from civilisation. We had to leave Lauren in one of the huts because her blisters were playing up, while Sean, Kate, and I carried on trekking through beautiful deserted tropical coastlines. Arrived at the trekking hut (in the middle of nowhere) and had to run around collecting wood for the fire. Stayed up playing cards under candlelight—another wild night out in New Zealand. Bed before 8 p.m. every night!

Day 391: 8 April 1991, Nelson, New Zealand

Finished the trek today, and about 5 minutes later, it pissed it down (talk about lucky). There are no roads for miles, so I had to catch a boat back, which took about 4 hours, covering the coastline that took us 4 days to trek. On the way, we passed a tropical island with a seal colony living on it. The boat pulled in really close, allowing us to get a good view of the seals. Had to catch the coach for the remaining trip back to Nelson. I couldn't believe it when I saw that the mountains surrounding Nelson were covered in snow (the first snow I've seen since I was in Nepal over a year ago).

Winter is drawing in over here in New Zealand. I'm enjoying it at the moment as it's the first cold weather I've experienced in a year. When I got back to Nelson, I checked into my garden shed that I left 4 days ago ($5 per night) and went to the chippy for a bag of chips and then a hot shower—civilisation again.

Day 393: 10 April 1991, Nelson, New Zealand

Another day doing fuck all, sniffing around the communal food basket every morning in the hope that someone has left some food in it. I haven't been too lucky lately as everyone's a bit tight. Watched *Coronation Street* and went to bed.

Day 394: 11 April 1991, Nelson, New Zealand

I got talking to an English lad today in the hostel and found out he's from Lincoln. I've been travelling for 13 months now, and I'm getting a bit pissed off with living like a tramp—eating dog food all the time, walking around with my arse hanging out of the back of my trousers, and never having enough money to enjoy myself. I haven't worked for over a month, and I'm not likely to work until I get over to America in about another 1½ months' time. I've only got $180 left (not including the money for my flight), that's about £60. I hate to do it, but I'm going to have to phone the old folks up and borrow some from them until I can get work again.

Day 395: 12 April 1991, Nelson, New Zealand

I picked up a couple of letters from Paula and a Viz comic from Mum at the Post Restante today. I was watching a film on TV tonight, when halfway through, I went back to my shed to get something and found some cheeky cunt asleep in my bed, in my sleeping bag. I couldn't believe it and had to look twice before it sunk in. He was pissed as a fart and found his way into my shed (as I hadn't locked it). I got Alistair, and we both had to drag him out—he didn't have a clue where he was, so Alistair took him to town and dropped him off. I wasn't too bothered about the incident as he'd dropped his money on the floor—only $2 (60 pence), but that buys about 3 meals.

Day 396: 13 April 1991, Nelson, New Zealand

Another lazy day in sunny Nelson, watching the grass grow. Geoff, Claire (the couple from Lincoln), and I bought a cask of wine tonight and began drinking at 7 p.m. By 8 p.m. we were all pissed and had finished the wine and so bought another one. By the time we'd finished that cask (even though I can't remember that far into the evening), Geoff and I biked down to the pub. We were both paralytic, and I ended up falling asleep in the pub. While attempting to bike home, Geoff fell off his bike, landing in the middle of the road, while, somehow, I managed to keep my balance. I made myself a sandwich and ended up being sick all over the garden.

Day 397: 14 April 1991, Nelson, New Zealand

I was a complete physical wreck today, surviving on aspirins and black coffee. Phoned home tonight in order to get £300 sent over.

Day 398: 15 April 1991, Nelson, New Zealand

Booked my flight home today, so in 3½ weeks' time, I fly to Hawaii. I'm there for a week before going over to the States for 9 weeks. I couldn't stay in the States for any longer because they wouldn't let me into the country as I haven't got enough money for any longer. I'm due to fly home from New York on 18 July. However, I might go down to South America instead. I'm going to have to phone Mum up again tonight to get £1000 sent over from my stocks and shares.

Day 399: 16 April 1991, Nelson, New Zealand

I got up at the crack of dawn this morning in order to hitch down to Queenstown—a very hard road to hitch down. I got a lift by a solicitor after an hour, but he was only going to the next town. It was then that I realised that I had forgotten my tent. After spending 4 hours trying to get back to Nelson with no luck, I went to see the solicitor in order to use his phone. He said that his wife (who was a doctor and had just finished for the day) would take me back. On the way home, she invited me for dinner this evening—I accepted straightaway as I've been living on two-minute noodles for the last 3½ weeks as I can't afford anything else. Even baked beans are an expensive luxury! I dressed up smart in case they had any daughters. They did. However, the eldest one was 12. I had to watch my Ps and Qs while remembering not to burp or fart at the table, but it was worth it for the good food.

Day 400: 17 April 1991, Nelson, New Zealand

I was a bit embarrassed today as several people who left the hostel a couple of weeks ago have toured the South Island and have come back, while I'm still here, and I haven't done fuck all.

Day 401: 18 April 1991, Greymouth, New Zealand

I got up at the crack of dawn again in another attempt to leave Nelson. The girls dropped me off at a hitch-hiking spot (I wasn't looking forward to it as it's at least a 15-hour drive to Queenstown, and the road is very hard to hitch on. It also rains a lot). Two other hikers came after me, meaning there were 3 of us on the road. I waited 1½ hours before getting my first lift. Beautiful scenery during the drive, getting dropped off in the middle of nowhere, 125 km down the road. The next car that passed me gave me a lift about 80 km down the road. I got out in the middle of nowhere and got a lift 10 minutes later from a scruffy Maori and then by some bloke in a large van. We stopped off at his house for a cup of tea before getting dropped off at Greymouth at 2 p.m. (300 km from Nelson). A good day's hitching.

It started to rain, so I checked into a backpacker's hostel. I'd only been there ten minutes when I got asked if I wanted to go on a trip to a brewery for $4.450. I went on it and crammed as much free beer down me as I could afterwards but got really bloated. We all got kicked out before I had time to get pissed.

Day 402: 19 April 1991, Punakaiki, New Zealand

Began hitching 70 km back up the coast today in order to get to a farm, which I'm going to work on for a couple of hours a day, getting *free* accommodation and food in return. I walked to the outskirts of Greymouth, and it began pissing it down. I got a lift 13 km down the road, where I sheltered in a bus stop as there was a heavy rainstorm. It pissed it down on and off for the rest of the day. I tried for over 2½ hours to get a lift—no chance, so I went to borrow someone's phone, who ended up taking me to the farm.

A really relaxed place. My first job was to sort pollen out that had been collected from the hive and is used as an anti-hay fever remedy. I had to sort out the pollen granules from the waste bits.

Day 403: 20 April 1991, Punakaiki, New Zealand

I did a couple of hours' work this morning before going down to the dairy farm next door. I helped the farmer milk the cows. There were a 100 of them (50 each). They were milked by machines, and I had to connect the udders up to the suction pipes. The cows were nervous because I was new, and so they shat and pissed everywhere. I was covered in shit—in my hair, on my face, and all over my clothes. After this, changing a baby's nappy will be a piece of cake (but don't quote me on it when later on in life I might have to do it). I can't chew my fingernails for about a week because of all the cow shit that's lodged down in them.

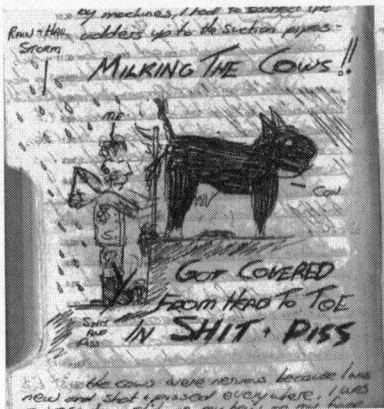

Day 404: 21 April 1991, Punakaiki, New Zealand

Did a couple of hours' work this morning, picking raspberries, weeding, etc.—we found a little nest with 3 kittens in the barn from a wild cat. I set several traps today in order to catch one of the many opossums in the area that are destroying all the vegetation.

Donna dropped me off at the Pancake Rocks this afternoon—strange rock formations along the rugged coastline, which look like hundreds of pancakes piled up on one another. I hitched back to the farm (only 6 km). I'm thinking about moving down the coast, but it's virtually impossible to hitch-hike, and it's hardly stopped raining since I got here!

Day 405: 22 April 1991, Punakaiki, New Zealand

I set opossum traps last night with Roland, and we caught one. We killed it this morning. I wanted to eat it, so Roland showed me how to skin and cook it. I boiled it for 2 hours before eating it, sharing half with the cat. I spent 2 hours cleaning the skin—I'm keeping it as a souvenir from New Zealand.

Day 406: 23 April 1991, Fox Glacier, New Zealand

Cunt of a day, trying to hitch down to the Fox Glacier. Only 300 km away, but with fuck all traffic on the road, it was a nightmare. I've only got $50 left to get me down to Queenstown (900 km away), a couple of days hiking at least, and that's if I'm very lucky. It took me nearly an hour to get my first lift, which took me to Greymouth, and nearly another hour to get my next lift—from a really good-looking Maori bird (the only good-looking one I've seen).

It kept raining on and off all day. I managed to get a couple more lifts down to Hari Hari in the middle of nowhere. It was pissing cats and dogs, and I got soaked to the skin and had to wait 4½ bastard hours for a fucking lift. It was from a van load of lumberjacks, and they dropped me off at the next town. Cold, wet, and shivering, I was forced to catch the coach for the remaining 60 km to the Fox Glacier. A bad day, and I've still got worse to come. It's twice as far to Queenstown with half the traffic.

Day 407: 24 April 1991, Fox Glacier, New Zealand

I've only got $21 (£7) left to get me down to Queenstown, which is 5 hours away and very hard to hitch-hike down. I managed to get work on a farm, with free accommodation and food. It was warm when I started work, so I left my shorts on. I was working in the field surrounded by amazing scenery—snow-capped mountains, glaciers, etc. I was working on the tractor, putting fence posts in when it began pissing it down. I had my shorts on, and I was freezing. I was so cold, I had to piss on my hands to warm them up. Got soaked to the skin again.

Day 408: 25 April 1991, Fox Glacier, New Zealand

Another day working like a twat for only free accommodation and food. I drove the tractor down near the river, where I had to dig several trenches in order to bury the cables that are part of the electric fence. Hard work but enjoyable. Every so often, I'd just stop and take in the scenery. Then a big cloud came over, and it began pissing it down (again).

That's the third day running I've been soaked through to the skin, and I'm getting more than pissed off with it. I had a rain mack on and a pair of size-14 wellington boots on with big holes everywhere. I nailed my possum skin on to a board tonight in order to dry it out Then I had a walk in the woods, looking for glow worms.

Day 409: 26 April 1991, Queenstown, New Zealand

I got up at 6.30 a.m. this morning in order to bike down to Lake Matheson in the middle of the mountain range, but by the time I got there, the mountains were covered in clouds. I went on a glacier tour of the Fox Glacier, lasting about 3 hours, spending over an hour walking about on the glacier. Neil (whom I was working for) went down to Queenstown this afternoon and gave me a lift (5 hours), saving me a couple of hard days hitch-hiking.

Day 410: 27 April 1991, Queenstown, New Zealand

I've run out of money—I've only got $10 (£3.50) to my name. I have to wait until Monday, when I can, hopefully, pick up £300 that Mum and Dad have sent me. I'll be in shit alley if it doesn't come.

I met 3 English hooligans today (all from up north) and went round with them all day. We climbed to the top of a massive hill or mountain. It took fucking ages to get to the top, but it was worth it for the views we got of Queenstown. We bought a couple casks of wine between us tonight and got completely arseholed in the room. I can't even remember leaving, but we all staggered down to a nightclub. I had a cask of wine rammed down the front of my trousers so that I didn't have to buy any drinks. I ended up unconscious on the floor, curled around a table leg, before getting thrown out. Dennis got thrown out as well for trying to start a fight. We went to another nightclub. Dennis and I were dancing when Dennis fell over, cracked his head, and knocked himself out—what a night!

Day 411: 28 April 1991, Queenstown, New Zealand

I woke up on the settee, next to a massive pile of sick that I'd thrown up last night. I had to sneak back to my tent as I'm supposed to be sleeping in there as I've no money.

The lads went paragliding today, jumping off mountains with a parachute on. Lee had a go and crashed. The instructor went mental. Then Craig had a go and crashed into a bush halfway down the hill. The instructor was really pissed off as the parachute got stuck in the bush. Lee had another go and forgot to put his brakes on when he landed and ended up spraining his ankles.

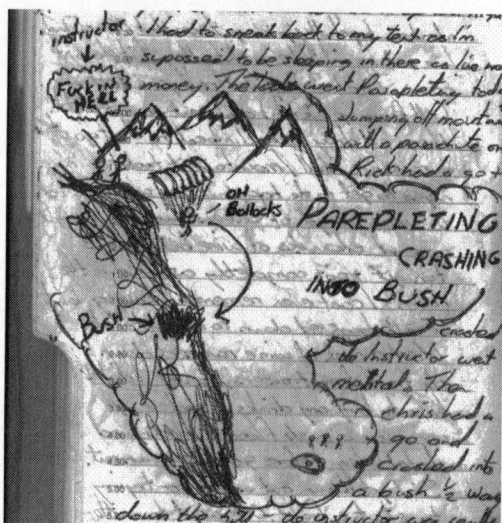

I went out on the piss with Craig tonight. We took a cask of wine out with us. We went to a nightclub but couldn't drink in there as we were the only ones in the place—no chance of sweeping. We went to a pub and drank the wine there before coming home.

Day 412: 29 April 1991, Milford Sound, New Zealand

Woke up this morning freezing cold and soaking wet—it had been pissing it down all night, and my tent had leaked. I've got about £15 to my name and went down to collect some money that my parents had sent me. I was shitting myself in case it hadn't come. It had and was there waiting for me.

I'm travelling around the South Island with Lee, Craig, and Dennis in their hired car. We drove for most of the afternoon through mountains, where it had snowed, and down to Milford Sound. I've only got about $30 a day to spend until I get home (6 June), and so when the lads checked into a hostel tonight, I sneaked in. We had an exciting game of Monopoly before going to bed.

Day 413: 30 April 1991, Milford Sound, New Zealand

I sneaked out of the hostel this morning, and we went on a cruise around the Mildford Sound ($30—I treated myself and then felt guilty afterwards). It's going to be touch and go as to whether I'll get back to England before I run out of money. The 2-hour boat trip was good—sailing through the Milford Sound, where massive mountains rise straight out of the sea up to a mile high. Lee, Dennis, and I got soaked trying to catch some water from a waterfall but won a small bottle of whiskey each, which we all downed.

We spent the rest of the afternoon driving to Bluff Point—the southest part of South Island NZ. Only South America goes further down. It was fucking cold. The lads slept in a hostel tonight while I put up my tent down an alleyway to save me from going over my daily budget.

Day 414: 1 May 1991, Taieri Mouth, New Zealand

I woke up down the alleyway—my tent was soaking because of the rain last night. Packed up and met the lads.

We drove up the coast, stopping off at Invercargill. We got lost in the middle of nowhere and nearly ran out of petrol. We drove to a small, quiet fishing village where the waling boats come in. We called at a place where you can work for fee accommodation and food. It turned out to be some old bloke with a small allotment. His house was a right tip, with junk and shit lying around all over the place. The good thing was that he didn't want any work done. Will was about 90, looked like a tramp, and all he talked about was how good life was in the old days and about the greenhouse effect.

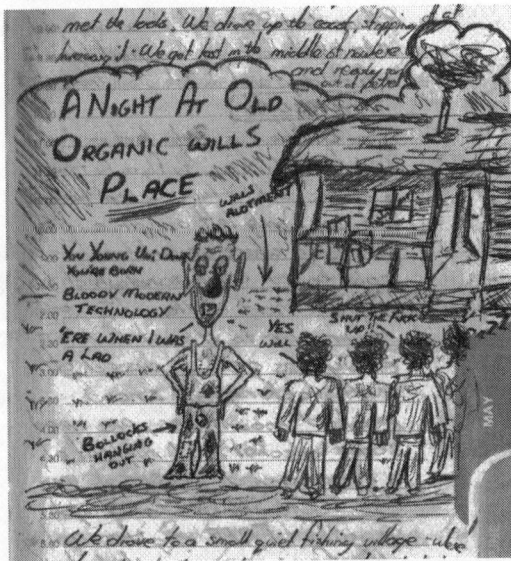

Day 415: 2 May 1991, Mount Cook, New Zealand

Will gave us another lecture today about food additives. His fly on his trousers is broken, and his bollocks kept hanging out. We finally left and drove up to Dunedin, where we had lunch—cold baked bean sandwiches.

Spent most of the afternoon driving up to Mount Cook. Everyone's getting pissed off with looking at snow-peaked mountains. We need some alcohol and nightlife! I managed to sneak into the youth hostel and got another *free* night—making the few pennies that I have got last a little longer.

Day 416: 3 May 1991, Geraldine, New Zealand

Sneaked out of the hostel this morning and drove to a few scenic spots around Mount Cook. We were driving in the country and stopped to ask a farmer directions and talked to him for about an hour. He was shearing the wool off the fannies off the female sheep, to give the ram a better chance of getting his wicked way with them. They've got a breed of sheep here in NZ called Lincoln, which originated from back home where I live. We called for some bloke whom Craig's parents vaguely know. Got invited in and ended up getting a slap-up meal and a bed for the night in return for spending several hours listening to his tale of his holiday in England.

Day 417: 4 May 1991, Christchurch, New Zealand

Had a great night's sleep and had a big breakfast this morning before being shown around Edward's deer farm. He gave us his sister-in-law's address in Christchurch for us to stay tonight.

On the way up the coast, Lee wanted to visit a farm, so we stopped off at a small town for a couple of hours. We arrived at Edward's sister-in-law's and stayed in a caravan in their back garden. We got some wine and got arseholed in the caravan before going out. I took a cask of wine with me and shoved it down my pants. We went to a disco/pub and spent half the time on the dance floor and sweeping drinks.

Day 418: 5 May 1991, Christchurch, New Zealand

Woke up with my head still spinning from last night—had a good night out on the town. My hangover lasted for most of the day. The 2 old ladies of the house, Kristi and Sharon, cooked us all a Sunday dinner—the best meal I've had in ages. We even got a few beers as well.

We went for a drive in the afternoon and drove to a small town called Lincoln. Only about 1000 people lived there, and it looked just as exciting as the Lincoln back in England.

Day 419: 6 May 1991, Christchurch, New Zealand

Got up at the crack of dawn (5.45 a.m.) with Lee in order to go and visit a dairy farm. It was pitch black as we drove around looking for the farm. We got there just in time to see the farmer milk the last few of his 40 cows. Lee was getting excited (being a farmer) because the quality of the cows was the best he'd ever seen. They all look the same to me. The highlight of the visit for me was the free breakfast we got afterwards. I drove home (leaving Lee at the farm) and got invited to breakfast by Kristi, so I had another pig-out. I didn't tell her that I'd already eaten.

Went uptown with Craig and Lee and sorted out various things. I used my visa card for the first time ever today—buying a 7-day Greyhound bus pass for £75 in order to get me across the states. I'm leaving for Kiakoura tomorrow—whale-watching.

Day 420: 7 May 1991, Kiakoura, New Zealand (60 Weeks Away)

Packed our bags and left Christchurch, heading upcoast to Kiakoura in order to go whale-spotting. I was pissed off when I got there as I had fuck all money with me and couldn't get any money out of the banks as they didn't have my branch. I had fuck all food and had to pinch 4 pints of milk from someone's doorstep to keep me going until tomorrow afternoon, when I, hopefully, get back to Christchurch.

Went along the beach, where all the wild seals hang out, before putting my tent up in the school field—it was dark, so no one could see.

Day 421: 8 May 1991, Christchurch, New Zealand

Got up at 5.30 a.m. and packed my tent away. Left the school playing field in which I camped last night. I met the lads, and we went on a whale-watching trip—I had to pay $25 by visa. A great trip on the speedboat. Saw whales, seals, even a penguin. After the trip, I said goodbye to the lads and hitched back to Christchurch. I only had to wait ten seconds before I got a lift most of the way, then had to wait a further 45 minutes after that to get to town.

Day 422: 9 May 1991, Waikiki Beach, Oahu, Hawaii

What a weird day. I got up at 10 a.m. and washed my clothes (which had only been washed once in 7 weeks). I went to town and closed my bank account and got some traveller cheques before going down to the airport. I flew to Auckland and hung around for 3 hours before going on a 7-hour flight to Hawaii, arriving in Hawaii at 5.30 a.m. the same day. I managed to smuggle my possum skin through customs.

I didn't have a clue where to go when I left the airport, so I caught the local bus and got off an hour later at Waikiki Beach. I checked into a hostel and ended up working there for 2½ hours, changing the bed sheets for a free night's accommodation. A long day. I had to turn my watch back 22 hours, meaning that today was 46 hours long.

Day 423: 10 May 1991, Waikiki Beach, Oahu, Hawaii

I got up at 10 a.m. to do my chores—cleaning the shithouse out.

Went straight down the beach after and relaxed in the sun. A tramp walked down the beach, stripped off down to her knickers and bra, and dived into the sea for a swim and a wash. She came out, dressed, and walked off pushing a supermarket trolley with all her possessions.

I went for a run in the park in the early evening and couldn't believe my luck when I saw a Harry Krishna food van. I went up and got a free feed before going back for seconds. I bought a bottle of vodka with Vicky, Bobby, and some Aussie twat. We all drank the vodka and went out to explore the nightlife. Great-looking women everywhere. We all ended up back at the room, smoking Bobby's cone, getting really stoned. Bobby and Keith (the Aussie storyteller) were both trying to get into Vicky's knickers. Keith was a typical Aussie, telling the biggest bullshit stories I've ever heard, and I couldn't stop laughing at the twat. Everyone else was laughing, and he was getting very pissed off with it.

Day 424: 11 May 1991, Waikiki Beach, Oahu, Hawaii

Spent the day down at the beach, trying to learn Spanish for when I get down to Mexico. I went for another run this evening, trying to get myself in shape for when I get home (only 3½ weeks). Went on the piss with Vicky and Bobby again tonight. We bought a large bottle of vodka between us and drank it down on the beach.

I phoned home to wish Michelle a happy 21st—no one could believe I was in Hawaii. We all got arseholed and ended up talking to some prostitutes in the street. One of them undid my zip in my trousers. I wasn't wearing any pants, and she couldn't believe it when my knob flopped out. We all got stoned again on Bobby's pipe. I used my passport to get into a nightclub and can't remember seeing it again. I fell asleep on the pavement on the way home.

Day 425: 12 May 1991, Waikiki Beach, Oahu, Hawaii

Woke up as pissed as a twat and had to go down to reception to get my chores for the morning—cleaning the shithouse again. I nearly threw my ring up.

I don't know why, but I lost my passport last night and don't feel too pissed off. I looked for it in my room, went to the police station, and even got the security guards to open up the nightclub for me to have a look—still couldn't find it.

Went to the north of the island with Vicky as its only 40 miles away, but it took 2½ hours to get there. It only cost 60 cents, the only thing that's cheap in Hawaii. We stopped off at a tropical golden beach and walked down the beach for a couple of miles—palm trees and coconuts along the beachfront, with giant volcanoes in the background. The 2½—hour bus journey seemed to take forever on the way back. I had a sore arse as I had loads of sand down my trunks, and with the bus going up and down, it was like some twat sandpapering my arse for 2½ hours.

Bought a bottle of vodka with Vicky tonight and got pissed down at the beach with her. Tried to get in a nightclub, but I didn't have any ID.

Day 426: 13 May 1991, Waikiki Beach, Oahu, Hawaii

I couldn't believe my luck this morning when I moved my pillow and found my passport underneath it. I was in a state of shock for at least 5 minutes as I couldn't believe it.

I went to visit Pearl Harbour today with Vicky. I couldn't believe it when they wouldn't let me in because I was barefoot. I had to sneak in and hide in the crowd all the time. We had a half-hour picture show on the Pearl Harbour before going on a free boat ride around the harbour to the *USS Arizona* ship, where over 1,100 men lost their lives in the attack.

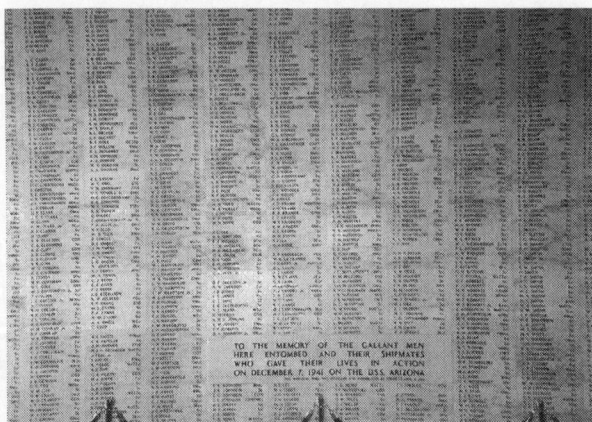

Drank another bottle of vodka on the beach tonight with Vicky, getting arseholed. We couldn't get in any clubs as we didn't have any ID.

Day 427: 14 May 1991, Waikiki Beach, Oahu, Hawaii

I hired a boogie board today in order to do some surfing. I got down to the beach, and there weren't any waves—it was like trying to surf on a lake. I bumped into Lee, Dennis, and Craig and spent the day on the beach with them. Some Japanese birds tried to chat us up, but we soon fucked them off.

It is like paradise over here. Everywhere you look, there are great-looking birds with fit bodies. There are a lot of posers as well. We all went on the piss tonight, and I got pissed on my bottle of vodka while the lads drank beer. We all got arseholed and went for a walk around town. We couldn't get in a club as we were too pissed.

Day 428: 15 May 1991, Waikiki Beach, Oahu, Hawaii

I moved into a motel with Dennis, Craig, and Lee ($41). It's meant for 2 people, but we all sneaked in. I went around the food bars today, applying for the many job vacancies available at the moment. It's illegal for me to work over here, but my chances of finding work are good. I went walking around a very posh shopping centre today and ended up going into a shop and trying a suit on—it cost just over £1000.

Went down the beach and met the other lads. We spent the afternoon watching all the posers making twats of themselves. My tongue was hanging out half the time at all the gorgeous birds—I'm surprised it didn't get sunburnt.

Another mental night on the piss, I drank nearly a full bottle of vodka (750 ml) to myself before going on the rampage round the town singing Rolling Stones songs. Went to a bar where I fell asleep on the table—got home about 3 a.m.

Day 429: 16 May 1991, Waikiki Beach, Oahu, Hawaii

We all got up still spinning from last night and caught the bus to Hanouna Bay—created years ago from a huge volcano. A scenic tropical beach surrounded by huge volcanoes. I saw a small weasel-like animal run across the beach. I ended up with it eating bread out of my hand. Dennis and I went for a walk along the rocks and nearly got washed in several times by large waves. We ended up climbing to the top of a volcano, ripping my feet to shreds as I was in bare feet. It took ages to get to the top but was well worth it. It was like walking on the moon, with all the molten lava that had cooled down. Walking along the cliffs on the way back, we saw a 2-foot turtle swimming around in the turquoise sea.

It's the lads' last night tonight, so we all got pissed (again). We went to some bar and sweeped a few beers before going to another bar. I had some Swedish bird after me but was too pissed to respond. Walking around the streets, we bumped into a gang of prostitutes, who came up to us and started rubbing us all up for about 5 minutes until they realised that we weren't interested.

Day 430: 17 May 1991, Manoa Valley, Hawaii

We all got up early this morning (9 a.m.) as the lads are going to LA. I had a couple of glasses of vodka and was arseholed again. I went down the beach, wobbling all over the shop, and just crashed out in the sun for several hours. I couldn't believe it when I woke up and looked at myself—the colour of my skin was purple with sunburn. I moved to a hostel at Manoa Valley tonight, using my hostel card for discount. It's 3 months out of date, but they never noticed.

Day 431: 18 May 1991, Manoa Valley, Hawaii

Went around Waikiki with Bobby. I treated myself for the first time in ages and bought a cheap Chinese meal for $4 and enjoyed every bit of it. We went for a walk up to Diamond Head, an inactive volcano. It took a good couple of hours to get to the top but was well worth it for the view.

Had yet another free meal tonight thanks to the communal food shelf—it didn't look or taste too good, but it filled the gap. I drank some of my vodka and then got stoned out my tree with Bobby. We were going to go to a club, but we couldn't be arsed.

Day 432: 19 May 1991, Waikiki Beach, Oahu, Hawaii

I moved back to the hostel on Waikiki Beach today. Watched a bit of MTV and then spent the rest of day on the beach, taking in the sun and watching the women go by. I can't believe that I'll be home in just over a couple of weeks, after travelling the world for 1½ years. I'm looking forward to it in a way. I don't know what I want to do. I might go over to Amsterdam for a month or work in London, but my main goal at the moment is to travel (in about

6 months' time) over through Europe to the bottom of Spain, then catch the ferry to North Africa, across the Sahara Desert, and hitch down to South Africa. It will take about 3-4 months getting there, after which I plan on getting a job in electronics in Durban.

Went on the piss again with Bobby tonight, taking my bottle of vodka along with me. Walking down the street, some local bloke offered us some blow for $50. We got him down to $30 and went for a walk in order to get a good look at it. There were too many people around—we decided not to buy and walked off. We went back to where we'd met him as we knew he hid the stuff in the flowers. We waited for 5 minutes until he walked away, then we dived into the flowerbed, found the stuff, and fucked off. We couldn't believe we'd actually ripped off a dealer. We got down to the beach, only to find that it was a tobacco mixture combined with spices—talk about pissed off. Had to settle for a cheap bottle of wine. Got completely rat-arsed before getting refused entry from several clubs. Some restaurant had thrown loads of food in the bin. I couldn't believe my luck and ate loads, taking a full carrier bag home.

Day 433: 20 May 1991, Waikiki Beach, Oahu, Hawaii
Woke up with a hangover. The room stunk from all the food that I'd taken home last night. I had to throw it away fast!

Day 434: 21 May 1991, Waikiki Beach, Oahu, Hawaii

Went down to the beach with an Aussie lad today. Got talking to an American bird who had just arrived here. We got on well, and I ended up going back to her hotel for a Jacuzzi. I went back to the hostel and managed to get another meal from the communal shelf. Met the American bird later on in the evening. We both bought a big bottle of wine and drank it down at the beach. We ended up going to the park—got home 3 a.m.

Day 435: 22 May 1991, Waikiki Beach, Oahu, Hawaii

I was knackered when I got up this morning. Spent most of the day running around like a twat, sending parcels home, etc. Went out with the American bird again tonight, down to the park again with a big bottle of wine. I couldn't believe it when the bastard police drove up on motorbikes. They saw the wine and made me pour it on to the grass. It broke my heart, and I felt like crying—what a waste of good plonk. The American bird started crying when I left her. I sneaked back into the hostel and found a spare bed. Went to bed at 2.30 a.m. as I have to be up at 5 a.m. to go to the airport.

Day 436: 23 May 1991, Venice Beach, California, Los Angeles

Complete physical wreck when I got up at 5 a.m. I staggered to the bus stop and caught the bus to the airport before catching the plane to LA.

I was going to sleep at the airport when I arrived, to save money, but ended up going to a backpacker's hostel down on Venice Beach with a lad I'd previously met in New Zealand. We got pissed tonight before going down to Santa Monica for a night out. I bought a small bottle of vodka and smuggled it in the bars with me, got arseholed, and danced the night away. I lost Ady and walked home. I ended up getting a lift with some bloke but soon fucked off out the car when he tried it on with me—dirty bastard.

Day 437: 24 May 1991 Venice Beach, California, Los Angeles

Got up at 10 a.m. Felt like shit. I caught several buses in order to get to Hollywood. I saw the big Hollywood sign and a few shops before coming back to the hostel, where the Alarm were playing a free concert 20 metres away from my hostel on Venice Beach. The concert was good, and I got talking to some bloke and ended up going back to his place, where I got completely stoned. He made me a meal as well.

Went out on the piss in Santa Monica again tonight. Pissed as a fart sweeping other peoples beers—another great night out. Hawaii a couple of days ago, California today, Mexico tomorrow—what a life!

Day 438: 25 May 1991, Mexico

Got up still pissed from last night (it's becoming a habit). Caught the bus to downtown LA and booked a bus to Mexico. I had an hour to spend and so walked around the streets. I've never seen so many people. I had a full cone on me and couldn't find any place to smoke it. In the end, I went in the toilets in some food bar. Got really stoned off it. Walking around in a world of my own, I ended up going down the rough end of town.

I stayed pretty well stoned for most of the 3-hour bus ride down to Mexico, where I got dropped off at the border. It was 5.30 p.m. and I had fuck all Mexican money. The banks were closed, and I had to cart my bastard heavy bag around for miles while looking for accommodation. I'm going to burn the fucking thing when I get home and buy a rucksack for my next trip. I asked a lad if he knew where a cheap hostel was and ended up going back with him. I got a room next door to him and his mate, both US Marines back from the Gulf War. I ended up going out with them tonight. We had several tequila slammers before going out to a *free* nightclub, where I danced for ages. I sweeped a few drinks and then went outside with one of the lads to get a small bottle of tequila. They wouldn't let us back in without ID, so by the time we fetched our ID, we'd drunk the bottle and so had to buy another one. They searched us both on the way in but never found it. Then once we got in, the lad dropped it, and it smashed on the floor—excellent night.

Day 439: 26 May 1991, Mexico

I caught a cab to a beach 20 miles away with the other 2 lads. One could speak Spanish, so we got there for $1.25 each. The beach was full of Mexicans and poor people selling food on the beach, from sweets to corn on the cob. The beach looked like a tip, with scrap metal, tyres, etc. hanging about all over the beach. We bought a litre of Tequila for about £1 and 3 limes and kept doing Tequila slammers on the beach until the bottle was empty. We all ended up pissed as farts. The lad who could speak Spanish pulled a Mexican bird, leaving me and the other lad to find our way home.

We couldn't speak Spanish but managed to get a taxi driver to take us home for $1.25 each. When we got back, he asked for $15—he got a bit angry when I told him to fuck off. I did a runner. He did a big wheel spin and fucked off with the other lad still in the car, but the lad just opened the door and jumped out.

On the Tequila's again tonight, getting even more pissed—I don't think my liver can take much more abuse. I've been arseholed every night for 2½ weeks and loving every minute of it! Another night on the piss in wild Mexico, where anything goes. They even have donkey shows here, where a donkey fucks a woman on stage.

Day 440: 27 May 1990, San Diego, California

The lads next door had a massive argument because one tried to shag the other one's bird. She was a right old slag but looked like a model (as most Mexican birds do).

I left Mexico this afternoon and caught the bus to San Diego (California), where I had booked the Greyhound bus to Dallas, leaving this evening. This gives me a couple of hours to explore San Diego—a great place with a really relaxed atmosphere. I could definitely live in California. Great beaches, great weather, great birds—what more could a bloke ask for?

Caught the Greyhound coach at 6 p.m. I was knackered, but getting to sleep on the bus was about as easy as getting inside a nun's knickers.

Day 441: 28 May 1991, Arizona and New Mexico (63 Weeks Away)

Totally fucked. The bus kept stopping every hour or two during the night, ensuring that I got fuck all sleep. As we drove for hours, the scenery changed slightly, from flat cactus-infested deserts to a slightly greener-type of baron land. When we reached Texas, the security police boarded the bus and began checking everyone. They let a sniffer dog go around the baggage compartment checking for drugs. I was shitting myself as I had a small amount of grass on me. The person in front of me was told to open his suitcase. The police took him off the bus, and we drove off while they were arresting him. At the next stop, I got my bottle of Tequila out and had several large mouthfuls. Some bloke got a joint out, which I kindly shared with him. Spent the rest of the day stoned, dazing out of the window, in a world of my own, swigging Tequila every now and then to keep me going. Got to Dallas at 2 a.m.

Day 442: 29 May 1991, Dallas, Texas

Got to Dallas at 2 a.m. completely fucked and dirty. My clothes were virtually rotting away from my body. I tried to sleep on the floor at the bus station and got covered in shit, spit, and chewing gum, etc. I kept getting bitten and so had to get up. I waited till it got light, then went out and tried to sleep in the park. The police thought I was a tramp and moved me on!

I spent the day wandering around Dallas and saw the place where J.F. Kennedy got shot back in 1963. Caught the 5 p.m. bus to New Orleans in Louisiana. I sat at the back of the bus, getting pissed on my bottle of Tequila, when some bloke saw me as he came out of the toilet. He asked me if I wanted to buy any cocaine. I said no, so he got some out and smoked it himself from a coke cone. I couldn't believe it. He got off his rocker smoking several cones of cocaine.

Day 443: 30 May 1991, New Orleans, Louisiana

Got into New Orleans at 5 a.m. and had to wait until about 7 a.m. until it was light enough (and safe enough) to walk to the hostel. I was knackered and just wanted to sleep but had to wait for half an hour for reception to open. I never got to sleep as I ended up working for 2½ hours, shifting furniture around with a couple of lads, in order for *free* accommodation. I had my first shower and bed in 4 days—it was great.

I went around the French quarter with an Aussie lad, watching all the buskers etc. in the street. We saw the Mississippi River and then got pissed in the street on cheap beer from the bottle shop, listening to all the live jazz music. We caught the tram home and had something to eat before going out on the piss again.

We went to a disco bar. I had some fat middle-aged woman clinging on to me tonight, and I couldn't get rid of her. She was pissed and wouldn't let me go. I pulled a nice Canadian bird and offered to buy her a drink. She said 'yes', so I took her outside to the bottle shop and bought her a can of beer. It's almost impossible to pull a bird when you've got no money, your clothes haven't been washed for a month, and your hair is so greasy that you could fry chips in it. Fell asleep at 3 a.m. waiting for the tram ride home. Someone woke me up. I shat myself as I thought I was being robbed.

Day 444: 31 May 1991, New Orleans, Louisiana

I got up at the crack of dawn this morning (9 a.m.), feeling like a bag of shit, and had to mow some bastard lawn for 2½ hours in order to get another free night's accommodation. Sweated like a twat in the 30°C sun. I broke the lawnmower and put it back in the shed without telling the bloke. Spent the day walking around the French quarter again, listening to all the buskers. I went to the Greyhound bus station to book my onward ticket to New York. I didn't have a shirt on, so some arsehole cop with nothing better to do started hassling me, telling me to get out. The manager of the Greyhound came out and gave me some shit as well (I think they both hate travellers). I took the piss out of them and nearly got arrested, and so I left in the end. To cut a long story short, I ended up losing my bus pass and had to go back to get it sorted, and I had to deal with the arsehole manager whom I had offended earlier. I have to buy a new ticket ($140, £80, to New York). Bollocks.

Went on the piss tonight with a Scottish and a German lad, buying beers from the supermarket. I was supposed to be meeting the Canadian bird from last night in a nightclub but didn't get there till 1 a.m. I don't know if she fucked off home early because I wasn't there or if she stood me up, but she wasn't there. Swept beers all night, and can't remember anything else.

Day 445: 1 June 1991, New Orleans, Louisiana

Woke up in the street at 8 a.m. completely pissed. Don't know what I was sweeping last night, but it must have been good. I didn't have a clue where I was but still managed to find my way home

(eventually). I had about 2 hours' sleep before getting up in order
to sort my bastard Greyhound ticket problem out. I never believed
in miracles until today, when I found out that someone had handed
my Greyhound pass in—*whew!* I couldn't believe it. I had to run
around like a twat for over an hour this morning (still pissed from
last night) in order to pick up my lost ticket. Got back just in time to
catch my bus to Akron Ohio, where the American bird whom I met
in Hawaii lives. She told me that I could come and visit her (free bed
for a night, I can't complain).

Day 446: 2 June 1991, Akron, Ohio

After spending 28 hours on a Greyhound bus in order to get
to Akron to meet some bird, she wasn't there to pick me up when
I got there at 4 p.m. I phoned her up and spoke to her mum, who
had no idea what was going on and told me that her daughter had
gone out for the day with a friend. The bitch. Spent 28 hours on
a bastard bus only to get stood up. I nearly phoned her mum up
again to tell her that I'd fucked her daughter in Hawaii. I was fuming
and went for a walk in the country town of Akron. I met a couple
of local hooligans and got talking to them and ended up going out
on the piss with them. We got loads of beer from the bottle shop
and got pissed in the street. It was a rough area full of street kids.
You don't need a TV over here. You just sit in the street as there is
always a scene going on. I decided to stay with these lads for the
night. Some bloke, paralytic drunk, drove us to someone's house in
order to get some acid tabs. On the way, some young kids threw a
rock at the car. We couldn't get any tabs, so we carried on drinking
and had several joints.

Day 447: 3 June 1991, Akron, Ohio

I caught the Greyhound bus to the Big Apple—New York.

Day 448: 4 June 1991, Manhattan, New York

I got to New York at about 3 a.m. shattered and dirty after
spending 86 hours on a Greyhound bus over the last 7 days. I had

to wait 3 hours in the bus station until it was light and safe enough to venture out on the underground to find some accommodation. Went to 103 Street to find a place and saw some bloke ripping a car door off. I went back later on, and there was hardly anything left of the car.

I checked into a hostel safely and then caught the tube into the city centre. I went down to see the Statue of Liberty and then went up to the top of the World Trade Centre building—the highest building in the world. You could see for miles from the 107th floor. It was like being in a plane.

Spent the afternoon walking around down Broadway etc. and past the Empire State Building. When I got back to the hostel, there was a big siege going on at the old people's home just around the corner. Police everywhere, 14 police cars and ambulances etc. and I'm staying in the respectable area (still rough as fuck!).

Went out on the piss tonight—*my last night*! I took all my jewelry off before going out. I've been robbed 3 times on my travels and don't want to make it 4. I went to a bar where it was only 25 cents (17 p) for half a pint of beer. It was watered down but still value for money. I got talking to a couple of local birds. They loved my accent and couldn't get enough of me. I though I was in luck until they both fucked off home as they had to be up for work in the morning. I stayed in the bar, getting completely arseholed. I can't remember anything else. Don't know how I got home.

Day 449: 5 June 1991, Manhattan, New York

Had a great night last night. Today is a sad day, as I go home to sunny Lincoln. I packed my bags and left the hostel. I had the morning to waste and so went down to Wall Street and saw the stock exchange in action. It was very full of loud-mouthed hooligans in suits, shouting to get in their bids. Caught the bus to the airport and caught my plane home.

Day 450: 6 June 1991, Lincoln, England

I arrived at Gatwick airport at 7.30 a.m. and was in a state of shock—home after 15 months of travel. I smoked a cigarette that I found on the floor, drowning my sorrows. I phoned up Paula, but she was still in Thailand, so I was going to hitch-hike home, but I couldn't be arsed, so I changed my last travellers cheque ($40) and ended up forgetting my passport—bastard. I had to run to catch the train to Victoria Station, where I got a coach to Lincoln. I met a few foreign travellers, which made it worse for as I'm on my way home.

I got to Lincoln at 6 p.m. All the money I had left was 15 pence. I had to scrounge 50 p at the bus stop in order to get back home. Everyone was pleased to see me when I got home—it just feels as though I haven't been away. Dad took me down to the pub and bought me a few beers and a cigar.

It felt strange sleeping in my old bed again.

Kevin moved down to London to live with Paula in July 1991. He remained with Paula for a few years, and she joined him later on in his next travelling adventures in Africa.

AFRICA, 1992

5 September 1992, Croydon, England

Pete came down to Croydon this morning with all his kit. Then Paula drove us both to Godstone, where we said our goodbyes. Pete and I started hitching from Godstone (J6 M25). We had to wait nearly an hour for our first lift, which only took us to the next junction. We got dropped off on the hard shoulder on the M25 (in which it is illegal to hitch-hike). We had to run across 2 busy lanes on the M25 in order for us to get on the correct road, on which, after 20 minutes, a van picked us up and took us both all the way to Dover Port. I tried to smuggle some dope over to France by shoving it down my sock along with a packet of ritzlers. Pete and I walked through customs and got stopped. We were asked lots of questions and had our passports taken away—I shat my pants in case I was going to be searched. After ten minutes, the customs chap came back and asked us a few more questions and then let us go—*whew!*

The ferry was 1½ hours We tried to get lifts with lorry drivers, but no joy. When we got to Calais, Pete and I walked down the motorway trying to hitch a lift—no one would stop after trying for an hour, so we set camp along the beach of Calais in the sand dunes. Great view of the beach. We put the tent up and then got pissed on whiskey and stoned, listening to the BBC World Service, then came along a Polish guy who set up camp beside us.

6 September 1992, Calais, France

Got up this morning feeling a bit hung over. My mouth was as dry as a nun's crotch, and we had no water left. Pete and I soon finished off the remaining food that we had—a small piece of cheese and a couple of Oxo cubes. We walked about 3 miles down the road to a better hitching spot—still no lift. By now, we were getting hungry and had to pinch some sweet corn from a field and eat it raw. We had some whiskey and some dope so remained buzzing for most of the day.

After hitching in Calais for 8½ hours, we managed to get a lift to Paris with a mad Frenchman—he couldn't speak English, so there wasn't any conversation in the car. He dropped us off in Paris, where we found a cheap hotel. We got chatting to the manageress, who ended up driving us around Paris, showing us the sights etc. Very interesting.

7 September 1992, Paris, France

Tried hitching all day, still no lift. It was getting dark by now, and no one would pick us up. We were just about to put our tent up (in the middle reservation of the motorway) when a police van stopped. Pete had a joint in his hands at the time and had to throw it. We got in the police van, and they took us to the airport—I was off my face and couldn't stop laughing. They dropped us off, and we sat on the side of the road, getting more stoned and drinking beer. Still no bastard lifts—slept in the airport. Spent 8 hours today trying to hitch out of Paris—no chance.

8 September 1992, Paris, France

Another night spent sleeping rough, getting woken up first thing in the morning in the airport. The police took us miles away from the motorway, so we had to find our way back on it, stocking ourselves up with local produce along the way (wine). After a couple of hours, we managed to get a lift a few miles down the road to a big service station. It was crammed wall to wall with hitch-hikers. I saw the Geordie lad whom I met yesterday, trying to hitch out of Paris a few miles back down the road. Had another bottle of wine while waiting for the lift that never comes.

The French are really tight when it comes to picking up hikers. We were just about to call it a day when it was getting dark at 8 p.m. when a French lorry driver picked us up and took us to Orange—600 km down the road. What a result. We got there at 3 a.m. at a roadhouse. We put our tent up, had some wine, and fell asleep.

9 September 1992, Orange, France

Woke up this morning freezing cold as it had pissed it down last night. The tent had leaked, and everything was wet. Packed everything away wet and then stood by the side of the road for 5 hours, freezing cold, until we got our next lift. This is the last time I hitch in France as the tight bastards never pick you up. Finally managed to get a lift from a Spanish lorry driver, who only took us 180 km to a place called Narbonne 'Knob-on'. There were already 3 sets of hitch-hikers trying to get lifts. We tried for 3 hours before calling it a day. We put the tent up behind the service station, next to a couple of Polish lads, and got pissed on wine before going to sleep. We hadn't had a wash for several days now, and we both look and smell dirty.

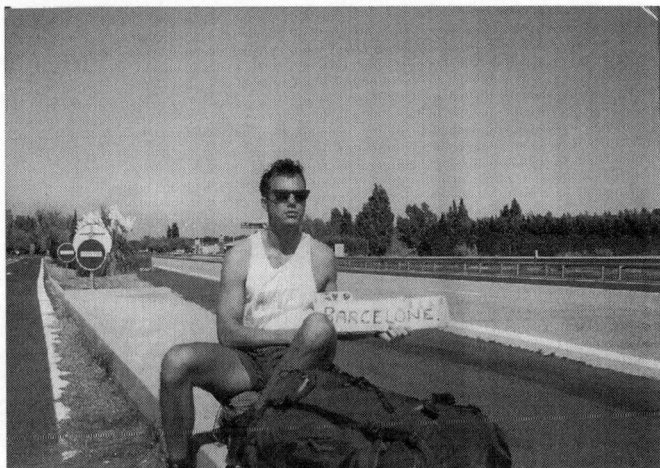

10 September 1992, Perpignan, France

Got up at 7 a.m. today in order to catch the early morning traffic. On the road at 7.30 a.m. Still no lift after 2 hours. We're both sick to death of standing hours on end on the roadside, only to get a pissy lift a few miles down the road. Haven't even had a hot meal or even a hot drink since I left England. We've both been surviving on bread, biscuits, and water. Four hours passed by—no lift. By now, Pete and I were really fucked off with our slow progress. Then a couple of good-looking Polish birds turned up in skintight tops. By this time, we'd been waiting for 10 hours in total—they got a lift within *five minutes*. We tried for 8 hours today to get a lift, and with yesterday's 3 hours, it meant that we'd spent 11 hours at this shithole of a place with no lift. Pete was suffering slightly with sunstroke. We decided to call it a day and catch the bus to Gibraltar. We flagged a car down and got a lift to the next town 10 kms away and caught the bus to Copignan 60 km away. A nice ride driving through small French villages. We bought a couple of bottles of wine each—9 Francs each (90 pence). We found a deserted area to camp, next to the maintenance shed for the railway. The floor was concrete, so we had to tie the tent poles to a drainpipe and to a couple of heavy poles alongside the tent. We drank about 2½ litres of red wine between us and got completely rat-arsed.

11 September 1992, In Transit, Spain

Woke up this morning to find several workmen outside our tent—they couldn't believe that we had camped right outside their depot. I was still completely arseholed for the first several hours today after last night's binge.

We caught the bus to Barcelona and spent a few hours walking around looking at the sights before catching the bus to Malaga. While walking around Barcelona, we got chatting to an old merchant seaman from Istanbul, who ended up giving us some top-quality dope from Poland.

On the 17-hour bus trip to Malaga, I saw a Spanish bloke nearby smoking a joint. He saw me looking and gave me some. Pete and I downed a bottle of wine and crashed out for the night.

12 and 13 September 1992, Fuengirola, Spain

We arrived at Malaga at about 9 a.m. where we caught the tube to Torrimalinos. We changed some money and found out that there was a livelier resort about 20 km down the road. We walked for about half hour to a campsite, where I paid for one person, and Pete sneaked in through the fence. All my clothes stink (as well as myself), so I had a shower and washed my clothes at the same time.

We had a couple of joints and a bottle of wine and spent the rest of the day lazing around the pool. In the evening, we walked into town, taking 2½ bottles of wine with us, which we bought for about 75 p each. Pete and I ended up in a nightclub called the 'Jaguar Club'. It was underground and full of the weirdest-looking people I'd ever seen. I got there at about 5 a.m. and stayed until it closed at about 7.30 a.m. I walked home and went to sleep for a few hours before going down the beach with Pete, taking a bottle of wine.

We both went around town again tonight with another bottle of wine and a microdot. I got off my head and woke up on someone's front garden at about 5 a.m. I made my way to the Jaguar Club and stayed there for a few hours until it closed. Then I sat outside for an hour, talking to a lad from Norway. Two blokes came out of the club, one about 35 and the other about 60, both from England but living in Spain for the last several years. They were right arseholes and tried to start a fight with the Norwegian lad and slapped him around the face.

I got back to my tent at about 8.30 a.m. Pete wasn't in the tent nor was his rucksack. All I found was some pissy little note saying that he'd gone home to his girlfriend in England.

14 September 1992, Tangiers, Morocco

I could not believe it. Pete had fucked off home. I was still off my head from last night and really pissed off. I've always wanted to go across Africa, but the thought of going on my own scares the shit out of me. It was 8.30 a.m. I had just got back from a night out to find my travelling companion had pissed off without me. I thought about going home and knew that if I thought about it any longer, I would. So I packed up the tent and headed 100 km down the road to Gibraltar. I had a look around Gibraltar and found out that there were no ferries going to Morocco today—bollocks. So I had to catch the bus to Algeciras, where I had to walk for another 3 miles to get to the ferry port. I managed to get on a ferry, where I met a couple of Dutch guys. We arrived at Tangiers and walked to a cheap hotel, getting hassled severely on the way by local paupers trying to get money off us. I hadn't slept or eaten for 2 days, so I had a meal and went straight to bed.

15 September 1992, Marrakech, Morocco

Got up at 6.15 a.m. completely shagged and caught the 6-hour train to Casablanca, where I picked up a letter from Paula and changed some money, before catching a four-hour train to Marrakech—an ancient city in the mountains. All the hotels were full, so I ended up sleeping on the roof of a hotel. Not bad, but I woke up at 4 a.m. when the Mosques belted out prayers and singing over the whole town.

16 September 1992, Fez, Morocco

Met a couple of English lads and went around the markets with them. Some local hastler kept following us around, trying to become our guide for money. We tried everything but couldn't shake him off. We told him that we didn't have any money, so he said that he'd show us around for 3 hours for 30 pence (10 pence each). So we agreed. He took us through a maze of narrow market streets and Mosques—very interesting and well worth the money. Afterwards, I caught a taxi to the train station and caught an 8-hour train to Fez, passing through wasteland and deserts. I was in a compartment with 2 Muslim women with their heads covered and a load of screaming kids, crying their eyes out for nearly the whole journey—talk about a headache. Got to Fez at 10 p.m. completely shagged. I had to go to 3 hotels before I could find a spare bed for the night.

17 September 1992, Fez, Morocco

I'm really fucked off with life at the moment and just want to get out of Morocco—England, Kenya, South Africa. Anywhere.

I met some English lads who were going to the Moroccan airline, so I went with them to see what was available and decided that I wanted to fly to Egypt, spend some time there, then fly to Kenya and go overland to SA, when I'd meet Paula for Christmas. I had to cut out my original route as it is becoming very dangerous in Algeria at the moment, and there isn't any traffic south due to armed bandits. I hardly know any French and wouldn't want to attempt it on my own. I got a guide this afternoon, and he took me around the old Medina—a massive maze of 7th-century buildings forming a massive market. If you went on your own, you'd never find your way out. We walked past stalls selling everything from goats' heads to bags full of dirty syringes. He took me down some narrow streets to a big opening where it was full of men dyeing wool in massive clay pots full of coloured dye. There we also saw men curing leather, in which they'd soak the leather in piss and then rub shit into it to soften the leather. The whole place stunk, and there were streams of piss pouring down the narrow streets. This place is amazing. I even saw a donkey walking up the cobbled hill, with an old washing machine strapped to its back.

I went around with the English lads this evening. We just sat in the middle of the market, drinking mint tea for a couple of hours, soaking in the atmosphere.

18 September 1992, Rabat, Morocco

Got up at 1 a.m. this morning after only 4 hours' sleep. Caught a taxi to the train station in order to catch the train to Rabat (4 hours). I had to go today in order to get to the Egyptian Embassy as I need a visa so that I can fly on Sunday (hopefully to Egypt—I just want to leave Morocco. Everyone is just trying to rip you off). I got talking to a Moroccan lad on the train, who was also going to Rabat. We got there just after 6 a.m. and found a cheap hotel together. I spent most of the day running around getting my visa and a ticket for Egypt. The ticket cost £320 but only £170 with a student card. I got my YHA card out and talked the bollocks off them for an hour before they would accept it. I've got a standby ticket for Sunday to Cairo. I tried to get a travellers cheque cashed today, but every bank I went to, I was directed to another bank. The 6th bank I tried (and 2 hours of walking around sweating my tits off) managed to cash it for me. I wanted about £3 of it in change so that I could phone Paula up tonight, but they didn't have enough change. I couldn't believe it. I was in one of the main banks in the capital city of Morocco, and they didn't have £3 worth of change. He told me to follow him—I did, and he took me through 2 security gates.

I went out around Rabat tonight with the Moroccan lad, after spending nearly 2 hours in this Mickey Mouse country, trying to phone Paula up. We had a bowl full of snails each and then had a Moroccan sandwich—very similar to a doner kebab in England, except that it doesn't give you arse burn in the morning.

19 September 1992, Casablanca, Morocco

What a nightmare of a day—the Moroccan sandwich I had last night from a street seller didn't agree with me, and I spent most of the day running from toilet to toilet. I was just pissing out my arse. My poor ring was red raw and in agony—any more of this, and I will need a skin graft on it. I caught the train to Casablanca, where I found a decent hotel (although I saw more of the toilet than the room). I felt really weak as well. This is the first time ever that I've had an arse as bad as this while travelling. I went for a walk later on and caught some cheeky twat with his hand in my pocket. He was about to pinch my Ray-Bans when I grabbed his arm and swung him around before he ran away. Then on the way back to the hotel, I saw a Dutch lad fighting with a local lad in the street—but the local lad ran off, He too had been trying to pickpocket. In the hotel, I got talking to a middle-aged English bloke, who travelled for several years and was now on his way across Africa. He'd been to 58 different countries compared to my 25. While in the hotel, a

Norwegian lad came in, who'd just been pickpocketed by 2 young boys, who stole about £65 (1000 drams) from him. A witness in the street knew the address for the boys and gave it to him. When he told the police, they told him to go away as they were too busy—what a shithole of a country.

20 September 1992, Casablanca, Morocco

My arse is still on the blink. I went for a shit 10 times yesterday and another 7 times today (even though I've hardly eaten anything). I got up early today and caught the bus to the airport, where, after waiting several hours, I caught the plane to Egypt (Cairo). It was a day flight over Alderia, Libya, and Egypt, so I made sure that I got a window seat. I did but right above the wing, so I couldn't see anything. The flight was 4½ hours, and I had to put my watch forward by 3 hours, meaning that I arrived in Egypt at 10 p.m. The centre of Cairo is 35 km from the airport, and it was hard work trying to find which bus to take as everything was written in Arabic. I got sent on 4 different buses. The people would tell me that I was on the wrong bus. I got on the right bus in the end and got chatting to some local bloke, who paid for my ticket (only 25 pesos). Not bad value for money—4 pence for a 40-minute bus trip into town. When we got to the town centre, the bloke went out of his way to show me where the hotel was.

21 September 1992, Cairo, Egypt

The so-called hotel I'm staying in is a complete shithole. It's on the 8th floor of an office block, right down the grotty back streets—a bit how you would imagine the slums of Hong Kong or New York. I got chatting to a lad from Mauritius, who'd been travelling for about 5 years, and he show me around a bit. I spent all day going from travel agent to travel agent, enquiring about a one-way ticket to Kenya. The cheapest I could find was for about £230. I found my way to the train station, but trying to get a ticket was a different kettle of fish. The people are animals when it comes to queuing up for things—it took me an hour to get my rail ticket for tomorrow.

I can't believe how cheap it is in Egypt (about half the price in Morocco). My room costs me about £1.20, including breakfast. The people are also very friendly and helpful, without expecting money for the slightest bit of help—it makes a nice change after Morocco.

I had a walk around with Ricky (the Mauritius lad) tonight, trying out various local food—even though my arse is still on fire from Morocco. I went to bed tonight, and Ricky (who hasn't had sex for 4 months) wanted me to suck him off (seriously). I told him to get on his bike.

22 September 1992, Cairo, Egypt

I had a shower in the middle of the night to cool down and left my watch in the bathroom—I never saw it again. I think the manager stole it.

I caught a bus to the university and got a student union card (very valuable—it will save me about £80 on my flight to Kenya). On the way back, I visited the Egyptian Museum—quite interesting if you're into that type of thing.

I caught the train to Luxor (12 hours) with an English lad from the hotel. Egypt is nothing as I expected—99% per cent of the population lives on the edge of the Nile, which is very green and tropical (similar to Malaysia). Yet about 500 metres either side of the Nile, the lush vegetation instantly turns into desert. Every now and then, we would pass through small Egyptian villages, with the local women washing their clothes in the Nile etc. Egypt is a lot more backwards than I'd expected—similar to that of a Third World country.

We arrived in Luxor at 10.30 p.m. (3 hours early) and went to a small hotel along with a couple of French girls, an Ozzie, and a Kiwi. I didn't go to bed until 1.30 a.m. and have an early start tomorrow.

23 September 1992, Luxor, Egypt

I got up at 5.20 a.m. today after less than 4 hours' sleep. The reason being is that I'm going on a donkey trek to see some of the ancient burial sites of Egypt. There were 6 of us in total, including the guide. We got on our own donkeys and travelled through a couple of villages. Then leaving the lush vegetation behind, we entered the desert (a complete contrast). We trekked through the desert up to a mountain range, which the poor old donkeys struggled to get up. We travelled along very steep and dangerous cliff edges with an excellent view of the Egyptian landscape, passing ancient temples from time to time.

We visited the 'Valley of the Kings', where various kings had been buried in about 2000 BC. Their tombs took years to construct, with a maze of underground tunnels painted and carved with hieroglyphics. A very enjoyable day—my best so far.

When we got back to Luxor, I caught the 3½—hour bus to Aswan, getting there about 8.30 p.m. It's Paula's 25th birthday today, and I spent 1½ hours walking around, trying to find an international phone (mission impossible). I managed to find it in the end, but you had to pay for 3 minutes (no less). It was about 9 p.m. in England by now, and Paula would probably be out, so in the end, I didn't phone (after all that running around).

I bumped into the 2 French girls from my previous hotel, and we all got a room together before getting something to eat from a poxy food stall on the side of the road.

24 September 1992, Aswan, Egypt

I am completely knackered due to the last 3 weeks of non-stop travelling, but today's the day when I have a short rest, as I'm spending 3 days and 2 nights on board a Fluccka (an old Egyptian sailing boat). I'm going with the 2 French girls, along with 2 Dutch guys and 2 German women. The trip was delayed slightly, so I ran to the telephone exchange and gave Paula a ring. She's probably going to fly into Johannesburg (South Africa) on about 8 December, which basically means that I've got to get my arse into gear if I'm going to get across Africa in that time.

We all got on board the Fluccka and sailed down the Nile to a small island, where we stopped off for half an hour. We went around a small village—very interesting to see how the local villagers live. Back on board, the skipper passed a joint around the boat, and I got stoned for my first time in Africa. And I couldn't think of a better place to be, lying on the boat, in the sun, sailing up the Nile, watching the tropical scenery go by. Great. My best day so far by a long way.

Spent most of the day relaxing and dozing in the sun. The sun went down until gradually it became dark. We carried on sailing, when the cook brought a small stove out and cooked us all a big meal of pasta and tomatoes. Nearly burnt the boat down in the process. It was so peaceful lying on the boat, looking up at the stars and listening to the drumbeat and singing from various villages alongside the Nile. I hardly slept tonight as the boat wasn't very comfortable, and we didn't stop sailing until 4.30 a.m.

25 September 1992, Sailing along the Nile, Egypt

Got up about 5.30 a.m. in order to watch the sun rise over the Nile—the skies instantly awoke with the sounds of the local wildlife awakening. I had been desperate for a shit all night, and now was my first chance. I ran ashore and dived behind a bush—what a relief. I had to wipe my arse on some dried corn on the cob that I found lying around. After breakfast and a cup of tea, we were back on our journey up the Nile. Another day doing nothing but lazing around in the sun. It got too windy later on, so we had to pull into the bank of a river—I wanted to explore the local village but was advised not to as the villagers were supposed to have been quite hostile (a German tourist had been killed there a couple of years ago). We'd only been there half an hour when some of the locals started gathering along side the riverbanks. Before long, there were 2 groups of about 10. Somehow, they both fell out with each other, and a big rock fight erupted. It got quite violent as they threw rocks (sometimes the size of a brick) at each other—we had to leave sharply and carry on up the Nile.

After the sun had gone down, we pulled into another local village. One of the Dutch lads and I needed a crap badly and couldn't find anywhere to go. It was dark, and we were desperate. We were virtually about to go a few metres from some bloke's doorstep and were just about to go when some woman came out the house, saw us, and invited us in. They were from the ancient Nubian tribe—the head of the house wanted me to marry one of his daughters, so I had a cup of tea and made my way back to the boat, where we carried on sailing up to Edfu. I had a really rough night trying to sleep on the boat as my back felt as if it was bent in two—it was so uncomfortable, I kept waking up every half hour in agony.

26 September 1992, Cairo, Egypt

Woke up at 6.30 a.m. in agony and could hardly stand up. Thank God I haven't got to sleep on the boat again tonight.

We all visited a local temple and then caught a taxi to Luxor (1½ hours, £1.40 each). We said goodbye to everyone. Then I went to my original hotel in Luxor with the French girls. We had a quick shower (my first in 3 days) and then caught the train to Cairo—the French girls left me halfway at Asyut, where I continued up to Cairo (9 long hours). I had some Egyptian pervert talking to me for about 2 hours about how he wanted to marry an English girl—not a hope in hell for this poor twat. I persevered with him until he ran out of cigarettes, so I changed seats.

Arrived in Cairo at 11 p.m. and found my way to a cheap hotel E£6 (about 90pence). It was full of weirdos—I was in a room full of 3 people, a really slow English lad, a 45-year-old woman from England, dressed as a tart and who has been living here for 2 years, and a pathetic retarded lad from Israel who had become a Muslim (from a Jew) last Wednesday in order to stay in Egypt. He's now changed his name and walks round saying prayers to Allah.

27 September 1992, Cairo, Egypt

Changed hotel first thing this morning and spent most of the day walking around Cairo, trying to organise my flight to Kenya. I managed to get it for £210—saving £80 (after a lot of persuasion) with my new student card. I bought myself an English newspaper (the *Daily Express*), and when I was reading it later on, I realised that the crossword had already been filled in.

I got talking to a couple from New Zealand in the street. They saw a dead woman floating down the Nile a couple of days ago. Just then, an Egyptian man walked past and rammed his hand right up the girls arse. She chased him and slapped him in the face. He couldn't believe it. Then she slapped him again. He spat at her. Then her boyfriend ran over and smacked the bloke—they had a quick scuffle in the street before the crowd pulled them apart.

I went to catch the local bus to Giza (in order to visit the pyramids). There were about 150 locals in the bus queue, so when the bus finally turned up, it was like a gang warfare trying to get on it. I only just managed to squeeze on.

I spent about 3 hours walking around the pyramids—not too bad, although all the flocks of American and German tourists get everywhere.

28 September 1992, Sharm el-Sheikh, Egypt

Hung around Cairo for most of the day before catching the afternoon bus to Sharm el-Sheikh (7 hours). We passed underneath the Suez Canal to Sinai and travelled through desert and mountains to Sharm el-Sheikh. I ended up getting off the bus 10 minutes after my stop and ended up walking back up a pitch-dark road for 40 minutes, trying to find my way back. It is a fairly expensive holiday resort here, so I just found the cheapest accommodation I could—I paid just over £1 to sleep on the floor of a campsite.

29 September 1992, Scuba-Diving in the Red Sea, Egypt

Woke up in the middle of the campsite, covered in flies. I went down to the dive centre and booked myself on a scuba-diving trip out in the Red sea (one of the best places in the world to scuba-dive). On the boat, I met a couple of English lads and a bunch of tossers from Belgium. It took us 2 hours on the boat to get to Ras Mahamed, one of the best diving spots in the Red sea.

The reef was good but nothing compared to the Great Barrier Reef in Australia. I swam down to a depth of 115 feet (35 metres) and still couldn't see the bottom of a massive ridge—supposed to be 400 feet deep. I saw a moray eel (6 feet long) swim and hide under a rock. So I swam to it and started poking it to get it to swim out—I found out later that it could have taken my arm off.

I got a headache from the first dive as I went down so deep, and my dive buddy ended up with a nose bleed. We moved to another site and did another dive—swimming around the bottom of the reef for about 40 minutes.

Caught the 5 p.m. bus to Dahab (a hang-out for travellers). The bus was jam-packed with people—I managed to get a seat, but there wasn't any room left in the boot, so my rucksack ended up wedged in the toilet along with several other bags. The 1½-hour trip took 4 hours due to the fact that the bus broke down in the desert halfway there. I wouldn't mind, but I'm out of water. In the end, the bus started again, and everyone crammed back on to the bus.

When I got to Dehab, I found myself a small hut for E16 per night (95 pence) and then scored some blow—about £50 worth for only just over £4. I bumped into the 2 Dutch guys from the Fluccka trip and spent the rest of the night with them, getting off my mind and going around from cafe to cafe.

30 September 1992, Dahab, Egypt

Got up and got stoned. Dahab is one of the most relaxed places I've ever been to—it's great. There is nothing to do all day apart from lying around in the sun, listening to the music from the cafes and having the odd drink or game of backgammon. The cafes are all the way down the beachfront, all of them blasting out mellow music. They have large carpets on the sand, covered with cushions—so you just slob around in the sun, with your feet up.

I had breakfast in one of the cafes and lazed around there for a couple of hours before going for a walk. I only went about 30 metres down the beach, where I ended up at another cafe—this time staying for four hours before moving on to another cafe. Popping back to my hut every now and then to skin up. I spent all day and night slobbing around from cafe to cafe. I bumped into the 2 French girls and the 2 Dutch guys who were on the Fluccka trip. We all sat around chatting until the cafes closed down at about 1 a.m.

1 October 1992, Sinai Desert (Camel Trek), Egypt

Got up early this morning as I'm off on a 2-day 1-night camel trek through the mountains in the Sinai Desert along with the 2 Dutch lads and 2 French girls. We spent half an hour arguing with the guide as the price had somehow gone up from the arranged price last night.

We eventually got on our way and slowly trekked through the mountains. My balls were in agony as my saddle was very uncomfortable. I just had to grit my teeth and grin and bear it. When we stopped for lunch, Hans (the Dutch lad) and I climbed to the top of one of the mountains, getting a great view of the desert. We then carried on through the mountains on camel back until we arrived at a small oasis in which we'd be spending the night.

Hans and I decided to climb to the top of one of the mountains to watch the sun set. It took us both ages, but we finally made it. After the sun set, we climbed back down, going a different route for a change. Before long, it was getting dark, and we found ourselves trying to climb down a cliff face—very hard as the rocks kept crumbling away. I was shitting bricks and thought I'd never get down, especially when I ran out of foot holes. I had to jump off the cliff, on to a large rock on the side, cutting my leg and hand in the process. Had a very basic meal to eat, cooked by the camel guide, before lying out in the open, staring at the stars and nodding off to sleep.

2 October 1992, Sinai Desert (Camel Trek), Egypt

Woke up this morning covered in dust and dirt and set off on the ball-breaking camel trek back to Dahab—I've never been so relieved to get off my camel. Soon as I got to Dahab, I was back in slob mode again, lying around in the sun all day (34°C), going from cafe to cafe.

I met 5 lads from Peterborough, who had just finished working a season in Crete—good lads. I caught a taxi at 10 p.m. to Mount Sinai with them, 80 miles away. We all took some opium and smoked several joints, getting us all on our way by the time we arrived in Mount Sinai.

We all staggered off into the mountains in pitch darkness, not even knowing which mountain was Mount Sinai. Luckily, we found a track and followed it to Mount Sinai, where we began to climb it. We were all knackered, especially Jay, who kept hallucinating. It took us 3 hours to climb to the top, getting us there at about 4 a.m., where we had a few joints and crashed out on the mountain (2228 metres).

3 October 1992, Dahab, Egypt

Woke up at about 5.30 a.m. nearly missing the sunrise over the mountains, which we had come for. Got a few photos and then went back to sleep for a couple of hours before making our decent down.

My leg was playing me up from when I fell over on it last night. We got back to the taxi at 10 a.m., which drove us all the way back to Dahab—the return taxi only cost us about £4 each. Not bad value, seeing as we went for 160 miles, and the poor taxi driver had to sleep in his car all night.

Got back to Dahab at midday, where I gave Paula a ring as she's at my parents' house for the weekend. It was good to get back to Dahab—although as soon as I got back, I bumped into the French girls who had been waiting for me. Shit. They're beginning to get on my nerves as I can hardly communicate with them.

I washed some clothes and then spent the rest of the day (and night) slobbing around in the sun, getting stoned and browner by the minute (temp 37°C).

4 October 1992, Cairo, Egypt

Got up at 6.30 a.m. and caught the bus to Cairo (8 hours). I fly to Kenya tonight and so finished the last of my grass at every available chance and ended up sleeping most of the journey. I hung around Cairo for several hours before travelling to the airport 5 hours before my plane leaves—a rough day of travelling and hanging around all day.

5 October 1992, Nairobi, Kenya

Arrived at Nairobi airport at 6.20 a.m. Going through customs, I was only given a visa for 1 week as I had no ticket out of the country. So I argued with the tight sod, and he gave me 2 weeks—which means I'm going to have to get my arse into gear and do some fast travelling.

I caught the bus from the airport to Nairobi. The bus was empty when I got on it, but after a few stops, it was crammed solid with people. I ended up with a large bag shoved in my face as we drove through the shanty towns. When the bus arrived at my stop, I couldn't squeeze past everyone to get off the bus, and the bus started off again. At the next stop, before I could get off, about 10 more people jumped on, pushing me back like animals, and the bus started off again. I managed to get off at the next stop, miles from where I wanted to be.

I arrived at a cheap-budget hotel at 9 a.m., where the manager told me that there had been a cancellation on a safari trip to the Masai Mari and that I could go for a really cheap price—I played on the fact that I had jet lag and that I wasn't really interested and got it for even less. The only trouble was that it left in 20 mins' time. I had to run to the bank, change some money, and run back where the van was waiting for me. I was knackered as I had virtually been travelling for the last 26 hours, had just arrived in Nairobi, and 20 mins later, I was on a minibus, going on a 4-day safari ($120). Also, on my trip were a Polish couple and a Dutch couple (on their honeymoon). It took about 7 hours to get to the game reserve, stopping off at a small town on the way. There were lots of Masai tribes people in the village, very colourful and with massive holes in their ear lobes as part of their tribal decoration. We arrived at our camp at 4.30 p.m. and went straight out on a drive through the Masai Mari. I couldn't believe how many animals there were and how close we could get to them. Saw loads of zebras, wilder beasts, giraffes, and lions, etc.—a great trip. It was back to the campsite for some food, then straight to bed for me as I'm shattered.

6 October 1992, Masai Mari Game Reserve, Kenya
Got up at 6 a.m. Had a good breakfast—sausages, beans, toast, coffee, etc. and then went out for a drive. It is a good time of year to view game here as the wilder beasts are beginning to

migrate to Tanzania. Everywhere you look, you can see herds of wilder beasts forming and heading off to Tanzania.

We stopped off beside a river in which there were about 20 hippos bathing in the water. Then we carried on and saw a lion dragging half a dead wilder beast home to her family. Also saw a cheetah chewing away on a gazelle, with a couple of very young babies next to it.

You hardly need a good camera or a zoom lens here as you are able to get so close to the animals. We got back at 1 p.m. after 5 hours' driving around, had lunch, and then went to sleep for an hour. Later on in the afternoon, we visited a Masai village—complete mind-blowing experience. There were about 20 mud huts in a circle, with all the men in a group singing tribal songs and taking it in turns to jump up and down the middle. They were actually singing hunting songs, and the jumping was aimed at strengthening the legs and warming up before a hunt. I went into one of the mud huts, which the whole family sleeps in—very dark and grubby. They even had leather hides pegged out on the ground, drying out in the sun—a great trip. One of my best travelling experiences.

We then drove around for a couple more hours, spotting various game—the whole savanna is littered with occasional skeleton or dead animals being torn apart by vultures, hyenas, etc. I saw a giraffe being ripped to pieces by vultures and other birds of prey. On the way back, we got really close to a herd of elephants and some ostriches.

Back at camp, I had dinner and drank several bottles of the local brew, 'Tusker Lager'—it went down a treat. It was about 40 pence (25 Kenyan shillings) for a half-litre bottle, I don't know the strength of it, but it did the job. My first taste of beer since Pete pissed off home while we were in Spain 3 weeks ago.

7 October 1992, Masai Mari Game Reserve, Kenya

Up again at 6.25 a.m. Put my boots and was in the van at 6.30 a.m. I was in a daze and could hardly see out of my eyes as I was that tired. Saw a group of hyenas lazing around in the sun as well as the usual game. Got back for breakfast and then went out to view some more game. We got to a few metres away from a king lion and lioness. I took loads of photos. Then when I looked around again, the male was shagging the arse off the female. I learnt a few new positions to try out on Paula when I meet her in South Africa. Everything else I saw was an anticlimax after seeing the lions as they were only metres away from me.

Got back, had lunch and a sleep before going for a walk in the reserve with a couple of Masai tribesmen. They brought spears and clubs with them in case we got attacked by a dangerous animal. We walked up to the top of a tall hill, admired the view, and then came back again. I started on the good old local brew again tonight after dinner and had more than my fair share, getting pissed and going to bed at midnight.

8 October 1992, Masai Mari Game Reserve, Kenya

Felt very hungover today after last night's session. I felt very rough on the five-hour trip to Nairobi. Back in Nairobi, I got a visa for Rwanda for K$H200 (about £3.60).

I went to an African bar tonight called the Modern Green Bar—full of prostitutes, slags, down-and-outs, and many local characters. The place is open 24 hours a day, 365 days a year, and the front doors haven't closed since 1968 (the year I was born). It's really rough inside and always a few people sleeping on the tables and music blasting from the Juke box. The bar is completely enclosed in a cage, which you pass your money through first and then you receive your drink. I'd only been in there about 5 minutes and had my arse and balls pinched by several different local women. The beer is really cheap as well at K$H18 (21 pence) for a half-litre bottle—They're strong, so you don't need many. I was getting harassed by the local women, so walked off and began chatting to one of the very few white people in the bar. He was from England and had been living in Africa for several years, teaching the Kenyan Army various anti-guerrilla tactics. It wasn't long before the local slags were sniffing around again, so we left and went to a nightclub, where it was £1.70 to get in and 40 pence a pint. Even in there, the birds were gagging for it—I'm not surprised that there is so much AIDS in this part of the world. I know that I certainly wouldn't go near any of them, but that don't stop them trying. Left the club at 5 a.m.

9 October 1992, Nairobi, Kenya

Got up at 9.30 a.m. Still wrecked from last night and feeling bollock rough. I changed some US dollars cash into Kenyan shillings on the black market (the bank rate is K$H34 for US $1) at a rate of K$H42 for US $1, making 25%. Then I went back to the Modern Green Bar with an English lad I'd met. I had a few beers and then had to catch the night train to Mombasa, where I met another English lad (a fireman). We got pissed together on the train before nodding off on the 13-hour journey.

10 October 1992, Mombasa, Kenya

Walking through Mombasa, we saw a petrol station that had just burned down, taking a bus with it. Got a shithole of a hotel. Then Seth and I made our way to Diawa Beach, 2 hours south of Mombasa. We had to catch a bus, a ferry, then another bus. An interesting drive, passing through small mud-hut communities and tropical vegetation, with various local characters on board the bus.

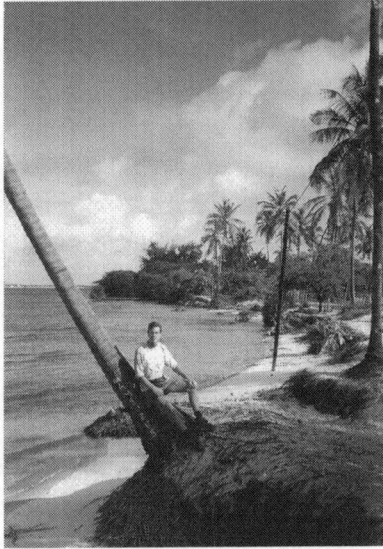

We got there in the end, and the beach was beautiful, light-blue sea and palm trees. The only thing spoiling it was the tourists (as it's a fairly expensive holiday resort). We spent most of the day drinking beer and lying around in the sun. Some local woman came around selling bananas and was after Seth's cock (no chance). I ended up buying some grass for just over a quid (worth about £30 in England) and got stoned on the beach.

On the way back to Mombasa, we had 5 black birds sitting behind us, all dolled up, on their way to a nightclub. They were all over me and Seth (probably prostitutes). We were glad to get off the bus. Went to bed at 8.30 p.m. knackered.

11 October 1992, Mombasa, Kenya

Caught the bus to Malindi this morning with Seth (2½ hours). We'd only been off the bus for 5 minutes when we had a couple of local girls following us and whistling.

Malindi is an old coastal town, and I spent the afternoon on the beach and wandering around the town. We both went around several local bars tonight, down the back streets, in which loud music blasted out, and half the people in there were rat-arsed.

12 October 1992, Malindi, Kenya

I cut my leg open in Egypt over a week ago, and ever since, it's been getting worse. It's now septic and full of puss, and the gland at the top of my leg is swelling up. I had a couple of large joints before catching a 6-hour bus to Lamu. We had to wait for over half an hour while someone fixed the bus before we could leave. The journey was a real boneshaker (a very bad road). We had to stop along the way as a large herd of wild antelope crossed the road.

After the bus, I had to catch a 20-minute ferry to the island of Lamu. Lamu is a very old town in which there are no cars or motorbikes, etc. Everyone gets around by donkey, walking, or dhow (ancient sailboat).

I got a room with an English bloke living in South Africa. We had a walk along the coast until we reached the beach—very scenic. After sunset, we caught a boat back. Out hotel is right on the harbour front, and sitting on the balcony tonight was very relaxing as there was a full moon right opposite me, glistening on the water. Had a few joints and took it all in. Had a massive plate of yellowfin tuna, chips, and salad, for just over a quid—good meal.

13 October 1992, Island of Lamu, Kenya

Woke up this morning feeling very weak and sick. I'd already arranged a fishing trip, so I went on it, hoping to feel better along the day. The fishing trip cost K$H150 (£2.30). It was on an old dhow. We sailed for over an hour before we started fishing for red snapper, using a line with a prawn as bait—I didn't catch anything, but the old man caught several.

We then stopped off at Manda Island—great beach—while the old boy cooked his fish and prepared lunch. I still felt very sick and weak and just wanted to get back. I didn't have anything to eat, and the sail back was a nightmare.

Got back at 3 p.m. and spent the rest of the day in bed. I feel as if I have some form of fever. I've got to go to the hospital tomorrow anyway because my septic leg is getting worse.

14 October 1992, Island of Lamu, Kenya

Got up this morning feeling a lot better yet still went to the hospital. At the reception, they told me it would cost K$H40. I pretended I knew someone who came last week and didn't have to pay, so they let me in for only K$H20 (you can even barter at hospitals). There was only one doctor on duty today, and there were over 30 people in the queue. After waiting for 2 hours to get my bad leg sorted out, I was 6th in the queue, and I kept wondering why no one was behind me. Then the doctor came out and said that it was now lunchtime and to come back in 1½ hours (bollocks). So when I came back, there was a new queue to join. I finally managed to see the doc, who only gave me a prescription for some antibiotics. I went downstairs to get them (another queue), and we all had to wait an hour for it to open. So it took me all day to get some pills for my leg.

15 October 1992, Island of Lamu, Kenya

Tom and I were up early to catch the 8-hour bus to Mombasa. I rolled a couple of spliffs to make the journey more bearable. After the half-hour ferry to the mainland, we caught our bus—very rough and bumpy. We stopped off at a small town called Witu after a couple of hours. A small town in the middle of nowhere—definitely a safe place for a quick spliff. I lit up right beside the bus and smoked it. I was almost finished when some lad came up to me and asked what I was smoking. Then some of his mates gathered around. The lad grabbed the joint out of my hand and started pulling me away from the bus. I struggled free and started fighting with them before realising that they were secret police in plain clothes. They started dragging me away to the police station. My bag was on the bus, yet I couldn't get it as I had some more grass in it—so I just shouted to Tom a hotel in Mombasa in which to leave it. I also had another joint in my cigarette packet, which I managed to get out and eat without anyone seeing me.

Everyone at the police station was an arsehole. They made me strip down to my shorts and started pushing me around. I thought they were going to beat me up. They took 4 sets of fingerprints and then threw me into a cell, really dark and grotty, completely empty apart from a few turds scattered around. I didn't know what was going to happen to me and was shitting myself.

I read in the paper last week that someone had been hanged for stealing. After a few hours, they took me out, handcuffed me, and took me back to Lamu. The worst thing about it was that we had to catch the bus there, so 3 armed guards walked me through the street, and we had to wait at the bus stop for half an hour. I felt such a prick standing there handcuffed. It wasn't long before I had a crowd of people around me just staring.

The bus arrived, and we all got on. Everyone on the bus was shocked to see me. I went 2 hours on the bus and half an hour on the ferry, handcuffed all the way back to Lamu, where I was thrown in jail. I shat myself when they opened the prison door. It was very dark, and I could see all these eyes staring at me. I was pushed in, with the door slamming behind me. Luckily, one of the blokes could speak English—he was in for virtually killing his wife with a club when he caught her with someone else. Another one was in for rape, another for stealing, and the 5th one was just pulled off the street by the police, who claimed that he was drunk.

After a few minutes inside, I could see better as my eyes got used to the dark. The cell was a total hellhole, covered in stale turds and piss, which acted as a sauna in the immense heat—it was like a sweat box as we're only less than 100 miles from the equator. We all had to lie around in the stale piss and shit on the floor, counting the minutes away. I was worried about my septic leg as it is an open cut and very septic. The guards kept treating us like animals and dirt. So humiliating. At mealtimes, we had a large scoop of sloppy shit called ugali, which I wouldn't feed my worst enemy—it's made from maize, with hardly any flavour, and you eat it with your fingers along with a grotty mug of stale water. When you watch the news on TV and you see starving people eating slop—that is ugali.

The night was very long and very rough (still very hot), and all you can smell is stale shit and piss (with a few fresh puddles in each corner). Luckily, there were only 5 of us in the cell (which was still crowded) as last night, there were 15 people crammed in. I was so fucked off with being here and so frustrated that if I had to spend more than a few days here, I'd definitely lost my mind. There are thousands of small bedbugs and creepy-crawlies hiding behind the flaking paint on the wall, and at night, they all come out, so you spend most of the night just scratching your body. As well as these, there are also mosquitoes and flies, which make it unbearable. The cell must have been rife with disease.

16 October 1992, Lamu Jail, Kenya

I hardly slept at all last night, rolling around on the sticky concrete floor and scratching myself every 5 minutes. I've never felt so disgustingly dirty. My hair feels like it's turning into dreadlocks. Woke up really early and couldn't get back to sleep again. I've never been so fucked off and felt so down in my life.

Breakfast came—3 slices of bread and a cup of tea. After a couple more hours (that seemed like days), I was taken out of the cell and escorted through the streets by 2 armed guards to court. Here I met the man who is directly below the judge—he seemed very friendly. Then came the catch. He wanted me to give him K$H 2,000 (about £35) in order for him to give me a low fine of about K$H 1500, telling me that an average fine is K$H 4000-6000. Bollocks. I'd been told by several people that the maximum fine would be about K$H 3000, though, because I was caught with a very small amount of grass left in my joint, that my fine would be about K$H 1500. So I didn't pay this corrupt tosser anything. It was a complete kangaroo court, with about 30 locals watching my case. My case was put across in a very bad way, saying that I was fighting with the police and that I should be made an example of.

My punishment was K$H 10,000 (US $300) or 12 months' hard labour in jail. I couldn't fucking believe how badly I'd been set up, paying nearly 10 times the amount I should have been fined just because I didn't give some arsehole a backhander. I wanted to run over and smash his face in, but I knew that if I did that, they would lock me up and throw away the key.

I had the chance to appeal, which meant that I would have to go back to jail for another week until my next court case came up, but there is no way that I'd survive another week in that hellhole without ending up permanently fucked up in the head. I had to wait for the next case to drag on and finish before the court was adjourned for 15 minutes. All I wanted was to pay my fine and fuck off, a free man again, but there weren't enough spare policemen to take me to the bank, so I had to sit in the court for another 2 hours, like a spare part, while the next case dragged on. I didn't have a clue what it was about as everyone was talking in Swahili.

Finally, the court adjourned again, and I managed to get a policeman to escort me to the bank. He kept telling me that he was doing me a favour (basically, he was after a backhander), so I played along with him until I got my money changed. Then I didn't need him any more and gave him a mouthful about how everyone in Kenya was after money all the fucking time. The cashier whom I had to pay the fine had gone to lunch, which meant that I had to go back to jail for an hour till he got back.

I'm so fucked off with this whole ordeal. It's really beginning to piss me off bad. Eventually, a guard took me down to pay my fine. I nearly smacked the bloke who tried to bribe me, but instead, humiliated him by shouting at him in front of his colleagues, asking why he wanted me to give him money—he soon shot off. I paid my fine (it was very hard handing over $300) but at the same time felt great to be a free man again.

Just as I was walking away, the high commissioner of Lamu came looking for me—he'd heard about my ordeal from contacts in

Nairobi and had come down to see me (an old English man in his late 80s). Half an hour later, I was drinking tea and eating scones at his place, while having my septic leg seen to. I could have stayed there all night, but I couldn't be arsed with all the nice talk (watching my Ps and Qs all the time). I went back to my old guest house and told Jermaine what had happened to me—he was great and let me stay the night for free, even taking me to his friend's house for some food.

17 October 1992, Mombasa, Kenya

Said goodbye to Jermaine and caught the 6.30 a.m. ferry in order to catch the bus to Mombasa (my second attempt). It felt so good to leave Lamu as most of the locals have seen me being escorted around the town in handcuffs, and they recognise me in the street. I'm still very edgy and very suspicious all the time—I suppose it may take some time to get over my stint in jail. My main concern now is to pick up my bag that Tom had left for me at Mombasa as Tom wasn't sure which hotel to leave it at.

I arrived at Mombasa very shaken and covered from head to toe in dust and couldn't believe it when my bag was waiting for me at the hotel. I changed some US Dollars on the black market in order to buy my train fare for Nairobi tonight. On my way to the train station, I met a Dutch woman. We got chatting, and we're both heading over to Uganda, then Rwanda, so decided to travel together for this period as it is much safer. Caught the 5 p.m. train to Nairobi and had several well-deserved beers that I'd looked forward to when in jail.

18 October 1992, Nairobi, Kenya

Supposed to arrive in Nairobi at 7.30 a.m. but being Kenya, we arrived at 9.30 a.m. (making the train journey 16½ hours). Monica (my temporary travelling partner) and I are off to climb Mount Kenya (the second highest in Africa at 5200 metres—about 3¼ miles above sea level). So we had to change more money on the black (which wasn't easy on a Sunday). We bought 7 days' worth of food, packed only essentials that we needed, and headed off to the bus station. On our way, some little shit jumped up and ripped my necklace off. I had my pack on, and my hands were full of various things, but I turned around and chased him for about 500 metres down the road until I realised that I still had my necklace on and that he'd just missed it. I turned around to walk back, and the whole street had come to a standstill, with me being the main attraction. Everyone came up to me to see if I was OK.

We finally got to the yard from where all the privately owned buses go, and straightaway, we had about 7 people run up to us asking us where we were going, trying to get us on their bus. They were almost coming to blows with each other. We got on the nearest bus going our way. You couldn't hear yourself think on the bus as Kenyan music was being blasted out the speakers so loud that it was very distorted and bassey. You have to wait on the bus till it fills up with people before it leaves. While the bus is waiting, you have at least three street vendors on the bus at anytime, walking up and down the aisle, selling anything from quilt covers, spades, watches, belts, bread, bottle openers—everything you could think of, and they don't understand why you say 'No' when they are trying to sell you a shovel.

Eventually, we got on our way, stopping off at a small friendly town called Embu along the way to have the exhaust pipe welded back on. The whole 6-hour journey to Chogoria, we had deafening African music blasted down our ears. We got dropped off in the middle of nowhere and had to walk for 15 minutes down a small track to the town of Chogoria. We both checked into a room, paid our money, then realised it was one bed. I went up the wall and asked for my money back. After half an hour of arguing, he finally gave in and gave us a room each.

19 October 1992, Chogoria, Kenya

Had a look around the small village of Chogoria before buying a few bananas, carrots, passion fruit, etc. for the trek up Mount Kenya. We paid a local man to take us up the first 15 km of the track. After he dropped us off and turned back, I felt for the first time that I was in Africa. We were stood on a dirt road with dense jungle either side of us, with various bird and animal sounds coming from all directions.

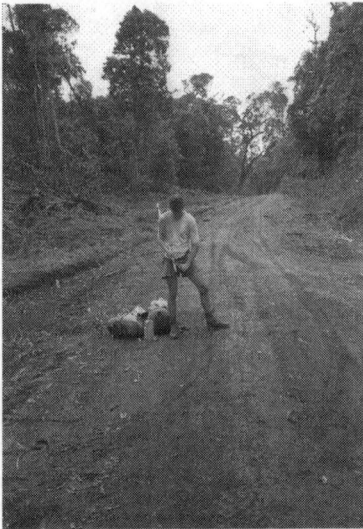

The first thing I did was to get a stick and sharpen the end, to protect myself against any wild animals that came my way. We walked for hours uphill to the entrance of the game reserve (15 km). Hard work yet interesting as the countryside kept changing the higher we climbed. Initially, it was a thick tropical jungle, turning into forest, then bamboo forest, and finally highland shrub (similar to that in the Scottish Highlands). All along the way, the trek was littered with elephant dung. There are plenty around here yet (thankfully) very shy. I also found a footprint in the mud, which, I found out later on, was that of a snow leopard. I kept stopping along the way to explore into the jungle etc. but didn't see anything.

We set up camp on a hillside, with a great view of shrub land below, where several deer and antelope were grazing. Sod's law—I put the tent on an ants' nest. No ordinary ants either as these bastards have big claws, and they know how to use them. I kept getting bit as I was sorting out the tent. Had a very rough night in the tent—firstly, the tent was on a slope, so I spent all night sliding down, ending up squashed in a ball near the tent entrance. Secondly, as we are so high up (10,000 feet), it gets very cold at night, and I could hardly sleep, it was so cold. My sleeping bag is meant only for summertime in England and so was about as much use as a paper bag. Finally, it pissed it down for half the night—the tent isn't waterproof. Hence, the inside of the tent got soaking wet.

20 October 1992, Kenya, 4-Day Trek to the Top of Mount Kenya

Woke up a physical wreck, crammed up in the corner of the tent, and pretty wet due to last night's rain. I was freezing cold, and it took me half an hour to thaw out a bit. Packed the tent away and had breakfast—squashed soggy bananas.

We entered the park and made our way along the track (mostly upwards). Very scenic until mid-morning, when the clouds and the mist came over, by which time you could only see about 10 metres in front of you—very weird and spooky (a bit like being in a set for a horror film). The path got steeper, which was very hard due to the altitude, making you go out of breath very easily. We couldn't see the top of the ridge we were climbing, which was just as well as it seemed to go on forever. There would have been some great views if it wasn't for the fact that we were walking in the clouds, as you could hear massive waterfalls about 100 metres away yet couldn't see a thing.

Things started getting tricky, especially when it started to rain, and we had to start climbing up rock faces, usually fairly safe yet a different story when wet. After about 9 hours of sheer sweat and effort, we finally made it to the 'Minto Hut' at about 14,500 feet above sea level. It was on a small plateau in the mountains—a very strange setting, weird tree-like plants everywhere. A turquoise lake and mountain matrix running about everywhere—similar in looks to a hamster yet the size of a large football. There was snow scattered everywhere. We were about 14,000 feet, which meant that it would be a lot colder tonight than last night (and it was). It even started snowing for a short while. The hut was very basic (made of corrugated iron). I spent most of the night shivering with cold and hardly sleeping at all and just lay there waiting for daylight so that I could get warm again.

21 October 1992, Kenya, 4-Day Trek to the Top of Mount Kenya

Got up at the crack of dawn (5.30 a.m.), freezing cold. It was still dark but was more or less daylight by the time we left.

My legs are so knackered from climbing that I found it very hard today. It was a tough 3 hours to the last hut. By the time I got there, I could hardly walk, breathe, or think. I was that exhausted. I had a few minutes' rest before leaving my rucksack and climbing the final peak. It was about a foot deep in snow and ice and on a very steep slope. I was falling about all over the place and didn't know where I was. After about an hour, I made it to the top. I was completely bollocked. Sod's law, as when I reached the top, the clouds moved in. I didn't really care. At least I'd made it to the top (it was all downhill from here). 3½ miles above sea level—it felt good.

I climbed down a glacier back to the hut and had to lie down for half hour to get some energy back. I think that this is by far the most physically demanding thing I've done (yet well worth it for the sense of achievement). It was great walking down the other side and felt so easy—even though it was raining. We arrived at a hut, where it cost $9 a night to stay. I gave the man a sob story about being ripped off in jail last week, so he let me off and even cooked me a hot meal—my first hot meal or drink in 3 days. We're back down to 14,000 feet and in a good solid hut, yet I still spent most of the night shaking with cold.

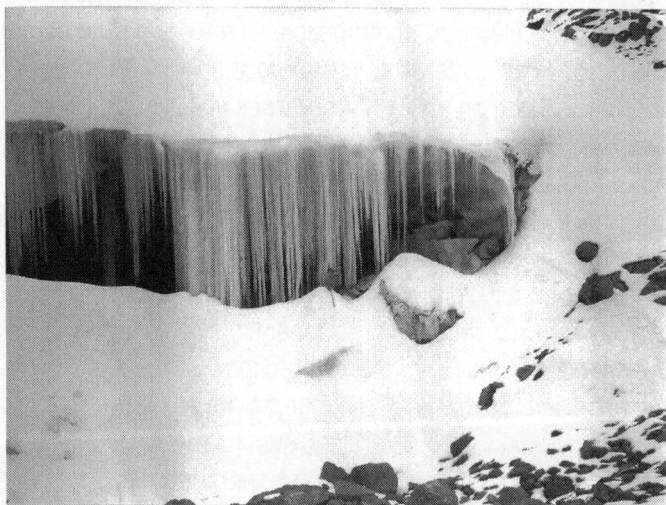

22 October 1992, Kenya, 4-Day Trek to the Top of Mount Kenya

Last and final day, and still a tough one as we had to go down across very steep marshland. It was raining fairly hard, and the marsh had virtually turned into a swamp. I spent about 3 hours crossing over it, up to my knees in mud and water half the time.

Arrived at the road, wet and very muddy, and managed to get a lift to the next town, Naro Moru, where I spent the next 4 hours in a matatu (minibus crammed with people about 3 times over the limit) on my way back to Nairobi. What a relief to get back to Nairobi—civilisation again (well, almost). I picked up some mail from Paula, had a hot meal, a shower, and then went straight to bed—my first decent night's sleep in 4 days.

23 October 1992, Nairobi, Kenya

I feel very fit after climbing Mount Kenya—but as a result, my feet are covered in blisters, and I'm finding it very hard to walk. My leg is also still septic from when I fell over in Egypt over 3 weeks ago.

A very busy day today—washed some clothes (only essentials that were beginning to rot and fester), got a Ugandan visa, $35, changed some money, got a Cholera vaccination, and a train ticket to Malaba for tomorrow. I also met some people who were on the same bus as me when I got arrested for smoking a spliff in Witu. They told me there had been an article in the paper about it, so I went down to the paper's head office in Nairobi and looked through the library pictures and couldn't believe it when I saw it. I ripped it out of the library copy and went down to the printers to get a few more copies. It was in a really grotty industrial estate, but I managed to get a few back copies for old time's sake—after all, it's all I have to show for $300. It was in the *Nation* newspaper (similar to the *Telegraph* in England), and I managed to get on page 3. They spelt my name wrong and used my middle name, but it's me all right.

Went out for a few beers tonight at the good old local Modern Green Bar. I'd only been in the place 5 minutes, and my arse and nipples were sore from all the AIDS-ridden slags molesting me. I had to sit in the corner to avoid them all. It's only about 23 pence for a (warm) bottle of strong beer—½ litre, so I treated myself to about ten bottles as I sat and chatted to the locals. Got completely rat-arsed and staggered home at about 3.30 a.m.

24 October 1992, Nairobi, Kenya

Got up this morning feeling very rough and hungover. I spent most of the morning sitting in a café, drinking black coffee until I caught the 3 p.m. (18-hour) train journey to Malaba—on the Uganda border. A very relaxing and scenic journey across the Great Rift Valley. Had a couple of beers on the train before going straight to bed.

25 October 1992, Malaba, Kenya

Got off the train at about 9 a.m. and walked through the small town of Malaba—a very friendly town with loads of money changers shouting at you from every direction to change your Kenyan shillings to Ugandan shillings.

It took about an hour to pass through both Kenyan and Ugandan customs. A lot of petty paperwork but no hassles. Walked through the border and got on a matatu and had to wait for an hour for it to fill up with enough people for us to leave. The journey took us 5 hours (including the waiting around), taking us past some very tropical areas—mud huts everywhere.

Arrived in Kampala (the capital) by mid-afternoon. Uganda is just recovering from a civil war which virtually destroyed half the country along with 300,000 people. As a result, most of the towns are still war-scarred slums with many derelict buildings almost everywhere—very sad yet interesting. Kampala is among one of the slummiest towns I have come across (outside India), with burnt-out buildings along the roadside. It is also the rainy season in Uganda at the moment, and the reddish-brown dirt roads become rivers every time it pours down (which is at least once a day).

I checked into the YMCA, which looked like a derelict building from the outside with broken windows—it turns out that it is an old school and still used as one during the day. My room (if you can call it that) was actually a classroom, and I had to clear some tables and chairs out of the way in order to lay my sleeping bag down, moving the blackboard in the process. I went to sleep virtually as soon as it got dark as there were no lights in the classroom.

26 October 1992, Kampala, Uganda

Had to get up at 7 a.m. and get out of the classroom before the school children arrived. The school is for 5—to 10-year-olds and looks more like a borstal. I went to the toilet, and there were turds rubbed all over the walls.

Because of the civil war here, inflation is really high (as much as 1,000% at one stage). The money is virtually useless, and you get nearly 2,000 Ugandan shillings to the pound. I changed $50 in the bank and got a massive wad of notes (about 120 notes), and they were in large nominations.

I got a matatu to Luwero (an area that the guerrillas were based in during the war and that the army completely wiped out, massacring everyone in the village and in villages in the neighboring area). A small village that has now been completely rebuilt. I wanted to visit one of the mass graves in which many people were buried but found out that you needed permission to go there, so I just walked to the village. Very interesting to see a small (typical) village, but they aren't used to white people and weren't exactly friendly.

Got a matatu back to Kampala and then from Kampala to Fort Portal (5 hours), a scenic drive until it got dark. The majority of the journey was on a rough dirt track. We were in the middle of nowhere, pitch black outside, and someone had just been telling me that there were still guerrillas killing people in the area, when all of a sudden, we came across over 50 men (in civilian clothes) walking down the road—all with rifles. I nearly shot my load when they stopped the matatu as I thought they were going to kill us all. Luckily, they were civilians being trained as part of their national service—*whew!*

Arrived at Fort Portal at about 10 p.m. Found a cheap tacky hotel and went straight to bed.

27 October 1992, Fort Portal, Uganda

After half an hour of bartering with the local drivers, I finally managed to hire a vehicle to take me 60 km through the Ruwenzori Mountains (a very rough 2-hour drive through the mountains along the Zaire border). Along the way, we passed dozens of mud huts and visited a hot spring. Then after driving through dense rainforest, we arrived at a Pigmy tribe camp in the Semiliki valley. I felt like a giant walking around the pigmys (most of them are about 4 feet tall), although there were a few taller ones who had mixed blood in them). They tried to sell me various tribal items that they'd made, including a big bag of grass for about 25 pence, worth well over £100 in England. I was very tempted, but after being put in jail for it in Kenya, I wasn't going to risk it. Spent 2 hours driving back through the mountains to Fort Portal.

Once back, I had to wait on another matatu for over an hour until it was crammed with enough people for us to leave. The journey should have only taken one hour yet took 3 hours as we broke down 2 times. It was absolutely pissing down, and the poor driver had to get out and fix it. Eventually arrived at Kasese (a beautiful town in the mountains). I went to check into a hotel and was told that I must first register with the police. The police station was over a kilometre away. When I got there, the twat wanted to take all my passport details down, see my currency declaration form, and asked me lots of pathetic questions before writing a letter to the hotel, giving me permission for me to stay there—what a load of bollocks. Then after that, he wanted me to buy him a beer—I told the twat to get on his bike.

The hotel was a right shithole but cheap—the showers and toilet didn't work, and the bed was full of bugs. I was scratching so much, I had to sleep on the floor.

28 October 1992, Kasese, Uganda

Got up at the crack of dawn (again). I'm totally shattered from spending about 6 hours a day going from place to place—it's wearing me out. I could really do with a day's rest yet can't afford the time if I've got to get to South Africa in time to meet Paula (5½ weeks to travel across 7 large and very slow countries). I should have a rest day today as I have only got to travel for just over an hour down the road to Katwe (the entrance to Queen Elizabeth National Park).

I managed to get on the back of a truck going that way, but he spent nearly 2 hours twating around, picking up various items of merchandise, (mostly sacks of maize) with me in the back, before telling me that he had to delay his trip until the afternoon (what a waste of fucking time). So I had to go back to the matatu park and wait on the back of another truck until enough people got on the back (only another hour). Thank God that we were finally on our way, but it was crammed full of people and huge sacks of maize powder. We'd only got about 10 minutes down the road when we stopped again and filled the back of the truck with even more large sacks of maize and massive branches of green bananas. The back of the truck was overhanging with people and luggage. I had to stand up and hang on to the top of the truck. Even so, it was a good drive through savannah, with lots of gazelles and antelopes along the way.

Finally arrived at the National Park gate 5 hours after leaving my hotel (it should have only taken one hour). I got to the entrance and was told that I had to wait for a vehicle to pass through the park to take me to the lodge (about 8 km away) but that I'd probably have to wait several hours for a vehicle. Bollocks to that. I decided to walk (after being advised not to as there are many lions, elephants, buffalo, etc. in the park, and it is dangerous to walk). I began to walk (keeping my knife handy) and spotted several lions' paw prints along the track—but only saw a few antelope and wild boar.

It was getting very hot, so I stopped to rub some suntan lotion on my face. Before I finished, it began to absolutely piss it down with rain—I had to shelter under a bush for quarter of an hour. I eventually got to the lodge after spending over 2 hours walking in the hot sun, with my full pack on. I was supposed to report to the ranger and pay $5 to camp the night but sneaked past and camped right out of sight next to a lake. The lake was full of hippos, and all you could hear was them grunting at each other—one even ran past my tent. Went to bed as soon as it got dark—knackered.

29 October 1992, Queen Elizabeth National Park, Uganda

It pissed down last night, and my tent is wet. I got up at 5.45 a.m. in order to take one last look at the hippos and sneak out of the park before the ranger found me and charged me for last night. I got out OK and spent an hour walking out of the park before managing to get a lift the rest of the way. From there, I had to wait an hour for a truck to come past and give me a lift to Katumbra (one hour), where I caught a 6-hour bus (which seemed to take all day) to Kabale. I planned to cross from here over to Rwanda, but fighting has broken out again, and the border is closed—another spanner in the works. Now I'll probably have to spend an extra 2 days travelling from Uganda to Tanzania to Rwanda (time that I can't afford).

Managed to find a very good hotel—nice room, balcony with view over the town, and friendly staff, for only 50 pence (U$H 1,000) a night.

30 October 1992, Kabale, Uganda

Got up early in order to have a look around Kabale and several beauty spots around the mountains. I was just about to go when it began pissing it down with rain (for about 2 hours), so I had to give it a miss and catch a matatu to Mbarrara and then to Masaka—near the Tanzanian border that I hope to cross. Both journeys only took 4 hours in total, yet it took most of the day due to the hanging around, waiting for the vehicles to fill up. In the first car, we managed to squeeze 12 people into it, including 4 in the front—it was a good job we didn't crash (although we came very close to it several times).

I arrived at Masaka with hardly any money left as I don't want to change any more because I'm leaving Uganda tomorrow. I haven't got enough money to afford both the bus to the border and a hotel for the night, so I had to give the woman at the hotel a sob story. In the end, she let me sleep on the floor for a fraction of the price. Some Friday night! No money, no beer, very hungry, and no food, and I have to sleep on the floor—good night.

31 October 1992, On the Way to the Tanzanian Border, Uganda

Got up very early again this morning in order to catch a couple of matatus to the border of Tanzania. Along the way to the matatus park, I passed several bombed-out buildings—completely destroyed, with the odd bullet hole in the wall (more reminders of their civil war).

Caught a matatu to a town halfway to the border and then didn't have enough money for the next matatu—I had to barter with the man for 5 minutes before he let me on. It was a really run-down matatu, with cardboard replacing half the windows. We had to wait 1½ hours before it left, but it got us there.

Arrived at the border crossing at about midday and got through both border crossings within an hour. I had a bit of hassle trying to change money on the black market because the rate was fairly bad—got some changed in the end (only $10) and caught a Land Rover to a place only 2½ hours away, although very rough dirt roads all the way. I'd heard that the transport system in Tanzania was very unreliable, which was proved when the Land Rover broke down. The suspension went at the front, and we all had to wait on the side of the road for 3 hours, while the driver bashed it with a massive hammer and ended up doing a complete bodge job on it, tying it back together with rope and a log. Eventually, we got going again and ended up stopping later on when we got a puncture, getting to Bukoba in the late afternoon.

Changed some more money on the black market (for a better rate $1—TSh 400) and then waited around for several hours before catching the night ferry across Lake Victoria to Mwanza. I had to pay $5 port tax (a complete rip-off) before boarding the ferry. I told the customs officer that I was a resident in Tanzania (even though I'd only been in the country half a day) and that I was a doctor visiting the poor areas of the country, helping the people out. So in the end (after a small bribe), I ended up paying about 75 cents.

The lake was massive and was more like the sea—we sailed at 9 p.m. I hung around on deck for a while before going to sleep in my cabin.

1 November 1992, Ferry Across Lake Victoria, Tanzania

Got up at the crack of dawn in order to catch the sunrise over Lake Victoria (not bad).

Arrived at Mwanza at 7 a.m. and made my way straight to the train station. There were loads of people queuing, but everything was closed up, so I went to a knackered old cafe and sat there for about 3 hours, drinking cups of tea for about 4 pence a cup. In the end, I bought my train ticket which leaves for Dodoma in 6 hours' time, so I went down to Lake Victoria and lazed around in the sun for several hours. Very hot, and I couldn't go in the lake because it contains Bilharziasis. It's the first time in a long time that I've been able to lie around and do sweet FA.

Arrived at the train station at 5 p.m. with sunburn. The train takes 26 hours to get to Dodoma, but as long as I'm moving south, I don't really mind. I'm going to be travelling everyday, going straight across Tanzania—I expect it to take about a week (although it will probably feel like a month as the transport system in Tanzania is very rough and unreliable). Hard travelling.

There are 6 people to a cabin in the train, and it got very hot and sweaty.

Day 59: 2 November 1992, Train to Dodoma, Tanzania

Could hardly sleep in the train as it was very hot, with a few people snoring next to me. One bloke came in pissed and started talking very loud. I was knackered and got pissed off when everyone got up at 6 a.m. and started shouting, etc., even turning up the radio to full volume.

The day seemed to drag on and on and on. It was very hot, and there wasn't alot to see from the train as the countryside was a very dry savannah with many dry bushes. It got a bit better later on when we passed through the Great Rift Valley, but nothing to shoot my load over.

The train finally arrived at Dodoma at 7 p.m.—I was glad to get off the train after spending 26 long hours on it. I spent nearly an hour, waiting around Dodoma (knackered), trying to find a cheap hotel that had a spare room. I got one in the end—it wasn't fit for a pig to sleep in, but I was just happy to find somewhere. I walked around the bus station, trying to organise a bus for Iringa tomorrow, but hardly anyone could speak English. I managed to get one in the end, great value at TSh 1,000 (£1.60) for an 8-hour journey. I can't believe how cheap it is here. I spent about 50 pence on 2 plates of rice and beans and 4 cups of tea and couldn't move because I was too full. Back at the hotel, my room had a massive swarm of mosquitoes. I lit about 10 mosquito coils to get rid of them. The whole room was full of smoke. I could hardly breathe, yet the mosquitoes were still there, so I gave up as a bad job.

3 November 1992, Bus to Iringa, Tanzania

Got down to the bus station for 8.30 a.m. (departure time) and had to wait an hour for the bus to turn up. Luckily, I had a seat reserved as there were nearly as many people standing as there were sitting. It was very hot and crowded—a long 8-hour (uncomfortable) journey over dirt roads. I couldn't bear it inside the bus as there were dozens of kids on board, and when one starts crying, they all start. Another kid near me threw up all over his clothes. After about an hour, I climbed out of the window and lay on the bags on top of the roof—brilliant, lying in the sun, watching the Tanzanian scenery pass by (although very bumpy).

Typical Africa—we'd only been travelling about 2 hours when the bastard bus broke down. We were in the middle of nowhere apart from a small tribal village just beside the road. As usual in Africa, when the bus broke down, the driver got a very large metal sledgehammer and started bashing it as hard as he could against the front wheel (apparently the bearings had gone). The driver said it would be a long time, so I walked right out into the countryside. Very dry and remote. In the distance, I could see local men herding their cattle across the plains, kicking dust up everywhere. There were baobab trees everywhere. Had to come back after a couple of hours as my nose was almost purple with sunburn. Waited around for several more hours and still no sign of the bus being repaired. When it got dark, I got some wood together and built a fire. I bought a few bottle of 'port wine' from a dingy shop looking like a shed. The wine was 24% volume and tasted like vinegar but did the job. About 10 local tribesmen came past at about 10 p.m., all pissed on their local brew. Black Box was playing on the bus, and they all started dancing to it. By 11 p.m. I was very merry and just about to fall asleep by the fire when the bus was ready for leaving. I climbed on the roof of the bus and made myself comfortable as the bus drove through the night. A greet feeling being pissed, looking up at the moon and stars while helping myself to free sodas that were part of the cargo on the rooftop.

4 November 1992, Bus to Iringa, Tanzania

Woke up on top of the bus, covered from head to toe in dirt, and with my back almost bent in two. I felt rough as hell. Driving across the dirt roads, taking in all the scenery, all of a sudden, I got the shits (very bad). I had to go there and then. I had to crouch over a plastic bag, with my shorts around my ankles, hanging on to the top of the bus as it bounced up and down over the dirt road. What a relief to get it out (and manage to get it all in the bag). I threw the bag on to the road, and there were a group of kids nearby who saw me throw it. They must have thought I'd dropped something as they all ran over to the bag, ripping it open to see what it was!

Finally arrived in Iringa at 8 a.m.—not a minute too soon. The bus to Mybaya left in 5 hours' time (and it was standing-room only for 6 hours), so I decided to hitch-hike. There wasn't much traffic, and I walked for ages in the heat, with my full pack on. In the end, a local bus came past, so I got on it—it was going halfway to Mybaya. I was glad to be moving again. However, the 3-hour journey was very uncomfortable as I had to stand all the way, and the roof was too low, giving me a sore neck. Finally got there and had to wait 2 hours for the bus I was originally going to catch from Iringa. There were about 70 people waiting on the side of the road for the bus (which was already crammed with people). I thought I'd never get on. There was mass panic when the bus turned up, and everyone tried to get on. I used the local tactics and pushed and shoved everyone else out of the way to eventually get on board. The bus was so crammed with people that many didn't get on. There must have been about 130 people (plus luggage) all crammed on to the bus. I was standing up again for the whole 3 hours—very uncomfortable as the bus was so packed, I couldn't move (or even bend my legs). It was very hot and humid, especially when some kid was sick all over herself and her mother. What a relief to finally arrive in Mybaya.

Day 62: 5 November 1992, Bus to Malawi Border, Tanzania

Caught a bus to a small town halfway to the Malawi border, where I had to hang around before catching another bus. The road was very dry, and I was covered in dust by the time I got off. I got off 5 km before the Malawi border and had to walk the rest. As soon as I got off the bus, I had about 15 kids with pushbikes fighting over each other to give me a backy to the border. I chose the one with the comfiest seat and climbed on the back (with my full rucksack on). The poor lad was sweating buckets as he peddled in the heat, uphill and against the wind. I gave him 30 pence for his efforts.

What a relief to finally arrive at the Malawi border after 6 days solid of hard travelling across Tanzania. I'd heard that this Malawi border was hard to cross—girls must wear long skirts, lads must have long trousers. If you've got long hair, they cut it off. My guide book is illegal in Malawi, so I ripped it apart last night and hid sections that I needed in my tent. They didn't even search me at the border. I just passed straight through and caught a matatu to Karonga—it was luxury after Tanzania to be on a Tarmac road again.

Arrived in Karonga and went straight down to Lake Malawi. The lake is just like the sea. It's a massive clear blue freshwater lake

with beaches and even waves. I had a swim and lazed around in the
sun, taking a long-deserved rest. In the evening, I went to a local
bar and got pissed on bottles of Carlsberg (4.7%) at about 30
pence per bottle. By closing time, half the locals were asleep in the
bar, while I was pissed and staring at the 1000s of ants running
around all over the bar.

6 November 1992, Livingstonia, Malawi

Caught the bus to Livingstonia (the local bus, which meant that
it stopped every 100 metres). It took 3 hours to get there. There's
a hard 10-mile walk (climb) to get to the top of Livingstonia (similar
to the Lake District). There are no buses as the road is too steep.
I was told at the bottom that a jeep was going up in about an hour,
and I could get a lift. So I waited in the cafe at the bottom for over
3 hours—still no lift. In the end, I decided to walk. It was hard going
with all my gear on my back and the heat. I was just dripping with
sweat. It was worth the effort as the higher I climbed, the better
the view of the lake became. I'd been sweating my bollocks off for
over 2 hours, and it was just getting dark when a jeep pulled up
and offered me a lift—I turned the ride down as I thought I was
nearly there, not knowing that I was only just over halfway. I walked
another couple of hours in the dark—not knowing where the hell
I was and getting very tired and pissed off as I was beginning to
get blisters. I walked straight past the campsite and didn't realise
until I'd walked on for another 20 minutes, so by the time I'd walked
back, I'd gone an extra 40 minutes out of my way.

I was so glad to arrive at the campsite, especially as someone had
cooked up a big pot of rice and tomatoes, and I managed to get a
large plate of it. Went to sleep completely knackered, too tired to
put my feet up. I just slept under the stars.

Day 64: 7 November 1992, Livingstonia, Malawi

Had a large plate of pancakes for breakfast before heading
over to the manchewe waterfall with all my gear. I sat down there
for a couple of hours, taking in the views. I met a doctor from

California—Kurt (38). We both walked down to the main road (another 10 long miles), passing small communities of mud huts along the way. Finally got down to the main road and waited a couple of hours to catch the express bus to Mzuzu (3 hours).

From here, we found a cheap dormitory, 1 kwacha per night, including breakfast (10 pence). Kurt and I went to check the nightlife out—3 bars/nightclubs next door to each other, all packed with locals pissed as farts. We went into the 'Fuka Fuka' nightclub—an amazing and wild place full of local characters drinking themselves silly. I was drinking bottles of Carlsberg Special Brew for 30 pence a bottle. African music was blasting out full pelt with all the locals bopping away to it—I've never seen so many sights in one place. We went to the other bars. Same old story—everyone drunk and enjoying themselves. I got pissed on about £2 and went back to the dorm—full of local dropouts. I had my rucksack locked away for the night but still managed to get my tracksuit and trainers stolen during the night—the bastards!

8 November 1992, Nkhata Bay, Malawi

Woke up this morning when someone in the dorm started to have an epileptic fit. I was still drunk and pissed off with having my tracksuit and trainers stolen.

Got a matatu to Nkhata Bay—a small scenic village alongside Lake Malawi. From here, we walked to Chikale Beach 2 km away—a great little half-deserted beach beside the lake. I put my tent up on the beach and spent the rest of the day lazing around in the sun. A well-deserved rest as I've been travelling for almost everyday for the last month since leaving Lamu (Kenya), and I'm about shagged. It's just good to be in one place for a few days, especially here, one of my favourite places. I just lazed around on the beach all day, going browner in the sun. Occasionally, local children came past selling food (mangoes, banana cake, filled rolls, bread, etc). All you have to do here is jump in the lake every half an hour to cool off.

I'm having real problems in Malawi trying to change money on the black market (you can get up to 25% more this way). I went around town this afternoon but couldn't find anyone willing to change. I went down to the beach and bought a couple of fairly big butterfish, took them back to my tent, cut them up, and cooked them on an open fire right outside my tent on an old pan I'd managed to scrounge. I also bought a load of grass wrapped in bark for about £1.80 (worth about £500 in England. There's loads of the stuff). I got stoned and ate the fish before lying my sleeping bag outside and going to sleep on the sand next to my fire—no mosquitoes either.

Day 66: 9 November 1992, Nkhata Bay, Malawi

Woke up at 4.45 a.m. (sunrise). Had a quick swim and went back to sleep on the beach. Got stoned this morning and had the munchies really bad. Some local boy came around selling pieces of banana cake. I ended up buying the whole cake and pigging all of it within 20 minutes.

I've still got my septic leg from a cut I got in Egypt over 6 weeks ago—it's not getting any worse, but neither is it getting any better. Along with that, I've got a weird form of septic scab infection spreading over my legs—I've no idea what it is.

Another day doing bollock nothing—I was going to catch the ferry tonight going down to Monkey Bay, but it takes 2 days and is fairly rough travelling, and I need some comfort for a while after going hell for leather across Uganda and Tanzania.

I bought another fish tonight, filleted it in the sea, then cooked it over the fire—this is what life is all about. Then I got stoned and went snorkelling with a big flashlight I'd borrowed and a face mask—very different to the day.

10 November 1992, Bus to Lilongwe, Malawi

Woke up on the beach again and bought various foods from the local kids on the beach—life is so easy here. I packed my tent away, and Kurt, Monica, and myself walked back to Nkhata Bay, where we caught a bus to Mzuzu. Then from Mzuzu to Lilongwe (7 hours), we caught the express (fast) bus, so it was only half full, giving us loads of room to lounge around. We all had some of my grass. Then about ten minutes later, we had a police check on the side of the road. We had to get off the bus and take all our bags with us—shit. I had to hide all my grass (loads of it) plus my pipe down the side of the bus before I got out. I got away with it, but it shit me up a bit, especially after my bad experience in Kenya.

We all got back on the bus, and I gave the driver my U2 tape to play. A great journey, sprawled over 4 seats in the bus, sun in my face, stoned off my face, listening to U2. It just knocked me out for about 3 hours until I got woken up at Lilongwe. Kurt and Monica were also very stoned and having difficulty in walking, talking, etc. We seemed to be walking around in a daze for ages until we found a room.

I was totally bollocked and fell on the bed as soon as the door opened. We had some strange-looking character who followed us into the room, closed the door, and said, 'Right, now let's talk business'. I nearly burst out laughing—who was this prick? Apparently, he was a local dude who wanted to change money with us on the black market. We were too out of it to even consider changing money. Kurt kicked him out, and we all crashed out to sleep even though it was only 5 p.m.

11 November 1992, Lilongwe, Malawi

Woke up this morning still stoned from yesterday's bus trip—I slept for 14 hours last night, not including the 3 hours on the bus.

I'm going to Monkey Bay today, but there is only one bus, and that is in the morning. I decided to miss it and give Paula a ring. First of all, I I went to the post office—no mail. Then I tried to phone Paula. By the time I'd been connected, she'd gone to work, and no one was at home—a waste of a morning.

Lilongwe is very expensive, and I just wanted to get out of town and get to Monkey Bay. I caught a bus to the Mangochi turn-off—a 3-hour bus ride but very interesting as the road drove along the Malawi-Mozambique border for about 50 km. On the right hand side (Mozambique), there were only a few derelict buildings, burnt and shot down as a result of their 13-year civil war that is still going on. The whole area was deserted. While on the left hand side (Malawi), there were lots of large villages full of Mozambique refugees. You could see mud huts as far as the eye could see in some areas.

We arrived at the Mongochi turn-off at 5.30 p.m. and got hassled straightaway by money changers and local traders trying to sell to us. We hitched alongside the road for half an hour before getting a lift in one of the few cars in this country. He wanted us to pay 7 kwacha each, but I got him down to 5—the same price as the bus. He took us 80 km down the road to Mongochi. He drove like a madman in the dark and never spoke once. We got dropped off in the dark and tried to hitch to Monkey Bay—only 70 km away, but very little traffic. We tried for an hour and had a group of about 8 kids hanging around, all taking the piss. We were just about to give up and find somewhere to camp when a Land Rover stopped and gave us a lift to Monkey Bay (5 kwachas each). It took us most of the day to get here, but as least we got here. Found a cheap room, dumped my bags, and spent 1½ hours walking around looking for somewhere to buy food—no chance. It was 8 p.m. The whole town was closed.

12 November 1992, Cape MacLear, Malawi

Got up this morning and had a look around Monkey Bay before trying to give Paula another call. 36 kwacha for 3minutes (£5.50). I tried to catch Paula before she went to work. I got connected, and Laura picked up the bastard phone. So I ended up shouting down the phone for 3 minutes, trying to tell little Laura to pass the phone to someone—I got very pissed off and ended up swearing very loudly down the phone. Then my 3 minutes were up, and I got cut off—what a waste of fucking time. I was so pissed off that I phoned back, this time reversing the charges. I got through to Sarah (Paula's mum) and had a chat with her—Paula was out trying to get her car repaired, so after all my effort and frustration, I still never managed to speak to her.

We managed to get on one of the few daily vehicles going to Cape MacLear. Hanging off the back of a combi van along with about 10 locals. It's a very dry windy dirt road through the hills. Arrived in Cape MacLear—a great little beauty spot right alongside Lake Malawi. Golden beaches, turquoise water—what more can I say? Cape MacLear is a small tribal village full of mud and straw huts. The people are very friendly and always smiling. We got a small hut just on the beach. It's nice to settle down in a place for a while after being constantly on the move. I'm getting to stay here a few days before moving on to Zambia and the Victoria Falls. I spent most of the day lazing around in the sun before exploring the local village and finding a small cafe, where you can buy pints of tea. Since I began travelling, I've managed to get a sweet tooth and now have 3 tablespoons of sugar in my tea.

Went back to the hut. Had a joint and a few beers (warm) in the candlelight as there isn't any electricity in this area. Took my sleeping bag out with me and went to sleep on the beach next to the lake.

Day 70: 13 November 1992, Cape MacLear, Malawi

Had a good night's sleep on the beach—the only trouble being that sunrise is about 4.45 a.m. and once it's light, I'm awake. If anything, this place is too hot, and between 8 a.m. and 4 p.m. you can't walk barefoot in the sand as it really burns your feet bad.

Kurt and I went scuba-diving today off one of the tropical islands in Lake Malawi. The motorboat broke down, so we ended up rowing the boat to the dive site. A lot of the tropical fish in this part of the lake are exported all over the world, so you can imagine how colourful it was underwater. We did a backward roll ascent into the lake (it was like a bath with the surface temperature at 27°C). There were 5 of us, including the dive master. The dive was good but not as good as the Great Barrier Reef or the Red Sea. We went down to 15 metres, where a few people saw a freshwater snake swimming around. An interesting dive—especially as it was in a freshwater lake. You can swim around and drink the water.

Came back to surface after 35 minutes and climbed back on the boat, where we threw dead fish into the lake and watched the massive sea eagles swoop down and grab the fish. It was great just to be away from Monica (the Dutch girl who has been following me for the last four weeks since Kenya) for a few hours. I'm so fucked off with her but haven't got the heart to tell her to piss off. I've never met anyone so dopey or thick—she's 27 years old and a vet. I don't know how as she's got no common sense. She's got no sex appeal whatsoever—in fact, since meeting her, my sex drive has really gone down, and I hardly think about it any more. She's really trying hard to get into my pants—not a chance in hell. I feel physically sick just thinking about it. Kurt's also getting very pissed off with her—she's just like a vegetable, no mind of her own, hardly speaks, and couldn't organise a fuck up in a brothel. It's like travelling with a child as I have to organise everything. I'm really beginning to get fed up with her—especially as people think she's my girlfriend.

Got back and went for a walk along the beach and watched the sun set over the mountains. Had another meal of rice and beans, a couple of joints, and a few beers, then lay on my sleeping bag on the beach, staring at the stars and listening to the waves crash on to the beach. Only another 25 days until I meet Paula in Johannesburg—I can't wait.

14 November 1992, Cape MacLear, Malawi

Up at 5 a.m. again on the beach, another day doing sweet FA—sun, sand, and warm bottles of Carlsberg Special Brew (5.7%) for 2 kwacha, 40 tambala a bottle (thirty pence). Almost paradise.

Kurt and I managed to shake off Monica and went to our local hang-out—a small cafe where you can get a pint of tea for 6 pence (with about 3 tablespoons of sugar in it). We've been here several times and never seen anyone else use it. Kurt and I had about 3 pints of tea each before walking through the village, with about 10 local kids following us.

Spent most of the day stoned, lying in the sun and drinking pints of tea, recovering from all my bone-shaking journeys. I like this place, but it's the place you would appreciate more if you were with a woman—certainly not Monica, who seems to be coming on stronger to me each day. Kurt feels sorry for me.

Well, we organised a BBQ on the beach tonight with a local boy—we cooked a large catfish, cooked over the fire on the beach, along with rice, tomatoes, and onions. It wasn't too bad, but I'd spent most of the day eating mangoes and buns with peanut butter and syrup, so I wasn't too hungry. Since arriving in Malawi, I've spent most of my time eating as it's so cheap and available—it also passes the time of day. Had a few beers and crashed on the beach again.

15 November 1992, Cape MacLear, Malawi

Woke up at 4.45 a.m. on the beach with the sunrise. Had a couple of pints of tea at one of the local mud-hut cafes. I got talking to one of the locals last night and arranged to hire his dugout canoe today. I waited on the beach with Kurt and Cling-on (the dopey Dutch girl who follows me everywhere). The local turned up in his dugout canoe, and we rowed along the beach to a very scenic spot called Otters Point—a larger lagoon full of massive boulders and beautiful turquoise water. I spent a few hours snorkelling in the lagoon and around the rocks. There were lots of colourful fish, and the water was crystal clear.

We paddled back to Cape MacLear for lunch. I ordered a plate of rice and beans and had to wait 2 hours until it was finally ready. In the afternoon, we paddled over to a small channel between a peninsular and a small island. It didn't look very far but took over an hour to paddle there. Spent the rest of the day lazing around before paddling back, stopping off on the way to visit a small tribal village of mud huts and local characters. There is no electricity here in Cape MacLear, so there isn't a lot to do once it gets dark (6 p.m.) apart from drinking beer and getting stoned in the candlelight or on the beach. Got my sleeping back out and slept on the beach again.

16 November 1992, Cape MacLear, Malawi

Spent most of the morning hanging around trying to get a lift back to Monkey Bay. Cape MacLear is in the middle of nowhere, alongside Lake Malawi, so there weren't many vehicles on the road. I waited 3½ hours until the first vehicle came past and gave me a lift—I was going to phone Paula up from Monkey Bay but got there only minutes too late (she'd already gone to work). So instead, I spent the money on a couple of attractive modern art wood carvings (about £6 for the pair—my first real souvenir of Africa).

Kurt, Monica, and I got a single room in the government rest house as the prices had gone up 50% since we were here 5 days ago. Spent most of the day talking to Kurt, taking the piss out of Monica (who is really getting on my nerves), and smoking joints. Africa's really beginning to wear me out. Whenever you ask people directions, bus times, etc. they all give you different answers—it's no wonder the countries so fucked up. No one's got a clue about anything. Everytime you go to a cafe or restaurant, they give you the menu. After 5 minutes of looking at it and deciding what you want, they tell you that they only have eggs and bread.

Kurt and I fell out with Monica tonight. Kurt called her a 'fucking arsehole' twice. She's dying to get in my pants and is always nice to me no matter how bad I treat her, but I've never met anyone with so little sex appeal and so little character—she relies on me for everything. I feel a bit sorry for her as I think I've given her an inferiority complex. Kurt and I had several (very warm) beers tonight before sleeping outside on the beach.

17 November 1992, Monkey Bay, Malawi

After asking 10 people yesterday what time the bus left to Lilongwe and getting several different replies (typical of Africa), we managed to catch the bus (at 5.30 a.m.). It was a local bus full of people and took 7 hours (although it seemed a lot longer) to arrive in Lilongwe. Along the way, we passed several stops in which locals sold food to the people on the bus. One of the food items was BBQ mice on a stick. I would have tried it, but it still had its fur on.

All 3 of us got a room near the bus station—Kurt and I leave for Zambia tomorrow. Monica is not coming (only because I told her Dutch citizens were not allowed in the country). She was making an all-out attempt to get in my pants, so I went to bed early and left Kurt with her. As a last resort, she ended up climbing into bed with Kurt in the hope of a shag. Kurt just rolled over and went to sleep.

Day 75: 18 November 1992, Bus to Lusaka, Zambia

What a relief. Kurt and I left Monica and caught the 6 a.m. bus to Lusaka in Zambia. It took us a couple of hours on an old bumpy bus to get to Lusaka—we had to stop off for 1½ hours so that the bus could have a service. Then another 1½ hours later on, the bus got a puncture. We stopped off in some town for half an hour, where Kurt and I walked around everywhere, trying to get a cup of tea, but all the tea shops said that they didn't have any tea. Very strange—until we found out that there is a big outbreak of Cholera in Zambia, and people are dying like flies, with mass graves being dug daily. Hence, it's not safe to drink the water.

Back on the road again, the bus had to stop at a couple of police checkpoints, where everyone had to take all their luggage off the bus, queue up for 15 minutes, then get back on the bus again—what is the fucking point! Apart from making the bus even later.

Well, we eventually arrived in Lusaka after 16½ long hours on the bus. By now, we were both knackered, and it was pitch dark, not the best time to arrive in a city renowned for its violence and theft. The bus station was on the other side of town from where we wanted to be. People came from all directions to offer help, but the bus station was full of dropouts and about 200 people sleeping on the floor, so I wasn't going to trust anyone. In the end, someone who worked at the bus station showed us where the Salvation Army was—it was about 3 km away, and I kept my knife in my hand while we walked there. Got there in the end and paid about 12 pence to camp in the grounds.

19 November 1992, Lusaka, Zambia

Kurt and I went to town to change some money and arrange transport to Livingstone. We'd only been walking for 5 minutes when the man from the bus station (who helped us out last night) spotted us—he came over and started talking to us and then followed us everywhere. We just couldn't shake him off. Normally, when I get a cling-on, I tell them where to go, which usually does the trick. The problem is this man helped us out last night, so I didn't want to be rude to him. We ignored him for ages, yet he still followed, trying to make conversation (without much success). It took us 1½ hours to finally shake him.

We went to the bus station to enquire about buses to Livingstone. We went to the ticket office, where the man said that there was one bus in the morning and one in the afternoon, but he didn't know what time they left. No wonder the country's in such a fucking mess! I just want to be out of this country asap. It's not very safe to travel in due to corrupt soldiers and policemen who can arrest you for nothing. It states in the guide book: 'Expect to be arrested at anytime'. With this problem and the Cholera outbreak, I don't fancy hanging around. Yet it's virtually impossible to get any information about the buses and trains. We went to the train station, but the ticket office was closed. Someone said it would be opening at anytime, so we had to hang around for a while before getting fed up waiting. We came back about 3 times during the day, and the ticket office was still closed. In the end, I was so pissed off, I went to see the station master, who was reasonably helpful yet didn't know if there were any places left in the 2nd-class sleeper and told us to come back in one hour. The train left in 1½ hours' time, and the campsite was 20 minutes away. So totally pissed off, we went back to the Salvation Army, packed away the tent, and walked all the way back to the station—not knowing if we would have a place on the train or not. We managed to get a reservation and then had to queue for 1½ hours to get the ticket. The train was supposed to leave at 5 p.m. but was late (just as well, as people were still queuing up for tickets after 7 p.m.). Kurt and I waited for the train that never arrived. We'd spent all day trying to get out of this shithole.

This is the last diary entry for his African adventure. He did send home postcards to his parents, which follow on his story. The postcards are as follows:

Day 77: 20 November 1992, Victoria Falls, Zambia

Hi,

It's no wonder Africa is in such a state—I spent nearly all day yesterday trying to get a damn train ticket to Livingstone. It took me several hours to get. Then the train turned up 5 hours late. A 22-hour train journey costing 850 kwachas (£1.60). I arrived (eventually) at Livingstone and hitched to the Victoria Falls, where I set up my camp for the night. It is dry season at the moment, and there's a bad drought. Hence, the falls were not in full force—along the Zambian side, it had virtually dried up, allowing me to walk along the edge of part of the falls usually flowing with water.

Day 78: 21 November 1992, Victoria Falls, Zimbabwe

Hi,

I spent the morning on the Zambian side of the Victoria Falls and visited some local craft stalls and bought 2 beautiful ebony carvings (made from the roots), both of African faces, one 18" high, the other 12" (you have to see them to appreciate them!). I used a lot of my salesman techniques to really barter hard and eventually got them both for 3 old T-shirts and a knackered old pair of jeans, plus about £1 in local currency.

Kev xxx

22 November 1992, Zambezi River

What a great day—I spent it on a white-rafting expedition down the Zambezi River. (One German woman died 2 weeks ago, but that only made me want to do it even more!) We started only several hundred metres from the base of Victoria Falls and rafted 25 km down the Zambezi. Great scenery as the whole way we had massive cliffs 100 metres high either side of us. Went down several grade-5 rapids. I got flipped out at one of them and lost my paddle.

Kev xxx

24 November 1992, Zimbabwe

Hi,

Well, after spending about 3 days at the Victoria Falls (Zimbabwe side), hanging around by the falls in the day and drinking several beers at night before staggering back to my tent, I finally made it to Bilawayo. I caught an old 19th-century steam train (overnight) with a second-class sleeper for 35 Zimbabwe Dollars (£4.30), arriving in Bilawayo this morning. I was in a state of shock for the first several hours as this is a modern city (the first I've seen since leaving England)—fast food and sit-down toilets.

Kev xxx

Day 93: 6 December 1992, Johannesburg, South Africa

Hi,

I arrived in JoBurg about a week ago and spent a few days with my aunty before hitching down to Durban and staying with Granny (spending a few wild nights out with my cousin). I hitched back to Joburg yesterday, and now I'm just waiting for Paula to fly in.

Kev xxx

Day 100: 13 December 1992, Cape Town, South Africa

Hi,

Well, Paula and I arrived here in Cape Town yesterday after catching a bus halfway and then hitching the rest of the way (no problem). We're staying in a house in between the mountains and the beach. We've rented out the house for a month, after which, who knows. Bye for now.

Kev xxx

19 December 1992, Cape Town, South Africa

Hi,

Well, we've been in Cape Town for almost a week now, and getting to know the place a bit better. We've spent a few days on Clifton Beach, lazing around, getting browner in the sun. It is here that we will be spending Christmas Day (bringing plenty of Christmas spirit along with us!). Clifton Beach is only a few minutes away from where we live, but there are supposed to be some better ones along the peninsular. Merry Xmas.

Kev xxx

24 December 1992

Hi,

Yesterday, I went on a wine route with Karl (Sonia's boyfriend). We got driven around several wineries, all located in scenic areas within the mountains. At each one, you are given a glass and can then sample as many wines as you want before moving on to the next winery. A good day out for all the family—although it was a bit blurry in places.

I also climbed the Lion's Head—hard work but worth the effort. Next week, I hope to climb Table Mountain. MERRY XMAS. Kev xxx

28 December 1992, Cape Town, South Africa

Hi,

Well, last week, I went on a wine route with Karl, getting driven around various wineries and drinking as much free wine as we could at each one.

Xmas day was spent on Clifton Beach. It was very hot at 32°C, and my ears got sunburnt, but luckily, we had a 5-litre cask of wine to cool us down (costing about £3.50). Then in the evening, we came home and cooked the turkey on the Braai Place—it took 3 hours but was well worth it. On Boxing Day, we went to a 12-hour concert at the waterfront, and after countless beers, I woke up the next morning with really bad neck ache from headbanging too much. I must be getting old—Bye for now. Kev xxx

2 January 1993, Cape Town, South Africa

I'm still recovering from a drunken New Year's Eve in which 20 of us piled into a minibus and drove down to Blouberstrand. We spent the night in a bar, where we had a meal while listening to a band and a couple of comedians. We started drinking at 7 p.m. and didn't get home until 5 a.m. after a good night out. Someone was picking us up at 8 a.m. to take us out for the day, but we didn't make it.

Kev xxxx

7 January 1993, Cape Town, South Africa

Well, we're still in Cape Town, living in Seaport. Cape Town is full of arse bandits, but they usually keep to themselves. We spend most of the days on the beach, Clifton, Camps, Sandy, etc.—There's a heatwave at present with temperatures reaching up to 37°C. The nights are usually spent beside Bob (the Braai Place), cooking dinner and drinking cheap wine.

9 January 1993, Cape Town, South Africa

Went down to the waterfront today and watched the start of the Cape sailing race. Not much of a spectator sport—the starting gun went, and the yachts sailed away! It was a good day, though, as we spent the next several hours drinking in the sun (a pint of strong beer, 80 pence). We are buying a 1972 VW Kombi tomorrow for about £1,400 in order to travel up the garden route to Durban—it had a large tent that fixes alongside it. We've knocked down the price a lot, and it seems a bargain at half the price!

Kev xxx

13 January 1993, Cape Town, South Africa

We drove 'Colin' (the camper) down to Cape Point yesterday—not a bad day out but very windy. We found a deserted beach surrounded by cliffs and spent a few hours down there getting burnt. Driving through the nature reserve, we saw several bonteboks (small antelopes). I couldn't believe it when we nearly ran over a couple of tortoises that were crossing the road. Write to you soon

Kev xxx

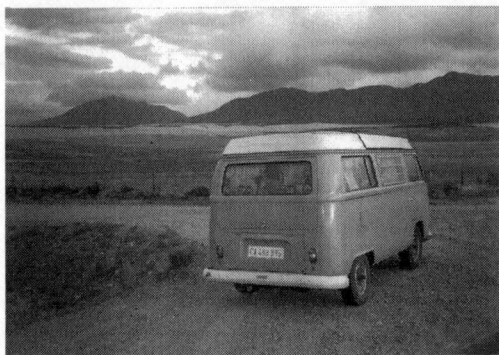

16 January 1993, Cape Town, South Africa

Well, I'm now a 25% share owner of a VW Kombi called 'Colin'. He's going fairly well apart from 2 flat tyres. We've left our house in Seaport and are now camping around Cape Town—sneaking in and out of campsites everyday without paying. Yesterday, Karl and I climbed to the top of Table Top Mountain and met the girls at the top—great views of Cape Town from the top. Somehow, I managed to lose my camera and may ask you to send one to me in Durban as they are so expensive here. I'll need the receipt as I'm going to claim for it on Paula's insurance.

18 January 1993, Betty's Bay, South Africa

Hi,

Well, we've finally left Cape Town (a beautiful city, although it's good to be on the move again). We drove down to Betty's Bay today and saw a penguin colony before collecting mussels along the rocks and cooking them on 'Bob', mixed with garlic and butter—not a bad change to steak or chicken.

Kev xxx

19 January 1993, Hermanus, South Africa

Another lazy day on the road. Got up around midday. Cooked baked beans and toast on the open fire before sneaking out of the campsite and driving 100 km down the road (along the coast) to the next place—today being Hermanus. We're camping right out on the coast—very scenic but very windy.

Kev xxx

21 January 1993, Waenhuiskrans, South Africa

Well, it was a bad day for 'Colin' today as he spent several hours in the garage—he had a dirty carb, which only cost us about £5 each to have sorted out. Then we went to Waenhuiskrans, a small coastal town surrounded by massive sand dunes and turquoise water. Stayed at a campsite, cooking dinner again on the open fire and drinking cheap wine.

Kev xxx

23 January 1993, Oudshoorn, South Africa

Today (believe it or not), I rode a big black bird with a bag over her head, and no, it wasn't a loose floppy woman but, in fact, an ostrich. I had a job hanging on the back of it while it ran around all over the shop but managed to stay on.

Kev xxx

24 January 1993, Oudshoorn, South Africa

Today, we went to the Kango Caves in Oudshoorn (very large and deep caves). We spent about 1 1/2 hours underground, going deeper into the caves. The further we went, the smaller and tighter it got—it was fairly dark and good fun.

Kev xxx

25 January 1993, George, South Africa

So far, since we left Cape Town 12 days ago, we've only paid for one night—so we felt a bit ripped off when we sneaked into a campsite tonight and got found out. To avoid paying, we left and drove towards George, stopping along the way and setting up camp on some farmland. At about 10 p.m. the farmer came along, told us that it wasn't safe, and let us sleep in some of his empty chalets used for his workers.

Kev xxx

28 January 1993, Wilderness National Park, South Africa

Today, we went for a trek in the Wilderness National Park to a scenic waterfall. On the way, Paula saw a snake on the path, but by the time she'd screamed and run away, it had gone—so I never got a look at it. In the evening, driving around looking for a campsite where we could get away without paying, we asked someone for directions and ended up camping in his back garden. He lived with a band, which were rehearsing all evening while we cooked our meal in the back garden and drank cheap wine.

Kev xxx

30 January 1993, Knysna, South Africa

Well, as you can probably tell by the postcard, we're currently bumming around Knysna—we left Cape Town about 3 weeks ago and have only travelled about 10-15 miles a day along the garden route towards Durban (nothing too strenuous!). Karl and I have bought ourselves a very basic fishing rod each—a line with a hook on it. Whenever we stop off anywhere, the girls lie in the sun while we go off and fish from the rocks—we've never caught any fish yet, but we only go to get some peace and quiet!

Kev xxx

2 February 1993, Plettenberg Bay, South Africa

At the moment, we're camping right alongside Plettenberg Lagoon—a very scenic and pretty spot renowned for its excellent fishing. I was straight out there with my line and bait—cheese, as it's all we had. Nevertheless, I never caught a thing! Next time maybe.

Kev xxx

3 February 1993, Storms River, South Africa

We're at Storms River at the moment (still a long way from Durban!). No more problems with 'Colin' thankfully. Storm River is a very scenic spot along the coast, where we went on a 5-mile trek along the coast today, past caves and lagoons etc. to a waterfall 20 metres high.

Kev xxx
PS Should be arriving in Durban end of Feb.

4 February 1993, Tsitsikamma, South Africa

Staying at another beautiful location along the coastal region of the garden route—Tsitsikamma National Park (try saying that with a glass of wine in your hand!). Today, we borrowed someone's boat and sailed up a river (I don't know whose boat it was as we found it). We had to use branches as oars to paddle ourselves along the river—hard work yet good fun! Kev xxx

6 February 1993, Jeffrey's Bay, South Africa

At present, we're at Jeffrey's Bay—a very popular surfing spot. 'Colin's' poorly again. This time, the solenoid has gone, which means that we have to bump start him everytime we go anywhere. We left Cape Town 4 weeks ago and should arrive in Durban in about 2 weeks.

Kev xxx

10 February 1993, Kenton-on-Sea, South Africa

Bad news I'm afraid. We went for a walk along the beach today through some massive sand dunes—when we came back, 'Colin' had been broken into. Luckily, not much stolen, and I only lost my wallet with about £11 and my visa card. I wouldn't have minded so much, but I've only got about £25 left to last me. Heading for Port Alfred.

Kev xxx

13 February 1993, Kenton-on-Sea, South Africa

Well, we've just come back from a 2-day canoeing trek up the Kowie River (Port Alfred). My arms were burning as it was 21 km both ways—it was a 2-man canoe, so I made Paula sit in the front to make sure she was paddling. It was very scenic and peaceful until we capsized, and I lost my sunglasses! We were supposed to spend the night in a little hut beside the river, but the girls wouldn't go in as it was full of massive hairy spiders—so we ended up sleeping on the jetty after we'd finished our 5-litre cask of wine. Saw lots of wildlife along the way, including otters and a lynx.

Kev xxx

14 February 1993, East London, South Africa

Went fishing yesterday evening using live mud prawns—not very easy putting live prawns on your hook, I can tell you! I felt embarrassed getting my stick and line out next to all the experienced fishermen. I couldn't believe it when I cast out for the first time. I was about to sit down after casting off when I got a bite—it was a 2 kg 'grunter' and tasted great on the old Braai. Today, we went to East London and were about to set up camp in the sand dunes on the beach when some local bloke invited us to his place for the night. We stopped off on the way and got drunk. When we eventually arrived at his home, his wife was furious as he'd come home drunk again, and his dinner had been ready 3 hours ago. He had a few more drinks and passed out. It turned out that he was an alcoholic.

Kev xxx

16 February 1993, Coffee Bay, Transkei

At present, we're travelling through the Transkei (an independent Republic of South Africa). A lot of the people have warned us not to travel through as there are a lot of vehicles getting stoned and robbed. We've taken the risk as it's a long way around Transkei to Durban. It is full of blacks and closer to the 'real' Africa, with mud huts everywhere. We spent last night at Coffee Bay, and today, we're making our way to Margate (SA). 'Colin's' running fine, but we still have to bump start the damn thing.

Kev xxx

17 February 1993, Margate, South Africa

What more can I say—I'm thousands of miles from home, yet I've ended up in bloody Margate! And believe it or not, it was a cold, windy, and drizzly day. We ended up getting a R 200 (£50) fine for parking 'Colin' on the wrong side of the road. Well, we've been travelling around like gyppos of no fixed abode for the last 5½ weeks, and I'm looking forward to reaching Durban and looking for work. I'm still trying to grow my hair long, but it's like pissing in the wind—you get nowhere fast!

Kev xxx

27 February 1993, Durban, South Africa

Hi,

We all arrived in Durban last Sunday. Paula and I stayed with Granny for a few nights while Karl and Sonia slept in the camper. It took us a few days to sort ourselves out accommodation-wise—we are now permanent residents of 'Marine Sands'. It is like a penthouse as it has just been refurnished, including TV, air con, even a maid who cleans up for us everyday and changes the towels etc. What more can a young man ask for! It also has an excellent view—we're on the 16th floor (2nd from the top) and have great views of the

Indian Ocean as the lounge window and our bedroom window face the coast. They want R 1850 per month but, we managed to get them down to R 1,400, including a security car park space for 'Colin' that works our at about R 11 each per day.

Kev xxx

Kevin remained in Durban looking for work and continued travelling around Africa in 1993. Unfortunately, he didn't continue with his diaries for the second part of his adventure.

CENTRAL AMERICA 1996/7

7 November 1996, Paris, France

Said my goodbyes to Connie at the airport, got on the plane, and started drinking the free booze. Had too much to drink. Didn't know where I was when I arrived in Cancun Mexico. Thought I was in transit. Before I knew what was going on, I'd picked up my rucksack and was through immigration etc. Supposed to be meeting Neil Kerfoot at the hostel but had lost his address. No guide book or anything, didn't know where I was going—got a taxi to a youth hostel. Luckily, it was the right one, but Neil had already moved on down the coast. Got some more beers, pizza, bought some gear, and sat on the beach.

8 November 1996, Mexico

Woke up and caught the local bus to the centre of Cancun—only ten minutes. Although, it took me 2 hours as the driver didn't tell me where to get off. I went too far and had to come all the way back. Caught the bus to Player del Carmen (only an hour). Went straight into the post office to pick up my mail from Neil, telling me where he was staying, and I bumped into Neil at the post office as he was posting the letter to me at the time.

I dropped my bags off in Neil's room and went down to the beach with him, where we spent the rest of the day getting pissed at a bar on the beach. Several hours later, Neil had to go to the local school and teach English (3 lessons). I could hardly stand up, so went for a sleep, leaving Neil to cope on his own. Went out tonight with Neil and Andy—saw a good-looking English girl. Had a 'chewing gum challenge' with Neil. He gave the girl a piece of chewing gum, and by the end of the night, I had to retrieve the chewing gum from her (by kissing her) and give it back to Neil. It was a long night. I lost the challenge, and we all went home at about 6 a.m.

9 November 1996, Playa del Carmen, Mexico

Got kicked out the hotel after the first night for being too noisy last night—moved into a hostel the other side of town with Neil. Spent most of the day hanging around on the beach (a beautiful spot on the Caribbean).

Drank loads of rum tonight and met up with the girls from the night before—the chewing gum challenge was on again, and I won. We all went to the local nightclub. I nearly had a fight in there with some local prat. It took me over an hour to get home as I couldn't remember the way.

10 November 1996, Playa del Carmen, Mexico

Woke up about midday in a bit of a daze. Went out again in the evening to some reggae band on the beach. Had a few beers and a laugh with the lads and girls. I ended up swapping my clothes (all) on the beach with Rosa and spent the rest of the night wearing her clothes. Got some right looks from people, especially when we went to a gay nightclub for a laugh. Tried to chat up some naive American lad. He shat himself, as he was straight as you like and half my size, as I towered over him, wearing a dress. He must have thought I was a right queen, especially when I asked him for a snog.

Went into the women's toilet with Rosa to swap our clothes back. Came out the toilets, and got some looks when we came out. Got lost on the way home again.

11 November 1996, Chetumul, Mexico

Woke up feeling rough as you like after a 4-day drinking binge. The 3 of us, along with the 2 English and 1 German girl, made our way down to Chetumul—a 6-hour and quite a painful journey with a hangover. Arrived at night, wandered around the town, had a few beers in a bar. Met some German lads, and we all went back to our room for a tequila party that went on till the early hours of the morning.

12 November 1996, Belize City

Left Mexico and spent 5 hours in a bus going down to Belize City. Arrived at night, and it was pissing it down with rain. Got a taxi and dorm for 6 of us—scored some gear and got stoned. Belize is a complete contrast to Mexico. It's English-speaking, everyone is of black Caribbean, and it's very funky yet dangerous.

Sat outside watching the rain, stoned, and some mad Rasta man came up and started preaching me in his Rasta beliefs in a strong Creole accent. I didn't have a clue what he was saying. Got the giggles and burst out laughing in his face and had to walk away. Sat on the balcony, watching rainy Belieze, and saw a huge mud crab walking slowly down the main road in Belize City.

13 November 1996, Ladyville Army Base

Belize is one of the strangest places I've ever been to—it has a very strong Caribbean influence and is full of Rastas who are constantly off their heads on grass and cocaine.

Phoned my mate up from school—Damon Blackband (Boris), who is in the army here as a sergeant. Met him in town at about 4 p.m. Went down to the bar in town, had several beers, and a lot of chat before getting a couple of bottles of cheap turps and going back to the dorm to meet everyone else and carry on the party. A few spliffs later and 2 empty bottles, we all went out to another bar. There was no music in there, so we started our own karaoke, which got very loud and abusive. I ended up singing 'New York, New York', with my pants around my ankles. Got home at about 2.30 a.m.

14 November 1996, Ladyville Army Base

Got up this morning in a daze and made our way to the British Army base in one of their Land Rovers, along with Boris, Neil, Andy, Rosa, and Fay. I was pissed off with the girls hanging on us as we've come to the army base in order to try and organise a jungle survival course to help us with the Darién Gap project.

Moved into the Sergeants' Mess. Luxury—washing machines, TV, lounge, etc. Went on a piss up this afternoon with Boris's lads (about 20) at the American section of the camp. The girls were very popular. Boris had to stand on the table while his boss bollocked him for a sexist comment he'd made to one of the female staff. Everyone got drunk. A good party, except one typical loudmouth American staff sergeant, who couldn't drink to save his life, so I challenged him to a drinking competition. He cheated and still lost. Boris nearly smacked him during the night but held back.

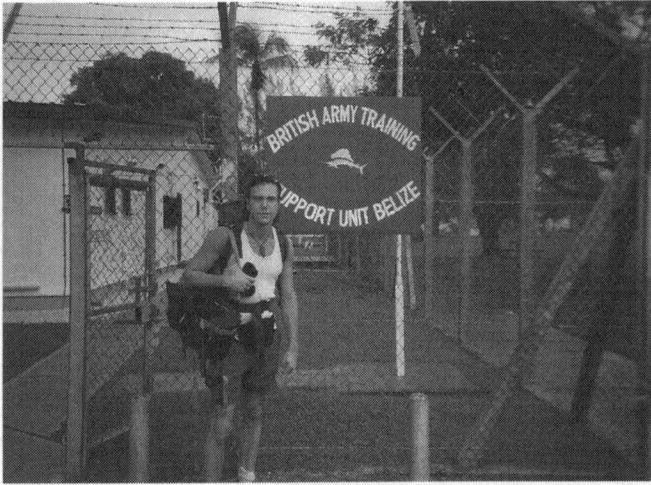

15 November 1996, Ladyville Army Base

Went for a run this afternoon and swam 20 lengths in the pool and chilled out for the rest of the day.

Went out clubbing tonight with about 20 of the army lads. Was half pissed by the time we went out—went to a nightclub in Belize City. It was a bit empty at first, so Neil and I sat out in the street, drinking a cheap bottle of rum and chatting. When it was finished, we bought another bottle but asked for the strongest bottle they had and got a small bottle of petrol for about 30 pence. We were told that it couldn't be drunk neat and had to be diluted with 4 parts water to 1 part gin. We took no notice. Had a mouthful, which nearly stripped the skin off the insides of my mouth. Tried to give the bottle away to some tramp who wouldn't take it. Another man took the bottle, stuck his finger in the gin, then set fire to his finger—talk about firewater.

Finally, went back to the club with Neil. After about half an hour, I ended up taking my clothes off and dancing on the stage naked. The funny thing was that no one really noticed me for about the first 5 minutes, until the bouncers threw me out. Still naked, standing in the street with my clothes in my hand, I decided to call it a night.

16 November 1996, Caye Caulker, Belize

Went to Caye Caulker today with Boris and about 10 other army lads. Caye Caulker is a typical tropical island in the Caribbean. It took us about 1½ hours to get there on the small boat, getting stuck on a sand bank at one stage. Then we had about 3 dolphins following us.

Got some looks when we arrived and unloaded about 8 crates of beer. Found some cheap digs and spent the rest of the day chilling out on the beach. There was a big beach party tonight with a Rasta band playing. We all bought a load of cheap rum and sat on the beach, getting slowly pissed, listening to the music until it began pissing it down with rain. To cut a long story short, Boris and I ended up going for a naked run in the rain around the town, which seemed like a good idea at the time—until we got lost and couldn't find our way back.

Found our way back in the end. Still naked, jumped into bed with Andy and tried to shag him for a laugh, and he was getting really annoyed. Ended up sleeping in the same bed as Boris—both bollock naked and drunk. Woke up this morning on a soaking-wet mattress—someone had swamped the bed in the night, but we didn't know who.

17 November 1996, Caye Caulker, Belize

Woke up naked next to Boris in a big puddle of piss. Another one of life's drunken mysteries. The army lads were supposed to be playing a football match with the local team with a BBQ and piss-up after. Luckily, it was raining, so we went straight on to the food and beer. Didn't go too mad today as I'm about worn out from the last 11 days' binge. Had a really good laugh this afternoon with the army lads, and coming back on the boat, some of the lads came back in the helicopter.

We were very close to running out of petrol on the way back as someone had loaded 3 metal containers on the boat, which turned out to be diesel (it was me yesterday morning—although I didn't tell anyone!). Managed to make it to an island on the fumes left in the petrol can before we ran out. Managed to get back in one piece, although Neil and I were looking forward to being shipwrecked for a while before being rescued by the British Army.

18 November 1996, Dangriga

Got up at the crack of dawn this morning and left the British Army base. I headed on south to Dangriga with the 2 girls while Neil and Andy went off to Guatemala.

Dangriga is another African town on the Caribbean coast, where a 48-hour African festival is being held. Good weather and a good atmosphere. Met a young American lad called Ruben, and we all went out to the festival and shared a bottle of rum. The festival was very ethnic, and it was like being in Africa rather than Central America as a lot of the blacks had their traditional dress on.

19 November 1996, Dangriga

Wandered around the festival today—plenty of people had drunk too much last night and were lying around unconscious in the street. There wasn't too much happening tonight, so Ruben, I, and the 2 girls played 'Arse Hole', meaning you had to do a forfeit, which got a bit out of hand as the forfeits got more stupid, i.e. going to the shop to buy more booze with their own money, crawling down the street and into the shop on their hands and feet, with 10 press-ups in the middle of the road on the way back. We were all sitting out on the balcony so could see if any cheating went on.

20 November 1996, Flores, Guatemala

Said goodbye to Belize today and the girls—I was pleased about that as they've been getting on my tits recently.

Ruben and I caught a couple of buses (5 hours) to the border, then another to a small island called Flores. Only about 400 metres across but with plenty of old and very colourful buildings. Moved into a cheap hotel and, within 10 minutes, had scored some grass from the hotel owner.

21 November 1996, Tikal, Guatemala

Got up about 3.40 a.m. and caught a minibus to Tikal, an hour away, in order to see the sun rise over the famous Mayan Ruins at Tikal. The ruins were built well over 2000 years ago by the Mayan Empire. They stand over 45 metres high and are in the middle of a vast and dense jungle. When you climb to the top, you can see jungle in every direction as far as the eye can see. Howler monkeys can be heard in the trees from miles away and red Marquis birds flying around.

I had no money, but Ruben said he would lend me some. When the minibus arrived at the entrance gate, we had to pay to get in. Ruben had left his wallet behind. We had no money between us and had to scrounge the money so that we could get in.

Walked along the path in the dark and climbed up a large temple in order to watch the sunrise. The sunrise was OK, seeing the sun come up over the jungle and ancient temples while listening to the monkeys and other wild life. Spent the rest of the day wandering around the ruins, thirsty and hungry (and no money!). Had to wait till mid-afternoon to get back.

Wandered around this evening and bumped into Andy.

22 November 1996, Poptun, Guatemala

Ruben and I caught the bus down to Poptun to stay at a small farm in the forest/jungle. It took about 4 hours on a very bad road to get there. Sod's Law—as soon as we got off the bus, it began pissing it down cats and dogs!

The farm was about 5 km away. We were originally going to walk, but by the time the rain had stopped, it was also getting dark. We got someone to organise a taxi—which turned out to be an open-back truck that Ruben and I had to help bump start! Not your conventional taxi but a lot more fun. Got stoned tonight and tried to sleep in a hammock—not the easiest thing to do after a smoke! The hammock was too small and felt like an old fishing net—I grazed my face just trying to turn around. I was determined to sleep in it but gave up after an hour after nearly falling out several times.

Ended up sleeping on the floor.

23 November 1996, Poptun

Got a guide today, who took us caving. It was a 2-hour walk through the jungle to get there—very scenic and plenty of exotic birds.

The cave was an underground river that you could follow for about a kilometre. The trouble was that it had rained for the last 3 days, and the water level was very high. The current was very fast and strong, making it a lot more exciting. The entrance was flooded, so for the first part, we had to go totally underwater—a real adrenalin buzz! We climbed along the cave walls alongside the underground river—several times, we had to swim across to the other side, which was quite dangerous as the current was so strong, and the river was like a rapid. If you didn't get across quick enough, you could have ended up getting swept down the river in the dark (there is no way it would be allowed in any civilised country). Made it down to the end, where there is an underground waterfall about 15 feet high that you can jump off into a pool below. You need diving gear to go any further. Coming back was a lot harder as it was upstream.

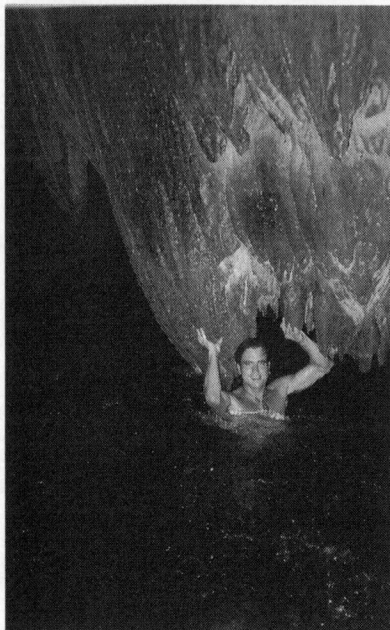

Got chatting to a Dutch girl tonight, who was a tour rep for a hopeless gang of Dutch tourists. Had a few drinks with her—I didn't really fancy her. It was just the fact that she's a tour guide. Managed to find my way home—I stayed in a tree house tonight, but you've got to be careful as sometimes tarantulas and snakes get in.

24 November 1996, Flores, Guatemala

Caught a bumpy bus back to Flores today—it felt good to be back in civilisation again. Had a few joints in our room with the hotel owner (same bloke as before). Went for some food tonight and bumped into the Dutch tour guide. Sat in the street with her, drinking beer and smoking a few joints. I didn't fancy her but just looked at it as a bit of a challenge (as she was going home next week to her boyfriend and didn't want to go any further). It was a bit of a tough one. I had a grope but nothing else despite various different tactics.

25-29 November 1996, San Andres, Guatemala

Ruben and I went over to San Andres today (a half hour away by boat to the other side of the lake). We are to spend 5 days at a Spanish school, learning Spanish, one-to-one teaching in a large relaxed classroom with a great view of the lake and the surrounding countryside.

I was really pissed off at first because none of the teachers spoke any English. I ended up sacking my teacher after the first day as in my first ever Spanish lesson, I had to correct him 3 times in his Spanish (and I don't even know any Spanish). It was a very intense course, 5 hours a day. I stayed with a poor Guatemala family, who cooked me 3 meals a day (it only cost £65 for a week at school, food, and accommodation).

It was a bit embarrassing at first, getting dropped off at my family and not understanding a word they said. It was a very tough and frustrating week to say the least. The mother kept telling me about robbers about twice a day—I thought she was warning me about San Andres but thought it's not as bad as she makes out as it's only a small village alongside the lake. It wasn't until my last day that I realised she was talking about *ropas* (clothes) and wanted to do my washing for me.

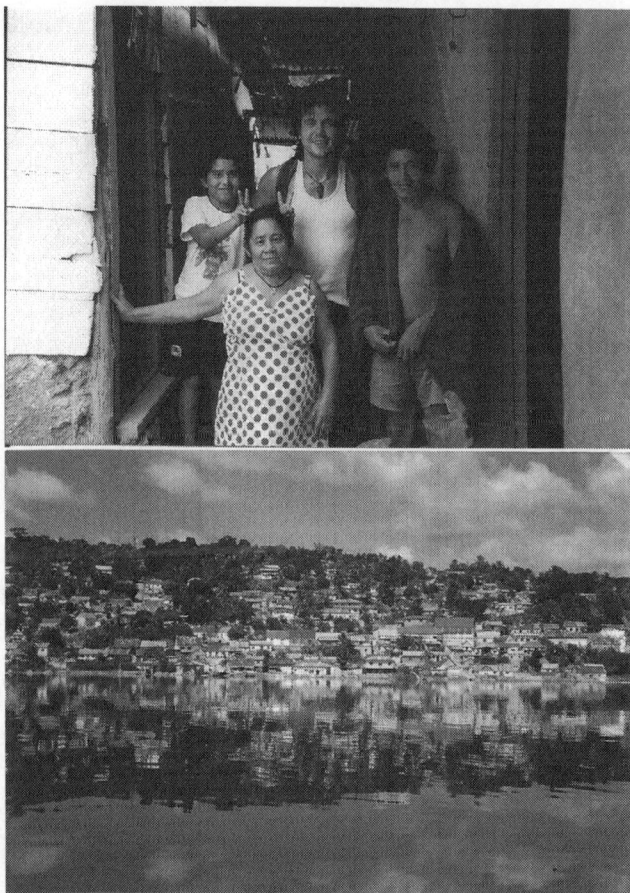

I stayed sober for the week and had a little binge on my last night—there was a big festival on in the village, and I went out on the piss with Ruben and a few other people on the course. Not a bad night, but the festival was nothing special. The next day, my family's son found his father unconscious in the street, and I woke up in a wet bed (I must have swamped during the night!). It was a bit embarrassing. I was leaving anyway, so I didn't tell her, said my goodbyes, and left for school for my last lesson. Halfway in the lesson, the mother came down to the school and gave me a bollocking for wetting her bed. A bit embarrassing to say the least! It's a good job I'm leaving today.

The lesson finished (*whew*), Ruben and I caught the boat back to Flores, where we went back to our old hotel for a few joints before catching the 12-hour night bus to Guatemala City—on a very bumpy road (I made sure I had a small bottle of plonk to help me sleep). It's quite a dangerous bus trip as there are a lot of guerrillas (bandits) in the area who are renowned for robbing the night bus. Only a couple of weeks ago, a couple of travellers were shot (1 died) in this area. Anyway, we survived the journey in one piece.

30 November 1996, Antigua, Guatemala

Woke up when we arrived in Guatemala City after a good night's sleep on the bus. Spent about an hour looking for the next bus station for the 2-hour bus to Antigua. Arrived and checked into a hotel with Ruben and had a wander around.

Antigua is a pretty little colonial town in the mountains, with 3 volcanoes right beside it. All the streets are cobbled, and there is a large church or cathedral on almost each corner. I've never seen so many in such a small area (at least 20 to 30 in this town). There is a pretty park in the centre that is really chilled out and has lots of the local Indians walking around in their traditional dress, selling various items. Bumped into Neil and Andy, who have been here a week already, studying Spanish. We sat in the park till late, drinking a cheap bottle of rum and coke and getting nice and merry.

1-5 December 1996, Antigua, Guatemala

Spent the next 5 days at a Spanish School, 5 hours a day and very intense and frustrating. I moved in with another local Guatemala family, who treated me really well. The first night I was with them, I went out on the piss. I was a dirty stop out and came home about 7.30 a.m. the next morning for my breakfast before going to school. The woman looking after me had been worried sick all night as she didn't know where I was!

Every night, we all went out on the piss (about ten of us). The next morning, only about half turned up for school. Neil was sick in his lesson. I had to go and sleep it off a bit on the school roof, and the teacher told me to wake me up after a couple of hours. I don't think anyone learnt anything in that lesson.

6 December 1996, Panajachel, Guatemala
Finished school at 1 p.m.—thank fuck for that. I've had it up to my ears in Spanish. Went up north with Andy to Panajachel (about 4 hours and 3 buses).

It felt so good to be out of Antigua and on the road again. Arrived as the sun was going down and checked into a hotel—got the dance music on full blast and had a few spliffs with a chilled-out Canadian guy. A cheap bottle of plonk and a stroll around town—couldn't really find anything happening. I sat on the street and rolled a joint while Andy went to the bar next door. I was going to meet Andy in there after the spliff, but he had a quick beer and came back—it was a gay bar.

7 December 1996, Guatemala
Got up early. Hired a mountain bike with the intent of biking up a volcano. We came down it yesterday on the way here—really steep and about 3-4 miles constant uphill. Andy said there was no way I could do it, so, of course, I had to try. I made it about halfway up before calling it a day. I could have managed it if I really wanted to, but it was putting so much strain on my legs that if I carried on to the top, I wouldn't have been able to walk for the next week.

Andy and I caught the ferry across Lake Atitlan to San Juan. Lake Atitlan is a huge volcano crater about 20 miles across, filled with water, with small villages along the edge and a few volcanoes on the skyline—very scenic. Got chatting to 3 American lads on the ferry—we were all lying out on the deck in the sun, listening to music and watching the world go by. Smoked a couple of spliffs, which rounded the trip off nicely.

San Juan is a small village on the side of the volcano—very chilled out and relaxed. There are no police here, and you're allowed to wander around, sit in cafes, etc. smoking spliffs. Which, of course, is what we did—sat in a bar (about 8 of us), drinking and smoking. Went for a lie-down at about 5 p.m. and that was me for the rest of the night.

8 December 1996, Chichicastenango, Guatemala

Moved on again this morning—a couple of hours back on the ferry, then a couple of buses to Chichicastenango. We came here for the Sunday market—very large and colourful. We had all our bags with us and didn't want to carry them around all day. So we found a posh hotel, made up a story about our friend coming later on, and we were all going to stay in the hotel there (in order for us to leave all our bags with them), which worked a treat.

Wandered around the Indian market. The Indians still wear their traditional dress here—women have very colourful embroided tops and dresses. Men—bright red flares with sequins sewn in flashy tops, waistcoats, and a cowboy hat. They look really funky, as if they've come out of a trendy club in the 70s. Picked up our bags from the hotel and hitched back to Antigua. Got a lift straightaway on the back of someone's truck. The sun was going down, and it got painfully cold as we drove around high up in the mountains—had a laugh, especially as somehow, in the wind, I managed to knock off a couple of spliffs on the back of the truck. After a couple of hours, the cold was unbearable, and we had to get off at a town and bus it for the rest of the way.

9 December 1996, San Salvador, El Salvador

Caught a bus to Guatemala City—spent over an hour looking for the other bus station, where we caught a bus to the El Salvadorian border. Left Guatemala and walked over the river on a bridge to El Salvador, where, about 3 buses later (6 hours in total), we were in San Salvador—the capital of El Salvador and renowned for being a rough and violent city.

You only pass through this way once, and if you're going to do it, you've got to do it properly, so Andy and I headed straight for the rough-and-ready end of the city for a real San Salvador experience. Got a cheap yet secure hotel—hid our valuables and went out to explore. Went into a seedy bar with 20-year-old Latin American music blasting out of the duke box—plenty of characters in the bar.

10 December 1996, San Azul, El Salvador

Caught the bus to La Luidad on the Pacific Coast this morning to meet up with Neil. La Luidad looks like a small friendly coastal village (however, it's quite violent and dangerous). A lot of people in El Salvador carry guns due to the excess leftover from the civil war that only ended several years ago! Got a hotel. Went around looking for Neil. Got a message that he'd moved on further up the coast to a surfer's hangout at San Azul. Bollocks. Went back to the hotel and did a runner and caught a bus 20 minutes up the coast to San Azul, where we eventually met up with Neil.

11 December 1996, Camping on the Side of the Volcano in Cerro Verde, El Salvador

San Azul is a very small village on the coast yet is the best place in Central America for surfing. However, there were hardly any waves when I was there. Left this afternoon, hitch-hiking up to Cerro Verde, one of the most scenic areas in this country—a huge volcano with great views.

I went on my own, and it was a great adventure, hitch-hiking in this often violent country, not knowing hardly a word of Spanish (it's different here than in Guatemala), and not knowing if I was going to make it. Got a lift after about 5 minutes, on the back of a truck, along a lovely coastal road. Crazy driver, flying around corners—good buzz. Got dropped off after about 1½ hours. Wasn't sure which direction I needed to go. To cut a long story short, ended up catching several short buses right out in the middle of the mountains to eventually arrive at the turn-off for Cerro Verde. A 14 km steep road to the top of the volcano.

There was no traffic, and I began walking up the never-ending road, at a fairly fast pace, with all my kit on my back. Very hard going. Passed a few small communities along the way. Got a short ride on the back of a lorry (only a couple of km), then back to walking again. The sun went down, and with the last remaining light, I went into a coffee plantation on the volcano. Cleared a spot (very rough and on a steep angle) and spent the night there in my tent. A great day full of adventure.

12 December 1996, Metapán, El Salvador

Got up early and packed my tent away and continued the climb to the top. I was feeling very exhausted and weak after all the strenuous exercise from yesterday's climb. I had to wait on the side of the road, too tired to continue. Waiting for a lift either up or down. Managed to get a short lift on a truck taking up water to the next small village. Pissed off, hot and bothered, and a physical wreck, I waited for about 1½ hours for a lift, only to find out the top was only about 500 metres away. Sod's law. I was too knackered to appreciate the view by the time I reached the summit. Waited a few more hours for the bus to Santa Ana and from there to Metapán, where I met up with Neil

13 December 1996, Cloud Reserve, Montecristo

Up at the crack of dawn this morning in order to go on a 3-day jungle trek to the peak of the Montecristo Mountain. At the summit are the borders for Guatemala, Honduras, and El Salvador—originally, we wanted to come out in Honduras but couldn't get the correct information and decided to leave most of our luggage in Metapán and come back the same route.

The Montecristo Cloud Reserve is 2,418 metres above sea level. The jungle has 2 metres of rain in a year with an average humidity of 100%, so it is always soaking wet. The trees are about 30 metres high, with their leaves interweaving at the top, stopping most of the sunlight from reaching the ground. Also home for many rare tropical birds and mammals as well as pumas and coyotes. We'd been planning this trip for a while and had to get written permission from San Salvador. Managed to organise a lift from an American Peace Corp worker, who took us the first 7 km to the beginning of the reserve.

A right result as there are a lot of bandits on the first stretch. From here, it was a 23 km climb to the summit. We'd only been walking for about 5 minutes when the ranger drove past and offered us a lift to within 5 km from the summit. Not bad going as we'd planned

1½ days to get this far and had managed it in under 2 hours. The last 5 km was spectacular and nothing like I'd ever seen before. Very green, tropical, wet, and misty. It was like being in a fairy-tale setting—unbelievable. Although we hardly saw any wildlife, it was well worth it. It was freezing cold at the summit as we sat in the middle of a cloud right at the point where the 3 countries of El Salvador, Honduras, and Guatemala meet. Had lunch there before coming back down the 5 km we'd just climbed. We were just about to set the tents up when the ranger offered us a lift down. We'd already seen everything we'd come to see and came back down with him back to Metapán. Moved into a room and went out on the piss, intending to move on to Honduras tomorrow morning.

Got drunk and ended up going to the circus for a laugh—it was absolutely shite (probably the world's worst!). To cut a long story short, we ended up asking at the end if we could join—they didn't really take us seriously but said that we could if we really wanted to.

14-24 December 1996, Working a Gypo Travelling Circus

Didn't have enough money between us to pay for our hotel—it was a Sunday, so we couldn't change any money. The woman was a right battleaxe and didn't believe us. Out of both Neil and my possessions, we found it really hard to give her anything of value to cover the cost until tomorrow.

Went down to the circus with our rucksacks—they couldn't believe it at first as they didn't think we were serious last night. We spent most of the next 2 weeks working for this travelling gypsy circus. The first night we just spent setting the chairs out and packing them away. By the second night, we'd talked our way into doing a duo act on stage as a couple of clowns. Neil and I were both pathetic to say the least, but the sense of humour over here is different, and the audience loved us.

We were both drunk for our first appearance on stage, which was a right laugh. I did Charlie for the first 3 nights, snorting it behind the stage while the audience were coming in—it's amazing how I didn't get caught. I also trained up on the trapeze—talk about shitting a brick, hanging upside down about 20 feet off the floor, with all the blood rushing to your head, and you have to catch someone who is flying through the air at quite a speed towards you—a real adrenalin buzz, believe me!

I had a tacky Lycra, all in one body suit, riddled with holes and a few sequins sewn in. I looked more like Eddie 'the Eagle', and my stage name was 'Avion Gringo' or, in English, 'Flying Whitey'. There was a really old safety net at the bottom, only about 1 metre wide and about as useful as a paper bag. I absolutely shat myself everytime.

For a laugh, we both went on stage as transvestites. A bit scary walking out on stage not really knowing what we were going to do dressed in women's clothes. Neil looked more like an old witch than a dolly bird—it took some doing in front of 700-800 people, without a beer inside.

It was a travelling circus full of gypsies—about 22 of them in total (including all the snotty-nosed kids). It was great how they all adopted Neil and me into their family (they couldn't speak English, and we only know a few words of Spanish). They are all as fit as you like, hard as nails, and respected by everyone. They have nothing but would give you everything!

We used to get paid about £4 a night (not bad in a country with 50% unemployment) and sleep on the stage after each show. The place was a shit hole and a deathtrap. I used to get at least a couple of electric shocks everyday. It was a typical Third-World travelling circus.

They had a really old and knackered car (and I mean knackered). I've never in all my years of travelling seen such a bad car on the road. The whole of the back end was smashed in, holes everywhere, pieces hanging off left, right, and centre—a total banger. It had a huge speaker tied to the roof, and they used to drive it around town, blasting music out and advertising the circus.

I had a go at driving it—it was unbelievable. I was driving around the streets for about 10 minutes and then back to the circus. The guy directing me kept pointing to the right, so I kept doing right turns. It wasn't until I got back to the circus that I realised that I'd been driving on the wrong side of the road and didn't understand him when he kept telling me to drive on the other side. Luckily, there was hardly any traffic on the road.

Went out with them one morning. They took me to a brothel for my breakfast. We had several beers each throughout the morning and just drove from brothel to brothel—a right laugh. They were a bit surprised to find that I wasn't interested in paying for it. Drove back to the circus in the deathtrap of a car, pissed up.

On the last evening in Metapán, once the show had finished, we all had a quick bite to eat and then spent most of the night packing everything away and taking the big top down.

It was about 3 in the morning, when, the next thing we knew, we were surrounded by police waving their sub-machine guns and pump-action shotguns in the air (basically, Charlie, who's bent as you like, tried to get off with a drunk man tonight in the cafe—the drunk got offended and went to the police and told them a greatly exaggerated story). The police were in full force and meant business, but all the gypsies weren't taking any shit and straightaway picked up iron bars and tools. The police took their safety catches off and got their handcuffs out. There was a lot of shouting, and it was a very tense situation—it went on for about 10 minutes until the drunk admitted that he'd made the story up. He got a slapping from the police and taken away and banged up. A bit of excitement in this war-torn and trigger-happy country.

Managed to get about 3 hours' sleep before getting up at the crack of dawn to carry on packing away the big top. Everything was thrown into the back of a large truck and tied on to the top of the other vehicles before heading on to the next town, Ahuachapán, about 60 km down the road. We drove out of town and looked like a convoy of refugees leaving a war-torn country. All the vehicles were old and knackered. I was in the car that I drove around in last week. I couldn't believe it when they tied a huge trailer to the back of it—literally tied it on to the inside of the car, with the boot open. I went the whole journey with one of the lads and his scruffy 1½-year-old son, who was sitting on my lap and wet himself after about half an hour (no nappy) and then started crawling all over me—covering me from head to toe in piss. We had to stop about 4 times to fill the radiator up with water. All the other vehicles broke down several times—the one Neil was in ran out of petrol, and they had to hitch to a garage. All in all, it took about 7 hours to get 60 km down the road—yet looking at the state of the vehicles, it was a surprise we made it at all.

Couldn't believe it when we arrived as this site was even worse than the last—it was on some wasteland that looked more like a rubbish dump. We spent most of the next 1½ days unpacking the vans and putting up the big top—good hard physical work but good fun at the same time. Ahuachapán is quite a rough area with a lot of thefts, robberies—there was a small shoot-out one night outside the circus while we were there, although we couldn't see anything as it was too dark.

I couldn't believe it when one of the lads climbed up a telegraph pole in the night, using two small pieces of rope—he tied himself to the top while with his bare hands he wired up the electricity for the circus by tapping it off the telegraph and electricity cables. It had to be seen to be believed. These guys know all the tricks in the book.

There were no toilets or washing facilities at this site, and day by day, it got more and more like a minefield, with turds and used nappies lying all over the place. Tramps in England have a better and more hygienic lifestyle than these gypsies in the circus.

To advertise the fact that the circus was in town, Neil and I and a few others got dressed up in our clown outfits and sat on the bonnet of the car while we got driven around town, with the music blasting out of the speakers.

Xmas Day, 1996

Woke up mid-morning in a bit of a blur from last night's party. It didn't really feel like Christmas one bit in the circus. I treated myself to some Charlie. Spent the afternoon wandering around town, drinking beer (compulsory on Christmas Day). Got plastered and went back to the circus for our final show—I was totally wasted and was sitting there in my clown's outfit and make-up and asked Neil if we'd been on yet! (Half an hour before we were due on!)

We both went on stage pissed as farts in front of a full house (about 1000 people) and forgot which act we were supposed to be doing—talk about dying on stage (although it wasn't the first in our pathetic little circus career). Thank God it was our last night as I'm sure we'd have been sacked.

Boxing Day, 1996, San Salvador

Got up in a drunken blur, packed my tent away, which has been on the stage every night for the last 2 weeks, said goodbye, and then spent 3½ hours on a bus to the capital, San Salvador.

Spent the rest of the day vegging out and recovering from the last couple of days' binge. Still haven't seen another white person in about 2½ weeks.

27 December 1996, Honduras

Got up at the crack of dawn and went down to the Tika Bus Station to catch the direct 2-day bus to San José (Costa Rica). Bastard—no seats left. Got a taxi and rushed over to the other end of San Salvador and caught the 6 a.m. bus to the capital of Honduras. Long day on the bus (8½ hours), with about half an hour at the border. The bus almost caught on fire going up a hill (smoke everywhere). Everyone had to get off the bus and find their own transport. Luckily, it was only about 5 km to the city centre—Neil and I caught the local bus.

Had a look around the capital and went out on the town tonight—not too much happening, so we came back. The taxi driver tried to rip us off, so we ran away—he chased us in his taxi around the streets and ended up banging on the hotel door. He came back an hour later, but we still wouldn't let him in.

28 December 1996, Managua, Nicaragua

Got locked out this morning and was in a rush to catch the bus—ended up smashing all the wire netting in the window and climbed back into the room. Left Honduras this morning for Nicaragua in order to be in Costa Rica for New Year's Eve to meet Andy. Went to the bus station and bumped into Andy—small world. Spent the whole day on the bus, watching the world go by through the window.

No problems entering Nicaragua and arrived in Managua (the capital) in the evening. Got a room with Neil, Andy, and some Aussie bird, who turned out to be a right bossy slag. Got some food and went out clubbing. Neil fell out with the old dragon and went home while the 3 of us went to a club. Quite westernised and full of the elite, trendy Nicaraguans. Had a couple of dances with the local girls before coming home for a smoke. Got the munchies and spent 1½ hours walking around looking for some food.

29 December 1996, San José, Costa Rica

Got up at the crack of dawn again after only 2½ hours' sleep and caught the bus to Costa Rica (San José)—10 hours. It was funny watching Andy getting stressed out because he couldn't have a cigarette—I gave up about 2 weeks ago at the circus, more for financial reasons as it was costing me a fortune. Everytime I got my fags out, all the lads were coming around and asking for one—I needed to stop as in the end, I was smoking about 25 a day.

Stopped off at the border for about half an hour. I went for a short walk to a lake to take a photo—not a good idea, but what the hell. As soon as I got there, a soldier jumped out of nowhere, waving a machine gun and shouting in Spanish. He wanted to see my passport, which I didn't have as it was at the border immigration post, being processed. I tried to walk away a couple of times, pretending that I couldn't understand him. He got angry and tried to pull me back to his army base. I couldn't go, otherwise I'd miss my bus. Luckily, another soldier turned up, who let me go—*whew!*

It was good to be back on the bus—great scenery, plenty of volcanoes and mountains, very tropical.

Arrived in San José at about 4 p.m. then caught a bus to Limon 3 hours away. Limon is a very black and Caribbean town along the coast. I was starving hungry but had no money as it's a Sunday, and I've just entered the country.

30 December 1996, Puerto Viejo, Costa Rica

Left Puerto Limon this morning on a bus jam-packed with people (all Caribbean blacks—plenty of characters) for the 2-hour trip to Puerto Viejo. Quite expensive here as it's a bit of a tourist resort yet only a fairly small one. Good to be here, though, as I've spent the last 4½ days with my arse stuck to a sweaty bus seat!

Had a look around and waited for Neil to arrive. When he finally turned up, I hid in the room, pretending I was out. He got pissed off and went to the reception, leaving his bag outside. I quickly opened the door pulled his bag in the room and shut the door. Neil came back and shat himself as he thought someone had stolen his bag.

Went out tonight, had a few beers, and bumped into Petya—the Swedish girl who went to the same school as us in Antigua Guatemala.

New Year's Eve, Puerto Viejo, Costa Rica

Chilled out this morning in a small bar on the beach and caught up with loads of writing I've been avoiding. Had a couple of beers in the afternoon and a spliff.

New Year's Eve on a Caribbean beach in Costa Rica—I'd never have dreamed of that last year, when I spent it in Hong Kong.

Went out tonight and wandered around the 3 discos in the village (combination of reggae, disco, and more reggae). There were quite a few people around on the beach, although it didn't feel like New Year's Eve, especially when at 11.30 p.m. there was a power cut in the whole village. Everyone just sat in the dark until it came back on about an hour later. No one had a watch in our group, so we never really knew when New Year arrived.

New Year's Day, Puerto Viejo, Costa Rica

Got up quite early, seeing that it was New Year's Day—must have been one of my soberest New Year's Eves in my drinking history.

Neil and I had to meet a couple of pretty Caribbean girls we'd met on the bus to Limon a few days ago. I'd been in contact with them, and they were going to spend 2 hours on the bus going home (although if we had anything to do with it, that wouldn't be until tomorrow morning). Anyway, we went to meet them off the bus, and they didn't turn up—strange, as they were very keen.

Bought a cheap bottle of plonk, sat on the beach, and slowly got pissed during the afternoon while relaxing on the beach in the sun. Bought enough gear for a spliff—smoked it. Got nicely stoned before coming home and calling it a day.

2 January 1997, Bocas Del Toro, Panama

Neil, Petya, and I left for Panama this morning. It was a 7 km walk to the main road, which was enjoyable as most of it was along the rugged and tropical coast with jet-black beaches (volcanic). Passed a shipwreck on the way—it must have been there for some time as it had a tree growing out of it.

We planned on hitching but ended up walking most of the way to the main road, where we caught a bus to the border. No problems at the border, although Neil saw a punch-up that ended up with 2 guys getting arrested. On the other side, caught a taxi to the port half an hour away—a great trip as it was in an open-back truck, with a mad driver hammering it through banana plantations and whizzing around corners at full speed while I stood up on the back and hung on for my life.

We nearly ran over a 3-toed sloth that we had to swerve around—the sloth was moving slower than a tortoise and didn't have a care in the world.

Arrived in Almirante in one piece and caught a half-hour water taxi to Bocas del Toro—a beautiful Caribbean island within a marine national park. I left Neil and Petya. Walked for about half an hour along the coast, passing a huge plane crash along the way—it looked like an army plane, about 35 metres long, that had crashed into the hill. Put my tent up in a remote area alongside the coast nearby. Eagles and hummingbirds were flying around.

3 January 1997, Remote Tropical Island, Panama

Found out that someone was murdered last night on this island with only 2000 inhabitants—must be a bit more cautious in future when camping out on my own.

Neil and I rented out a couple of kayaks and paddled to a nearby island. Got a motorised dugout to take us to a remote island half an hour away. The engine broke down halfway, and we had to paddle to a small island community. Went to a small shed playing music and selling beer while the guy got his engine fixed.

Carried on to a deserted beach on a real typical Robinson Crusoe Island. Right behind the beach was dense tropical jungle with a wide range of tropical birds, sloths, and iguanas (lizards about 1½ metres long). Put the tent up on the beach, built a fire, and opened a cheap bottle of gin.

4 January 1997, Remote, Tropical Island Panama

Got a bit of rain last night but not too much. Rebuilt the fire, had some breakfast, and went for a swim and snorkel. Before I knew it, I'd been swept out to sea—the current was very strong, and I started to panic a bit as I was swimming as fast as I could and getting nowhere. Luckily, I managed to grab hold of a rock, where I could rest for a while before managing to get back to shore. Close shave!

Saw loads of fish, though, before I got swept out—big shoals of fish about 1 and a half feet long. If only I had my speargun.

There's a footpath running through the jungle over a hill to the other side of the island to a small Caribbean community. I managed to find the path. It was hard for me to follow—nearly got lost a couple of times. It took me about 40 minutes to get to the village, where I had some food in an old wooden shack and a couple of beers. Chatted to a local bloke who could speak English and who told me all about the dictatorship of Panama that only ended about 6 years ago when the Yanks came in force and bombed parts of Panama City.

Came back through the jungle with a couple of black lads taking a semi-wild horse to the other beach. Got back to the beach I'm camping on to find about 7 black girls getting pissed on the beach and a small music box and about 5 scruffy kids crawling around. All the girls were as rough as you like—most had teeth missing, others had curlers in their hair. This was an opportunity I couldn't miss—I invited myself to their party and pulled out a small bottle of gin that I'd bought for tonight and joined them. Could hardly communicate with them, but it was a good laugh. Then a couple of Rasta lads came down the beach on horseback. I got chatting to the lads and had a go on his horse—bareback. The horse was really knackered and sweaty by the time I got on it so didn't go too fast—just as well, as by now, I was quite pissed. Then I changed horses and had a go on the wild one. It was a bit faster, and I ended up clinging to its neck as it shot down the beach.

Had a quick swim and went back to see Neil and Petya down at the beach. Went for a walk and met a local Indian family. The man had his front teeth filed to points so they looked like saw blades. The man's wife was 18, and she had a 5-year-old daughter—they start young over here.

Still very merry, I staggered back through the jungle in order for someone to catch me a giant iguana so that I could take it back to the beach—skin and cook it. Found out it wasn't the right season at the moment, and they're hard to find. Instead, I had some food in the same shed I ate in earlier. By the time I'd finished, it was totally dark, and I still had to find my way back home through the jungle (about half an hour's walk). I bought a candle and a box of matches and another bottle of rum and attempted my way home. I had a good idea of the route as I'd already done it 3 times in daylight. I was still merry and stopped a couple of times along the way for a quick tipple. I was running out of time as I only had one candle, and it was burning down quite fast—in the end, I had to run as it had burnt right down to my fingers. I slipped and fell over, catching my arm on a barbed wire fence, cutting it quite badly, so it will probably leave a small scar. I was dripping in blood and running through the jungle, pissed up in the darkness as my candle completely burnt out, leaving me without light. Luckily, I was about 100 metres from the end of the jungle and managed to get back to my tent in one piece—had a top day.

5 January 1997, David, Panama

Packed the tent away and caught the dugout canoe we'd ordered to take us back to Bocas del Torro—the main island area. From here, we caught a 3-hour cargo passenger ferry to the mainland (felt like I was on a cruise as we passed over a dozen small uninhabited islands along the way). From here, it was a 3½-hour bus trip to David—the 3rd largest town in Panama and very relaxed. Got there fairly late—had a Chinese meal and went to the room to find a bat flying around inside.

6 January 1997, Boquete, Panama

Neil and Petya went to Panama City today while I shot off on my own to visit Boquete 1½ hours away in the mountains. Got there and had a stroll around in the hills for a while. I was going to camp here tonight but couldn't be arsed to hang around until dark as there was nothing else to do, so I caught the bus back to David and then another bus (5 hours) to San Carlos—a beach not too far from Panama City. Got drunk on the bus.

7 January 1997, Panama City

Woke up in my tent at about 5 a.m. by some local man shouting outside my tent—he wanted me to move. I told him I would in a couple of hours and went back to sleep. I didn't have a clue where I was, and when I finally got up, I found out that I was camped outside a car alongside the main road and about 1½ hours before San Carlos, where I was supposed to be heading—must have been a heavy night.

Caught the bus down to San Carlos—supposedly one of Panama's best and most popular beaches. I got off the bus dying for a shit—too many houses around, so I headed quickly for the beach, looking desperately for somewhere to go along the way. The beach was miles away, and as I rushed down the road with houses on both sides, and my rucksack on my back, I couldn't hold it in any longer, and logs started falling out my shorts and on to the road. I ended up going on some ground between 2 houses. Got to the beach and washed my shorts. Wasn't too impressed so caught another bus to Panama City. Checked into a hotel and walked to the yacht club a couple of miles away—ended up going through a really rough area, where the police stopped me and made me catch a bus as it was too dangerous.

Went to the yacht club to try to get a place on a yacht as a crew member sailing through Panama Canal—left a message on the board. Met up with Neil and Petya, tonight who are staying at the same hotel.

8-13 January 1997, Panama City

Spent the next 6 days in Panama, finalising our expedition through the dense and hostile jungle called the Darién Gap—between Columbia and Panama. Went to various consulates and embassies, all of which said, 'Don't go as it's too dangerous'. Had a contact in the US army serving in Panama, whom we met on the British Army base in Belize who, after a lot of effort, gave us some army supplies.

The hotel we were staying in turned out to be a brothel and a right shithole—rats and huge cockroaches everywhere. It turned out to be great fun as there were peepholes everywhere, so you could occasionally watch the shagging that went on. Neil and I turned into right perverts during our week there. I had a room to myself, with a few holes into the girl's room next door, while in Neil's room, he had a few holes into his next-door neighbour's room, a local Panama girl—not bad-looking but a bit of a tart. On the other side of his room, he had a few holes into the shower—that after a few days we had to make bigger.

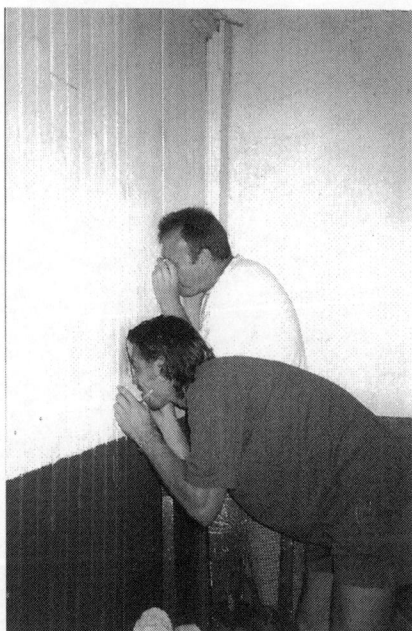

The trouble with Neil was that he was sharing a room with Petya (the Swedish girl), who couldn't understand how excited Neil got when something was happening in the next room, and he was running around like a teenager from peephole to peephole, trying to get a better view.

Went to see the Panama Canal, which I'm glad I've seen, but it's nothing special.

I had a really enjoyable time in Panama City—that is renowned for its crime. Most people I'd met here had been robbed. Even walking around the High street in daylight on your own was dangerous.

Kevin and Neil carried on to do the Darién Gap (next chapter).

DARIÉN GAP 1997

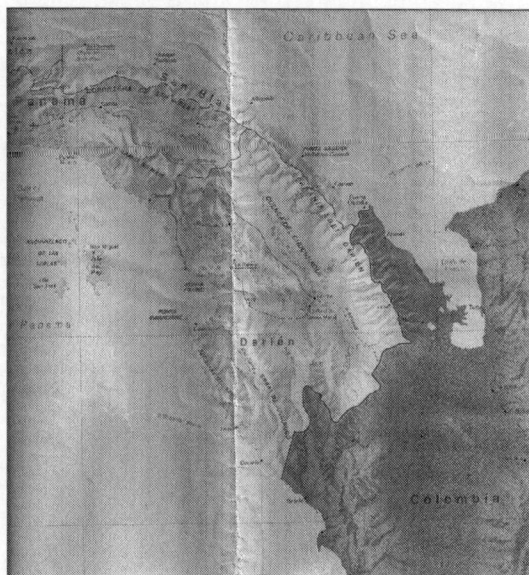

The Darién Gap is a huge and hostile dense jungle between Panama and Columbia. There are no roads through this area—you must either fly across or take a ship around in order to reach Columbia. The expedition that we are undergoing is to go through the jungle on foot and come out on the Columbian side. This expedition is in aid of charity for 'Children In Need' back in England and is the main reason I left Hong Kong last year.

This trip has been done before by adventurous travellers in the past, although the area is becoming more hostile day by day, and we haven't heard of anyone attempting this trip over the last two years, when a Canadian guy attempting it was shot in the back of the head by guerrillas. Previous to that, three American missionaries were kidnapped and are still held hostage in this area.

It is a very dangerous jungle due to all the drug traffic coming over from Columbia. The main problem is with the Columbian guerrillas, who are renowned for their violence and kidnapping. They are presently at war in the Darién with both the army and Panama guerrillas (who are fighting for their share of the drug trade).

For this expedition, we've had help from both the British Army in Belize and the US Army here in Panama. We've contacted various people and consulates, all of whom have said the same thing: 'Don't go as it's too dangerous'.

Time will tell, but between the 4 of us, we have about 24 years of travelling experience and are looking for more than conventional travel. This is the type of adventure I've been looking for, and all going well will be a real adrenalin buzz and certainly an adventure of a lifetime.

Day 1: 14 January 1997

Left Panama City this morning for Yaviza—the main village in the Darién. Originally, we were going to catch a 12-hour banana boat down the Pacific Coast and up river to this jungle trading post. However, there were no spaces left last night, so we had to catch the bus this morning.

The bus was an old bright-yellow US school bus that took us for eight and a half hours on a very rough and bumpy dirt road, where it dropped us off at Meteti. We thought the bus was going to take us all the way, but obviously not.

We weren't really sure where we were—just at a 3-way junction. This is the end of the line for the bus as the road to Yaviza from here gets too bad.

We ended up getting stranded for the day as there was no transport and had to set up camp at the bus stop in the middle of nowhere. Three hammocks, my tent, and a fire. A paramedic stopped and said he was going to Yaviza and would give us a lift—the problem was, he was leaving at 3 a.m.

Day 2: 15 January 1997, Yaviza

Didn't sleep too well last night at the bus stop—got woken up at 3 a.m. by our lift to Yaviza. Took about 5 minutes to pack up camp and load it on to the back of the ambulance for our 3-hour trip down a very bumpy road (only passable in the dry season).

The driver of this 4-wheel-drive ambulance was a madman and thrashed it completely through this jungle dirt track in complete darkness. I've been down plenty of dirty roads in my time, but this was by far the worst—God help the patients who travel in the back of it.

Arrived in Yaviza at about 6 a.m. Still pitch black. We found the only hotel in this town, woke up the manager, got a room, and crashed out.

Spent the rest of the day acclimatising to the jungle and relaxing before heading off tomorrow. Yaviza is the biggest village in the area, with about 500 people—mostly Caribbean blacks, all of whom live in wooden shacks about 6 feet off the ground on stilts. Neil went to the so-called post office to send a book back to Panama City. The man held it in his hands for a few seconds and said '*Oooh,* that will be about a dollar'. They don't have scales here.

Day 3: 16 January 1997

Left Yaviza this morning and headed off into the unknown. Had to cross the river before we could start (about 50 metres across). I traded my old boots that I was going to throw away for a local guy to take us across in his dugout canoe.

We've got really good (or so we thought) army issue maps for this area. It should have taken us one and a half hours to reach the next village, yet the path on the map was wrong, and we soon found ourselves lost in the jungle, with no one around to ask. Managed to find a path going in our direction, which was OK until it veered off into 2 directions. Shit a brick, everyone was hot, sweaty, and tired by now. It was our first day's walking with full packs on, and we'd climbed several steep hills.

Looking at the map, we knew if we carried on south, within an hour or two, we'd hit a main river—the same river Pinogana was on. We all agreed on it and carried on south. Andy was beginning to crack under the pressure, but luckily, after one and a half hours, we finally hit the river—what a relief! We all stripped off and went for a swim. The only problem was that we didn't know whether Pinogana was up—or down stream. We just sat on the riverbank and waited before a dugout canoe came past. Andy and Neil managed to get a ride to the village, while Eddie (the Aussie guy with us) and I carried on walking.

We all decided to stay in Pinogana tonight after quite a physical day (5 hours in the jungle). Pinogana is a very quiet village alongside the river. Had a wash and got some water from the river and set up camp.

Day 4: 17 January 1997

Left Pinogana this morning for a 5-hour slog to the next village along the river—an Indian tribe. We'd only been walking for about 5 minutes when we met a local man with a horse. After a bit of negotiating in broken Spanish, we'd got ourselves a guide and, even better, a horse to carry all our bags (a bargain at £1.50 each). It took us about half an hour to tie 4 heavy rucksacks (100 kg) to the back of the poor horse before we began. We'd only been going for ten minutes when we hit deep mud. The horse was up to its knees in the mud, panicked, and ended up ripping the waist belt of my rucksack—bastard. That will take some repairing.

KEVIN COURTNEY

Carrying the bags on the back of the horse seemed like a good idea at the time, but it was putting a big strain on the bags (not to mention the horse) as it went along the narrow path, with the branches ripping the bags. They kept going lopsided, so in the end, we had to retie 3 bags on the horse and take it in turns carrying the other. It was quite muddy, and the soles of both my boots began falling off. I had to fix them temporarily with gaffa tape. We've only just begun this expedition, and already, all my things are falling apart.

Saw some interesting wildlife today. First, a bird eating a spider the size of your hand—a lot bigger than a tarantula, with its body the size of a mouse. Then I saw a snake dart quickly into the bushes. It was black with a silver belly, quite thick, and must have been at least 1½ metres long. Also saw several small bright-red crabs near the swamps, with huge claws almost the size of their bodies.

Finally made it to a remote Indian village alongside the river. They were pleased to see us and very friendly. Their village consisted of about 15 huts (all on stilts). We asked them if we could camp in the area, and the chief came over, shook our hands, and took us to a spare hut, where we spent the night—unreal. Within about ten minutes, our hut was full of the village Indian kids (about 25 of them), who just sat around and watched our every move in amazement.

One of the Indians invited us all around to his hut for dinner (then he asked us if we had any food for him to cook). It was great to be in the jungle miles from anywhere in a local Indian's hut, having dinner with his family.

Got back to our hut, and within 5 minutes, all the kids were back. We decided to sing them a song and ended up with 'Get Your Tits Out for the Lads' as it was the only song we all knew the words to. They obviously didn't understand the words but clearly enjoyed it.

Day 5: 18 January 1997

Spent about 2 hours this morning repairing my boots with Araldite and sewing my rucksack belt back on. I had to wash my rucksack first as it stunk of horse sweat (really bad) from yesterday.

There was a really big festival going on in Union de Choco today—a fairly large Choco Indian village about 45 minutes' walk away. So we all went down, taking a couple of Indian kids from our village to show us the way and help us across the river crossing. As soon as we arrived, we were met by the prime minister's legal adviser, who was here for the festival. We told him that we were going through the Darién to Columbia. He told us that we were all mad as it's a very violent area, and there are many problems with the guerrillas in the areas which we are going through. Only 3 days ago, 2 men were kidnapped, not far from here (one Indian and one Panamanian), with a ridiculous ransom of $3,000,000. Yet this area is only on the edges of the Darién and considered fairly safe. There were still several soldiers patrolling the village with AK47s. From now on, as we move further into the jungle and further from civilisation, the risks are going to get a lot higher.

Anyway, back to the festival. The Indian chief came over and introduced himself and showed us around his Indian village—all the men were really drunk (especially the chief). Several of the Indians were curled up unconscious on the ground. On our tour around the village, we had a good sample of traditional Indian beer. A bit vinegary but not bad.

Neil and I saw a live tortoise (about a foot long) hung upside down outside someone's hut. Immediately, we wanted to buy, cook, and eat it to add it to our collection of exotic animals we'd eaten, but the Indian who owned it wouldn't sell it to us.

The Choco Indians were in traditional dress—typical Indian-style, but what was unique was their body painting. Most of the women and some of the men were covered in black dye from head to toe, with various stripes and patterns incorporated into their body. A rare and special site to see ethnic Indians in the middle of the jungle like this. The chief asked us if we wanted to be painted. We'd all had a few beers and agreed. It took over an hour for each of us to be painted from head to toe by one of the elderly women. We were all as black as the ace of spades from head to toe before we realised it takes about 8 days to wear off. Shit—there's no way we could go back to civilisation looking like this! We'll have to make sure that we stay in the jungle till at least the next week, until it wears off.

The chief came up to us as we were about to leave and invited us to a virgin ceremony. We weren't sure what he meant, so we followed him to the main hut in the centre of the village, where the ceremony was being held. This ceremony is to celebrate the coming of age (15 years old) for the local Indian girls who at this age officially turn into a woman and can get married. In this ceremony, 2 girls had recently reached the age of 15 and were brought in to the centre of the hut, where they sat down in front of the whole village. Both looked very young and very innocent—wearing the traditional body paint and a sarong around their waist. They were both topless with quite elaborate necklaces. They both looked very nervous, especially before they had their virginity tests. Intrigued to find out how their virginity was tested, we watched on—I got a bit nervous when I saw 2 towels being brought into the centre. However, for the test, a piece of cotton was tied around their neck—then an equal length tied at both ends placed in their front teeth. If the cotton was long enough to go back over their heads, then they were virgins.

Both passed the test, and the ceremony continued. The next stage was even more extraordinary. Both girls were then force-fed neat gin by their mothers while music played and the village watched. Still sitting in the centre of the hut and over a period of only half an hour, both girls were force-fed about 1 pint of gin each—even when they were virtually unconscious, their mothers were still pouring gin down their necks while the other Indians cheered. Then about 15 topless dancers came into the hut (ageing from about 16 to 80 years old). The mothers slung their daughters over their shoulders and in the long procession danced around the hut along with the other dancers while water was thrown over them. Then, still unconscious and over their mothers' shoulders, the girls were paraded around the village and then thrown into the river for some form of baptism.

That was one of the most unique and rarest ethnic experiences I have ever seen—and increasingly harder to find in this ever-changing world.

By now, it was dark, and the party was in full swing. The chief was staggering around, pissed as a fart, not knowing where he was. Traditional music was being played, and the villagers were doing their traditional dancing. I had a go. It was dark, and I ended up standing on most of the Indians' feet. Got some local kids to take us back (45-minute walk, plus short river crossing in a dugout canoe) to the Indian village we were staying at.

Day 6: 19 January 1997, Boca de Cupe

Despite the warnings yesterday, we carried on with the expedition and headed on further into the jungle to the next village, about 5 hours away, called Boca de Cupe. We said our goodbyes to the Indians we've been staying with for the last couple of days and who had been good to us.

Got ourselves a guide (a 6-year-old Indian—who was told by the chief to show us the way). We're getting into more dangerous territory now, so we had to keep more of a low profile. An interesting day's walk through the jungle, the highlight being when we reached the peak of a hill, and as far as the eye could see, in every direction was dense jungle—what a buzz!

Arrived in Boca de Cupe as the sun was going down. Our aim was to get an exit stamp from the police station so that we've officially left Panama (although we won't arrive for several days, this is the last place) and leave first thing tomorrow. Went straight to the police—the stamp was locked away in the post office, and the immigration man wasn't turning up until at least tomorrow afternoon. It was getting late now, and we had to make a mad dash across the river into the jungle in order to set up camp before the daylight had completely gone. The river crossing was exciting, to say the least—about 50 metres across and chest-deep at its deepest. Pretty nerve-racking as the river was flowing very fast, and I had everything I owned on top of my head. Set up camp, built a fire, had some Spam and noodles, went to sleep.

Day 7: 20 January 1997, Boca de Cupe

Felt really dazed all day. I'm sure it's due to the strong Malaria tablets I'm taking, 'doxycycline'. They seem to make you feel stoned all the time and don't half give you some weird dreams—they're great!

Boca de Cupe, strangely enough, is the last village of any size before Columbia and is full of blacks, probably originating from the Caribbean coast many years ago. It's quite dangerous but nothing compared to what we have waiting in front of us in the heart of guerrilla territory. There are 200 villagers living here and about 20 soldiers guarding it 24 hours a day. All very serious looking, tooled up with M16s (machine guns that very rarely leave their sides). Some serious shit has happened here over the last several months with guerrilla warfare etc. including a couple of kidnappings (who still remain hostages further in the jungle). Despite the problems and trouble here, most people have warned us about going further into the jungle and into Columbia as apparently it gets very bad further up.

We know this and the risks we are taking—but because of all the effort we've put into the expedition and having been warned too many times about the risks involved, we seem slightly brain-dead of the danger and are just focused on moving forward. Although, deep down, Andy is messing himself but doesn't want to be the first to turn back.

Anyway, managed to get our passports stamped, so officially, we've now left Panama—yet couldn't find a guide willing to come with us upriver.

Day 8: 21 January 1997, Boca de Cupe

Did some repair work today on both my boots and rucksack—it will be a miracle if both survive this trip. Managed to get a guy to take us upriver tomorrow to a small Indian village very far away, called Paya. After a lot of bartering, got the price down to $130 for the whole trip, which takes 9 to 12 hours on a dugout canoe. Had to make some hair-raising river crossing back to the village this evening—chest-high in water, about 30 kg of equipment on my head and shoulders.

Day 9: 22 January 1997, Paya

Got up at 5 a.m.—still pitch black. Packed up the tent and began our long upriver trip to the small Indian village of Paya. We all squeezed our bags and ourselves, plus 2 local lads, on to a dugout canoe. It was as stable as you like. Everytime you moved, the thing nearly turned over. We left just as light was beginning to fall on the jungle—an amazing sight. Very mysterious, with all the mist rising from both the jungle and the river.

After a few hours, we left the main river and went up one of the tributaries. It's the dry season at the moment, so the rivers are all fairly low, which meant the last 6 or so hours of the trip were quite hard work as everytime we hit a low point or a rapid, we all had to get out and push (not easy in flip-flops).

One of the local lads taking us to Paya heard a sound in the trees, picked up his rifle, and shot—we couldn't believe it when a huge green beautiful parrot came crashing down to the ground (it's the same type my granny has in England, and must cost over £100 in a pet shop). He shot it for food as parrot is quite a delicacy in these parts. As we drove off in the dugout, the poor thing was still alive—Neil ended up killing it by twating it over the head with the driver's bottle of gin (which, by now, was almost empty). The driver was pissed, with a big dazed grin on his face. How he managed to get us up the rapids and through the shallow parts without running his motor on the rock, I'll never know.

Saw lots of birdlife along the way—plenty of toucans, hummingbirds, kingfishers, parrots, and many other colourful species.

At one stage, we hit a large rock. The boat stopped dead. The guy in front fell off, and the boat nearly flipped over, throwing the bags with it. On a few occasions, there were fallen trees completely blocking the river—where we had to drag the dugout over the tree and in the other side. Hair-raising moments—if we were going to get ambushed, this is where it is likely to happen.

Arrived in Paya late in the afternoon. Paya is a small and pretty Indian village with about 30-40 Cuna Indians. The women wear a colourful sarong around their waist and walk around topless—although, when we appeared, they all covered themselves up, which was a shame. There are also about 20 San Blas Indians living here—originally from the Caribbean Islands. All the women still wear their traditional outfits.

We found this village fairly hostile compared to the previous Indians we'd met and lived with.

Set up camp in their village quickly as it was getting dark. Once the camp was set up, Neil and Andy went off to find the army base and register with them while I got the dead parrot out of my bag, took it down to the river, and plucked and gutted it ready for cooking. I ripped its top beak out of its head in order to make a necklace out of it.

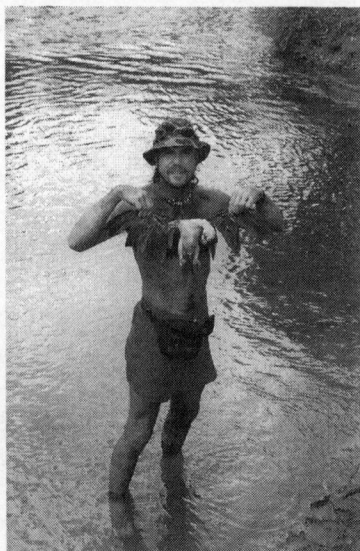

Then from out of the dark appeared about 5 fairly scruffy men carrying sub-machine guns (M16s), with very bad attitudes and a lot of shouting. They said they were soldiers and that we had to come to the army base with them *now* and were quite forceful about it. We didn't know who the fuck they really were, in this area renowned for it's Columbian guerrillas. We asked them if they had any ID—they said it was back at their base.

We had no choice but to go with them—we had to pack up our camp (while they virtually cut down Neil and Andy's hammocks). Then we were frogmarched away from the village with all our belongings, in pitch darkness, by these 5 men waiving their machine guns around (one guy had an M203 grenade launcher on the bottom of his M16). Serious weapons.

Not knowing what was really going on, whether these were so-called good guys or bad guys—and not having any choice—we walked through the jungle for about half an hour, when we arrived at the army base (that was a relief, believe me!). After about half an hour of the head incharge trying to get money out of us and us pretending that we couldn't understand, they let us go—bastards.

Made our way back to the village. Met Neil and Andy and set up camp for a second time that night. I got a fire going and cooked the parrot—not too bad. Young Indians everywhere stealing everything they could from us—luckily, I had most of my things inside my tent. Can't wait to leave this place first thing in the morning.

Day 10: 23 January 1997, Paya

After all the petty shit we've had in this village with both the army and the Indians, I couldn't wait to get going. Managed to hire a couple of Indians to take us 3 days through the jungle to Columbia. The most dangerous section of the expedition—they would only come in a pair as it was too dangerous for them to come back on their own. They wanted $150 for the trip. We got them down eventually to $100—still a rip-off, but they know we can't do it without them.

We all set off on the 3-day trek—after only ten minutes, Neil fell over and sprained his ankle. The worst part of it was that it was directly over a huge ants' nest, so we all got bitten to pieces while Neil was stumbling around.

Back to Paya again—we'll try again tomorrow. The Indian chief came over and helped Neil. He rubbed a lotion on the swelling, then strapped his ankle up using Sugar Cane bark—a very good job. Nice to meet a genuine person so willing to help you out—or so we thought until he tried to charge Neil with $5 for the treatment.

As soon as the sun starts going down in this village, the mosquitoes swarm around you—I've never know a place like it.

Heavy rain tonight.

Day 11: 24 January 1997, Columbian Jungle

Finally managed to leave Paya first thing this morning. Neil's ankle is a bit better, and he paid one of the Indians extra to carry his pack. Started walking out at first light at a fairly fast pace—plenty of hills to climb up and then come down. There was a lot of rain last night, so the jungle was very muddy—we were all slipping around all over the place, sometimes up to our shins in thick mud. It felt like I had two breeze blocks tied to my boots.

Saw a few different types of monkeys along the way and some stick insects that I haven't seen before. The Indian guide also spotted and killed a small poisonous spitting snake that can be fatal if bitten by it.

Had to make several river crossings during the day, which slowed
us down a bit. By mid-afternoon, everyone was soaking wet from
sweat, covered head to toe in mud, and knackered. The problem
was that everytime we stopped for a rest, swarms of mosquitoes
attacked us from every direction.

Finally reached the Columbian border—nothing there. Just a big rock.
We all stripped off naked quickly and walked across just wearing our
boots and rucksacks so that we'd walked from Panama to Columbia
naked. Or even better, from Central America to South America naked.

Big problem today with mosquitoes and ticks—Andy had to have 2
ticks burnt off him during the day, while I managed to knock a couple
off my hands before they had the chance to dig into my skin.

Everyone, by now, was getting weaker. I fell over and ripped the
belt off my rucksack—a big problem as it now means that I have to
carry all the weight of my rucksack (about 25 kg) on my shoulders.
The soles of my boots fell off or partly off during the day, which
was a nightmare as I had to stop and tie them back on to my boots
using a rope—a right bastard trying to mend them as quickly as
possible as I sat in a swarm of mosquitoes, being bitten all over!

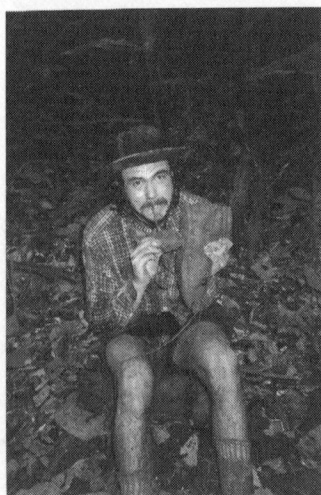

Everyone was knackered, and the 2 Indian guides told us that it was only an hour to where we could camp. When we got there, they told us that there was a better place to camp along the river—the only thing was, it was another hour away. We forced ourselves for another hour—still no river. The guides kept saying, '5 more minutes, 5 more minutes'. We were all on our last legs and very weak, covered from head to toe in mud, soaking wet from sweat, and slipping all over the place in the mud. It was getting dark, and tempers were getting very short, to say the least—especially as we kept going up hills. We very nearly lost our patience and came to blows with the guides—especially when we realised they were tricking us to get us to walk as far as possible so that they could finish their jobs sooner and go back to their village.

Found a stream and stopped there. By now, it was almost dark—none of us had any energy. We were all soaking wet, covered in shit, stunk really bad, bad-tempered, and very hungry. Couldn't get a fire going at first as the wood was wet. Took us about 40 minutes in the end to get it started. Had a wash in a stagnant pond in the dark, ate my 2-minute noodles, and went to sleep.

Day 12: 25 January 1997, Columbian Jungle
Different day—same shit! Woke up in a mouldy tent, smelling like an incontinent tramp. All my clothes stink and are soaking wet. My boots, rucksack, and tent all need some serious repairs. Felt great putting on wet, smelly, and dirty clothes before a hard day's slog through the jungle—however, with all the howler monkeys screaming in the trees, along with many colourful birds of paradise, it did put a bright side on things. Mended my boots by using rope to tie the soles on to them. Had my breakfast (a bowl of mashed potatoes as I'd run out of porridge).

Spent most of the day wading through the jungle, up to our ankles deep in mud half the time. My boots broke a couple of times, which was a bastard as everytime I stopped to mend them, I was hit with a swarm of mosquitoes and bitten everywhere, especially around my face. Very frustrating when you're trying to mend your boots asap and dripping in sweat.

Another physically hard and challenging day. Although, hopefully, tomorrow should be the last stretch to the next village of Bijao. The guides were getting very nervous this afternoon and wanted us to pay them fully this evening—no chance! We're not having those bastards running away during the night, leaving us on our own in the middle of nowhere. They say it's too dangerous for them to return with the money as there are a lot of bad people along the next stage.

Well, whatever happens, tomorrow, we'll all really have to keep on our toes and have a low profile—whatever. It should be interesting, especially as Andy is absolutely shitting himself.

Day 13

Unfortunately, I cannot find day 13 of Kevin's trip. He changed over diaries, ending one on Day 12 and beginning the other on day 14. However, day 14 starts on 26 January, so I think he may have got confused over the numbering of days. Or maybe he didn't want to have a day 13 (unlucky for some).

Day 14: 26 January 1997, Columbian Jungle

Dragged myself out of my tent this morning, a physical wreck and smelling worse than anything I had smelt before—at least the other 3 are in a similar condition. Neil got severely attacked by mosquitoes last night and is covered in bites. Andy got bitten all over his ankle, which has now swollen up really bad.

Had some mashed potatoes for breakfast—as that is the last food I have. Mended my boots quickly and then we were off. Another day of trekking through the jungle ankle-deep in mud. Got pissed off with the guides as they got lost a few times today, which meant that we had to waste a lot more time crossing several rivers. Neil walked into a wasps' nest and again got stung all over (walking disaster).

The guide spotted a piousness snake on a log I'd just climbed over (without noticing it!) and clubbed it to death with a stick—only a small snake yet very venomous.

Everyone was suffering from heat exhaustion, and the soles of my boots were virtually hanging off by the time we arrived in Bijao this afternoon. Bijao is the first village on the Columbian side of the border and the first village we'd seen in 3 days. It has a small black community renowned for not liking gringos (whiteys), which was no understatement. This was probably the poorest village I've seen since Africa. These people have nothing at all—just the clothes they wear and a knackered old wooden shed they live in. The hygiene standards were very bad. It was from here we left our guides and tried to arrange a dugout to the next village, Travesia, further down on the other side of the swamp. This proved to be real hard work as the starting price for a 3-hour boat trip was $400—a complete rip-off, but these people have you by the balls. You can't walk across the swamps, and they know you're not going to go all the way back to Panama—bastards. All you need when you're shattered, tired, and hungry. Managed to get them down to $110 for the 4 of us. Then we were out of this shithole for good.

The swamps were really interesting, with plenty of narrow waterways, overhanging trees, etc. You really knew you were in the middle of a swamp miles from anywhere. A lot of interesting wildlife as well—plenty of lizards, up to 1½ feet long, that run perfectly across the water without sinking. We came across an overhanging branch that had a 3-toed sloth hanging from it with a small baby clinging to its stomach. It was great to see some exotic and fairly rare wildlife until one of the men on the dugout pulled out his machete and chopped the branch off and then tied the poor sloths to the boat. He was going to take them back to his wooden shed and have the poor things as pets.

By now, the sun was going down, and we were getting very nervous to say the least as our lives were in the hands of these 2 arseholes driving the boat. We had no idea whether they were going to take us to Travesia or if they were going to take us to one of the many Columbian guerrilla camps in the area and sell us off. We just had to stay calm and wait.

Eventually, we hit a huge river about 500 metres across, and the dug pulled up on the side of a deserted village that they said was Travesia (the village we wanted to go to).

There were about 50 wooden huts in the village on the edge of the swamps. Every single one was empty—not a single person was here. We were told back in Panama that we would be able to stock up on food here and catch a boat to Turbo—which is a fairly safe area.

It was a ghost town! We didn't know where we really were or what the fuck was going on. It was dark, and we were getting eaten alive by mosquitoes. What do you do in a threatening situation like this—especially when everyone is really tired and ratty? If this really was Travesia then, why were no people here? Was it a set-up? Were these men dropping us off at the wrong village on purpose (where we'd have to spend the night) and coming back later with some more of them to do us over or, even worse, let the guerrillas know we were here and helpless!

Andy was almost shitting himself with fear. Neil nearly kicked off and wouldn't get out of the boat, while, for some reason, I was on a real adrenalin trip and wanted to spend the night here—all right, it was obviously very dangerous to spend a night in a ghost town in the swamps in a high-guerrilla-activity area. And why were there no other people here—not one? But we didn't have a lot of choice—and if we survived this one, then it certainly would have been an unreal adventure.

After about 45 minutes of arguing, Neil finally got out of the dugout, and it soon pissed off into the darkness—this was shit or bust! Fate is in our hands now.

First of all, Neil and I had a quick look around the village, which was built on stilts above the swamp. We found a house (wooden shed with several rooms) that looked OK for tonight—front and back door in case of any trouble. Andy and Eddie moved in, putting up the mosquito nets etc. while Neil and I looked for an escape route into the swamps in case we got attacked during the night.

We looked into several of the houses. These people had hardly anything—very poor. But why was the whole village totally deserted? Not even one person here in this place we'd intended to stock up on supplies. The scary thing was that in a lot of the houses, there were Christmas decorations still up and calendars on the wall for 1997, meaning that the place had only just been evacuated.

We were disturbed when a motorised dugout pulled up. We all shat ourselves senseless until we realised that it was only looters.

Built a fire on the stove and cooked our last meal—2 packets of 2-minute noodles between 4 hungry lads (it didn't even touch the sides). The house we're staying in is covered with about half a dozen huge spiders the size of your hand. Went to sleep in anticipation.

Day 15: 27 January 1997, Stranded in a Ghost Town

None of us slept too well last night, but at least we made it through until daylight in this Ghost Town in the middle of nowhere.

We were all weak with hunger and getting tired. Luckily, Eddie had about half a bowl of muesli left that we shared between the 4 of us.

Time would certainly tell now—we were stranded in the middle of nowhere, in a very dangerous guerrilla area, with no food!

Luckily, there were a few pet dogs still running around in the village that had been left behind. I spent an hour trying to catch one so that we could have a good meal and be able to think straight again. The dogs weren't having any of it as they were as hungry and cautious as we were.

Neil was staggering around trying to build a raft—if we were in Travesia, then, according to our map, if we went downstream for 60 km, then we should hit the coast (and relative safety).

By now, it was mid-afternoon. Andy was on boat watch when he spotted a boat coming downstream. We all quickly hid in our house until it got a lot closer, and we could see it better. It was far too big to be a guerrilla boat—it was a banana boat with passengers going downstream to the coast. We all ran on to the jetty, waving anything we could find and shouting until they spotted us and pulled in.

Thank fuck for that!

It was a knackered old steam boat carrying a cargo of wood and bananas, heading for Turbo (the next town about 4½ hours away) on the mainland.

That was it. We had done the Darién Gap—we were safe from now on, and it was all over. We hardly had the energy to lift our bags on to the boat, but what a relief.

No one could understand why we were there as, believe it or not, the government had closed the whole village down less than 2 weeks ago due to the place becoming too violent, dangerous, and vulnerable due to all the high guerrilla activity. Shit a brick, and there we were, stranded there on our own. Everyone was saying how lucky we were to be alive etc. and these people, who are some of the poorest people I've met, were giving us all their food—we were far too hungry to turn any of it down.

It felt great to be lying on the deck of a banana boat in the sun, watching the world go by (all the monkeys in the trees etc.) as we headed for Turbo.

Finally arrived in Turbo, a small Columbian town that felt like a city the size of Hong Kong or New York after the last 2 weeks. Got a cheap hotel—with first-class luxuries like cold showers and proper toilets. It was quite embarrassing when we first got there as it was obvious we'd been in the bush— everyone looked like tramps, with beards, sticks, and stinking to high hell.

We were going to go on a drinking binge tonight, but everyone was pissed and knackered after the first pint.

But as stupid as it maybe *we crossed the Darién Gap*

Kev's travels continue in his South America Chapter.

SOUTH AMERICA 1997

27 January 1997, Turbo

Got up this morning and went down to the Columbian Army base and got our entry stamp into Columbia (as officially we had been in no-man's-land for about the last 10 days).

Rushed about and got stressed out in order to get on the Banana boat (the same one we were on yesterday) before it left at 10 a.m. After a lot of effort, managed to get one just in time. The boat was loaded up with wood and bananas. Neil, Eddie, and Andy found ideal places and put their hammocks up while I put my tent up on the top deck (I've never camped on a boat before). After about half an hour on the boat, we were all settled in for the 20-hour coastal trip to Cartagena. To cut a long story short, we ended up waiting around all day for paperwork etc. to be authorised. I ended up eating all my food for the trip within the first hour. Spent the rest of the day hanging around waiting to go, occasionally jumping overboard to cool down. Finally left at 1 a.m.

28 January 1997

Spent the whole day chugging around the Caribbean coast of Columbia on the knackered old boat. It was very rough for the first part of the morning, with many people being sick everywhere. It was impossible to either avoid standing in sick or being sprayed by it. The day seemed to last forever (it's now the 3rd day we've been on this boat). When the wind picked up this evening, my poor tent took a battering—I thought it was going to blow off the top of the boat.

29 January 1997, Cartagena

Finally arrived in Cartagena some time in the early hours of this morning, but stayed on the boat until daylight, when we all got a taxi to a cheap hotel in the centre.

Cartagena is noted as one of the most colonial and beautiful old towns in South America and is also a big holiday and beach resort for Columbians. In the old section of town, the architecture and condition of all the colonial buildings were amazing and fascinating to walk around.

First things first though—as we'd just spent the last 2½ weeks in the Darién Jungle, with all our food on rations, it was time for our first big pig-out. We found a posh hotel with a breakfast buffet and went mad eating everything in sight until we could hardly move.

Met 3 crazy lads from New Zealand and went out on the piss with them this evening—drank a shedload of booze at their hotel. Then one of the lads wanted some Charlie, so I went with him to find some. It only took 5 minutes to find a local dealer, who lived around the corner—as we went into his house, 3 good-time girls (probably prostitutes) were walking out. I managed to get the price down to £2.50 a gram, and between us, we bought 10 gm. I tried a bit—good shit, man. Only in Columbia can you get the best at a ridiculously cheap price. As the money was being changed hands, the man's 7-year-old son was rushing around giving the change out (he's probably got a bright future in front of him, when he takes over his father's business in a few years' time!).

We staggered back to the hotel with about 10 gm between us, only to find the hotel had been raided by the police (we had been making a lot of noise in the street earlier). They were checking ID, and we managed to dodge them.

All charlied up to the eyeballs, we went down to a very trendy club on the beachfront, with a combination of Salsa and House music.

What an atmosphere—it seemed that most people were on the same buzz as us. You can't seem to get away from it in Columbia as everywhere you go, day or night, people approach you with slogans such as 'Anything for the nose, sir?' We left the club at 4 a.m.

30 and 31 January 1997

Spend the next couple of nights in Cartagena, abusing myself to the limits as I had done on my first night here. Had a great time partying in this party town (which was great after the physical Darién experience). Sleeping all day and partying all night.

It's great when you're travelling on a budget as you always end up staying in the rough end of town in the cheapest of hotels. You see and experience a lot more than you would if you stayed in a posh hotel in the nice area. Obviously, it's a lot more dangerous in these rough areas, but as long as you use your common sense and keep one eye over your shoulder, you're normally OK.

A lot of the hotels double as brothels, so you've always got a lot of seedy (yet interesting) people around—prostitutes, pimps, drug dealers, drug addicts, glue sniffers, drunks sleeping on the pavement. There's never a dull moment in the seedy areas of town—much more fun than watching TV.

1 February 1997, Santa Marta

Managed to get my arse into gear today and left this mad town with Eddie to another town on the Caribbean coast called Santa

Marta—a 7-hour bus trip, which was great as I managed to catch up on a lot of sleep on the way.

Moved into a hostel, which was a real travellers' hang-out. One of the best places I've stayed in on this trip as it's really chilled out, and everyone is on full-on party mode. They had no rooms left, so Eddie and I had to sleep on the roof. Met up with Neil and Andy here, who arrived a day before us. They had both been recovering all day from a rough night from which none of them remember coming home.

Several drinks in the hostel, I then out around a few of the bars and discos (which, around the area of the hostel, all seem to be girly bars full of old prostitutes). It was a good night.

2 February 1997, Santa Marta

Spent most of the day lazing around the hostel, recovering from all my Columbian nights out, and playing chess with some of the lads.

3 February 1997, Tayrona National Park

Went to Tayrona National Park today with Neil, Andy, Eddie, and the 2 German lads and a straight Ozzie who tagged on.

Tayrona is a huge and wild national park on the Caribbean, about an hour away from Santa Marta—very beautiful with crystal-clear water and, strangely enough, palm trees and large cactuses growing next to each other. The hostel had a bus leaving daily to the park in the morning. I nearly missed the bus today as I had to rush around to the bank, buy food, etc. Only just made it back to the hostel in time before the knackered, old, and colourful hostel bus left.

Bastard—halfway to the park, I realised that I'd left my food bag behind. Shit a brick. I intended to stay for 3 days, and armed with a bag of weed, it's going to be murder when I get the munchy attack and haven't got any food. In my pathetic Spanish, I tried to tell the driver to pick it up and bring it with him on the bus tomorrow. The problem was that from where the bus dropped us off, it was over 2 hours' walking through forest along beaches, etc. to one of the best spots. I would have enjoyed the walk if I wasn't haunted by the fact that I'd have to do the whole thing twice tomorrow to pick up my food bag!

Finally arrived at the beach—set up camp (I put my tent up while the other lads set up their hammocks). Then I sat back and smoked a big jay and watched Eddie getting stressed out as he was the only one getting firewood (which was very hard to find). No one couldn't be arsed to help.

A relaxing day of smoking, drinking, and bodysurfing in the huge waves. Carried on until I couldn't smoke any more.

4 February 1997, Tayrona National Park

Dragged myself out of my tent this morning for a 4½-hour round trip to the bus stop and back in the chance that my food bag was on the bus. I'd be pissed off if it wasn't on the bus. I've come here to relax. The last thing I need is a 4½-hour walk to pick my food up.

Luckily, my food was on the bus—I dived in straight away and pigged out on a packet of biscuits.

Two lovely Argentinian girls in bikinis got off the bus, looking lost—so I did my good deed of the day and directed them along the path. It's moments like these you really wish you'd tried harder to learn Spanish. Had a good laugh with them, especially when one of them pulled out a bag of grass, and we stopped off at a scenic spot for a nice big spliff.

Eventually arrived back at the camp, where the jays were being passed around. Spent the rest of the day stoned and lazing around the beach.

5 February 1997, Tayrona National Park

Got woken up at about 6 a.m. this morning (just as it was getting light) by the Columbian police. The bastards had come first thing in the morning on purpose. They got everyone up and then searched us all, finding about ½ oz of grass at the bottom of a sleeping bag. Shit! Everyone comes here to relax on the beach and smoke—they know that, and that's why they come first thing in the morning, when you're still asleep.

The starting bid was a $100 backhander in order to be let off. An officer stayed with us while the other police officers (dressed in jungle outfits and carrying sub-machine guns) went on to catch other travellers. Managed to get them down to $30—it was like an auction, getting the price down. We had to write our names in his book, which I took great pleasure in doing, writing down 'Piss Flap' as my name. I couldn't keep a straight face when the policeman repeated it out loud. The funniest thing was that once you've paid them a backhander, they give you your gear back and let you get on with it—can you believe it!

Caught the hostel bus back to Santa Marta. It was good to be back at the hostel again—a crazy and interesting place that has its own drug dealer who comes around several times a day, taking people's orders. The funny thing is that he's about 50 years old and fairly well dressed—looking more like a respectable grandad rather than a Columbian drug dealer.

Went out tonight with a mad Ozzie, his girlfriend, and another lad. Started off sitting next to the beach, chatting and drinking a bottle of gin, before popping back to the shops for another one. It was great getting merry and watching the world pass by. Then we went into a bar that was fairly quiet (apart from us, there were about 5 prostitutes in there). From then on, the night seemed to phase out.

6 February 1997, Santa Marta

I don't know what happened last night, but I woke up half naked on the floor of the dormitory. Another one of life's drunken mysteries. Spent most of the day sleeping it off in bed, when I was finally given my own one to sleep in. Neil and Andy came back from Tayrona today along with the Argentinian girls.

Tonight is the first night of the carnival—the biggest party of the year in South America (especially in Rio de Janeiro—Brazil). The best place to celebrate the carnival in Columbia is Barranquilla (about 1½ hours away), where apparently it kicks off big time. Neil and Andy went down tonight with some people from the hostel while I'm off down tomorrow with Eddie and a few others.

7 February 1997, The Carnival Barranquilla

Armed with a huge bag of Charlie and some spending money, Eddie, 3 others, and I made our way down to Barranquilla for the big carnival. We checked into the same hotel as Andy (and about 10 other travellers from Santa Marta). We quickly made our way to the procession of the floats. Everyone and everything was covered in white flour that had been thrown around during the beginning of the procession. We had missed the first half of it, and by now, everyone was drinking quite heavily in the street as thousands of people partied in the carnival.

As Eddie and I watched the tail end of the floats, some kind and well-plastered local man left me incharge of his bottle of whisky. We couldn't understand a word he said but made polite conversation with him until the bottle was empty. Went back to the hotel for more Charlie and booze. The party was already in full swing. Andy was doing his best to chat up all the Danish girls at the same time and, as usual, was getting nowhere.

We all went down to a disco bar that was full of drunk people dancing to the Salsa music and ended up staying there for most of the night. Everyone was charlied up to the eyeballs and running around like headless chickens. We all left about 4 a.m. because we couldn't take any more Salsa music. Went back to the hotel room, where about 8 of us smoked joints until daylight. Great night!

8 February 1997, Santa Marta

Had about 2 hours' sleep before catching the bus back to Santa Marta. Went out tonight, and a big gang fight nearly erupted a few metres away from us, between about 6 lads all waving big bowie knives with blades about 8" long. It would have got very messy if it wasn't for one side running away with the other side in pursuit.

9 February 1997, Venezuela

Left Columbia today with Eddie—2 buses and 5 hours later, we arrived at the border, where we were all taken out of the bus. We were faced up against a wall, with legs spread, and searched. What a nice welcome to Venezuela (the most unfriendly border crossing I've ever been to). We had it lucky—a couple from New Zealand were stripped naked and forced to squat on the floor for 10 minutes.

It was another 2 hours in the back of a van to Maracaibo, where we met some fun-loving Venezuelans still on the piss from the carnival.

At Maracaibo, we caught the 12-hour night bus to the pretty little mountain town of Mérida.

10 February 1997, Mérida

Arrived in Mérida first thing this morning and spent a couple of days here relaxing in this quiet little tourist town high up in the Andes Mountain Range.

Went to see a bullfight, which is renowned to be value for money as the crowd (nearly all men) get very drunk and always end up fighting. We got there to find lots of sober families with children, only to realise that it was a fun one for the children.

The highest cable car in the world is here in Mérida (12,500 feet), although I didn't go up it as it cost £10, and the weather was cloudy.

They also have the world's largest ice-cream selection here—with an ice-cream parlor with over 200 hundred choices. I had 3 flavours together—spaghetti, cheese, and meat (this was disgusting and had pieces of meat and fat in it), followed by beer flavour. I must admit, I didn't feel too good afterwards.

Met 2 German lads we knew from Santa Marta and went out on the piss with them. Mérida is quite a happening place at night, being a university town, and for a Tuesday night, it was very busy. We went to the student club, which was very good. I went home half an hour before it closed at 2.30 a.m. Both the German lads stayed, and when it finished, 2 girls came up and asked them if they wanted to go home with them, which, of course, they did—bastards. If only I'd stayed another half hour.

12 February 1997, Caracas

Caught the 13-hour night bus with the 2 German lads and Eddie (full bus, didn't sleep too well).

13 February 1997, Caracas

Arrived in Caracas (the capital of Venezuela) this morning and checked into a cheap hotel. We didn't realise at the time, but it was a love hotel, where men bring prostitutes to shag and pay by the hour. It was really interesting to see all the couples check out an hour later. I quite enjoyed it until I realised that I was probably the only one in the hotel not getting any sex.

Went out tonight to experience the local nightlife on a Friday night. Unfortunately, we got sent to the posh and friendly end of town—with lots of false people and high prices. We got talking to a couple of local lads—one who turned out to be very well known with the Crown and knew a lot of people in the know. The other was a right prat, who considered himself 'really cool'. They took us to a very trendy and elite dance club, where we went straight to the front of the queue and got in for free. There were a lot of rich people in there (most of them were buzzing with cocaine). They played some excellent dance music, but where's the charlie when you need it? Left about 3.30 a.m. and went to some seedy bar full of prostitutes, which was great apart from the price of drinks, so we left and came back to the hotel.

14 February 1997, Valentine's Day

Walked out of the hotel this morning, only to find Neil off his face, staggering out of a taxi—he'd just arrived from the night bus after taking a very strong prescription-only sleeping tablet that totally knocked him out cold.

Eddie caught a bus south tonight while I went out with the 2 German lads again (I've known them for 2 weeks now and still don't know their names). Neil was still spaced out from last night's sleeping tablet, so we left him behind. Caught a taxi to the nightlife, where the taxi driver offered us some charlie (it would have been rude not to). He stopped off at his mate's house and picked up a couple of bags, then drove off. The bags were small and expensive. I told him we didn't want them (in a ploy to get the price down). Then as he waited at some traffic lights. he poured a bag on to his lap and snorted the lot. I couldn't believe it. You only get this in downtown South America—a taxi driver snorting charlie at some traffic lights. There we were, driving through Caracas, in a huge American car the size of a small limousine. It was like sitting on a sofa. Ended up going to another trendy dance club (yet also cheap). Probably the best club I've been to yet on this trip.

It was a great atmosphere, and one of the Germans and I managed to get chatting to a couple of stunning local girls, whom we spent the rest of the night dancing and partying with. I thought they were prostitutes at first, but it turned out they weren't. When the club finished, the German lad and I spent about half an hour trying to get ourselves back to their place, but they weren't having any of it. Got back to the hotel at about 4.30 a.m. and managed to steal the keys to the fridge, where we pulled out a handful of beers, replaced the keys, and went back to the room, where we drank the beer and smoked until daylight.

15 February 1997
Spent most of the day in bed before packing my bags and catching the 22-hour bus with Neil to Santa Elena on the Brazilian borders.

16 February 1997, El Dorado, Venezuela
Got woken up at about 7 a.m. by the bus driver, who told us the bus wasn't fit enough to go any further and that we'd have to get off the bus. We were in a small town called El Dorado, about 6 hours from Santa Elena. The driver gave us enough money for the next bus, but Neil and I were like zombies. We expected to be on the bus for another 6 hours and were still unconscious from the super-strong sleeping tablets.

El Dorado is a small town in the middle of nowhere. It sprung up when gold and diamonds were discovered here—it's a very interesting place to be stranded in. It's full of gold and diamond hunters. Then of course, there are lots of prostitutes here as well to provide the men with their needs. Neil found one after only being there for ten minutes. He flirted with her for a while until she realised that she wasn't going to get any money out of him and buggered off.

It's very dangerous around these parts as life is very cheap. People are constantly going missing in the bush—robbed of their gold and diamonds and killed and buried.

Finally, after hanging around for about 5 hours, another bus turned up, which took us 6 hours down the road to Santa Elena on the Brazilian border.

The scenery along the way was stunning—plenty of savannah and hills covered in yellow grass like a carpet of yellow. Two stunning girls got on the bus from some small Indian community along the way. Neil and I were straight in there at the first chance and fixed ourselves up with them for tonight.

Went to the local disco, which was the equivalent to a Venezuelan working men's club in the middle of nowhere. The 2 Indian beauties never turned up, so I pulled another girl, who turned out to be a Brazilian travel agent who was here on holiday for a week. After several beers and an invitation to come back to my hotel to pick up my Portuguese phrase book (that I don't have), she came with. Everything was going well until I got lost in this two-horse town. I felt a right prat as there are only a few streets, and it took me over an hour to get back to the room. Neil was already in bed, pretending to sleep, with one eye open. To cut a long story short, I didn't get anywhere with this girl and went to sleep.

17 February 1997, Boa Vista

Got woken up at about 6 a.m. when the Brazilian girl left. Went down the bus station and bumped into Eddie, who was just leaving on the bus south to Brazil, the same one as us except we're on the next one. Bumped into the 2 Indian girls, who were very apologetic about last night and took us to the immigration, where we got our exit stamps for Venezuela. Got the bus for the 6-hour trip to Boa Vista (Brazil). As soon as we crossed into Brazil, we all had to get off the bus while it was fumigated.

Arrived in Boa Vista and found a hotel (after a lot of effort and walking)—it's a lot more expensive in Brazil. Shit, at these prices, I can't stay around for long. Bumped into Eddie, who was on cloud nine as he'd pulled some Brazilian piece on the way down here and spent most of the journey snogging.

18 February 1997, Manaus

Neil and I were up at the crack of dawn this morning and caught the 4-hour bus south to Caracarai, in the hope of finding a cargo boat heading downriver to Manaus (about a 3-day trip).

Spent 2 hours wandering around the docks in this jungle town, trying to find a boat going today or tomorrow. No luck, although it was a bit of an adventure trying.

Got back to the bus station soaking wet with sweat and waited a few more hours for the bus to Manaus. When the bus turned up, Eddie was already on it as it had come from Boa Vista. The bus to Manaus was an interesting 16-hour trip through the jungle, stopping occasionally at small lumberjack communities along the way—basically houses, a few shops, and plenty of wooden shacks selling beer or liquor, similar to the old gold-mining towns.

19 February 1997, Manaus, Brazil

Arrived in Manaus first thing this morning, found a hotel with Neil and Eddie, and had a few hours' kip. Manaus is a big city alongside the Amazon, which sprung up out of nothing when gold was discovered by the Spanish a few hundred years ago. It used to be a very rich city until the gold dried up—yet still very interesting.

It pissed down with rain today as I went for a look around and changed some money. I went to enquire about a boat down the Amazon to Belém on the Pacific Coast. There was one leaving today at 5 p.m. although it was almost full. Eddie and I decided to go for it. Rushed back, packed our bags, and ran back to the boat before it left. Unfortunately, didn't have time to say goodbye to Neil, who, in a few days, is going to the States for a week, then over to the South Pacific Islands before spending the next year in New Zealand and Australia. Although I'll probably meet up with him later on next year in Mongolia for a horse-riding adventure.

Arrived on the ferry, and both decks were jam-packed with hammocks hung all over the place. It looked like a refugee boat fleeing a war-torn country. We managed to squeeze in and find a space. Then the boat left for the 5-day trip down to the end of the Amazon. There were a lot of goodbyes and a lot of tears as the boat pulled away.

Five-Day Boat Trip Down the Amazon River
The next 5 days were great, very relaxing, with some good and interesting people. The whole thing cost about £50, with 3 good meals a day.

Typical day—wake up, go for breakfast, go back to sleep in my hammock, read a bit, sleep some more, dinner, have a spliff in the toilet, read, chat, sleep, get up for the evening meal, up to the bar for some beers, spliff, more beers, a bit of a party, then back to my hammock until the next day.

Met a few good travellers on the boat—a couple of Germans who were cycling around South America, an American lad who was permanently stoned, and an Italian who wanted to shag every woman on the boat. The trip was excellent as you were forced to do nothing for 5 days. Just lie in your hammock, relax, and watch the world pass by. Although, there wasn't a lot to see as the Amazon is huge, and the riverbanks are so far away. At Manaus, the Amazon River is almost a mile wide and gets wider all the time, up to 20 miles wide as it reaches the Pacific Ocean.

In Brazil, everyone speaks Portuguese, and with my pathetic Spanish, I have no chance, so I must admit, although I made a lot of Brazilian friends on this trip, I hardly spoke to any of them. I'm only going to be in Brazil for a couple of weeks, so it's not worth me trying to learn Portuguese and then getting even more confused when I go back to Spanish-speaking countries.

A few of us were at the back of the boat one evening, having a spliff—the whole deck smelt of ganja, and the next thing we knew, some bloke came up and gave us a bollocking. I was holding the spliff at the time and had to get rid of the evidence, so I ate the rest of it rather than throw it over the side.

23 February 1997, Belém

Finally arrived in Belém after 5 days—I enjoyed it so much, I wanted to spend another 5 days going back to Manaus. Went straight to the bus station in the hope of finding a bus to Salvador tonight. There was 1 bus, and it left in a couple of hours—perfect. Belém is one of the rainiest cities in the world—we were only there a couple of hours, and it pissed it down.

The other travellers we'd met on the boat turned up at the bus station, so we all went down some back alley for a last spliff together. The randy Italian lad was with some piece of fluff that he'd only just pulled on the boat. They were getting a hotel for the night. On the way to the station, the German cyclists sheltered in the rain, and some local girl with a beer in her hand ran up and offered one of them sex. I bought a bottle of turps for the 36-hour bus journey to Salvador, then dropped and smashed it as I was getting on the bus.

24 February 1997, 36-Hour Bus to Salvador

Spent the whole day on the bus with Eddie on this marathon bus journey to Salvador. A long but enjoyable trip—Eddie bought a large bottle of something strong, and we somehow managed to wait until 3 p.m. until we opened it for a mid-afternoon tipple. That was when the party started and didn't stop until the bottle was empty.

25 February 1997, Salvador

Got woken up at about 8 a.m. when we arrived in Salvador—I felt as sick as a dog after that cheap liquor we drank yesterday.

Checked into a cheap hotel that included breakfast—although we got there too late for it and had to sweet-talk the maids into giving us some.

Spent most of the day walking around the old streets of Salvador—one of the best towns I've ever been in, in terms of beautiful and very colourful colonial buildings, both restored and run-down, although very touristy. I went down a side road and all of a sudden had lots of girls hanging out of the windows and doorways, whistling at me and offering me sex. It turned out that the whole street was just brothels.

Walked back to the main street, only to find a huge demonstration—about 2000 plus locals were waving banners and shouting slogans outside some government building. There were about 60 riot police protecting the building—it was getting a bit rough. I went straight into the middle to get some better photos, when it all kicked off around me. Several scuffles broke out with the police right beside me as I was standing on a dustbin taking a photo—the batons were being swung around and blood was being spilt as I was in the middle of it, trying to take photos. Then the tear gas came out, and it all came under control again just as it was about to kick off big time. A great adrenalin buzz though—it's not every day you get the chance to be in the middle of an almost riot.

Salvador is one of the best towns I've been in so far on this trip. Not only is it beautiful, but it's also got a very good party atmosphere—some say that the 4-day carnival is a lot better here than in Rio. Went out around the streets tonight with Eddie (you have to be very careful here as it can be very dangerous—especially if you go away from the main street).

There was a big street party in the main square, several street bands playing with 100s of locals drinking and dancing in the streets—an unbelievable atmosphere (the Brazilians certainly do know how to party). Eddie pulled a local girl (although I think it was the other way round—she pulled him!) while I bought a huge handmade bong for about £6. As soon as I bought it, I was like a kid with a new toy and just wanted to try it out. I found a dealer whom I'd met earlier today and went off with him to score a small amount of grass. He wanted me to give him the money first, which, of course, I didn't, so I ended up going with him. Which was great as it allowed me to go right into the rough and violent parts of Downtown Salvador—where you wouldn't even dream about going down in the day. It was relatively safe as I was with one of the locals and obviously doing business. Went down some back alley into some guy's back passage. There were a few guys smoking a joint, who soon came in my direction. I was smoking the spliff when the police came in—everyone ran off. I followed some guy and dived into his wooden shack of a house, where his 2 kids were asleep (still with the spliff in my hand).

The police went. I bought my gear and left, although I must have looked very suspicious walking back to my hotel with a bong in my hand.

Had several hits on the bong—not bad. Then I was back out again to meet Eddie. I wandered around the street for another hour or so before calling it a night.

26 February 1997, Salvador

Brazil is famous for its beaches, and today, I caught a local bus about 30 km north of Salvador and got off at one of the beaches and walked for an hour or so. Not the best beach I've seen but very scenic, white sand and palm trees that looked a lot better after a spliff. Got chatting (in pigeon Spanish) to a couple of local girls on the beach and spent the rest of the day with them. They didn't live far from my hotel, so I took them back. Eddie was there and had already had a few beers. They stayed for another hour. They wanted to meet us tomorrow, but we'll be well gone by then.

I went out with the hotel maintenance man tonight to score some charlie for Eddie's 30th birthday in a few days' time. It was great as we went in a lot more dodgy areas than I'd been in last night. Right in the middle of the rough end of town, we ended up going into a crack den—unbelievable! Dodgy people all around just getting high on various things. Interesting yet sad to see. We were in some wooden shack where we could look down and see what was going on. A young black guy right next to me (barely 16 years old) was off his face smoking crack from an old yoghurt pot. Everyone was out of it—the charlie was too expensive, $30. I bought a bit more grass. There was an intense scene at the end when the guy said I didn't give him enough money—he grabbed my arm as I went to leave. I pulled away and carried on walking while he shouted at me. What an experience—you don't read about that in the guide books.

27 February 1997, 24-Hour Bus to Rio de Janeiro

Got up at about 4.30 a.m. (not easy) and caught a taxi to the bus station in order to catch the 5.30 a.m. bus to Rio. Managed to get to the station in time, only to find out that the bus didn't run any more (bollocks). Had to wait until 8 a.m. for the $62 bus (it's so expensive in Brazil, I can't wait to get out).

The bus trip was OK until some old man shat himself and stunk the whole bus out.

28 February 1997, Rio

Arrived in Rio first thing this morning, tired and ratty after hardly any sleep over the last few days. Moved into the worst hotel in Rio for $9—it was more like a hostel for homeless men (a shithole, but they don't come cheaper than this in Rio).

I'm only going to be in Rio for a few days, so I spent most of today running around trying to see and do as much as possible, although most of the day was wasted due to Portuguese being a huge language barrier.

I went to the post office and picked up a few letters, then spent 1½ hours trying to find the right bus to Cristo Redentor (a mountain with a huge 30-metre statue of Jesus Christ on the top). I was getting really pissed off as everytime I asked someone (or as least tried my best to), they would give me a different direction and bus number. I must have walked halfway across Rio trying to find this fucking bus that only takes 20 minutes. Finally caught the bus and arrived at the base of the mountain, only to find out that the scenic train that takes you up to the top had gone up in price from $3 to $15—sod that. I went to get a taxi instead, but the robbing bastard wanted $20 (for a 20-minute uphill ride). I would have walked, but it's very dangerous (as you have a good chance of being robbed). Also, it was late and cloudy. So after all that effort, I caught the local bus back and went to Coco Cabana Beach (a world famous beach similar to Venice Beach, LA). By the time I got there, the sun was going down, and people were leaving. I just lay on the beach and relaxed with a big spliff and watched the world go by—all the joggers, roller skaters, cyclists, and posers going past in this trendy and happening place. I got chatting to a local girl (not the best one I'd seen so far). She told me she was studying religion at college—within 5 minutes, I'd made my excuse and left.

Got back to the shady hotel at about 8 p.m. and went straight to sleep.

1 March 1997, Rio

Eddie wanted to move hotels, so I came with him, and we went to the youth hostel on Coco Cabana Beach. It was $6 more but 100 times better. Very clean, with kitchen—the dog's bollocks compared to the shithole we were in last night.

Eddie and I went off (despite all the warnings of danger about being robbed) today to climb the 800-metre high mountain to visit Cristo Redentor. It took us over an hour to find the right bus (even though I caught it yesterday). I can't wait to get out of Brazil, where it's a lot cheaper, and everyone speaks Spanish, so at least you have a chance of them understanding you. It was a long hard slog to the top of the mountain—and sod's law, as soon as we were almost on the top, the clouds came over. It was very touristy at the top with all the tourists who had come up on their tourist buses. Despite the clouds, it was an excellent view.

It's Eddie's 30th birthday tomorrow, so I bought a bottle of cheap plonk, which we drank at the hostel tonight. We gathered up a few other people and went down to Coco Cabana Beach for some more cheap booze. I went off with some guy from the street to get some charlie for Eddie. Before I knew what was going on, I was being taken down the back streets, and there were now 3 of them. I fucked off quickly before it was too late (they were definitely going to rob me).

Found my way back to the beach—Eddie and everyone else were going to a club. I was knackered and went back to the hostel. It's only a 15-minute walk at the most from the beach, but I was buggered if I could remember where—I spent 3 hours walking around the streets, trying to find the bastard hostel with no luck.

2 March 1997, Rio

Woke up on a car bonnet as the sun was coming up and, in the daylight, finally managed to find my way home. Eddie was already there—today was his 30th birthday. I opened the fridge, pulled out a couple of beers, woke him up, and forced him to down a couple of shotguns. Found out that he'd got robbed as he staggered home last night from the club. Two men held him against a wall and took his cheap watch and the few dollars change he had in his pocket. I couldn't think of anything better than being robbed in Rio on your 30th birthday (as he hardly had anything stolen), although Eddie didn't see it the same as I.

I went down the beach to find a huge festival going on—everyone was dancing and drinking in the streets. If anyone knows how to party, it's the Brazilians.

I said goodbye to Eddie (whom I have been travelling with for about 2½ months) and caught the 22-hour bus to Foz De Iguacu.

3 March 1997, Foz De Iguacu

Spent most of the day looking out of a bus window until I finally arrived in Foz De Iguacu later on in the afternoon. The bus trip was OK until the old man in front of me shit himself and stunk the bus out—that's twice now that it has happened to me in a week. Maybe old Brazilian men get incontinent with old age!

Found a cheap hotel and was slightly disappointed to find that it was in a fairly respectable area with no prossers, pimps, etc. hanging around the streets.

4 March 1997

Caught the local bus to the Argentinian border, then through to the town to Puerto Iguazu Falls—one of the natural highlights in the whole of South America. The falls are huge waterfalls as far as the eye can see. They are equal to the Victoria Falls in Africa in terms of size and beauty. I spent the whole day walking around the Argentine side—which was very good as they had balconies where you could actually walk directly over parts of the falls. Caught a bus back to Brazil, where I spent the night.

5 March 1997, Asunción, Paraguay

What a hectic day! Rushed around this morning and made my way to the Brazilian side of the Iguazu Falls, which was more stunning and beautiful than the Argentinean side as you get a panoramic view of the whole waterfall—very impressive!

Went back to my hotel, got my bags, then caught the local bus to Paraguay (only a few miles away). The bus crossed over a bridge and went through a *very* busy town. When I asked the driver where the immigration was, he told me that we'd passed it about a mile ago. I had to get off the bus into all the hustle and bustle of the crowded streets and walk a mile back to get my passport stamped. I had to walk another half mile back over the bridge to Brazil in order to get my exit stamp. Shit a brick! I've never had so much hassle trying to leave a country. The midday sun was blazing down, and I was sweating really bad. Anyway, after a lot of effort and twating around, I was finally in Paraguay.

I wanted to hitch to Asunción (the capital) and began walking down the road out of town—after walking about 4 miles, the road was still very busy with local traffic and no good for hitching. My face was badly sunburnt from all the sweat and the sun, so I decided to call it a day and caught the bus.

I got chatting to a local man on the bus, who seemed over-friendly, and I instantly thought he was gay when he invited me to spend the night at his place. I never turn an offer down as it's always an experience, whether good or bad. If he was gay, it wasn't a problem with me as long as he kept his hands to himself.

Went back to his house, and it turned out he had a wife and 3 children, who were all as friendly as he was. Chatted to them for a while, and they told me about the dictatorship of Paraguay and how violent the country used to be.

6 March 1997, Asunción

Spent the day relaxing with this Paraguay family and enjoying the home comforts (and great food). The man had a small leather factory and showed me around while his wife insisted on washing *all* my clothes—I must admit, I did smell a bit. My clothes were in a terrible state as they've only seen one washing machine in the last 4 months, and I'm always too lazy to wash them properly by hand. It took her 2 hours to wash them by hand, and I was more than embarrassed at the black water that was coming out. I got them back cleaner than when I bought them and all nicely ironed. They're so clean that I don't want to wear them (just keep them for a special occasion). Later on in the afternoon, the wife gave me a sightseeing tour around Asunción—the capital city, although no larger than my hometown of Lincoln back home in England.

A very relaxed city with plenty of colourful colonial architecture.

7 March 1997, Encarnación

The Paraguay family that I've been staying with gave me a big breakfast, plenty of food, and then a lift to the next town, where I caught a 5-hour bus to Encarnación (the Paraguay border town with Argentina). I was going to hitch but decided to begin tomorrow when I cross the border. Encarnación is another typical chilled-out town of Paraguay. Although I've only been in this country for several days, I have a very good feeling about the place—friendly and pretty.

8 March 1997

Left Paraguay this morning as I crossed over into Argentina—I was a bit weary at first as to how the Argentinians would react against me being English and the fact that we were at war with them only 15 years ago. However, to my surprise, I found them very friendly. Although everytime I saw someone in military uniform, I had a little smile on my face as I remembered we beat them.

Pasada—the border town was very modern and cosmopolitan. I wanted to hitch out of town, but it wasn't possible as the town was too big. I was trying to get to Colonia Pellegrini, a small village in the middle of nowhere, in order to have a look at the swamps and wildlife that are very famous here in Argentina.

I caught a bus to the turn-off for the village and got dropped off in the middle of nowhere alongside a dirt road that led to Colonia Peligini 122 km away. As far as I could see, in every direction was savanna grassland—this was cowboy country. There was very little traffic—the few cars that did go my way were full of rough-looking cowboys (whom I wouldn't want to mess with), who were both unfriendly and pissed. Every vehicle that went passed was a knackered old car full of pissed-up cowboys. Finally got a lift after 1½ hours, off a friendly Argentinian couple who were going fishing in one of the swamps. We only went 20 km down the road before they began fishing—I had a go and caught a couple of small piranhas about a couple of inches in length.

It was getting dark now, and I got dropped off a few miles up the road, where it was just flat grassland for cattle. It felt great to be in the wilderness in the middle of nowhere. I put my tent up, opened a bottle of cheap wine, read my book, and fell asleep—great.

9 March 1997, Argentina

Woke up in the middle of nowhere to watch the sun rise over the savanna, with cattle grazing in the distance. Flat grassland as far as the eye could see and flocks of green parakeets flying above my head—this is what travelling is all about. Cooked my porridge on my stove, packed everything away, and began walking towards Pellegrini along the long and lonely dirt road that went on forever (it's very similar to the Australian outback except greener). I only had about half a pint of water left and so was on strict rations. It felt so good to be in the middle of nowhere as I walked for about an hour, passing a few unfriendly cowboys along the way, herding up cattle.

Chilled out for a bit on the side of the road, then carried on walking—a couple of cars passed without stopping. I wasn't bothered as I was enjoying myself too much. Until I ran out of water and my mouth was as dry as a nun's crotch. By now, the midday sun was up, and it was very hot. I had to open a tin of peas just for a drink. I was soon thirsty again as I carried on walking in the hope of finding water.

Then from nowhere, I spotted a small puddle of water on the side of the road—a little oasis! I don't know how long it had been there, but it had a few beetles swimming around in it. That didn't bother me, though, in my state—I got my stove out and made myself about 6 cups of coffee, one after the other.

Then a van drove past—the driver must have felt sorry for me as he saw me cuddled up to my puddle of water and gave me a lift. Within 5 minutes, I had a sandwich in one hand and a large cold beer in the other. Luckily, he was going all the way to Pellegrini, so I enjoyed a few more cold beers on the way, watching the great scenery of nothing.

He dropped me off outside the national park, where I managed to hire a boat and a guide to take me around Laguna Ibera—a huge swamp famous throughout South America for its beauty and wildlife.

The swamp trip lasted 2 hours and was excellent—saw plenty of exotic birds as well as many camen (small crocodiles), Capybara (huge rat-like mammals about 60 kg in weight), and a few swamp deer. Went for a swim in piranha-infested waters (apparently they don't attack humans!) although it was still a bit nerve-racking.

Great trip—well worth the effort as we got back at sunset. I put my tent up in the national park, cooked my dinner, and then went to sleep in my tent.

Before I fell asleep, I heard a van being thrashed around the campsite and a pissed-up voice shouting my name. I looked out my tent, and it was the same man who drove me here this afternoon (and, by the state of him, he'd had another crate of beers). He was on his way back home to Paso de los Libres and offered me a lift. I was going to hitch that way tomorrow, and although he was drunk, I went with him—it would be an experience, whatever happens. Spent 3 hours in his van before arriving at his house, where his wife had a couple of huge pizzas waiting for us, and I was shown my bed for the night.

10 March 1997, Paso de los Libres

Chilled out in the morning with the Argentinian family I stayed with last night—had a big breakfast and huge dinner before I said my goodbyes and got them to drop me off on the road south, where I began hitching the 340 km to El Palmar National Park.

Got a great lift after only waiting an hour—it was on an open-back truck going all the way down to Buenos Aires. A good ride as it took me all the way to El Palmar—while I lay on the back of the truck, watching the world go by, lying in the sun and drinking wine.

I got dropped off as the sun was going down and managed to walk around the park entrance gate and avoid paying the $5 entrance fee.

El Palmar National Park is a huge area full of palm trees as far as the eye can see. As I entered the park, it was beginning to get dark, so I camped in the woods surrounded by palm trees in every direction. It wasn't too comfortable camping in the woods, and I had run out of water so went to the park office and found an outside tap. Had a job finding my tent on the way back. Although I had a good idea where it was, it was still very hard to find in the dark.

Pissed it down with rain tonight—which isn't much fun when your tent isn't waterproof. Luckily, the palm trees sheltered me from most of the rain, although I did have a sleepless night and woke up wet and cold.

11 March 1997, El Palmar National Park

Dried most of my things out this morning as I cooked my porridge, then hitched the 12 km into the centre of the park. Spent the morning wandering around the park, then hitched out to the main road south. This is where I began hitching the 300 km to Uruguay. I was sure I'd be in Uruguay today, but the hitching went slow. It took me 2 hours to get my first lift, which took me to a town 30 km away from the Uruguay border, then spent another 2 hours waiting until a young girl pulled up on a moped. She told me that I'd be better off 8 km down the road at a service station. I couldn't believe it when she offered to give me a lift—her little shopper moped was barely powerful enough for her. When I climbed on the back with my huge rucksack, and she had my daysack, I thought her bike was going to collapse under the weight. It was a slow yet fun ride, and by the time I got there, the sun was going down, so I set up my tent on the side of the road and called it a day.

12 March 1997, Hitching to Colonia

Carried on hitching this morning and managed to get a lift to the border in a huge transport truck. Then hitched a ride over the bridge to Uruguay on another truck. No problems getting into Uruguay (my 58th country). Then spent another 1½ hours trying to hitch to the next town 30 km away—managed to get another truck, taking me half hour down the road to Mercedes. The hitching was taking too long, and there were too many small towns in between Mercedes and the town of Cobnia I was heading for, 220 km away. I got a bus ticket and went for a decent meal while I waited—I ordered lamb and got a huge portion (at least ½ kg) South America is a great place for good meat.

Caught the bus to Colonia. By now, it was night-time—found the municipal campsite and put my tent up.

13 March 1997, Colonia

Had a look around the old Uruguayan town of Colonia this morning—a beautiful town with plenty of colonial buildings and cobbled streets. I would have liked to have stayed longer in

Uruguay as it had a very friendly and colonial feel to it, similar to Paraguay.

However, this afternoon, I caught the 1½-hour ferry to Buenos Aires (the capital of Argentina). I had a family to stay with—a sister of the family I'd stayed with in Paraguay. I went straight to a phone box to phone this family up. I had problems with the telephone and asked some young piece of fluff—the Courtney charm worked wonders (at long last) as within an hour, I'd moved into her place. Was lucky in more ways than one as over the next few days, she became my tour guide around Buenos Aires as well as someone to practise my Spanish on. The rock band Kiss came over. I wanted to go to their concert but couldn't get hold of a ticket.

I spent 3½ days in Buenos Aires and had a great time. It's a beautiful capital city, similar to London or Paris, yet isn't dangerous at all.

I was going to hitch 3,000 km south to the very bottom of South America, yet on the day I was due to leave, I phoned Connie (my girlfriend) up, and she told me that she wanted to meet me in Chile for Easter, meaning I wouldn't have time to hitch-hike. I was forced to pay $100 for the 38-hour bus ride to Rio Galliano right down in the south.

17 March 1997, Rio Galliano
Arrived in Rio Galliano this morning and booked a bus to Punta Arenas. Spent a few hours wandering around this very southern and isolated Argentinian town—it looked similar to how I'd expect a small Eastern European or Russian town to look. Caught the 250 km bus to Punta Arenas that took about 6 hours due to the fact that it was dirt road most of the way with the Chilean border crossing in between. The scenery was interesting—grassy coastal plains with occasional sheep grazing in the ice-cold wind. This is almost the bottom of the world.

Arrived in Punta Arenas—the most southern town in mainland South America (and one to the most southern towns in the world). I checked into a hotel and met an Argentinian girl who could speak English. I spent to the rest of the night taking the piss out of her—she was a great laugh and took it all well.

18 March 1997, Punta Arenas

Got chatting to a couple of Canadian lads at the hostel—they were heading south to Ushuaia in Tierra del Fuego (the most southern part of the world outside Antarctic). They had managed to get a ride on a Chilean war boat, taking 1½ days to get there and costing $50. I was tempted to go with them as from there, they were trying to head down to the Antarctic. I would have loved to attempt it with them, but I don't have the time or money.

Went for a skinny dip in the sea as this will probably be the furthest south I'll be able to swim (and the coldest!). Bloody freezing.

Caught the 4-hour bus to Puerto Natales and met a young American guy who had just finished a 6-month job in the Antarctic, working as a field biologist—an interesting bloke. He told me about all the parties that they have in Antarctic and how they grow marijuana there using hydroponics.

19 March 1997, Moreno Glacier, Argentina

Up at the crack of dawn and caught the 6-hour bus to Calafate back in Argentina, where I met up with a group of other travellers, and we hired a vehicle to take us 2 hours down a dirt road to Parque National De Los Glaciares. We visited the world-famous Moreno Glacier—a huge glacier 60 metres tall and about 14 km wide. Definitely one of the most spectacular sights I've ever seen in over 8 years of travelling. You certainly get a feel of the power of nature, standing right next to the glacier, listening to the ice constantly cracking and falling into the lake below.

Suddenly, I heard a huge roar of thunder and looked around to see a massive chunk of ice, the size of a 20-storey block of flats, shear off from the main face of the glacier and slide down into the lake below. Such an amazing and powerful sight to witness. I couldn't believe my eyes at first.

Went to the campsite about 8 km from the glacier—again probably one of the best spots I've ever camped at in terms of a view—right alongside the lake with a great view of the glacier in the distance. Plenty of autumn colours in the area, grass, trees, etc. with snow-capped mountains in the distant—excellent.

I went to make a fire but couldn't find enough wood so had to use dried sheep dung that I found scattered around the grasslands. Got chatting to a funny Argentina lad who turned up late and camped next to me and used my fire. Then an Israeli lad turned up, and we all sat around the fire, chatting and drinking mate (similar to tea yet very popular in southern South America). It's a ground plant called mate (that looks like sawdust) and is put in a metal or wooden cup. Hot water is then poured into the cup, and the liquid is sucked up through a metal straw, with a grid on the base to stop all the ground leaves coming up. Everyone in Argentina, Paraguay, Uraguay, and Chile seem obsessed with this drink as everywhere you go, you see men and women walking around with a flask of hot water in one hand and their mate cup in the other.

Anyway, I finally went to sleep in my tent yet was woken suddenly in the night when gale-force winds started blowing everywhere. My poor old tent (Wendy) isn't made for this type of stress and was almost bent in half under the pressure of the wind and was flapping all over the place. I heard the Argentinian lad cursing as his flysheet almost blew away, and he spent at least an hour in the darkness and in the ice-cold gale-force winds, trying to sort his tent out with no luck. I would have helped him but was acting as a human tent peg—holding my tent down with me on one side and my bags on the other to stop my tent blowing away!

20 March 1997, Moreno Glacier
Had a very cold and sleepless night as on several occasions, I was sure my tent was going to collapse under the pressure of howling gales last night.

Got out of my tent this morning to find the Argentinian's flashy 3-man tent in pieces on the floor, with the poor Argentinian lad asleep under all the carnage.

Managed to get a lift back to the glacier this morning for a final look, with a young Argentinian couple touring around. They offered to take me to the famous Mount Fitzroy—probably the most difficult mountain in the whole of South America to climb. It was several hours away, so I decided to go back to El Calafate and chill out for a while rather than rush around all the time trying to see everything.

Relaxed in the hostel this afternoon and opened a couple of wine cartons with an English lad called Les I met there. We both got slowly pissed as we talked shit and exchanged travelling stories.

22 March 1997, El Calafate

Began hitching down the very baron road to Puerto Natales today in Chile—there is very little traffic on this dirt road, and as I walked to a good spot, I saw another couple hitching. I expected it to take me a couple of days but could take a lot longer if I had to wait in a queue for a lift. So I made a decision straightaway to catch the 6-hour bus this afternoon—it turned out to be the right decision as later on, I saw the same couple. They had given up after 3½ hours with no lift.

I felt bad as Les was on his way to visit the Moreno Glacier, and I convinced him to hitch, saying he'd easily have a lift within half an hour. The poor lad waited on the side of the road for half the day with no lift and ended up coming back to the hostel—he is to catch the bus tomorrow (only 1 hour). I had half a day to kill and went off to climb some mountain in the distance. Quite a physical climb but well worth it for the view at the top. On the way down, I passed a lake full of pink flamingoes—I was a bit shocked at first as I thought they only lived in hot countries.

Later on in the afternoon, I caught the 6-hour bus to Puerto Natales, back to Chile. I couldn't believe it as I had the whole bus to myself for the whole trip.

23 March 1997, Puerto Natales

Spent the day relaxing and getting supplies for next few weeks.

Day 1: 24 March 1997, 7-Day Trek in the Andes

It was pissing down with rain when I got up at the crack of dawn this morning. A good day to start a 7-day trek in the Andes Mountain Range! Nearly missed the 8 o'clock bus (3 hours) taking me and a few other hikers to Torres del Paine National Park. Got chatting to an English guy, Adam, on the bus and ended up doing the trek with him. The rain had stopped, and we walked for about 5 hours in total wilderness. Spotted various wildlife, including foxes and huge condors soaring overhead. Beautiful autumn colours in the trees and plantation.

Camped in a great spot beside a lake, although very, very windy. I had problems holding my tent down as I haven't got any pegs. Took ages to cook my spaghetti due to the wind, which was so strong, I thought my tent would break several times during the night under the pressure.

Day 2: 25 March 1997, 7-Day Trek in the Andes

Had a quick breakfast. Then Adam and I were on our way. A tough day today. We walked for 9 hours through forests, lakes, rivers, etc. with the view of the snow-peaked Andean Mountains in front of us getting closer and closer. Came across a lake in the valley of the mountains, with a huge glacier pouring over the side of the mountain into the lake—stunning.

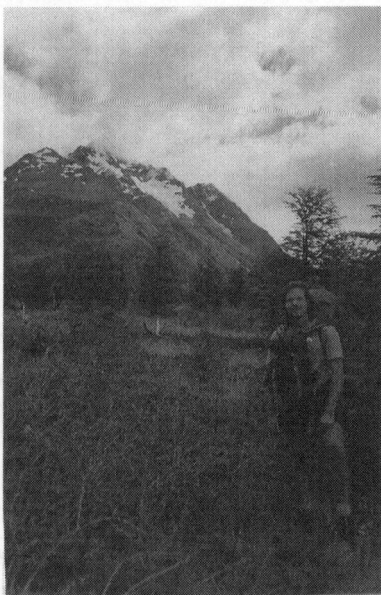

Camped nearby and got woken up in the middle of the night when it began raining, Wendy (the name I call my tent because it's so shit and is more like a Wendy house) isn't waterproof at all, so I had to stuff all my belongings into black plastic bin liners to keep them dry—even put the bottom half of my sleeping bag in a bin liner. A cold and sleepless night as I huddled up in the middle of my wet tent in a puddle of water.

Day 3: 26 March 1997, 7-Day Trek in the Andes

Woke up in a puddle of water. I hadn't wet the bed last night. It was from the rain. However, I managed to keep surprisingly dry

under the circumstances. I went for a quick dip in the glacier lake
this morning (not for fun but for a silly photo). I borrowed Adam's
sunglasses and waded out a few metres, past huge chunks of
glacial ice, to a huge ice block the size of a large shed—the water
was freezing cold, my whole body went numb, and I felt my heart
stiffen. I climbed on to the huge floating block of ice and lay down
on it with only a pair of boxer shorts and some sunglasses on. Had
a very quick photo before swimming back—fucking freezing!

It rained on and off all morning, and the heel of one of my boots
came off due to walking in the mud. Then to make problems worse,
the heel on the other boot came off as well. I had to tie them back
on to my boots using string. I've still got 3-4 days trekking left,
and it will be a nightmare if my boots don't hold out. Every now and
again, when I see another trekker, they've always got the latest
expensive equipment, yet I've got a shitty tent, my boots are in
pieces, I've got nothing more than a couple of shirts to keep me
warm in this freezing climate, and my water bottle is an old Coca
Cola bottle—I am the tramp of the Andes. However, I haven't got
all the correct clothing and equipment as I'm travelling for several
months, and it's not possible to carry everything you need. Anyway,
I'd rather do this trek with a bit of hardship (although it actually
turned out to be a lot) than not do it at all.

Began climbing a snow-peaked mountain—very steep and hard going and totally exposed to the elements. Very strong winds and heavy ice-cold rain at high speed. However, the view was amazing—beautiful mountain range with snow and glaciers. As we climbed the ridge, it was very physical, uncomfortable, and hard core, but at the same time, it felt great. The challenge of this mountain and all the elements against us—this is what adventure is all about. I felt like Chris Bonington out there on the mountain in the middle of nowhere.

As soon as we reached the top ridge, the wind and rain hit us in the face twice as hard. We could hardly stand up. But what a sight, for when we looked down the mountain, we could see the grey glacier as far as the eye could see—definitely the most spectacular natural wonder I've ever seen. The glacier was in a huge valley and must have been at least 20-30 miles long and about 5 miles wide of pure ice, of various shapes and tints of white and blue.

Stood there for a while in amazement—a great moment. Spent about 3 hours walking down towards the grey glacier, taking far too many photos—it was hard not to!

Camped inside a forest this evening before the sun went down. Had a very uncomfortable time tonight in a freezing-cold and wet sleeping bag. Woke up in the middle of the night with a very itchy scrotum—shit. I thought I'd caught crabs again. I realised a few days later that they were just chapped due to the wet and the cold.

Day 4: 27 March 1997, 7-Day Trek in the Andes

I camped on a slope last night, and when I woke up this morning, freezing cold, I realised that I'd slid down the tent during the night. The tent zip had opened, and the bottom half of me had slid out the tent.

Carried on walking down the ridge alongside the grey glacier for about 4 hours until we finally got to the bottom—very tough on the old knees. Had a quick stop, got lunch (a stale sandwich that I'd carried all the way), then we were off again.

The trek I'm doing normally takes about 9-10 days to complete. I have a boat to catch on Monday and am forced to do this trek in 7 days, which is possible but means it's a lot harder, and the days are a lot longer.

Spent a fairly physical 4½ hours trekking over a mountain pass to reach the next base. Bumped into Eddie (the Aussie guy I did the Darién Gap with) and his mate Lance coming the other way. A quick chat and then carried on. Adam and I were both physically knackered by the time we reached the campsite. It was about 5 p.m. and we'd been walking for 9 hours. We didn't want to camp at the campsite so carried on a little further along the trail, looking for a spot of our own. To cut a long story short, we ended up walking another 4 hours to the next campsite as there were no suitable spots along the way—too rocky.

We were physical wrecks and still walking when the sun had gone down, and we were in darkness. Adam fell over and smashed his head on the ground—luckily, no rocks, and he was well enough to carry on. Thank fuck for that. We finally arrived at the next campsite at about 9.30 p.m. after staggering the last hour in the dark, after a marathon 13-hour trek.

Day 5: 28 March 1997, 7-Day Trek in the Andes

Had another cold and wet night, with today being Good Friday or, in my case, 'Bad Friday', being just the same as last night. I ended up spending the whole day and night stuck in a freezing-cold and wet tent, with a continuous puddle of water on the bottom. A very miserable day to say the least, which turned out to be more of an endurance test than anything else. Talk about braving the elements—plenty of rain, even snow, and the wind was so unbelievably strong. I spent half my time in my tent with the ice-cold and wet sides of my tent in my face due to the strong winds. In the end, poor old Wendy (my tent) couldn't take any more punishment and collapsed in the wind with a few broken tent poles.

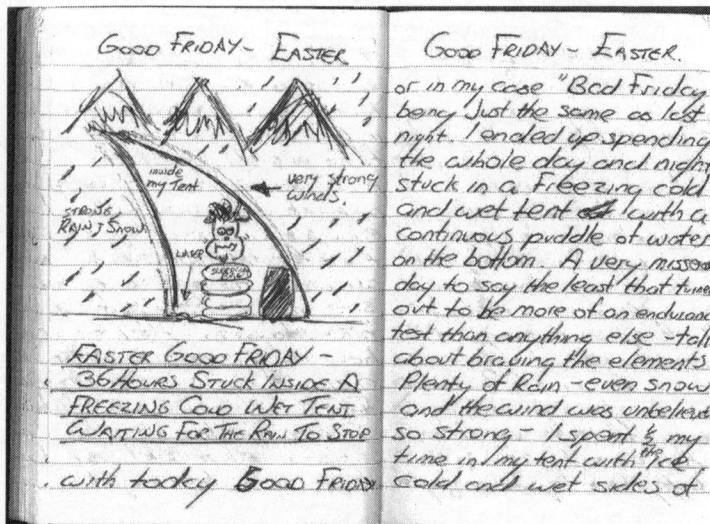

I was forced to quickly abandon tent and jump into Adam's, where we both spent the night. All in all, I was stuck in a tent for about 36 hours in very harsh and uncomfortable conditions. However, I'm not sure why, but I quite enjoyed it in a strange sort of way. Definitely a character-building experience that won't be forgotten in a long time.

Day 6: 29 March 1997, 7-Day Trek in the Andes

Dragged myself out of Adam's tent this morning—the weather was still bad, but at least the rain had temporarily stopped, although the sky was still very dark, and a lot more rain was still to come.

From where I was, it was a sturdy 9-hour walk to where the daily bus brings people back to civilisation—the small town of Puerto Natales. The only problem was that it left in 6 hours' time, and the weather was very unpredictable—shit or bust, I decided to go for it on my own and shot off down the track. It was going to be tight whether I got there or not in time for the bus, but what made it worse was that I had no watch so wouldn't know what time it was until I actually arrived there at the ranger's hut.

I went like shit off a shovel, taking it in turns to run, then walking fast—another tough day, although the thought of a good meal and a warm bed in Puerto Natales tonight, if I made it, gave me all the energy I needed.

All in all, it took me 5 ½ hours to get there with a total of about 15 minutes for quick stops. I felt so good and fit—haven't been this fit since my kick-boxing days many years ago. Anyway, after all that effort to get to the bus pick-up point in time, it was all in vain as, sod's law, the bus was 1½ hours late.

Arrived back at the hostel in Puerto Natales a physical wreck—all my clothes were in pieces, and I hadn't shaved for a week, although I felt great to be in civilisation again. A long hot shower, and I was as good as new again.

Andre, the Alaskan lad whom I'd met 2 weeks ago when he just finished his stint in Antarctica, was in the hostel and ended up dragging me out to the local disco tonight. I thought it was going to be a little shithole with a tin roof, but I was wrong. It turned out to be a full-on nightclub with 3 dance floors and packed with people, although the music and the mixing was really bad. Stayed until about 4 a.m. then couldn't take any more. The thought of a nice warm (and dry) bed was too great, and I went home.

30 March 1997, Easter Day

I was the happiest man in Chile today after I phoned Connie up in France, and she told me that she was going to come over to Chile in about 10 days' time to visit me—you can't blame the girl as I've been away for almost 5 months now.

31 March 1997 to 3 April 1997, 4-Day Cruise Through the Chilean Fjords on a Cargo Boat

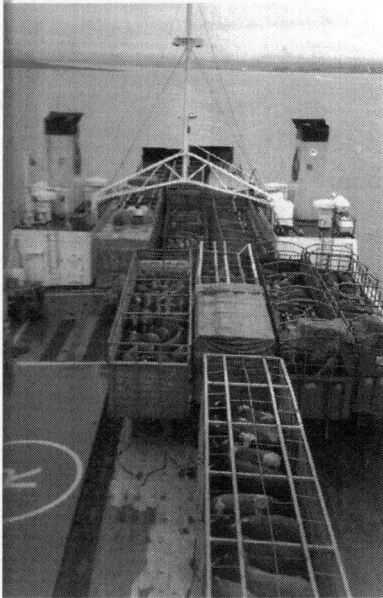

Spent the next 4 days and 4 nights on a cargo boat sailing up through the Chilean Fjords from Puerto Natales, up the coast to Puerto Montt. Supposedly one of the highlights in South America, although the weather was bad for most of the way. Saw plenty of small interesting islands, mountains, seals, and even a few penguins. There were plenty of other travellers aboard, including Ozzie Eddie and Lance. There was a very friendly atmosphere for the whole journey, which was more of a booze cruise than anything else.

There was a really rough stretch of sea for about 12 hours, which is great for people who don't get sea sick and can just sit back and watch everyone else being sick over the side.

On the last night, there was a big party (bigger than the previous 3 nights'). It was a bit like a school disco but still a good laugh. I found out that the tour guide (a Chilean woman in her mid-30s) had a crush on me, and I don't know if it was a compliment or not as she is blind as a bat. Eddie had some middle-aged German woman chasing him around the ship—as desperate as he was (very), she was still very round, and later on in the night, the alcohol had got the better of him, and he was running around like a headless chicken, looking for somewhere to shag. Successful as ever with women, he couldn't find anywhere and went to sleep on his own—pissed off.

He was woken in the morning by the same German woman, who put a condom in his hand and asked him to have a shower with her. It was now the morning, and being sober, without his beer goggles, he realised how rough she was and shat himself!

4 April 1997, Volcano Osorno (3-Day Climb)

Arrived in Puerto Montt this morning after a 4-day cargo trip through the Chilean fjords. Got chatting to a couple of adventurous lads on the boat (an English lad and an Israeli). We all wanted to climb Volcano Osorno. It's 2,652 metres tall, making it almost twice as high as Mount Snowdon or Ben Nevis in the UK. It's very dangerous to climb, and you can't do it without a guide. The problem was that it costs £120 a person for a guide.

The other 2 lads had mountaineering experience, so instead, we hired all the equipment and did it on our own—crampons, boots, harness, rope, thermal waterproof trousers, ice picks, etc. Went to the supermarket to buy 3 days' worth of food and ended up buying a 4 kg pig's head, called 'Colin', intending to take if to the summit for a laugh.

Hitched the 50 km to the base of the volcano. Then spent the next several hours walking up the track to the base camp—the weather wasn't too good, and we were in clouds most of the time. Finally arrived at base camp, knackered and an hour after dark fall.

There were several signs around saying that you could not go any further without a guide. We went straight to visit the park ranger, telling him that we were all mountaineers with plenty of experience. We had to fill out some forms, and I put 'Mile High Club' for the section under which club we belonged to. It was all fairly straightforward, and we were given permission to climb the summit.

5 April 1997, 3-Day Climb, Volcano Osorno

All 3 of us were up at the crack of dawn this morning. Porridge for breakfast, then with bags packed and our ice-climbing gear and 'Colin' the pig's head (our lucky mascot), we were on our way.

It took about 2½ hours of physical effort to climb up the scree slopes of the volcano before reaching the snowline, passing an amazing glacier along the way up.

It took us about half hour to get all kitted up—thermal trousers, boots, crampons, harness, rope, etc. and we were off. It was the first time for any of us to attempt anything like this (and very nearly the last).

There was a beautiful blue sky. The view was excellent. You could see the town of Puerto Montt, the sea, but the best view was of the summit—an amazing sight, but it looked so steep.

We'd previously asked the ranger the way to the summit, and he spent 30 seconds sketching a quick route on the back of his cigarette packet. We decided to find our own route and come back down the same way. There were no other footprints in the snow.

Initially, the snow was about 6" inches deep on a bed of ice that was several metres thick with huge crevices everywhere. We were all tied together at 7.5 metre intervals for safety reasons in case someone fell down a hidden crevice. After a couple of hours of this, we reached a more technical climb—a sheer face of ice at an angle of 45 degrees and an uphill length of over 100 metres. The ice was rock solid and was as hard as concrete. There were a couple of inches of snow covering the ice, but that was of no help.

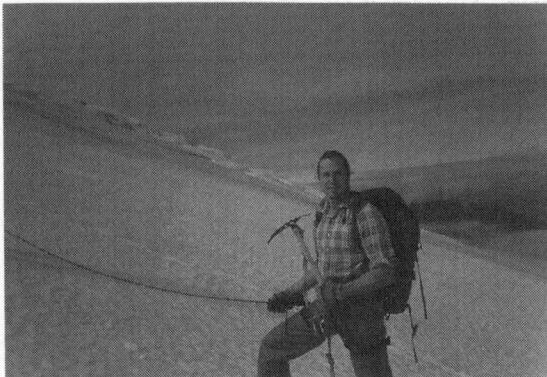

It was a very physical climb as you had to whack the ice very hard several times with either your ice pick or crampons in order to get a good hold before going higher. Hard work and very scary as the further you went up, the further you had to fall, and if one fell, the chances were that all 3 of us would fall (as we had no ice screws or a way of securing ourselves).

We were all physically tired by the time we reached the end of the 45-degree ice climb. We had a quick snack and tried to think about the view (rather than the height) as without a doubt, we were all absolutely shitting ourselves.

The next bit was the worst as it was at an angle of 60 degrees, solid ice, rock hard, and a climb of about 20 feet. Shit a brick! I've never been so scared in all my life. It looked so steep, and if I fell, it would probably be the end of it. I was doing this for the adrenaline buzz, but it had gone too far. There was no adrenaline. A great experience, though, as it was all mind over matter (it had to be). You had to forget the fear and put it to the back of your mind and focus on the climb. As soon as you think of fear, you get nervous, and accidents happen.

It was so dangerous as Jorrick (the Israeli lad) was above me, and if he fell, he'd come down on top of me, crampons first. We made it to the top of this bit, then had another rest. It was about another 100 metres to the summit. With the bright blue sky, you could see perfectly. However, it still seemed miles away and so steep. It got scarier with every inch going up. Then when we were only about 50 merers from the summit, Martin's ice pick broke—fuck! We all clung to the ice for a few minutes, and hardly a word was spoken. We were forced to go back down. I was relieved to be going down but certainly not with 2 ice axes between 3. It was then that we realised that no one knew how to get down. Jorrick (the one with the most mountaineering experience) just froze to the ice with fear—we had to come down inch by inch, but by now, the sun was coming down fast, and we still had a long way to go. Jorrick was still coming down far too slowly. We weren't going to make it before nightfall, but the more we hurried, the more he panicked.

I was having a quick rest in a crevice covered in snow when I heard Martin scream and his broken ice axe scratching the surface of the ice as he slid down—a sound I'll never forget. It was a good job I was in the crevice at the time as it was easy for me to dig in and take his weight on the rope. I honestly thought I'd never see another day as I watched the sun come down over the horizon, and we were still halfway down the ice face.

Then as we came down over a ridge, the ice had partly melted due to the exposure to the sun. It was as if a miracle had happened. The ice was softer and easier to climb down. We all climbed down as fast as we could and made it to the bottom of the ice face—thank God that we were safe (or at least the main danger was over). We still had to get below the snowline and still had a bit of twilight left. We ended up running down the hill (30 degrees) in single file and jumping over crevices one at a time (still roped up).

I fell over in the dark and ended up losing one of my crampons. We couldn't find it, and I had to carry on without it. We'd been on the ice in the dark for about an hour before we managed to get back to rock. *Whew.* It was about another 1½ hours down the scree until we arrived back at base camp about 9 p.m. safe and sound. I must admit, after that close-to-death experience, I'll be happy to hang up my traveller boots and live a normal life!

We were all physically drained, had some food, and went to bed.

6 April 1997, 3-Day Climb, Volcano Osorno
Made our way down the 16 km track to the main road—none of us were in the mood for it, and luckily, after only 10 minutes, the ranger was on his way down, and we managed to thumb a lift.

Then spent the next couple of hours hitching back downtown. Got several lifts, including one on the back of a truck full of apples. Went back to the hire shop and complained about the ice pick breaking and their equipment putting our lives in danger, but they still charged me £16 for the lost crampon.

I said goodbye to the lads and went off to catch the night bus to Santiago in order to meet Connie in a few days' time. While I was waiting for the bus, I watched an amazing sunset over the Volcano Osorno in the horizon—it looked so calm and friendly.

7 April 1997, Santiago
Arrived in Santiago first thing this morning (Santiago is the capital of Chile and the 2nd-most populated city in the world, after Mexico City). I went to the underground to get on a tube to the centre, but everyone was going to work, and all the tubes were full—no room for me to squeeze in with all my bags. Had to sit and wait for rush hour to end.

I found myself a cheap hotel (very hard to find in Santiago). It was a right shithole. Spent all day looking around and getting excited over Connie's visit tomorrow.

8 April 1997, Santiago

Got up this morning and first thing, checked into a descent hotel, then rushed over to the other end of town in order to catch the bus to the airport before Connie's flight arrived.

Got there in time and waited as everyone got off the plane. All of a sudden, I was standing there on my own—everyone had got off, but still no Connie. I waited another half hour in case she had problems at customs, but still no sign of her. In the end, I thought I'd just give her a ring in Paris to make sure she got on the flight, and the silly woman answered the phone—talk about being pissed off. It turned out she'd missed her flight but had managed to get another one, arriving in 2 days' time. It turned out for the better as she managed to get another 1½ weeks here. All that rushing about for nothing. Now I had to rush back to the posh hotel I'd booked and moved into this morning in order to postpone my stay. It was a reasonable room for £20 a night—a big splash out when travelling.

No problems with the hotel, and I didn't lose any money.

Then I phoned Anton, a Chilean lad, about 23, whom I'd met in Southern Chile, where he was working as a horse-trekking guide but is now living back in Santiago, studying to be a lawyer. Within about half an hour, I had met up with him at the underground station and moved into his flat, where he lived with a couple of other trainee Lawyers.

That night, I contacted Eddie (the Aussie lad I did the Darién Gap with) and Lance, his mate—it was his 30th birthday today, and we all went out for a party. Anton and I went round to their hotel with a couple of bottles, drank them, then went out. We all went to a trendy bar, where it was about £3 for half a pint. Sod paying that for a drink. I made mine last 3 hours before going home.

9 April 1997, Santiago

My boots are in a very bad state. Both soles are hanging off and tied on to the boots with string and wire at both front and back.

I went to buy a new pair and spent the whole day going from shoe shop to shoe shop, just looking for a pair that fitted me. The Chileans are all small, so it's almost impossible to find size 9-10. Ended up buying the shittiest and most unfriendly boots I'd ever seen.

10-12 April 1997, Santiago

Connie was due to arrive (again!) today, so I had another mad morning of moving all my things into a hotel and jumping on the bus to the airport. Typical, plane was delayed 2 hours. When the plane arrived, I waited for the people coming out—I couldn't spot Connie but noticed a pretty Japanese girl. We both looked at each other for a while, and I asked her, 'Is that you, Connie?' It was—we'd been apart for over 5 months, and neither of us recognised each other.

It was great to see the old girl again. We spent a couple of days together in Santiago and, on Friday night, went to a party at one of Anton's friend's house. The people there were very friendly. However, the majority of them were Americans, so hence, it was a long way off from being a wild party! But it was still good.

13 April 1997, Antofagasta

Got the bus first thing this morning with the intention of hitch-hiking all the way up to the Calama, about 1,000 km away. Connie, coming from Hong Kong, had never heard about hitch-hiking before and thought I was joking when I told her to stand on the side of the road and stick her thumb out.

There was very little traffic, and we were both tired, so after an hour, caught the local bus to the next town—a small fishing community on the coast. We had a look around for a while, then caught the 7-hour bus up the coast to Antofagasta. A fairly interesting journey through desert scenery.

14 April 1997, Rock Arch

Caught the bus half an hour up the coast and got out in the middle of nowhere. The coast was on one side and desert on the other. We walked down the cliff to a beautiful beach. About 50 metres in front of us was a natural rock arch about 12 metres high in the sea. It looked stunning in the sunlight with the turquoise-blue sea. Spent a few hours relaxing on the beach before going back to town and hitching up to Calama.

While hitching, a dirty old man pulled up in his truck, saying that he only had room for one in the van—the other would have to sit in the back of his truck with all the rubbish. There was plenty of room for 2 more in his cabin, but obviously, it would be me in the back while Connie sat in the front. I didn't like the man and turned the lift down. Connie said that we should have accepted the lift, and she would have sat in the back outside while I'd sit next to him to piss him off.

Managed to get a lift after an hour, but the man was only going 70 km through the desert to a huge copper mine.

We got out there and began hitching again. But the same old story—only perverts stopped for us, saying that they only had room for one person (obviously Connie). We hitched for an hour, but it was now late in the afternoon, so when the bus came past, we got on.

Arrived in Calama in darkness, and after some food and a beer, we caught a 2-hour bus to the small desert village of San Pedro, arriving there at midnight. It's a small village, it was pitch black, and there was no one around—I didn't have a clue where we were going to spend the night. Finally, I found a hotel, a very basic one, but no one was around. I walked into the hut, and it was the owner's house, and he was asleep in bed with his wife and child.

In the end, I put my tent up in a derelict building, and we both spent the night there.

15 April 1997, San Pedro

Got some strange looks from the locals this morning when they walked past and noticed two gringos camping in an old derelict building.

Moved into a room and had a look around this interesting village. San Pedro is a small oasis in the middle of the desert, and because of its altitude of 2900 metres, it gets very cold at night. In the distance across the desert is a mountain range consisting mostly of volcanoes, all of which are covered in snow—an amazing sight. The village itself is made from mud houses, and the people who live here have lived this way for hundreds of years. It is a very interesting place to visit.

In the afternoon, Connie and I went on a tour to see the Valley of the Moon, a fascinating trip through stunning mountain scenery that over the years had been carved into various shapes and forms due to the desert winds. Visited several different sights of the desert this afternoon. The last one, we climbed a huge sand dune about 100 metres high to watch the sun set over the mountains.

This is where Kevin's diary ends. I cannot find any more from this date, although he did write a letter home to his parents, dated 23 May 1997, from Peru. Kevin was still engaged to Connie when he died. The letter says the following:

Dear Family,

I've decided to write you all a letter as it's almost 60 pence to send a post card each time—bloody rip-off. Had a great time with Connie on her 4-week holiday here in South America and got engaged to the old girl—it happens to the best if us!

She went back to Paris on 6 May, and the following day, I spent 2 days on a bus going to La Paz Bolivia (saw 4 Bolivian men caught smuggling cocaine on the border). La Paz is the highest capital city in the world at 4,000 metres, and because of the altitude, you are always gasping for breath. La Paz is at a very interesting stage at the moment as elections are being held very soon. There are small riots almost everyday, and riot police with rubber bullets, tear gas, etc. are on almost every corner. Saw a teachers' demonstration a couple of days ago that got out of hand and ended up with a police motorbike being set on fire and exploding in the middle of the High Street.

Had a look around the prison last week by a prisoner. You pay him a bit of money, some of which he gives to the guards—very interesting to say the least and not the place to end up in life. The guards basically let the prisoners get on with it, and it's survival of the fittest, with many killings. Even managed to get into the guy's cell and saw all his weapons. There are also a lot of druggies here, and they've even got a cocaine production centre in the jail.

Had my first bash at skiing as well at the highest ski
resort in the world only a few miles from La Paz. It's at
5,300 metres above sea level and very basic—certainly
not the place to learn. I was affected quite badly by the
altitude and could hardly get my boots on. I had a few
small attempts but nothing special.

I've been with Martin the last week—the English lad
I climbed the Volcano Osorno with. Well, you'll be
pleased to know that we attempted another mountain
together, Mt Potosi, at 6,088 meters (over 20,000
feet). This time, we did the sensible thing and hired
a guide and porter—along with all the equipment,
crampons, harness, ropes, ice axes, etc. The first day,
we did a lot of ice climbing up vertical glacier faces,
using 2 technical ices axes and crampons. A great
buzz and physically exhausting at that altitude. Spent
the first night at base camp. The second day was very
hard as we spent the day tied together (in case of a
slip or hidden crevice) and trekking and climbing in the
snow—constantly out of breath with the altitude. Spent
the night at High Camp (5,400 metres), camping on
snow and ice (at these altitudes, it takes about 2 hours
to turn a pot of snow into boiling water). Everyone
was feeling the effects—from simple headaches to
diarrhea, nausea, and being sick. It was a very long and
cold night—29°C outside the tent and—10°C inside.
We all had the proper sleeping bags etc. although
it was freezing cold. The condensation on the inside
of the tent froze along with the bottles of water etc.
We were supposed to leave camp at 4 a.m. for the
final 5-hour snow climb to the summit. However, the
weather conditions changed for the worse, and we
had heavy wind and snow for most of the night—about
1½ feet, making it too physical (and dangerous due to
avalanches, hidden crevices, etc.) to continue, forcing

us to return back to base camp in occasional snow blizzards. We never made the summit. However, it was still a rewarding experience.

Martin and I are now on the final planning stage for our next expedition, which I've told you about, canoeing down an Amazon tributary for about 2 to 4 weeks. We begin this Monday, when we head off to a small gold-mining town called Mapiri—this should take us about 3 days' travel on the back of trucks via the small settlement of Guanay (slightly north of La Paz). These are real frontier settlements similar to the old west, where gold is legal tender, and saloons, gambling, fighting, and prostitution are normal in free-time activities.

Once we arrive in Mapiri, we intend to buy a small boat (and gun—for food in the jungle) and head down Rio

Mapiri (River Mapiri) through the jungle to Guanay, then up Rio Beni (River Beni) to Rurrenabaque and up to Riberatta near the Brazilian border.

All going well, this should be one of my best trips yet and in which I'll probably celebrate my 29th birthday—but don't worry, I'm sure I'll be able to find a cheap bottle of plonk somewhere!

No, seriously, although this trip takes us through some very remote and wild areas, it has been well planned out and is nothing as near as dangerous as the Darién Gap. Have a great holiday in Oz.

Thinking of you all,

Kev xxx

PS—Just found out that 3 Dutch lads attempted the Darién Gap a couple of months ago and were all murdered by Columbian guerrillas!

LETTERS FROM KEV'S FRIENDS

A few notes from some of Kev's closest friends.

Greg Dawson—school friend

32 Turner Street
Lincoln
LN1 3TL

Dear Mr. and Mrs Courtney and Michelle

I have just heard the devastating news about your beloved son Kevin. As the tears roll down my cheeks, I cannot begin to imagine the pain and sense of loss you will all be going through. Your son was respected and loved by everyone who knew him. Everyone admired him for his sense of adventure and free spirit and he touched everybody's lives with his kindness and humour. I first met Kevin in 1977, and even at the age of nine he had developed his own, very special character. Kevin knew how to enjoy himself and if it meant getting into trouble then so be it. But Kev never got into serious trouble, and there was one very good reason for this. Above all of his talents, Kevin was extremely intelligent. This was the one characteristic that made one of my best friends stand head and shoulders above the rest. As we grew up and went to school together our circle of friends began to increase, but whoever we socialised with, all the lads looked up to Kev. One of the reasons for this respect was Kevin's immense sense of loyalty. I remember one day at Branston School telling Kev about a boy who had been bullying me. Nobody saw the boy for two days after that because Kevin had sorted it out! That boy never spoke to me again. Kev and I spent many happy, carefree hours together throughout our adolescent lives. Homework would always get in my way but it would never bother Kevin. For several terms, maybe even years, the fact that Kev. never

455

worried about his school work was a constant puzzle to
me. I just presumed that he never did it. Then one day
the penny finally dropped. Kevin was so bright that the
homework just took a quarter of the time for him to
complete! If a person has a friend who looks up to him
that that person will feel proud of himself. Kevin had
dozens of friends who looked up to him. When Kev came back
to Lincoln I was always so proud that he always made
contact with me. I would spend hours listening to his
latest adventures and marvel at how he lived his life.
But Kev would never hold court and show off about his
travels in a group of people. This was another quality that
I loved Kevin for. He never forgot his roots and he repaid
our love with his loyalty and true friendship. It's been just
three hours since I have found out about Kevin and every
time I stop and pause I think about him. I can honestly
say that all of my memories are very happy one's. As we grew
older, I made new friends through work and the like. Even
though many of them had never met him, all of my mates had
heard of Kev Courtney. Then every so often Kev would turn
up again and within minutes he would have settled
himself in and we would all be laughing and joking
together. The best memories in the world. I loved Kevin like a
brother and will continue to do so. Although God has taken
him, Kevin's memory and spirit will live on through his family
and friends and we will all treasure that for the rest of
our lives. With this letter, I am sending my deepest heartfelt
sympathy. My thoughts are with you. With all of my love.
God be with Kevin,
                    Greg Dawson.

Paul Hedley—school friend

I was good friends with Kev and hung around with him since I was at school, and even back then, he was always the joker of the class. When we left school, we went out in town, drinking every week. There was the same old gang, but we always met up with lots of others in town. Our birthdays were on the same day, 11 June, so we spent many years celebrating together. Kev always had a way of making it a special occasion. We went out drinking together every week, we lived for our nights out, and we always made the most of it. Kev had a knack of making a normal night out into being a great night with lots of good memories. You never knew where you would end up or what might happen. He always seemed to know where there was a party or a good club in another town, and anything could happen, from being chased by a gang of lads to waking up in a strange place like a skip, not knowing how you got there or what had happened that night. We spent most of the time together laughing, joking, and having a good time. He always had a big smile on his face and was always looking for a way to have as much fun as possible. He always wanted to make the most of life and always lived it to the full.

Paul

Julian Elkington— school friend and beer buddy

'Some birds aren't meant to be caged.'

Kev made his cage global, a world worth exploring and experiencing, with lots of different challenges, fun, madness, and character-building along the way.

I can remember arriving in Ko Pang Yang to meet Kev, arriving at a set of beech huts. The huts were either side of a rock jutting out into the sea, sun shining, being very tired, thinking where the hell was he (a time before mobiles), then in the distance, beyond the rock in the sea, was KC dancing and darting about, with a big smoke on.

Great preparation for the full-moon party, which goes without saying, was 24 hrs of madness and fun.

Talking of dancing, the first time I was introduced to the dance scene of love was with KC at the 'Ministry'.

'Oh What a Night'. I danced like my dad all night. Kev danced Like a Duracell rabbit.

My short career in kick-boxing was with KC, funny as fuck. We were so keen, we used to jog 6 miles to get to the sessions. This career ended up at the York rooms. (I lost every fight, KC a bit more successful.)

The great thing about Kev was, amongst all his travelling, he still had plenty of time for good nights out back home and Stamford and would often pop down for pre—or post-travel nights, always full of travel and adventure stories.

These stories were the main inspiration for the three amigos (Me, Tim O'Conner, and another guy) to go to South America, particularly Bolivia, which Kev always rated as one of the best.

What more can I say? It was a privilege of a friendship, to be inspired, talk nonsense, have lots of nonsense together, fun, laughter, and rock 'n' roll.

Cheers, Kev, never forgotten.

Jte (Pooh)

X

Smell the flowers while you can!

Damon Blackband (Boris)—
school friend, and met again in Belize

During my 23 years' Army service, I had the honour and privilege to meet some truly remarkable people. However, most of these people were only in this category because the Army had given them the opportunity and training to realise their ambitions and potential and become what they now are. For Kev, it was different.

I remember running around the school cross-country course with Kev at Branston School, discussing beer, fags, and women and the normal niff-naff and trivia that fills the heads of 15-year-old schoolboys. I remember Kev as a warm, adventurous, and spirited individual who probably, like myself, did not really know what he wanted to do with his life (and I still don't). We lived for the weekends and the parties, the opportunity to be ourselves, and the uncertainty of what life would bring.

On leaving school in 1984, Kev and I parted company and went our own ways. For me, it was the Army, and for Kev, it soon became a life as equally challenging and exciting. Several years later, I was to be reunited with Kev in the jungles of Central America, I as an Army Sergeant and Kev as a Professional Adventurer!

It was like discovering a long-lost brother, both of us picking up where we left off in 1984. Belize soon became a whirlwind of parties, adventure, and excitement, from running naked around the island of Caye Caulker (and getting arrested) to dancing naked in the most dangerous nightclub in Belize City!

Kev was a true extrovert, living each day by the seat of his pants and always eager to try life's next great adventure. Whether it be parachuting, diving, trekking Central America's notorious and deadly Darién Gap, or working as a number 2 on the trapeze in an El Salvadorian circus, Kev was your man.

Kev's life could be summed up by Rudyard Kiplings poem 'If'—a fine blueprint for life if there ever was one.

The last time I met with Kev was shortly before he entered immortality. We sat drinking a beer at one in the morning on the roof of Lincoln's old telecom building (seemed the logical place to have a beer with Kev).

Kevin was an inspiration to me and all those he encountered, a true adventurer, and one of life's great characters. He is fondly remembered and sadly missed and will always serve as a reminder that 'life ain't a rehearsal', so enjoy it whilst you can.

Damon (Boris) Blackband

Our Jacks Lad Terry

Tim O'Conner—
friends since playschool, and met up in Sydney, Australia

Our Jacks Lad Terry

I often wondered what it would be like when we'd hook up later on in our lives and have a few cheeky ones together. Kev would always have a few good comical tales to tell. It could be anything from some jail bust in deepest Africa, to the time he bought his mum a souvenir T-shirt back from Hong Kong, with a lovely picture of a cat, and it had written across it in Chinese writing: 'I'm a lesbian'.

This guy had more balls than the National Lottery. He believed it was better to get out there and get it done than sit around watching Coronation Street *for the rest of his life, wondering what could have been.*

Bless you, Kev, mate, it was always a pleasure. I'll never forget those words that were played out when we were last together ' . . . regrets, I've had a few, but then again, too few to mention'. You certainly did it 'your way' although sometimes slightly harrowing and often messy!

Tim O'Connor

Neil Kerfoot—
travelling buddy in his later adventures,
completing the Darién Gap together

On first travelling with Kevin, I wasn't sure if he was brave or just foolhardy. I later realised it was raw determination that fuelled his voracious appetite for adventurous travel.

I've been to some very remote locations well off the beaten path and met some outstanding characters along the way but never met anyone with the passionate desire Kevin had for adventure, in whatever format it presented itself in.

Creed, race, language, or religion never seemed a barrier to Kevin's pursuits, and in fact, the more barriers that appeared on the horizon, the more likely the adventure would appeal to his tastes.

On discovering some of the travelling adventures Kevin had engaged in over the years, an acquaintance once asked, 'Why have you never mentioned any of this to us before?' Kevin replied very openly, explaining he knew all his own stories, so why would he tell them all again? He was more interested in what happens next and what would be the next great adventure. This logical bashfulness was both completely genuine and very disarming for the majority of the people he interacted with.

By the very nature of the life Kevin decided to lead, he was under no apprehensions that he would live to a ripe old age and eventually die in his sleep. But I believe he would never have anticipated the hole his void would leave in those around him who knew him and how devastated those of us who truly loved him would feel.

When Kevin died, his parents gave me some of his ashes. I take Kevin's ashes with me every time I travel. I have them with me now, in this hotel room. It started as a good-luck thing, then became a duty of care to take him for a trip out every now and then. Just by chance, the lid of the pot his ashes came in never fitted correctly. Over the years, and in the many countries I've visited since his death, normally, a little bit of his ash spills out, so inadvertently, I've been spreading his ashes all over the world, which I think is somehow fitting.

The first building I constructed here in Ghana for 'Village by Village', I honoured to Kevin and named it after a song he once taught me. It took eight long hard months to complete with the help and support of all the villagers, and I named the building after a song Kevin taught me one night as we both were lost walking back in the dark after some adventure walking through a tropical forest in a remote island in the Philippines. I taught it to all the kids in the village, and even the little ones who do not know English know the song. It was a lovely reminder of him every time they sing it, and they still sing it every time I return.

He once told me, 'The more unusual the things you do, the more normal they seem', and he did lead an amazingly unusual life.

Neil

KEV'S LAST WORDS

Below is a letter written by Kev just before he began his Darién Gap adventure. He sent this letter to his friend Tim O'Conner, who was to hand it over to the family should anything happen to Kev.

No more words are needed.

10th ~~Dec~~ January 97
Panama City ~ McDonalds,
To The Courtneys.

Well if you recieve this
letter it means that I didn't
make it through the darien
gap in one piece - don't
get upset (because I won't)
If it is the end then this
is the way I would have
wanted to have gone
doing a real adventure!!
rather than being run over
on my way home from
a boring 9-5 Job in
rainy England!!
I may only be 28 but
I've crammed so much into
my life and have done
alot more then your

average pensioner.
Ive had more fun, parties,
adventures and laughs
than anyone else Ive
met. Ive had a good life
and have no regrets

From Your Favourate
Son / Love Ya
all to bits

KEV xxxx

5591048R00272

Printed in Great Britain
by Amazon.co.uk, Ltd.,
Marston Gate.